THE FOX SPIRIT, THE STONE MAIDEN, AND OTHER TRANSGENDER HISTORIES FROM LATE IMPERIAL CHINA

The Fox Spirit, the Stone Maiden, and Other Transgender Histories from Late Imperial China

Matthew H. Sommer

Columbia University Press

New York

Columbia University Press
Publishers Since 1893
New York   Chichester, West Sussex
cup.columbia.edu
Copyright © 2024 Columbia University Press

Library of Congress Cataloging-in-Publication Data
Names: Sommer, Matthew Harvey, 1961– author.
Title: The fox spirit, the stone maiden, and other transgender histories
from late imperial China / Matthew H. Sommer.
Description: New York : Columbia University Press, [2024] |
Includes bibliographical references and index.
Identifiers: LCCN 2023033182 (print) | LCCN 2023033183 (ebook) |
ISBN 9780231214124 (hardback) | ISBN 9780231214131 (trade paperback) |
ISBN 9780231560207 (ebook)
Subjects: LCSH: Sex customs—China—History—18th century. | Sex customs—
China—History—19th century. | Gender identity—China—History—18th century. |
Gender identity—China—History—19th century. | Sex role—China History—18th century. |
Sex role—China—History—19th century.
Classification: LCC HQ18.C5 S66 2024 (print) | LCC HQ18.C5 (ebook) |
DDC 306.760951—dc23/eng/20230829
LC record available at https://lccn.loc.gov/2023033182
LC ebook record available at https://lccn.loc.gov/2023033183

Cover design: Chang Jae Lee
Cover image: Actors, ca. 1890. Fuchsia hand-tinting is original.

I dedicate this book to three old comrades from UCLA's Chinese history program—Christopher Isett, Karasawa Yasuhiko, and Bradly Reed—in gratitude for their friendship and in memory of the brave days of our youth.

Old age hath yet his honour and his toil;
Death closes all: but something ere the end,
Some work of noble note, may yet be done . . .
Tho' much is taken, much abides; and tho'
We are not now that strength which in old days
Moved earth and heaven, that which we are, we are;
One equal temper of heroic hearts,
Made weak by time and fate, but strong in will
To strive, to seek, to find, and not to yield.

—TENNYSON, "ULYSSES"

Contents

Acknowledgments ix

Conventions in the Text xv

Introduction 1

I Transgender Paradigms in Late Imperial China 25

II The Paradigm of the Cross-Dressing Predator 50

III Clergy as Wolves in Sheep's Clothing 81

IV Creativity Inspired by Torment? 108

V The Fox Spirit Medium 137

VI The Truth of the Body 173

VII The Hustler 207

Epilogue 248

Character List 261
Notes 281
References 333
Index 353

Acknowledgments

For the third time in my life, I have finally finished writing a book, and it is a relief and a catharsis to thank everyone who has helped me along the way. Needless to say, the views expressed in this book and any remaining errors are my sole responsibility.

Since I published my last book in 2015, I have lost both of my parents, and here I wish once again to acknowledge the vital role that their faith in me and their generous support played in whatever success I have enjoyed in my career. I also wish to acknowledge my brother Andy, who died eleven years ago of esophageal cancer—he is constantly in my thoughts.

I wrote the first draft of this book in what I will always remember as the plague year, 2020–21 (i.e. the high point of the COVID-19 pandemic), during which I had the great good fortune to be on leave. During the previous three years, I had served as chair of the History Department at Stanford, and, with the onset of COVID, my last few months as chair were very stressful. I am sure that anyone else who served in an administrative role during that period can sympathize. My service as chair ended at midnight on August 31, 2020, and my father died early the next morning.

A silver lining of the pandemic, however, was that my year of leave became the most productive I have ever had, simply because there was nothing else to do except work on my book, under conditions that amounted to a kind of house arrest. My wife, Ih-hae; our son, Joseph; and

I all worked at home—fortunately, we had enough room for separate workstations—and we would rendezvous at meals and in the evening to watch movies together. Our daughter, Anne, often visited from San Francisco, where she was in medical school. At dinner, I would tell them about what I had written that day, and I hope they found it entertaining; at least they did me the courtesy of listening and voicing encouragement. Ih-hae and I were fortunate to be able to take long, peaceful walks on Stanford's beautiful campus, which we had mostly to ourselves. On the whole, we were good roommates, and I am grateful for my family's tolerance of my idiosyncrasies in such close quarters, over such a long time—it was rather like how I imagine it would be to serve together on a submarine.

Further moral support during the plague year and its subsequent denouement was provided by friends who connected mainly over Zoom: Frank Borchert, Tristan Brown, Chris and Siu Li GoGwilt, Hirata Koji, Roger Inouye, Momoko Kishimoto, Tina Lu, and Alex Statman—and especially my old UCLA comrades Chris Isett, Karasawa Yasuhiko, and Brad Reed, to whom this book is dedicated. Closer to home, I owe a particular debt to Brent Carlson for our hikes in the redwoods at Sam McDonald Park, and more recently for our Friday evening "Low Stakes Tang Poetry Club." These friends' camaraderie played a vital role in sustaining my morale during a very challenging time.

Many friends and colleagues have helped with various aspects of this project, and I offer them all my deepest thanks. Early inspiration can be traced back to a graduate course on feminist theory and history that I team-taught with then-colleague Lynn Hunt at the University of Pennsylvania in 2000—I found that an extraordinarily stimulating experience. More recently, after I gave a talk about my research for my department's faculty seminar at Stanford, a group of colleagues and I decided to launch an experimental course, Trans History: The Long View, which we team-taught for several years. At first it was a one-credit lecture series, but gradually it developed into a real class. Participants included Estelle Freedman (who did the initial organizing and acted as our first lead instructor), Madihah Akhter, Adrian Daub, Paula Findlen, Fiona Griffiths, Ana Minian, and Laura Stokes. I drew great inspiration from their presentations and from their feedback on my own. I also wish to acknowledge the students at Stanford who have taken my courses Queer History in Comparative Perspective and Gender and Sexuality in Chinese History, for helping me think through many basic issues.

This project forced me outside my comfort zone in many ways, and I have relied shamelessly on the expertise of colleagues more knowledgeable than I. First and foremost, I wish to thank John Kieschnick, who shared his vast knowledge of Chinese religion and also provided copies of his own work and that of other scholars. In the course of his own research, John happened to notice the two illustrations in *Dianshizhai Pictorial* that appear in chapter 3, which enabled me to track down the corresponding news reports in *Shenbao*. John also put me in email touch with Vincent Goossaert, who patiently answered my questions about Daoism. Eileen Chow, Andrea Goldman, Tina Lu, Catherine Yeh, and Mengdie Zhao graciously answered many questions about Chinese fiction and drama, and I hope they are not embarrassed by what I have to say on those topics here. Byungil Ahn, Christian Henriot, Macabe Keliher, Qiong Liu, Zhijian Qiao, Gina Tam, and Jiayan Zhang shared their knowledge on various other matters, and I occasionally found it useful to crowd-source questions in the Sinologists' group on Facebook. Che-chia Chang, Ron Egan, Mark Lewis, Dongfang Shao, Yi-Li Wu, and Yiqun Zhou helped me interpret or translate difficult texts. My former student Janani Balasubramanian provided the metaphor of the brown dwarf for the epilogue. Finally, I wish to offer sincere thanks to the informant (she prefers to remain anonymous) who shared the story of the gender-ambiguous spirit medium that appears in the epilogue.

While I was writing this book, several friends and colleagues did me the honor of reading various drafts and their feedback helped me avoid errors and strengthen my argument. Wen-hsin Yeh was the first to take a look, and her generous encouragement helped motivate me to persevere. My old friend from Swarthmore '83 Chris GoGwilt read multiple drafts of most chapters, and Sam Huneke, John Kieschnick, and Barbara Voss all read a late draft of the entire manuscript. Margaret Kuo provided detailed comments on the Introduction, which went through multiple revisions.

In this connection, two events in the fall of 2021 stand out as especially gratifying and valuable experiences. First, several of my former students organized a manuscript workshop for me on Zoom, in which they discussed my entire first draft: Madihah Akhter, Janani Balasubramanian, Andrew Elmore, Annelise Heinz, Alex Statman, and Yvon Wang; Alex later commented on revised drafts of the introduction and epilogue. Second, my successor as department chair, Caroline Winterer, generously hosted a salon at her home for me to workshop a section of the manuscript with colleagues Paula Findlen, Fiona Griffiths, Ana Minian, and Laura Stokes. Sincere gratitude to all!

It took a long time for this project to come into focus, and over the past twenty-five years I have given many talks about different aspects of it. I wish to acknowledge those who hosted me and to thank everyone who offered feedback for their help in developing my ideas. To begin with, I presented some of the material in chapter 6 at UCLA's Center for Chinese Studies (1999) and later at a conference on Chinese forensic medicine at the University of Michigan (2011). I spoke about Xinxiang (protagonist of chapter 7) in five talks between 2000 and 2004: at the New York Gay and Lesbian History Seminar (hosted by Randolph Trumbach at his home); the Center for East Asian Studies, Stanford; the China Humanities Seminar at Harvard; the China Colloquium at UC Berkeley; and the Center for Early Modern History, University of Minnesota. I presented my preliminary thoughts about the Qing legal cases of "men masquerading in women's attire" (chapters 2–5) in multiple talks between 2012 and 2022: at my department's Faculty Seminar; the Center for Early Modern History, University of Minnesota; the Academia Sinica, Taiwan; the History Department, UC Davis; the Center for East Asian Studies, University of Chicago; the Stanford Humanities Center's Queer Studies Workshop; the Ming-Qing History Summer Retreat at Miura, Japan; the Institute of East Asian Studies at UC Berkeley; the workshop Acting the Part: Gender and Performance Onstage at Harvard's Fairbank Center; and Stanford's Michelle R. Clayman Institute for Gender Research. Finally, I presented previews of the finished book in two talks in the spring of 2023 at Cornell University and at the Zvi Yavetz School of Historical Studies, Tel Aviv University.

Readers should not assume that anyone named here necessarily agrees with me on any particular point. In fact, people I respect strongly disagreed with each other about certain issues that come up in this book (e.g., my policy on pronoun use; see the introduction). Since not everyone agreed, it was impossible to follow everyone's advice. In these instances, the friction between different perspectives helped me clarify my own views and realize my own vision of what this book should be.

Of course, this book could not have been written without the primary sources that are its foundation, especially original case records from the Qing legal archives, and I wish to thank the staff at the Sichuan Provincial Archive, the Nanchong Municipal Archive, and China's First Historical Archive for their vital assistance. Later, my former students Michelle Chang and Guo Yuxin secured several documents for me in Beijing when I could not travel there myself. Zhaohui Xue and the other staff at Stanford's magnificent East Asia Library supported me at every stage of the project.

In the end, what made this book possible was the generous financial support of several institutions at Stanford: the History Department; the Michelle R. Clayman Institute for Gender Research; the Freeman Spogli Institute's China Fund; the Stanford Center at PKU; and, most important, the School of Humanities and Sciences. I particularly want to thank my former boss Lanier Anderson, who was then the Senior Associate Dean for Humanities and Arts, for arranging a year of leave for me with no strings attached after my service as department chair had finished.

Finally, I would like to thank Caelyn Cobb, Monique Laban, Susan Pensak, Emily Shelton, and the rest of the staff at Columbia University Press for shepherding my book into print with such efficient and reassuring competence.

As this book was going to press, my former student Yvon Wang notified me that a fictional manga loosely based on the case of the gender-transing spirit medium Xing Shi (protagonist of chapter 5 in this volume) has been published in Taiwan: *Xing Da and the Fox Spirit* (Xing Da yu huxian), by Ai Mutu and Ming Yuping (Taipei: Gaiya Wenhua, 2012). I was pleasantly surprised to learn that the feedback loop between legal cases and fiction that I have identified in the Ming-Qing era continues to this day, and that it has produced a new perspective that is markedly sympathetic to the fox spirit medium. Xing Shi lives!

Conventions in the Text

I n this book, my use of "transgender" does not assume any stable, trans-historical identity, but instead is based on Susan Stryker's definition that focuses on practices in their specific historical contexts. For Stryker, "transgender" refers to "people who move away from the gender they were assigned at birth, people who cross over (*trans-*) the boundaries constructed by their culture to define and contain their gender."[1] She does not assume any particular motivation or endpoint for such movement. Similarly, I emulate Jen Manion in using "trans" as a verb, as in "to trans gender" and "gender-transing."[2] See the introduction for a detailed explanation, and also for my policy on pronoun use.

I use the terms "late imperial" and "Ming-Qing" interchangeably, to refer to the era of China's last two imperial dynasties: the Ming (1368–1644) and the Qing (1644–1912).

In imperial China, dates were expressed in the lunar calendar according to the current emperor's reign period (*nianhao*). The Gregorian calendar and the lunar calendar do not align exactly (with the lunar New Year falling in early spring), but, for convenience, when referring to dates I have converted years to the closest Gregorian equivalent. For example, instead of "Qianlong 20" (i.e., the twentieth year of the Qianlong emperor's reign), I use "1755," unless the date falls near the end of the lunar year, in which case I would use "1756." When giving exact dates (e.g., in citation of cases), I provide the reign period followed by the year, month, and day, in the

Chinese fashion (e.g., "Qianlong 12.10.2" means the second day of the tenth month of the twelfth year of the Qianlong emperor's reign). In citation of Chinese dates, "r" refers to an intercalary month, and "?" means that part of the date is unknown.

Unless otherwise noted, people's ages are expressed in *sui*, which are, on average, one more than the same age when reckoned in "years old." (At birth, a person is aged one sui, and gains another at each subsequent New Year.) For example, a person aged twenty sui may be eighteen years old but is probably nineteen years old.

Chinese women's names are rendered as found in original sources. Usually, a peasant woman had no given name of her own (aside from an indicator of birth order, such as "second daughter" or "older sister"). Instead, legal documents would identify her by the surname of her father and sometimes (if she were married or widowed) that of her husband, followed by the term *shi* (literally, "lineage"). For example, "Wang Li *shi*" refers to a woman whose father's surname is "Li" and whose husband's surname is "Wang." (In very formal contexts, this might be rendered "Wang *men* Li *shi*"—i.e. "Mrs. Wang née Li.") In the text, I have not translated or italicized *shi*.

Chinese names and terms are Romanized in *Hanyu pinyin* according to standard Mandarin pronunciation.

All translations are my own, except where noted.

Figure 0.1 Provinces of China Proper within the Qing Empire, ca. 1800.

THE FOX SPIRIT, THE STONE MAIDEN, AND OTHER TRANSGENDER HISTORIES FROM LATE IMPERIAL CHINA

Introduction

When male is distinguished from female (*nan nü you bie*), then father and son will draw together in affection. When father and son draw together in affection, a sense of moral duty (*yi*) will be born. When a sense of moral duty is born, the rituals appropriate to human relations (*li*) will be created (*zuo*). Once the rituals have been created, all things will find their proper place. Without distinction between the sexes there is no sense of moral duty, and that is the way of animals (*wu bie wu yi, qinshou zhi dao ye*).

—*THE BOOK OF RITES*

"The Way of Animals"

The Book of Rites (*Li ji*) is one of the "Five Classics" that formed part of the Confucian canon. It was tested in the civil service examinations and as such, memorized by all educated men (and not a few women) in China during the last five or six centuries of the imperial era. The original text was supposedly compiled by Confucius himself.[1]

In the famous passage quoted in the epigraph,[2] *The Book of Rites* teaches us that the distinction between the sexes is essential for human civilization.[3] That civilization is structured by "rites" or "rituals" (*li*), which are the norms that properly govern human relationships. These rites do not develop spontaneously; they must be "created" (*zuo*), and their creation amounts to the invention of gender. When the sexes are separated and socialized into their respective gendered kinship roles, the father/son axis emerges as the primary relationship, characterized by the core value of filial piety that links patrilineal ancestors to descendants through the present generation.

The text as a whole makes clear that the point of distinguishing male from female is to establish a correct foundation for the relationship between husband and wife. As a later passage explains: "Once male is distinguished from female, then husband and wife shall have a sense of moral duty (*fufu*

[1]

you yi). Once husband and wife have a sense of moral duty, then father and son can draw together in affection; and once father and son draw together in affection, the relations between sovereign and minister shall be established in the correct way. Therefore, it is said that the rite of marriage is the root from which all the other rites grow."[4] Note that the husband/wife, father/son, and sovereign/minister dyads parallel one other, as do marital moral duty (*yi*), parental/filial affection (*qin*), and political legitimacy (*zheng*). The gendered hierarchy of the family established by the distinction between the sexes thus serves as the template for a moral, well-ordered polity.

In this Confucian vision, the family is a web of dyadic relationships that define each individual in terms of the duties they owe others. For example, the same man may simultaneously be a son to his parents, a younger brother to his older brother, a husband to his wife, and a father to his children, and each of these hierarchical relationships imposes specific duties and expectations. If people are socialized to behave in the manner required by each overlapping kinship role, they will be domesticated to Confucian patriarchy writ large, because a filial son will be a loyal subject to his sovereign. As the first chapter of *The Analects* (*Lunyu*) tells us: "Those who in private life behave well towards their parents and elder brothers, in public life seldom show a disposition to resist the authority of their superiors. And as for such men starting a revolution, no instance of it has ever occurred."[5]

Some lines after the passage quoted in the epigraph, *The Book of Rites* explains the status of women in the family, as governed by the rites: "A woman is one who follows and obeys (*furen congrenzhe ye*): in childhood, she follows her father and older brother; after marrying, she follows her husband; and after her husband dies, she follows her son."[6] The principle articulated here—often abbreviated as "thrice following" or the "three obediences" (*sancong*)—is that a woman's status and obligations are defined by her immediate male kin, to whom she owes deference and submission.[7]

What does *The Book of Rites* have to do with transgender? The last line of the epigraph is key: distinction between the sexes—and their assignment to distinct gender roles governed by the rites—is ultimately what distinguishes humans from animals and therefore defines our humanity. What happens, then, when the sexes are not properly distinguished? What if the boundary between them blurs, is crossed, or collapses altogether? "That is the way of animals"—a threat to civilization itself. As the Confucian sage Xunzi observes, what sets humans apart from animals is our capacity for "discrimination" (*bian*): "It is true that birds and beasts have both parents and offspring, but they lack the affection between father and son that characterizes humans; they have both sire and bitch, but they lack the distinction between the sexes that characterizes humans (*you pin mu er wu nan nü zhi bie*)."[8] In other words, animals are certainly capable of biological reproduction, but not of the gendered "discrimination" necessary for the rite of marriage; they have no comprehension of the ritual norms that create human family and civilization.

We begin to comprehend how gender nonconformism might have been understood in China during the late imperial era, at least by the authorities and Confucian elites. ("Late imperial" refers to the last two dynasties, the Ming, 1368–1644, and the Qing, 1644–1912. In this book, I use "late imperial" and "Ming-Qing" interchangeably.) With few exceptions, gender crossing was understood as symptomatic of "heterodoxy," as was the indiscriminate mixing of the sexes—because distinguishing between the sexes implied their spatial separation, with women's proper domain being the inner domestic sphere of the household. In the Ming-Qing era, Confucian orthodoxy defined female chastity as the absolute sexual loyalty of a woman to one husband for life and elevated it as a value coequal to the filial piety of son to father and the political loyalty of subject to sovereign. In this context, spatial separation of the sexes to safeguard chastity acquired heightened significance, especially in the lifestyle of the elite; it was in the same period that footbinding became universal practice among elite Chinese women and widespread even among the peasantry.[9]

Because of its cosmic and ideological implications, the crime of heterodoxy appears in the Ming and Qing legal codes under the Board of Rites, rather than the Board of Punishment. In fact, "the way of animals" (*qinshou zhi dao*) is a good approximation for the concept of heterodoxy (*zuodao yiduan*, "deviant ways and heterodox principles"), which in Confucian terms is defined as the opposite of "the orthodox way" (*zhengdao*).[10]

My Path to This Book

Ever since my first research in Qing legal archives as a graduate student, over thirty years ago, I have benefited from serendipity. It has been my constant experience that while looking for cases related to a given topic, I encounter others, seemingly at random, that pique my curiosity because they reveal something completely unexpected and cannot be explained based on what I already know.

My practice has been to copy these outliers, file them away, and let them accumulate over time. Occasionally, they come together like pieces of a puzzle, showing me a clear picture of something new, and, when that happens, I have the basis for a new project. For example, a paper I wrote some years ago on the practice of abortion in the Qing developed in this way—and so did the present book.[11]

It seems fitting that a book about what was seen as an anomaly—situations where sexed bodies and gendered behavior did not align in normative ways—developed through the random accumulation of seemingly anomalous cases encountered unexpectedly in the archives. In a sense, my process of discovery paralleled the way magistrates encountered these cases back in the day—although my goal is as much to make legible how those magistrates made sense of the cases as it is to make legible the lives that came under their scrutiny. I have brought together this collection of case studies under the sign "transgender," however anachronistic that word may seem, because it has helped me discern connections and patterns and meanings that otherwise would have remained obscure.

The first of these cases that I encountered in the archives were a series of marriage disputes involving "stone maidens" (*shinü*), individuals assigned female at birth whose anatomy made it impossible to consummate marriage by means of vaginal intercourse (see chapter 6). These cases intrigued me, but their significance eluded me. Then, in the spring of 1998, while I was still teaching at Penn, I had the great good fortune to team-teach a graduate seminar on "feminist theory and history" with my then-colleague Lynn A. Hunt. In that seminar, we combined canonical readings in feminist theory with examples of historical scholarship that attempted to apply those theories. Some of the most stimulating works we read (e.g. Judith Butler's *Gender Trouble* and Thomas Laqueur's *Making Sex*) grappled with how to understand the relationship between sex and gender—that is, between the body and what society expected of it. I felt inspired to use the stone maiden cases (and others that suddenly seemed relevant, such as the husband whose penis was too small) to analyze how Qing magistrates interpreted the physical evidence of the body in terms of normative gender expectations and how they tried to solve the social problems created when the two did not match. I ended up writing a paper that, much later and much revised, became the basis for chapter 6 in this book.[12]

Next, I happened upon the case of Xinxiang (a.k.a. Zhao Jianlin), who is the protagonist of chapter 7. Xinxiang defied category, given their chameleon quality of switching roles: Buddhist monk; female impersonator in the opera; sex worker; and, finally, con artist who practiced a kind of identity theft. I saw these roles as parallel to one another—different kinds of masquerade or even "drag" that all seemed "queer" in some way—but, again, I was not really sure what to make of all this. I was especially perplexed by Xinxiang's statement that they were really a woman, when it was clear that they were treated as a man throughout the case record. It was only later (after reading Susan Stryker's work) that I came to perceive Xinxiang's career as a series of transgender maneuvers, with the underlying reality perhaps being their subjective identity as a woman.[13]

Finally, I came across the three cases of "men masquerading in women's attire" (nan ban nüzhuang) that are the focus of chapters 2, 4, and 5. These cases obviously related to one another—and to the concept of transgender—in that the protagonists all had what midwives described as normal male anatomy, but at some point started presenting as women. Moreover, all three were prosecuted and harshly punished for the same crime: a variation of "heterodoxy." Upon reflection, the cases of stone maidens and even of Xinxiang seemed finally to come into focus when read together with these cases of male-to-female (M–F) crossing, and vice versa.

Qing authorities understood the crime of heterodoxy fundamentally as a kind of confidence scheme, in which evil charismatic leaders exploited their gullible followers for sex and money, as well as to foment sedition; a frequent accusation was that they encouraged the indiscriminate mixing of the sexes. By the same token, for a man to "pretend" to be a woman was understood as the nefarious masquerade of a sexual predator whose true intent was to insinuate himself into the female quarters of proper families in order to seduce or rape the "chaste wives and daughters" cloistered therein. The themes of fraud and sexual predation linked M–F crossing with heterodoxy, as did the cosmic and ideological implications of "the way of animals" previously discussed.

In contrast, stone maidens were interpreted as women who suffered from a disability and deserved compassion, so a place had to be found for them that did not require sexual intercourse and reproduction. The most common solution to this "problem" was for a stone maiden to become a Buddhist or Daoist nun. "To leave the family" (chujia) by joining the celibate clergy required the renunciation of normative gender roles based on marriage and procreation and implied (at least in theological terms) an aspiration to transcend the dualities of sex and gender. For this reason, I interpret "leaving the family"—a term also used for entering imperial service as a eunuch—as another transgender paradigm, albeit one safely contained within a circumscribed institutional framework that rendered it acceptable.

In the end, I realized that the most fruitful way to make sense of these seemingly anomalous, disparate cases would be to interpret them as episodes in the history of transgender in imperial China. But what do I mean by "transgender"? How do we write transgender history?

Transgender as Identity

The term "transgender" is new (although people who trans gender are not), having come into widespread use in the United States as an identity category or label only since the 1990s. As an umbrella category, transgender (alternatively "trans" or "trans★") prioritizes community organization and political mobilization, and the history of trans activism closely parallels that of the self-conscious transgender community. Indeed, it is fair to say that the community came into being in order to fight for trans people's right to exist, and that fight in turn has helped foster trans people's collective identity as a community.[14]

Activists have sometimes disagreed on exactly who should count as transgender and where this category's boundaries lie, but it is generally understood to include (at minimum) all people who identify with a gender other than that which they were assigned at birth, regardless of whether they have taken measures to confirm that gender, such as surgery. In addition, people who identify as gender-nonconforming (i.e., those who accept their assigned sex but whose gender presentation does not conform to expectations) or nonbinary often include themselves under the transgender umbrella. (Intersex people, whose *bodies* defy simple binary classification, are usually seen as constituting a closely allied but distinct identity of their own, but opinions vary.) One thing all of these people have in common is the assertion that the body is not destiny—in other words, that each person's real gender identity is a matter of individual self-determination, irrespective of genes or anatomy. Gender is not determined by one's body, let alone by how parents, medico-legal authorities, or other parties judge that body. Moreover, gender can be dynamic, and one is free to change one's mind.[15]

This way of understanding the body's relationship to gender has required a profound reorientation in thinking. The body is still assumed by many to be the empirical, immutable ground of a person's being.[16] But transgender identity today is founded on the proposition that it is one's subjective gender that is real, and that the body is a plastic, malleable vessel that can be adapted to accommodate the identity inhabiting it. This evolution in perspective has occurred in tandem with the development of sophisticated new technologies of "gender confirmation" (another neologism of recent vintage), including surgical procedures and the use of hormones. It is now possible to modify the body safely and effectively in ways that could barely be imagined a century ago.[17]

In prioritizing self-determination, transgender identity resembles sexual orientation, which is a social identity determined by the sex of one's object of desire, such as homosexual, bisexual, or heterosexual. Sexual orientation as a *social identity* is also a relatively recent development, although same-sex desire has been present in all times and places. Sexual orientation is understood to be a matter of self-determination in the sense that being of a particular sex or gender should not automatically dictate whom one desires, let alone whom one marries or with whom one has sex. It is up to each person to determine what their own sexual orientation is and to live their life accordingly.

From a Foucauldian perspective, self-determination makes sense as the basis for identity in democratic capitalist societies like the United States, because these societies imagine the individual citizen to be a free agent who exercises choice (as voter and consumer) and whose lifestyle and identity are largely defined by their choices. Free elections are equated with popular self-determination, and egalitarian social and political relations (e.g., equal opportunity, equal rights, equality before the law) are idealized, if not always realized in practice. In a political economy of this kind, an individual's subjective perceptions and desires really matter (or, at least, are believed to matter) and are seen as rightly determining their social persona and lifestyle. The legal recognition of LGBTQ rights has been a logical development of these principles.[18]

Needless to say, not all societies either in the past or in the present day have been organized like the contemporary United States.[19] In most times and places, self-determination and egalitarian social and political relations have not been idealized, let alone empowered, and individual preferences and desires have had far less influence over most people's social identities and life chances.

The study of transgender history requires a somewhat different perspective from that of modern transgender identity. For one thing, if we project our new identity categories into the past, there is great risk of anachronism. These terms and labels did not exist in, for example, eighteenth-century China, and it is impossible for us to know how a gender-transing individual from that time and place would identify today. Insofar as self-determination is a core value of modern transgender politics, it would seem presumptuous and wrong to impose labels on people who cannot speak for themselves.

To mitigate these problems, historians have increasingly focused on transgender *practices* and avoid positing any stable, transhistorical identity based on what is familiar today. Susan Stryker pioneered this approach by using the term "transgender" to refer to "people who move away from the gender they were assigned at birth, people who cross over (*trans-*) the boundaries constructed by their culture to define and contain their gender."[20] As to *why* people might cross gender boundaries in this way, Stryker advocates a maximally inclusive approach:

> Some people move away from their birth-assigned gender because they feel strongly that they properly belong to another gender in which it would be better for them to live; others want to strike out toward some new location, some space not yet clearly described or concretely occupied; still others simply feel the need to challenge the conventional expectations bound up with the gender that was initially put upon them. In any case, it is *the movement across a socially imposed boundary away from an unchosen starting place*—rather than any particular destination or mode of transition—that best characterizes the concept of transgender that I develop here.[21]

As the phrase "in any case" suggests, Stryker is deliberately agnostic about the motivation for such movement; she also avoids specifying its endpoint, and whether it is permanent or temporary. For these reasons, her definition can be applied without anachronism to a variety of historical and cultural contexts, illuminating important parallels and differences between them.

Historians such as Peter Boag, Clare Sears, and Jen Manion have built on Stryker's approach by focusing on transgender practices and representations in specific historical contexts, rather than transhistorical identities.[22] To underscore this emphasis on practice, Manion uses "trans" as a verb, as in "to trans gender." As she explains, "To say someone 'transed' or was 'transing' gender signifies a process or practice without claiming to understand what it meant to that person or asserting any kind of fixed identity on them."[23] To be clear, in this context the meaning of "gender" and the significance of transing it are specific to a particular time and place. This approach frees historians to think about transgender in a more expansive and open-ended way than would be possible with a narrow emphasis on identity. For example, "trans-ing analysis" enables Sears to "assemble a wide range of cross-dressing practices that are rarely considered alongside one another, thereby facilitating a series of juxtapositions that expose the workings of cross-dressing laws."[24] Sears does not get bogged down trying to guess which nineteenth-century cross-dressers might identify as transgender, were they alive today.

Similarly, Stryker's definition of "transgender" enables me to consider together a number of paradigms and practices that are usually thought of as unrelated. For example, I believe that the act of "leaving the family" (to join the celibate clergy or to become a eunuch) fits Stryker's definition perfectly. Such people did not turn into the opposite gender, but there is no question that, by forsaking normative gender roles defined by marriage and procreation, they "moved away from" the gender they had been assigned at birth. From this standpoint, it is illuminating to compare clergy and eunuchs with figures who might more obviously seem to fit a presentist definition of transgender, such as the boys who performed female roles in the opera, and the M–F crossers who are my focus in chapters 2, 4, and 5. As we shall see, clergy make frequent appearances in the chapters that follow, appearances that are not dictated by my analysis so much as rendered legible by it. Thus, it seems significant that the first step in Xiong Mumu's M–F transition was to shave their head and pose as a runaway widow who sought to become a Buddhist nun in order to safeguard her chastity (chapter 2); that the most common solution for the "problem" of the stone maiden was to have her become a nun, making a virtue of necessity (chapter 6); and that Xinxiang's career as an actor of female roles was preceded by their vocation as a monk (chapter 7). Moreover, it is no accident that the paranoid stereotype of the M–F cross-dresser as a sexual predator was paralleled by similar fears about clergy in particular (chapter 3), but also eunuchs and actors of female roles.

In the passage quoted, Stryker maintains an agnostic posture toward people's motives for transing gender, but her word choice indicates that she sees movement away from "an unchosen starting place" as a matter of self-determination that reflects the feelings and wishes of the individual in question. Manion agrees that motivation is "one of the most elusive dimensions" of trans history, yet she, too, emphasizes that her protagonists "chose to trans gender and live fully as men."[25] It seems clear that both historians are projecting into the past an assumption that to trans gender represents an act of will that reveals a person's genuine identity, their true inner self. After all, such revelation is generally taken for granted as the point of transitioning today.

But it would be anachronistic to make any such assumptions about people who transed gender in the Chinese past. It is clear that many of the people I include in this category had little or no agency in the matter. For example, the most common way that boys became eunuchs or actors of female roles is that they were sold by their parents out of poverty; similarly, most boys who entered the clergy were donated by parents who could not afford to support them (this included some boys with disabilities). Some who became eunuchs were the young sons of convicted rebels or murderers, their castration being intended to cut off their fathers' lines of descent. But even grown men who made the drastic decision to become eunuchs also typically did so out of poverty, suggesting something other than free choice. This is not to say that individuals' own choices played no role whatsoever in their transing. If I had to guess, I would say that the protagonists of chapters 2 and 4, who were assigned male at birth but presented as women, are the two people discussed in this book most likely to have freely chosen to trans gender; but the very similar protagonist of chapter 5, Xing Shi, is a more ambiguous figure, as we shall see.

In *Transtopia in the Sinophone Pacific*, Howard Chiang reflects on the reception of his earlier edited volume, *Transgender China*: "Some Anglophone readers criticized the ways in which the term *transgender* was used to describe a range of phenomena in Chinese culture that they did not deem sufficiently genuine to the concept as it is understood in the West. Many of the examples discussed in *Transgender China* were simply not 'trans enough' for those readers. I was surprised by the degree of boundary policing imposed by its interlocuters."[26] Chiang does not name his critics or specify what they rejected as "not 'trans enough.'" But perhaps his own most important contribution to Chinese transgender history (previewed in *Transgender China* and elaborated in his subsequent book, *After Eunuchs*) is to trace a conceptual genealogy from the eunuch of the imperial era to Taiwan's first "transsexual" (*bianxingren*), Xie Jianshun, an apparently intersex person forced to undergo experimental sex reassignment surgery in the 1950s; their female gender was chosen for them.[27] Notably, neither of these iconic figures freely chose their fate—on the contrary, I would suggest that both are best understood as victims of state violence. As a result, no identitarian concept based on self-determination that purports to reveal the true inner self would likely recognize either as "transgender"—and this, I suspect, may be one reason for the "not 'trans enough'" complaint that Chiang received. But I agree with Chiang that we cannot understand China's transgender history without a sympathetic effort to understand such figures in their own historical contexts.

As a general rule, transgender practices that confirm the established hierarchy of status and privilege have not been prohibited or necessarily even considered controversial. Thus, for example, the male Harvard undergraduates who dress up as women for the Hasty Pudding theatricals suffer no stigma, let alone persecution; in fact, that club's alumni include some of the most prominent American men of the last 250 years. Their freedom to flout gender norms with impunity, albeit temporarily, is a sign of privilege.

In late imperial China, gender transing by clergy, eunuchs, and actors was accepted because it took place within narrowly defined institutional contexts where it did not threaten the normative order. Even the nominally prohibited sex work of boy actresses was tolerated, for the most part, precisely because it served the pleasure of elite men. If anything, these safely contained zones of gender transgression helped define, by contrast, the boundaries of the normative. But becoming an actor, a eunuch, or a member of the clergy generally did not represent a nonconformist act of individual self-expression; most people who entered these vocations had little or no choice in the matter, and their gender transing followed specifically coded protocols. These facts seem to have helped neutralize whatever transgressive implications may have attached to such deviation. In contrast, gender transgression that was understood to be an act of self-determination provoked paranoid fantasies of heterodoxy and sexual predation and therefore became a target for harsh persecution. This was especially true of the individuals we shall encounter who were prosecuted as "men masquerading in women's attire."

In my case studies, the single most elusive dimension is the subjective perspectives of people who transed gender, especially their motives and how they understood their own identities. I will explore these dimensions as far as the sources allow, but I will pay at least as much attention to how transgender people and practices were represented and understood by others—especially the Qing authorities who produced the legal cases I have collected, as well as the literati authors of fanciful fiction that explored gender transgression and anomalies of sex. All of these sources represent attempts to render gender nonconformism legible in terms familiar to those who produced them. To their efforts we can add my own, although my target is as much the officials and literati who grappled with nonconformism as the nonconformists themselves.

The Pronouns of People in the Past

A related question is what pronouns we should use in reference to historical figures who transed gender or whose gender identity is unclear in surviving sources. There is no simple answer to this question, and the best scholars working in the rapidly growing field of transgender history have pursued diverse strategies, each with its own rationale.

No Gendered Pronouns in Ming-Qing Sources

An important consideration for the present study is that, until the early twentieth century, gendered pronouns did not exist in the Chinese language, either in speech or in writing. Gendered pronouns do not appear in any of my Ming or Qing dynasty sources. Indeed, they do not exist in speech even today: for example, in spoken Mandarin, the words for "he/him," "she/her," and "it" are all pronounced *ta* with a first tone; the possessive is created by simply adding the particle *de*.

A separate written character meaning "she/her" was invented only in the early twentieth century.[28] Before the invention of this written female pronoun, the character *ta* that is now used exclusively for "he/him" could also refer to "she/her," depending on context. The old nonbinary *ta* appears primarily in vernacular texts, including Ming-Qing fiction and the oral testimony recorded in Qing legal case records. (The corresponding character in classical Chinese, *yi*, also refers to either men or women.) This *ta* is written using the radical *ren*, meaning "person" or "human being."[29] There is usually no ambiguity about the gender of the referent, but the default meaning of *ta* is masculine—just as the word *ren*, if unmodified, means "man" by default. This default masculinization is reminiscent of traditional English usage, such as "mankind" to refer to all humanity, and masculine pronouns to include both men and women (e.g. "to each his own").

The new character for the female *ta* replaced the person radical *ren* with the radical *nü*, meaning female or woman; the rest of the character remained unchanged. The main justification cited by the new character's advocates was the supposed difficulty of translating literature from European languages into Chinese: gendered pronouns were needed to ensure accuracy, and their lack was deemed a symptom of the backwardness and inadequacy of Chinese. The female *ta* was just one of a host of iconoclastic reforms proposed to "modernize" China's language and culture in order to "catch up" with Japan and the West. Activists debated whether to invent a new spoken pronoun that would denote the new character for "she/her," but in the end all of these characters continued to share a single pronunciation, so the modern innovation of gendered pronouns was limited to writing.[30]

When translating Qing legal texts into English, it is usually a simple matter to decide whether the nonbinary *ta* should be rendered "he/him" or "she/her." But, in the particular cases I introduce in the chapters below, we cannot rule out the possibility that pronoun ambiguity in the original Chinese carried a significance that is lost in translation. In fact, at least some fiction writers seem to have exploited pronoun ambiguity for specific narrative purposes. Judith Zeitlin addresses this point in her analysis of Pu Songling's seventeenth-century tale "The Human Prodigy" (*Renyao*): "The Chinese language, with its lack of gender pronouns or genderized endings, is ideally suited to stories about ambiguous sexuality. Since gender markers are not required, awkward constructions such as him/her or a definitive gender assignment can be avoided, something impossible to do in English. The narrator is required to lie less, to strew fewer 'snares,' to employ

Barthes's term. Instead, a vagueness of language can mask the uncertainty of gender."[31] In testifying about ambiguous individuals, the use of a single, nonbinary pronoun allowed witnesses to avoid voicing an explicit judgment about their gender, and this ambiguity carried over into the written transcripts of testimony. This feature of the Chinese language may have permitted suspension of judgment even on a cognitive level: in effect, both speakers and writers were free not to commit, without calling attention to themselves. It is impossible to know exactly what was in the mind of any given witness (or scribe) who used the nonbinary pronoun—but that very uncertainty deserves our attention.

Recently, trans and nonbinary activists in China have begun advocating for the revival of a gender-neutral written character for the third-person pronoun, one that matches the *ta* used in speech. At least three strategies have been proposed. One is to introduce a new written character that uses an "X" instead of either the person radical (for the masculine *ta*) or the female radical (for the feminine *ta*). A second strategy proposed by activists in Hong Kong is to adopt the character *keoi* (pronounced *qu* in Mandarin), which is the Cantonese equivalent of the old gender-neutral *ta*. A third strategy is simply to use the romanization "TA" instead of any Chinese character.[32]

Recent Scholarship and the Approach of This Book

In recent studies of transgender history (almost all of which focus on the United States or Western Europe), we find a range of policies about pronoun use. At one end of the spectrum, Rachel Mesch uses female pronouns for her three famous leading characters, all of whom in various ways presented as men, because in her view none of them definitively renounced their identities as women and because the category "transgender" did not exist in their day.[33] At the opposite end, Jules Gill-Peterson eschews pronouns based on the gender people were assigned at birth and makes a point of labeling them "trans" when "the available evidence is clear"[34] that they were "obviously trans."[35] In similar vein, Emily Skidmore names her protagonists "trans men" and uses exclusively male pronouns, because each of them "chose to live as a man for many years," and "they all expressed the sentiment that they were men despite their anatomy."[36] But Gill-Peterson and Skidmore have the advantage that surviving records show some of their historical figures giving explicit answers when directly questioned about their gender identities, so their confidence on this point may be justified. In contrast, Peter Boag, Howard Chiang, and Clare Sears opt to switch pronouns midway through narrating an individual's life (to indicate a change in gender presentation); Boag and Sears also use quotation marks to flag uncertainty and occasionally resort to "s/he" and "his/her."[37]

In *Female Husbands: A Trans History*, Jen Manion has pioneered a different approach, using "they/their/themselves" in order to refuse the binary straitjacket of gendered pronouns altogether. This refusal is an act of intellectual humility, an acknowledgment of the limits of what can be known about the past based on the sources that survive.[38] The "female husbands" whom Manion studies were individuals in eighteenth- and nineteenth-century England and the United States assigned female at birth who presented as men and married women. Who are we to judge whether they were "really"—for example—*butch lesbians* or *straight transmen*, when none of them used this anachronistic vocabulary themselves?[39] Manion further suggests that our familiar categories and labels may simply be inadequate to capture the dynamic reality of female husbands' lives. In the end, she decides, her protagonists were simply what they called themselves and were called by others in their own day ("female husbands"), with all the paradoxical ambiguity that term contains. Among other things, it fruitfully calls attention to the tension between bodily sex (female) and gendered social role (husband), without favoring or erasing either.[40]

I am fully persuaded by Manion's approach, which I emulate in this book, especially with regard to the protagonists of chapters 2, 4, 5, and 7. We actually know less about the people in my legal cases than we do about many of those studied by the scholars cited above, and nowhere in my sources can we be absolutely sure that any given individual is really speaking for themself, without duress. In fact, we will see clear evidence that testimony changed in response to torture, better to fit the expectations of interrogators. Therefore, caution seems warranted.

Any policy on pronoun use that I adopt in this book is likely to seem anachronistic in one way or another, and no policy is likely to please everyone. To be sure, gender-neutral pronouns can create some awkward turns of phrase, and, for someone of my generation, at least, they take a great deal of getting used to. But to use gendered pronouns in this book in an indiscriminate way might constitute the most insidious anachronism of all, because its apparent naturalness would mask my assignment of gender to whomever I was writing about. By using nonbinary pronouns for certain key figures, I am trying to suspend judgment myself and also to reflect more accurately the language of my sources. In fact, "they/them" appears to be the closest equivalent to the old nonbinary *ta* that English can offer. This approach seems especially appropriate for my protagonists who transed gender by presenting as women despite having been assigned male at birth, and for Xinxiang, the enigmatic focus of chapter 7.

When prosecuted, M–F crossers were "regendered" male as an automatic part of their punishment and as a necessary part of restoring normative order.[41] Thus, for example, in the legal case records they are always referred to by their original names—what we might now call their "deadnames"—rather than the new names they had adopted upon transitioning. In order to reject this regendering, I use the new names these individuals chose for themselves, as well as gender-neutral pronouns.

I should note, however, that after considerable thought I have decided to continue using gendered pronouns for some other figures who transed gender in different ways: the actors who performed female roles (*dan*); eunuchs; and Buddhist and Daoist clergy. My reason is that such figures seem to have been identified by others (and at least some themselves identified) primarily with the gender they had been assigned at birth, despite the various ways in which they had "moved away" from that gender. Thus, for example, *dan* actors were never confused with cisgendered women—in fact, their charm and erotic appeal derived precisely from the fact that they were *boys* who performed a particular standard of femininity—and, despite their female roles on stage and the effeminate personae they maintained offstage, they were consistently identified as male. Also, nearly all quit the theater by the end of their teen years and most presumably reverted to normative masculinity.

Most eunuchs were castrated and sold into imperial service as children and at their parents' behest, and had no say in the matter. They would preserve their amputated genitals in order be buried with them, in hope of reincarnation as an intact male, and, upon retirement, most became Buddhist or Daoist monks (never nuns).[42] Moreover, we know that many eunuchs regretted their condition, and at least some who had sufficient means attempted to approximate a normative masculinity by discreetly marrying and adopting sons (although this was prohibited).[43]

In the case of clergy, to transcend the dualities of sex and gender was an aspiration. But even as clergy understood the main social boundary as dividing them collectively from the laity, they remained aware of the difference of sex among themselves. This is especially clear for Buddhists, who maintained rigid sex segregation in their institutions, but it can also be seen in the elaborate efforts of Daoists to overcome that difference, the disciplines of their "internal alchemy" differing by sex. Moreover, the terminology used to refer to clergy consistently differentiated by sex, as can be seen in the language of the Qing code, which uses distinct gendered nouns for Buddhists (*sengren* for monk, *niseng* for nun) and Daoists (*daoshi* and *nüguan*), respectively.[44]

For all of these reasons, it makes sense to me to retain gendered pronouns for these categories of people, even though they all clearly moved away from the gender they had been assigned at birth in a number of significant ways.[45] In fact, for all of these categories, the gender status that resulted from such movement was contested to some degree, and its very ambiguity became the focus of suspicions and tensions, as we will see.

Sources and Methods

Qing Legal Cases

As with my previous work, the main source for this book is original records of legal cases from the Qing dynasty's archives that date to the eighteenth and nineteenth centuries. But, instead of attempting to generalize from a mass of material, as in my first two books, I have narrowed my focus to a close reading of a limited number of intriguing examples. Four of the chapters focus on a single case each.

The Qing Empire included "China proper" (equivalent to the territory of the former Ming at the time of the Manchu conquest) as well as vast territories on the periphery of China that were conquered in the seventeenth and eighteenth centuries. The dynastic ruling house of the Qing were Manchus, not Chinese, and they ruled their diverse, pluralistic empire by coopting local elites and incorporating them as junior partners in the regime. This strategy of rule necessitated preserving and upholding the traditional values and institutions dear to those elites. Thus, after conquering China proper (which region is the exclusive focus of this book), the Qing ruled it by adopting most Ming institutions wholesale, including a provincial bureaucracy staffed mainly by elite Chinese men who were recruited via civil examinations that tested their mastery of the orthodox Confucian curriculum. Similarly, the original version of the Qing legal code (initially applied only in the former Ming territories) was a near verbatim copy of the Ming code, although its statutes (*lü*) would be amended over time through the addition of many substatutes (*li*). Following the Ming system, China proper was divided into eighteen provinces, which were subdivided into approximately 170 prefectures, in turn subdivided into approximately 1500 primary local jurisdictions—most of the latter were counties (*xian*), plus some departments (*zhou*) and subprefectures (*ting*); for legal cases, these local jurisdictions served as courts of first instance. These numbers changed little over the course of the Qing, despite significant population growth.[46]

The legal case records used for this book come from two main categories, both held at the First Historical Archive in Beijing. The first is "routine memorials on criminal matters" (*xingke tiben*), which were reports of provisional judgments of major crimes submitted by provincial governors to the imperial capital for review. (The usual chain of command for reporting major crimes was county-prefecture-provincial capital-Beijing.) My previous research depends on these sources, and I have described them in detail elsewhere.[47] The second category is newer to me: "secret palace memorials" (*zhupi zouzhe*), which were intended to be a secure means for senior officials in the provinces to communicate confidentially with the emperor. These memorials would be delivered by express directly to the emperor and then returned to the memorialist bearing his "vermilion rescript" (*zhupi*), written in his own hand. An official copy (*lufu zouzhe*) would be kept on file at the palace, and after the memorialist had read the emperor's response, he was supposed to return the original to the capital as well.[48] Secret palace memorials usually concerned urgent matters of security (e.g., war, sedition, official malfeasance), and the fact that cases of "men masquerading in women's attire" were also reported through this extraordinary channel reflects the weight of the ideological implications such cases bore.

To make sense of these case studies, I draw on my experience with a much larger body of historical sources. In a fundamental way, this book rests on the foundation of all my research in the Qing archives over the past thirty-odd years. My first two books were based on a total sample of more than 2500 legal cases.[49] For my long-term research project on male same-sex relations and masculinity (the topic of my projected fourth book),

I have collected nearly 2000 more that are focused on the crime of *jijian*—that is, male-male anal intercourse (or, for convenience, "sodomy"). In the process of selecting these focused samples, I skimmed perhaps 8000–10,000 *xingke tiben* and 2000–3000 local court cases. It is on this basis that I am able to generalize about, for example, the typical features of male same-sex relations among beggars, and a number of other matters. This wide reading in the archives enables me to see more clearly what was truly distinctive about the case studies presented here.

The Fictional Genre of "the Strange"

In addition to legal cases from the Qing archives, I also cite the lively corpus of Ming-Qing fiction in the genre of "the strange" (*zhiguai*) that touches on gender transgression and sexual anomaly, including the work of such well-known writers as Li Yu, Ling Mengchu, Pu Songling, and Yuan Mei. Many of their tales take the format of a court case that climaxes when a clever magistrate manages to discover the truth. These authors' main purpose was to entertain readers, but a closely allied goal was to make sense of anomalous people and behavior by rendering them comprehensible in familiar terms, and, in this sense, the fiction provides an interesting alternative and complement to judicial sources. The literati who wrote these tales (as well as most of their readers) had received much the same orthodox Confucian education as the officials who dealt with such matters in the courtroom, and they were operating broadly within the same worldview. In fact, two of the most famous authors, Ling Mengchu and Yuan Mei, actually served as officials themselves.[50]

There appears to be a direct relationship between fiction and court cases—what one might even call a "feedback loop"—in which their mutual influence created a shared discourse about gender transgression that shaped the case studies presented in this book. Most obvious is the fifteenth-century case of the paradigmatic cross-dressing sexual predator Sang Chong. Sang was apparently a real historical figure, because a brief account of their alleged crimes appears in the *Veritable Records of the Ming Dynasty* (*Ming shilu*), which is a chronicle of major events produced by the imperial court. Sang's sensational story became the basis for an entire subgenre of popular literature, including works by some of the most famous authors of the late Ming and early Qing. Some versions narrate Sang Chong's story in a seemingly straightforward manner, as if relating the actual record of their trial, whereas others use it as the point of departure for even more bizarre scenarios that are pure invention (including shape-shifting sorcerers with retractable penises who disguise themselves as nuns). By the end of the Ming, local gazetteers from Sang Chong's home province of Shanxi were recording a version of their case that seems to be based largely on fiction.

As a result, Sang Chong's story was well known in the Qing, and its fictional versions contributed to a discourse of the cross-dressing predator that clearly influenced how magistrates interpreted actual cases of M–F crossing that they encountered. These cases fed the feedback loop in turn, fostering further fictional elaborations. For example, the case of Xing Shi (chapter 5) attracted widespread attention because it took place in the imperial capital, and at least one fictional version of the case was subsequently published. Moreover, it seems likely that the extraordinary "facts" of Sang Chong's case themselves derived from a long-standing literary discourse of sexual anomaly and transgression embodied in the figure of the *"renyao"*—variously translated as "human prodigy" or "human demon."[51] If Sang Chong did confess to these crimes, I suspect that they did so under torture, which had the effect of eliciting a confession that confirmed a preexisting "script" in the minds of their interrogators. If I am correct, then the feedback loop between literature and court cases already existed at that early date.

Late Qing Newspaper Reportage on Gender Nonconformism

I have also located a remarkable amount of material relevant to this study in Shanghai's late Qing press, specifically the newspaper *Shenbao* and the illustrated *Dianshizhai Pictorial*, which were published by the same company.[52] A regular theme in *Shenbao*, from the paper's earliest issues in the 1870s until its demise in 1949, was the transing of gender. Such reportage is closely related to the fictional genre of "the strange." As Rania Huntington has observed: "Alongside coverage of national and international politics, crime, and social events, late Qing periodicals recount stories of hauntings, monstrous births, and karmic retribution. Such stories suggest that the newspapers and pictorials were, among other things, a continuation of the *zhiguai* (tales of the strange) genre. . . . I contend that strangeness was central, not marginal, to late Qing periodical literature."[53] Huntington notes that "tales of the supernatural . . . are a recurring presence" in *Shenbao*, and that "in the years between 1872 and 1884, on the average one such story appeared every five or six days."[54] These periodicals blurred the boundaries between "the news" and "the strange"; as Huntington comments, "*zhiguai* are presented as unembellished reportage of bizarre events."[55] Although she does not address transgender specifically, her observations clearly apply to that theme as well.

Typically, gender nonconforming people appear in stories about their arrest and prosecution in Shanghai or occasionally elsewhere in China. Keyword searches in *Shenbao*'s full text database turn up dozens of articles about cross-dressing con artists, sex predators, and spirit mediums; male clergy masquerading as women; people of ambiguous anatomy who might today identify as intersex (often referred to in the paper as *yinyang ren*, or "yin-yang people"); miscellaneous individuals arrested in public places for cross-dressing; unhappy people found to have committed suicide while wearing the clothing of the opposite sex; and so on.[56] Some of these stories are illustrated with engravings in the *Dianshizhai Pictorial*. In fact, there is so much relevant material in the late Qing and Republican-era press that it deserves a separate study of its own. I present only a few examples in this book.

Most of this reporting appears to be based on actual legal cases that involved real people, although those cases have been rhetorically packaged in terms of familiar paradigms and normative expectations about deviance. We find constant references to Sang Chong, Pu Songling's *Strange Stories from the Liao Studio* (*Liaozhai zhiyi*, a classic of the *zhiguai* genre), Li Yu's fiction, the cross-dressing woman warrior Hua Mulan, scenarios from the Peking Opera, and other literary tropes. In this sense, the newspaper reportage is clearly part of the feedback loop between legal cases and fictional representations discussed earlier. Instead of being taken as an empirically accurate representation of the facts, such reports should be treated mainly as discourse—and, in that sense, they are useful for demonstrating the stubborn persistence of older paradigms and expectations about gender well into the twentieth century. But if we assume that most of these stories were based on actual events that bore at least some resemblance to what was reported, then the newspaper reportage also constitutes valuable testimony to the sheer ubiquity of gender-transing and nonconformist people—in other words, to the fact that such people existed and were not necessarily so rare. In addition to the more lurid, graphic stories, we find brief and relatively mundane reports of individuals being summarily detained and punished simply because they were caught cross-dressing in public.[57]

An Overview

Chapter 1 provides a broad overview of transgender paradigms in the culture of the Ming-Qing era to serve as context for the case studies that follow. We open with the theme of cross-dressing in popular literature, most of which features female characters temporarily adopting male attire or playing a masculine social role: the woman warrior, the female knight errant, and variations of the scholar-beauty romance (including the story of Zhu Yingtai). We also briefly discuss the genre of "the strange" (*zhiguai*), which is most pertinent to the case studies that follow. Next, we address the male performers of female roles in the opera, who were the objects of intense erotic and aesthetic connoisseurship by elite men. Finally, we take up the paradigm of "leaving the family" (*chujia*), which included male and female clergy as well as eunuchs: both vocations required an individual to renounce normative gender roles defined by marriage and procreation. We close by introducing a final paradigm, the cross-dressing sexual predator, which features prominently in the rest of the book.

Chapters 2 through 5 address the paranoid fantasy of transgender predation through a series of case studies from the Qing legal archives, *zhiguai* fiction, and *Shenbao*. Chapters 2, 4, and 5 each focus on a single legal case involving "men masquerading in women's attire": individuals assigned male at birth who lived as women, and who were prosecuted and harshly punished for this crime. Chapter 2 uses the case of the midwife Xiong Mumu to introduce the predatory paradigm and its locus classicus, the Ming serial predator Sang Chong, and to analyze how and why M–F cross-dressing was prosecuted as "heterodoxy." Chapter 4 uses the case of Zhang Yaoguniang to introduce the demonization of faith healing and popular religion under the rubric of heterodoxy, as well as the way interrogation under duress tended to produce confessions that conformed to the preconceptions and prejudices of the interrogators. Chapter 5 continues to examine these themes through the case of Xing Shi, who served as medium to a female fox spirit, and for whom we have three separate and complementary sources: confessions produced before and after torture, plus a posthumous fictional account. The latter illustrates how a feedback loop between legal cases and fiction produced and sustained the discourse of the cross-dressing predator.

Chapter 3 takes a closer look at the popular stereotype, which clearly influenced legal judgments, that not all clergy were what they claimed to be—that many used the pretense of "leaving the family" in order to engage in sexual predation and other crimes. I argue that this stereotype of clergy as wolves in sheep's clothing paralleled the Sang Chong paradigm of the cross-dressing sexual predator. In fact, they should be understood as two variations of a single paranoid vision of gender-transing as a dangerous and predatory fraud.

In Chapter 6, we look more closely at how the body itself was read for evidence. The three cases of "men masquerading in women's attire" (covered in chapters 2, 4, and 5) all involve individuals who had what midwives deemed to be normal male anatomy, but whose behavior failed to conform to that anatomy. In chapter 6, in contrast, we look at a series of cases in which the anatomy itself was problematic and failed to fulfill the expectations of the assigned gender: cases involving "stone maidens" rejected by their husbands, men with problematic penises rejected by their wives, and so-called two-formed persons of ambiguous sex. We also look at rape cases involving clergy to explore how magistrates understood the sex of individuals who had transed gender by "leaving the family"; these cases show that under some circumstances the sexed body took precedence over gender roles and expectations.

Finally, chapter 7 presents the enigmatic character Xinxiang, whose remarkable career included stints as a monk, an actor of female roles, a prostitute, and a con artist. Xinxiang also claimed really to be a woman, despite having been assigned male at birth. They adopted at least eight different personae that we know of and finally were arrested and sentenced to death for pretending to be an imperial official. Utterly defiant of category, Xinxiang provokes more questions than we can answer—indeed, the term "transgender" seems almost inadequate to encompass their protean behavior.

A source of frustration for me in writing this book has been the many inevitable gaps in the legal case records. Many of the questions I would most like to ask simply cannot be answered with certainty, based on the evidence that survives. For example, one of the most intriguing episodes in the life of Xinxiang is the four years they spent in Beijing being trained and then performing as an actor of female roles. But everything we know about that period is contained in the previous sentence, which paraphrases a single line in Xinxiang's recorded testimony. For whatever reason, the magistrate did not see fit to inquire further about this topic, or at least to include any further information about it in the edited transcript of testimony he sent up the chain of command for review. Fortunately, we know from other sources (and from the work of other scholars) a great deal about the theater scene in Qing dynasty Beijing, and I have used that information to sketch what I hope is a plausible picture of Xinxiang's likely experience there.

Wherever I have encountered gaps in the surviving sources, I have done my best to compensate in this way, while acknowledging the limits of what can be known for sure. I take comfort in knowing that Natalie Zemon Davis had to resort to similar measures when writing her masterpiece, *The Return of Martin Guerre*: "When I could not find my individual man or woman in Hendaye, in Artigat, in Sajas, or in Burgos, then I did my best through other sources from the period and place to discover the world they would have seen and the reactions they might have had. What I offer you here is in part my invention, but held tightly in check by the voices of the past."[58] In what follows, I have tried to distinguish clearly when I speak directly from primary sources from when I engage in informed speculation.

There are no happy endings in this book, although the lives of some of these people do seem heroic to me, in a modest way. In general, I do not advocate looking to the past for role models or for a golden age when things were better, especially with regard to gender relations. Rather, my own view is that the historical past is useful mainly for making us aware of what needs to be overcome, as we strive to invent a better future. I do hope, however, that the stories in this book will be of value not only for historians, but also perhaps for transgender people and other nonconformists today, who may discover intriguing resonances with how gender was transed, and its implications, in a time and place very different from their own.

CHAPTER I

Transgender Paradigms in Late Imperial China

Tang Ao said, "Jiugong, look at them! They are just ordinary women, but they want to masquerade as men—so unnatural and pretentious!"

Duo Jiugong laughed and replied, "Brother Tang, that's what *you* say. But I'll bet that, when they see us, they complain that we are not content to be 'normal *women*,' and instead put on a show 'pretending to be men!'"

Tang Ao nodded. "What you say makes sense. It's like the old saying goes: 'Whatever you get used to seems natural.' They look strange to us, but no doubt they've always been like that; and, naturally, we look wrong to them as well.

–But if the men here are like this, I wonder what the women are like?"

— "THE KINGDOM OF WOMEN," IN
ROMANCE OF FLOWERS IN THE MIRROR

I n Ming-Qing China, we can identify a rich variety of transgender paradigms. In this chapter, I sketch the most important of these paradigms in order to provide background and context for the case studies that follow. Certain forms of gender-transing were permitted and even celebrated, but only within specific, narrow limits where they tended to confirm rather than threaten the established order of status and privilege. In sketching these paradigms, I hope to justify my application of Susan Stryker's practice-based definition of "transgender" to include categories of people such as actors, clergy, and eunuchs. I end by introducing the paradigm that is most pertinent to this book—namely, the cross-dressing sexual predator.

Literary Paradigms

Cross-dressing is a favorite theme in the fiction and drama of the Ming-Qing era, with female-to-male (F–M) crossing being particularly common. The typical scenario is for cross-dressing to serve as a temporary expedient to deal with some predicament. The resulting awkwardness provides occasion for titillation and tension (will the heroine be discovered? what about her bound feet?), comedic double entendre, and escapist fantasy—especially, one imagines, for female spectators who watched F–M crossing being performed onstage. (Such performance could be complicated, with a male actor of female roles recrossing in order to "pretend" to be a man.) In the end, however, order is restored when the protagonists resume their assigned gender roles and don the appropriate attire. For this reason, the cross-dressing comedy is often seen as reconfirming the established order rather than challenging it.[1]

The Woman Warrior and the Female Knight Errant

No doubt, the most famous example of F–M crossing in the Chinese tradition is the legendary woman warrior Hua Mulan, whose tale dates to the Northern Wei dynasty (386–534 CE), but has been repeatedly refashioned to suit changing times. Probably the best-known version of Mulan's tale in the Qing dynasty was Xu Wei's late Ming play *The Female Mulan Joins the Army in Place of Her Father (Ci Mulan ti fu congjun)*. The basic plotline common to all versions is that Mulan's family must provide one soldier for the army, but her father is too old and infirm, and her brother is too young; so Mulan, at the age of seventeen *sui*, disguises herself as a man and joins the army in their place. Over the next dozen years she proves an outstanding soldier, and in the end she is offered high office, but she declines, finally revealing her sex, and returns to her parents. In Xu Wei's version, this happy reunion culminates in her wedding to a promising local scholar.[2]

The crucial point about Mulan is that she is motivated not by any selfish desire or ambition, but by filial piety, that most orthodox of Confucian virtues—in other words, she does not cross-dress in order to defy patriarchal authority, but to serve it. During her years in the company of men, she never takes advantage of the situation to indulge in sexual promiscuity or any other impropriety. On the contrary, she keeps her sex secret and resolutely guards her chastity, and, as soon as the emergency is over, she resumes her role as a filial daughter. Mulan's cross-dressing is an exceptional measure taken in an emergency; it confirms by contrast the truth that, in normal times, the normative must prevail.[3]

Related to the woman warrior theme is the "female knight errant" (*nü xia*), who uses masterful swordplay and magic to punish evildoers. Typically, her motive is some personal mission of blood revenge—for example, avenging a murdered father—but, as an extension, she may fight injustice on behalf of society. Like Mulan, her motive is righteous. But, unlike Mulan, the female knight errant usually does not cross-dress or otherwise pretend to be a man; her gender crossing is limited to her role as a violent avenger, and, when her revenge is complete, she disappears from the social world. This genre is characterized by a tension: her acts may be righteous, but, as vigilante violence, they are inherently subversive of the official order. The implication is that she must take matters into her own hands because the authorities fail to provide justice, and no man will act on her behalf.[4]

An underlying theme in much of this gender-crossing fiction is the collective failure of men in a time of crisis, such as foreign invasion or dynastic collapse. This theme featured prominently during the Ming-Qing transition, when female poets loyal to the Ming adopted a masculine voice and martial imagery in order to express their political sentiments. Mulan was cited with envy by women who lamented the gap between their heroic aspirations and their actual abilities—they could only write poetry. In this way, the crisis became an occasion for women to vent their frustration at the limitations of traditional gender roles.[5]

In the twentieth century, Mulan served as a powerful role model for women activists, who downplayed her filial piety in order to reinvent her as the feminist and patriotic heroine they needed.[6] More broadly, for revolutionary women across the twentieth century, to dress as a man—and, more radical still, in a soldier's uniform—signified that they refused the confines of the Confucian gender system in order to play a public, political role. What they retained from Mulan (aside from cross-dressing) was selfless commitment to a higher cause. This theme of politicized gender crossing runs right through the history of the revolution, from Qiu Jin and the early women Communists, through the "Amazons" of the Northern Expedition, down to the Iron Girls and Red Guards of the Maoist era.[7]

The Scholar-Beauty Romance and Zhu Yingtai

Cross-dressing can be found in many romances of the "scholar-beauty" (*caizi jiaren*) genre, in which an ideally matched couple are fated to marry, but must endure trials and hardships before they can be united.[8] One interesting variation appears in Zhu Ying's early Qing play *Lovebirds' Reversal* (*Dao Yuanyang*), which is set during the chaotic Ming-Qing transition. Unusually for this genre, both heroine and hero must cross-dress in order to avoid an even worse fate: the heroine, to avoid sexual assault, and the hero, to avoid shaving the front of his head to conform to the tonsure imposed on Chinese men as a sign of submission by the Manchu conquerors who founded the Qing dynasty.[9] (After its universal adoption, this tonsure—which included growing out the back hair and braiding it into a queue—would become the most obvious gender cue that signaled a person's identity as a man.) The hero's predicament is especially ironic: to avoid the symbolic emasculation of cutting his hair, he must dress as a woman. After many adventures, the two are restored to their respective gender roles and joined in marriage. The hero, who had justified his refusal to shave his head out of filial piety, submits to the tonsure when ordered to do so by his father.[10]

Mulan aside, the most famous example of F–M crossing in Chinese literature is the heroine Zhu Yingtai, whose popular story (a variation on the scholar-beauty theme) has been retold many times. The basic plot is that Zhu Yingtai leaves home in male disguise in order to pursue an education; during her studies, she rooms with a fellow student named Liang Shanbo, with whom she falls in love, but she keeps her sex secret from him and carefully preserves her chastity. By the time Liang Shanbo discovers the truth and asks for her hand in marriage, she is already pledged to another, and Liang soon dies of unrequited love. En route to her wedding, however, Zhu Yingtai visits his tomb: it miraculously opens, and she jumps in, to join him in death.[11] In Wilt Idema's words, "A mutual love that never should have happened can now be consummated only when the lovers are united in the grave."[12]

In modern times, Zhu Yingtai's tale has often been compared to that of Romeo and Juliet. In the Ming-Qing era, Roland Altenburger explains, it may have been understood mainly as a cautionary tale about the tragic consequences of a smart girl, who should have known her place, having too much ambition for her own good. There is no question that her masquerade looks bad from a Confucian perspective (especially in contrast with the selfless Mulan), and in many versions Liang reproaches her for her deception. She defends herself by saying that the deception was necessary to preserve her chastity.[13] The tale offers contradictory messages, however, and this ambivalence is no doubt one reason for its enduring popularity. On the one hand, Zhu Yingtai's masquerade is portrayed as a temporary expedient to enable her to get an education, and, although she is motivated by personal ambition, her ultimate goal is not to usurp the worldly power of men, but to serve as the wife of a worthy husband, for whom she zealously safeguards her chastity. In this sense, at least, her story confirms the established gender order. At the same time, however, Zhu Yingtai may have served "the subversive function of a fantasy of temporary excursion into the domain of masculinity," much as Hua Mulan seems to have provided a conquering heroine fantasy for frustrated women during times of crisis.[14]

To sum up, Ming-Qing literature offers a rich diversity of F–M cross-dressing themes and scenarios. In most cases, however, the subversive potential of transing gender is safely neutralized by the selfless motivation and chastity of the heroine, and by her eventual submission to her assigned gender role. Moralists who might otherwise frown at the heroine's hair-raising adventures could take comfort in this didactic message. As a result, she can appear in a sympathetic, even positive light.

The Kingdom of Women

Another intriguing paradigm is the "Kingdom of Women" (*nü guo, nü'er guo, nüren guo*), an imaginary realm located on the far periphery of civilization that is ruled by powerful, sexually aggressive women. This trope originated in traditional ethnography, which used Confucian gender norms to demarcate the putative boundary between civilization and savagery (i.e., what *The Book of Rites* would call "the way of animals"), especially along the empire's southern frontiers, where the Chinese encountered other peoples who had dramatically different customs with regard to sexual relations, marriage, and the gendered division of labor. Gender disorder reinforced the portrayal of such peoples as uncouth and even bestial. In many accounts of the Kingdom of Women, this bestial connotation is explicit: the women there are described as having strange anatomy, being exceptionally hairy, and mating with dogs or snakes. Maps from the late imperial era locate a Kingdom of Women on an island off China's southeast coast, and, in the Qing, Chinese travelers strongly associated it with Taiwan, where indigenous societies seemed to be dominated by women.[15]

In Ming-Qing fiction, the Kingdom of Women has two principal variations. The first, like the homeland of the Amazons in Greek mythology, is inhabited only by women. This version of the Kingdom of Women has an ancient provenance, its locus classicus being the mythic geography and bestiary *The Classic of Mountains and Seas* (*Shanhai jing*), which dates to the third century BCE.[16] In the Ming dynasty novel *Journey to the West* (*Xiyou ji*), the Kingdom of Women's exclusively female denizens are fascinated by the novel's exotically male protagonists, who are traveling through, and the travelers' leader, the Tang Monk, only narrowly escapes being detained by the local queen to serve as her consort. This is just one of many episodes in the novel when the Tang Monk's pure body becomes an object of vampiric desire on the part of demonic figures that are gendered feminine.[17]

In the second variation, the Kingdom of Women is inhabited by both sexes, but their gender roles are reversed from the Chinese norm: each sex plays the social roles and adopts the adornment and attire typically associated with its opposite. The most famous example appears in Li Ruzhen's early nineteenth-century novel *Romance of Flowers in the Mirror* (*Jinghua yuan*), in which the male protagonists travel by ship to a number of exotic countries located far from China's shores.[18] *Flowers in the Mirror* resembles Jonathan Swift's *Gulliver's Travels* in that the description of each new country implies critical reflection on some aspect of the travelers' own society. For example, in the "Kingdom of Confucian Gentlemen" (*junzi guo*) people actually live according to the Sage's doctrines, implying a higher moral standard than that achieved in China itself.

When the travelers arrive at the Kingdom of Women, the handsomest of their number, the merchant Lin Zhiyang, catches the fancy of the "King," who (in an echo of *Journey to the West*) orders Lin kidnapped and incorporated into the royal harem. This narrative is greatly facilitated by the absence of gendered pronouns in Chinese, which enables a playful ambiguity that is impossible to capture in English translation. Perhaps the most famous passage in the novel is a graphic (and hilarious) description of Lin's excruciating experience of having his ears pierced and his feet bound by the merciless "mistresses" of the harem, who beat him into submission when he tries to resist. In the end, Lin and his companions manage to escape, taking with them a young "man" (i.e., anatomical female) who begs to accompany them back to China and immediately changes into woman's clothing, with evident relief, as soon as they depart. (In the Kingdom of

Women, this change of attire would have been a gender transing move.) In this way, the episode ends on a note of ambiguity: Was Li Ruzhen a protofeminist, as some modern scholars have suggested?[19] Or does the rectification of gender roles that concludes the episode negate his insights into the agony of footbinding and the arbitrary nature of gender roles?

Significantly, Li Ruzhen set *Flowers in the Mirror* during the reign of Wu Zetian (690–705), who was the only woman in Chinese history ever to claim the title *huangdi* and rule the empire in her own name.[20] (*Huangdi* is usually translated as "emperor," but in fact the term is gender neutral.) Wu Zetian is the most famous example of the classical trope of a woman usurping masculine political power, a form of gender-transing that the Confucian canon associates with the collapse of states and cosmic calamity. Wu Zetian first acquired power via the traditional route by which women did so, as the favorite consort of a besotted emperor and then as the mother of an emperor. In the end, however, she dispensed with all pretense and took the throne and title for herself and even declared a new dynasty of her own, the Zhou, to replace her in-laws' Tang dynasty. In the process, she violated a host of Confucian taboos: as a wife defying the authority of her husband and in-laws, as a disloyal subject overthrowing her sovereign, and as a woman usurping the political power of men. Ever after, Confucian historiography would condemn Wu Zetian as a licentious and sadistic tyranness, and her reign as the epitome of moral chaos in a world turned upside down—echoing the orthodox admonition that failure to separate the sexes into their proper social roles is the antithesis of human civilization.

Thus, Li Ruzhen chose to stage his vision of the Kingdom of Women within a gendered role reversal of imperial scale. His fictional Wu Zetian wreaks havoc on earth by ordering all the flowers to bloom in midwinter; she even promulgates a new civil service examination to be taken exclusively by women. In the end, however, in a move that mirrors historical events, gender order is restored: Tang loyalists overthrow Wu Zetian, abolish her deviant Zhou dynasty, and sequester the novel's female characters back in the inner quarters where they belong.

In an ironic mirror image of China, *Flowers in the Mirror* illustrates the enforcement of gender roles and punishment of nonconformists. Like the other fiction we have discussed, this novel teases its readers with the suggestion that gender roles are not necessarily or immutably linked to sex (see, e.g., the passage quoted in this chapter's epigraph); rather, they must be learned and performed, can be reversed and exchanged, and may even be rejected. In this respect, our fictional sources echo the canonical view that rites and norms do not emerge spontaneously out of nature, but instead are something essentially artificial that must be created and maintained in order for civilization to develop. That artificiality in turn implies contingency and fragility: nothing can be taken for granted, and vigilance is required to safeguard the normative order.[21]

The Genre of "the Strange"

Further valuable context for my case studies appears in the literary genre of "the strange" (*zhiguai*): short fiction and essays that record a diverse array of ghosts, demons, anomalies, and other weird phenomena that do not lend themselves to ready explication within the orthodox order. Hence, the eighteenth-century writer Yuan Mei gave his famous story collection the tongue-in-cheek title *Zi bu yu* (*What Confucius Did Not Say*, also translated as *Censored by Confucius*), which is an allusion to a comment in *The Analects* that "the Master never talked of prodigies, feats of strength, disorders, or spirits" (*zi bu yu guai, li, luan, shen*).[22]

A significant proportion of this genre consists of bizarre anecdotes involving sex, with vampiric fox spirits who seduce unwitting humans being an especially favorite theme.[23] Many of these tales call into question the links between anatomical sex and gender performance, and the same judiciary that sought to regulate gender and sexual relations in society also banned much of this literature as "licentious."[24] In these works, the body exhibits an extraordinary plasticity, and anatomy seems to pose no barrier to any particular role: sexual predators with protean genitalia masquerade as women, attractive young ladies turn out to be sexual vampires, castrated males serve as "female" concubines, and animal spirits and "stone maidens" prove to be ideal wives.[25] One function of this literature, no doubt, was to define the normative by contrast. But, in the Ming-Qing era, its main purpose was entertainment, and its enormous popularity in the commercial book market underscores the eternal truism that sex sells.

For our purposes, the genre of "the strange" is helpful because it provides a broader view beyond orthodox texts (e.g., legal codes and cases) of how educated elites thought about such matters. After all, as mentioned in the introduction, the men who wrote (and read) these works had received much the same Confucian education as degree-holding officials, and some of the most famous authors in this genre (including Yuan Mei) had themselves served as magistrates. More specifically, the literature that seems to be part of a "feedback loop" with our court cases belongs to this genre—for example, the many tales inspired by the case of Sang Chong. In other words, this literature helps us understand how, beyond the law, literati tried to make sense of anomalous bodies and gender nonconformism.

The Boy Actress

Literary fantasies aside, perhaps the most obvious paradigm for transing gender in Qing dynasty China—and the only acceptable one for M–F transing—was the actor who performed female roles in the opera: the *dan*. As many scholars have documented, a distinctive feature of elite male culture in the Ming-Qing era was erotic connoisseurship of young males, most famously these cross-dressing actors. Such connoisseurship played an important role in elite male bonding and was expressed through shared poetry and an avid fan literature that ranked boys by their feminine beauty, charm, and talent.[26]

Since the Ming, virtually all opera troupes had been unisex, with the vast majority being all male.[27] In all-male troupes, the performers of female roles were boys typically aged about thirteen to eighteen years old (i.e., fourteen to twenty *sui*), although their training might begin as early as age nine or ten. Most of these boys were sold to opera troupes by their parents out of poverty (others were kidnapped), and, while their careers lasted, they were the property of the troupe's master—in effect, his slaves. Their tender age was a key criterion for recruitment because it was associated with femininity, and for this reason their careers were short; as soon as their unmistakably masculine features became too obvious, they would be sidelined.[28]

In Beijing, which was the empire-wide center of the theater scene during the Qing, the ideal recruit for *dan* training was "an effeminate, pale and delicate looking boy," and their strict regimen of diet and training was designed to enhance these features and to inculcate an exaggerated version of femininity that suited literati taste.[29] As one late-Qing source recounts, "after three months of such a programme the boys' appearance was as lovely and fair as that of a young maiden. When they looked over their shoulders the effect was charming beyond belief."[30] (This specialized training in M–F crossing may be compared to the defeminization training of Buddhist nuns and the demasculinization training of male Daoists that we shall address later.) To add to this effect, *dan* were given "flamboyant, feminized stage names": typical examples include "Pretty Orchid," "Jade Fairy," and "Marvelous Coral."[31]

Since at least the Ming, the theater had been closely associated with prostitution, and, in the Qing dynasty, the exclusive focus of this theatrical sex industry was the boys who performed female roles. In Beijing, the main public venue where literati gathered to watch opera was the "teahouse," which was really a sort of theater. Women were banned from teahouses, so this was an all-male scene, including both actors and clientele, and its atmosphere carried an intensely erotic charge. In the heyday of the Peking Opera, as Wu Cuncun has shown, performances at the teahouse served mainly to advertise the charms of the *dan*, whose really lucrative work took place offstage, in the restaurants and private apartments where they served as high-end escorts and catamites for their wealthy patrons.[32] Spectators did not mistake *dan* for women. On the contrary, the allure of the cross-dressing actor depended on everyone knowing that he was not a cisgendered woman, but, rather, a boy performing a female role; it was precisely this artifice that was the source of his charm. Andrea Goldman's translation of *dan* as "boy actress" neatly captures the paradox.[33]

How are we to understand elite men's passion for these boy actresses? As Wu Cuncun points out, Chinese sources often attribute it to Qing dynasty laws that prohibited officials from contact with female prostitutes. Supposedly, such prohibitions forced elite men in Beijing to use *dan* as surrogates for women—but what they really wanted was women.[34] This theory is clearly wrong. For one thing, the connoisseurship of boy actresses dated at least to the Ming.[35] Also, Qing law prohibited officials from "consorting with actors" (*xia you*—this term generally referred to sexual relations with actors), and from "sleeping with prostitutes" (*su chang*) of either sex; moreover, it criminalized anal intercourse between males (*jijian*), regardless of their status.[36] If the laws against female prostitutes really had such dramatic effect, why were these other prohibitions so ineffective? A related line of argument is that since literati were attracted to performers of female roles, this attraction should be understood as an expression of *heterosexual* desire. But, if that was the case, why didn't they just pursue women?

In contrast, Wu Cuncun argues that elite male fashion since the Ming had been to downplay masculinity, so that to some extent the literati themselves had come to resemble the boy actresses they so desired. Therefore, in her view, the relationship between literatus and *dan* was actually one between "feminized-male and feminized-male," and, given the fundamental similarity between the subject and object of desire, that desire should be considered "homoerotic." She also uses the anachronistic term "homosexuality" to characterize this phenomenon.[37]

I find Wu's argument no more persuasive than the surrogacy theory. What she considers the "feminization" of elite men, I would suggest, was simply another mode of empowered masculinity—after all, we are talking about elite men. Their attraction to *dan* was not, fundamentally, an attraction of *like to like*, as the prefix "homo-" would imply. (Nota bene: before the twentieth-century import of Western sexology, there was no clear equivalent to the modern, egalitarian concept of sexual orientation in China.[38]) Rather, it was the possessive desire of an empowered adult male subject for a feminized boy object of unfree status, who was being rented out by his master for sex. This was a steeply asymmetrical relationship of exploitation; there was nothing mutual about it. The two sides of the equation had absolutely nothing in common, aside from male anatomy—and, given the wide age difference between patron and boy actress, even the similarity between their bodies would have been quite superficial.[39]

Elite male attraction to boy actresses seems to have been neither straightforward *hetero*sexual attraction (of a man to a woman) nor straightforward *homo*sexual attraction (of a man to a man), nor even simple hebephiliac attraction (of an adult to an adolescent). Instead, it was precisely *a boy's performance of femininity* (i.e., his transing of gender) both on- and offstage that constituted the focus of fascination. (A limited analogy might be how some cisgender men today fetishize transwomen as sex objects.)[40] But, also, the asymmetry of objectification and the boy actress's sexual availability were fundamental to this genre of connoisseurship.

We should bear in mind the profound misogyny that undergirded this entire discourse. The boy actress was not simply a substitute woman; on the contrary, connoisseurs believed, no mere woman could hope to achieve the exquisite feminine allure of the boy actress.[41] The appeal of the *dan* represented a triumph of artifice over nature—or, one might say, of gender performance over bodily sex—that suggests comparison with the appeal of bound feet, *penjing* (bonsai) trees, and scholars' rocks. In this aesthetic system, to be "natural" was not a value, because nature simply provided the raw material out of which culture was to be fashioned.[42]

As a profession, acting was stigmatized and discriminated against by law. In the Ming and early Qing, actors and other entertainers had been among the occupational categories that in legal terms were defined as having "mean" or "debased" status (*jianmin*). The "music households" (*yuehu*) associated with prostitution are the most famous example. The reforms of the Yongzheng era (1723–1735) eliminated most of the debased legal statuses, at least insofar as they were ascribed and hereditary, but the official expectation was that the people who were released from these statuses would abandon their debased occupations and conform to the moral standards of conduct that applied to free commoners (*liangmin*). In other words, the occupations themselves—as conduct—continued to be stigmatized and were discriminated against in significant ways. Prostitution, which had been legally tolerated as a hallmark of debased status, was entirely criminalized.[43]

Nevertheless, acting was not prohibited, and female impersonation onstage continued to be tolerated by the authorities and celebrated by its aficionados—even as, paradoxically, the boy actresses themselves were stigmatized for their debased occupation, which everyone understood to include illegal prostitution. This fact poses a further question: If M–F cross-dressing was tolerated and even celebrated onstage, then why was it considered a heinous crime, punishable by death, for "a man to masquerade in woman's attire" *offstage*? The reason is that, far from challenging the normative order, the boy actress reinforced it by serving the pleasure of elite men. It was a very different matter for an individual assigned male at birth to live as a woman in an act of nonconformist self-expression.

"Leaving the Family"

Another major paradigm for transing gender was "to leave the family" (*chu-jia*), a term that applied to the process of becoming a Buddhist monk or nun, a Daoist monastic (either male or female), or a eunuch in the imperial service. Entry into any of these vocations required physically moving away from one's natal family, but also renouncing marriage, procreation, and sexual relations altogether. Given that normative adult gender roles were defined in terms of marriage and procreation, to leave the family in this way amounted to the renunciation of such roles, a renunciation that was marked by distinctive adornment and attire and enforced by imperial law. As the early Chinese monk Huiyuan wrote, "The monk who has left the household is a stranger dwelling outside the world of human relations."[44] Here, the term "human relations" should be understood to include Confucianism's web of gendered kinship ties that define each person's place and how they should behave toward others.

Buddhist Clergy

A Buddhist ideal is to transcend all dualities, of which sex and gender rank among the most important, and "leaving the family" marked the first step on the path to transcendence. Monks and nuns took vows of celibacy and chastity and generally lived in sex-segregated communities of fellow clergy, at least initially. Upon leaving the family, their heads would be shaved, and they would adopt gender-neutral clothing: a simple, shapeless robe. In fact, male Buddhist and Daoist clergy were the only Han Chinese men not required to conform to the Manchu tonsure, reinforcing the sense that they belonged to a distinct gender category of their own.[45] The original names of monks and nuns would be replaced by new Buddhist names (*faming*): the surname *Shi*, from the historical Buddha Sakyamuni (*Shijiamuni*), plus a two-character given name that was usually a phrase from a sutra. Their natal families would be supplanted by the monastic community, and blood descent by a ritual lineage of master-disciple relations. For all of these reasons, Buddhism's critics condemned it as the antithesis of Confucian filial piety, which holds that the foremost duty of a son is to marry and have sons of his own in order to continue his ancestors' family line.[46]

The case of Buddhist nuns illustrates this effort to transcend gender duality quite vividly. In her study of "women without men" in the Song dynasty, Hsiao-wen Cheng argues that a conventional two-gender model is inadequate for understanding nuns. Following Judith Butler, Cheng understands gender not as a stable state of being, but as a role that comes into being through performance. Therefore, "once a woman changes what she does, she changes who she is."[47] Having renounced marriage and procreation, Buddhist nuns acquired "a categorically distinct identity from other women. Through renunciation, women already turned into non-women."[48] Specifically, a "female renunciant . . . does not always identify herself—nor is she necessarily identified by others—as a woman. . . . Buddhist nuns in Chinese society, past and present, do not share the same womanhood with laywomen."[49]

Despite the passage of centuries, this basic gender ideology has persisted, largely intact. In Chün-fang Yü's account of the Incense Light Community of Buddhist nuns in contemporary Taiwan, we find strong continuity with the ideas described by Cheng. "Incense Light nuns often referred to themselves as 'neutral' (*zhongxing*), meaning that they have transcended the ordinary gender distinction between male and female."[50] In order to achieve this state of gender-neutral transcendence, novice nuns would undergo a specific kind of training: "Nuns were trained to eliminate their feminine mannerisms as soon as they began seminary training. They were told not to speak with a high and lilting voice. They were taught not to walk on tiptoes or with a swaying gait, but to take big steps with an upright carriage. They stopped wearing bras and tight underpants and wore instead a cloth to bind their breasts and loose boxer shorts. Their robes also obscured their women's figures."[51] In other words, renunciation of feminine attire was not enough. It was necessary not only to conceal the distinctively female features of their bodies, but also to unlearn whatever behaviors and habits had marked them as women. This process demonstrates an acute perception of the difference between bodily sex and social gender, and of the specifically performative nature of the latter. The Incense Light Community also strictly prohibited sexual activity, with particular emphasis on the risk of lesbian relations developing between nuns who lived in close proximity, and great care was taken to avoid intimacy or exclusive friendships.[52]

Given the Confucian mandate against celibacy, why would any parents have taken the seemingly radical step of giving a son or daughter to the clergy? No doubt some were motivated by piety, but it appears that leaving the family (like selling a son to an acting troupe) was often a last resort for poor parents who could not feed their children, or could not support a child with disabilities.[53] Stone maidens often became nuns (to obviate their disability), and becoming a nun was also a strategy for a widow facing pressure to remarry: in effect, Buddhist celibacy would safeguard her "Confucian" chastity. In the latter two scenarios, a vow of celibacy might be seen as making a virtue of necessity.

The model for transcending sex and gender by leaving the family was the historical Buddha. According to tradition, the Buddha's penis and scrotum were sheathed or retracted within his body, to be produced only when necessary—in some accounts, they had the superficial appearance of female genitalia. Because of the Buddha's absolute celibacy and the merit he had accumulated in previous lives, his penis had no sexual function, nor did it provoke sexual desire on the part of others if they saw it.[54] This anatomical manifestation of transcendence suggests comparison with the effects of Daoist ascesis.

Daoist Monastics

In terms of transing gender, there are significant differences between Buddhism and Daoism, but also some striking parallels. In Buddhism, all who became monks or nuns "left the family." In Daoism, however, the term applies only to that subset of clergy (both male and female) who took vows of celibacy: most of those were monastics based in large, officially registered temples where celibacy was required in part to secure the purity of the ritual space. In fact, however, the majority of Daoist clergy lived outside such temples within their own communities, and many of these "at-home" clerics married and had families of their own. The celibate monastic life is most strongly associated with the Quanzhen tradition, but some Quanzhen Daoists did marry; moreover, even some clerics of the less ascetic Zhengyi tradition lived celibate lives.[55]

Upon ordination, Daoist clergy would be given ritual names (*faming*, the same term used for the ritual names of Buddhists), although the at-home clergy might also retain their birth names for use in secular contexts. For monastics, the ritual lineage largely replaced the birth family, and they used kinship terms to address one another.[56] Daoist temples have apparently never been as strict about gender segregation as the Buddhist clergy, and many temples had (and continue to have) male and female clerics living together, albeit in separate rooms. In Adeline Herrou's view, the prohibition of sexual relations is strengthened by an implied incest taboo, given that the monastics view each other as ritual kin. In modern temples, at least, there is no gendered division of labor in the tasks they perform or the training they receive, and male and female clergy receive the same stipends.[57]

Both Buddhism and Daoism at times aspire to transcend the dualities of sex and gender, but they approach this challenge differently. If, for Buddhism, the body itself—as part of material existence—is an obstacle to be overcome, Daoist transcendence as practiced by its most ascetic adepts involves intense engagement with the body through physical and mental exercises that aim to sublimate sex difference and to return the practitioner to a nonbinary prepubertal or even infantile state. For advanced practitioners, these exercises are believed to result in the gradual disappearance of bodily sex differences: males cease ejaculating, and their penises shrink and disappear, whereas females stop menstruating, and their breasts shrink and disappear. With the attenuation of sex difference, the bodies of such adepts converge in a sort of neutral, desexed state.[58] But transcendence may also find expression in fluidity or even shape-shifting: Daoist tradition tells of immortals and other advanced personages who can alternate sex, with males appearing as females and vice versa.[59]

Like the Buddhist clergy, Daoist monastics wear unisex attire and hairstyle, but, instead of shaving their heads, the Daoists leave their hair long and tie it in a distinctive topknot that has important ritual functions. Apparently, the tonsure and queue mandated for men by the Qing dynasty were not imposed on male Daoists any more than on Buddhist monks.[60] The monastics' unisex appearance signals their conviction that they have "passed through and gone beyond all categories of gender."[61] Given that the True (i.e., fully realized) Person in Daoism is androgynous, male monastics are enjoined to embrace the feminine in order to balance the masculine in their nature. Thus, for example, they squat while urinating, in the manner of women, and try to avoid becoming angry or raising their voices. In general, they seek to adopt a "female attitude" by being soft and gentle, "weak and withdrawing."[62] In short, these male monastics must unlearn the gender cues that had marked them as men, in an intriguing mirror image of the Buddhist Incense Light nuns.

Eunuchs

Finally, "to leave the family" also denoted castration and entry into imperial service as a eunuch (in either the emperor's own palaces or one of the princely estates); this act corresponded to a monastic's vow of celibacy.[63] The use of the same term in both contexts underscores the many meaningful parallels between eunuchs and clergy. To state the obvious, castration—which, in the Qing dynasty, involved complete amputation of the genitalia—made the renunciation of procreation absolute.[64] But also, once they had entered imperial service, eunuchs were prohibited from taking wives or adopting children. They forsook their birth families, which were supplanted by the community of fellow eunuchs inside the palace. In effect, eunuchs would be "reborn" inside the palace, a rebirth signaled by the new names they acquired, which were different from their birth names.[65] It was this radical repudiation of normative gender roles that historian Mitamura Taisuke presumably had in mind when he characterized eunuchs as "the artificial third sex" (*tsukurareta daisan no sei*).[66] Eunuchs could not procreate biologically, but by initiating and mentoring novices they reproduced their community socially, creating a eunuch "lineage" that suggests comparison with the ritual lineages of Buddhist and Daoist monastics.[67]

The basic motive for employing eunuchs inside the palace may be obvious, but it is worth stating explicitly: a eunuch could be entrusted with the emperor's women because he was incapable of impregnating them and therefore could pose no threat to the integrity of the imperial lineage. For this reason, the separation of the sexes did not apply to eunuchs, and they could move freely between male and female spaces; this "transcendence of gender norms" is precisely what qualified them for service in the inner quarters of the palace. But, having forsaken their families, eunuchs were expected to have no personalistic ties that might conflict with their absolute loyalty to the imperial house.[68]

Individuals of various ages might become eunuchs, but the Qing court consistently preferred those emasculated in childhood, ideally before puberty. This preference is starkly explicit in eighteenth-century laws governing the punishment of rebels and mass murderers: such offenders would be put to death, their wives and daughters enslaved, and their young sons condemned to serve as eunuchs—but only if under the age of fifteen *sui*; older sons would be sentenced to slavery in Heilongjiang, along with the women. Very young sons were to be held in custody until they reached the age of eleven sui, when they would be emasculated.[69] From this stipulation, we can see that the ideal age of emasculation was believed to be eleven to fifteen sui, (i.e., nine to fourteen years old). Eunuchs castrated at an older age were generally used for exterior or even peripheral roles; the Qianlong Emperor made a point of sending them to the princely estates in exchange for younger eunuchs to serve in his own palaces. This preference was partly aesthetic, presumably because castration before puberty prevented the development of some secondary sex characteristics: in short, they looked and sounded less masculine, not unlike the boy actresses of the opera. But it was believed that the younger a eunuch was when he entered service, the more tractable and malleable he would be, and the less likely it was that he would retain any external ties that might compromise his loyalty.[70] The freedom of eunuchs was severely curtailed: most fundamentally, they could not leave imperial service of their own volition. A eunuch was enslaved to the imperial house from the time of his emasculation until he received permission to retire in old age.[71]

Unlike clergy, Qing dynasty eunuchs wore their hair in the tonsure mandated for ordinary men, but they were immediately recognizable from their distinctive uniform. There is some disagreement about the extent to which the physical appearance of eunuchs differed from that of ordinary men; no doubt it varied, depending on the age of castration. Those emasculated before puberty had distinctive high-pitched voices, and for this reason some were trained as actors to sing opera inside the palace.[72] The parallel between eunuchs and clergy is underscored by the fact that the two groups actually overlapped. Some eunuchs were ordained as Buddhist or Daoist clerics in order to perform religious functions within the Forbidden City and at certain temples elsewhere in the imperial capital. But emasculated men who were rejected for palace service often became monks; moreover, a common retirement strategy for elderly eunuchs released from service was to become monks, and a number of Buddhist and Daoist temples in Beijing functioned essentially as eunuch retirement homes.[73] Eunuchs who ran away from the palace often sought refuge in temples, taking advantage of what Norman Kutcher calls "a general fluidity of identity between eunuchs and (especially Buddhist) monks": "One of the synonyms for 'eunuch' that appears even in the Qing is *siren*, which literally means 'temple person.' Monks and eunuchs also looked similar, because both were generally beardless. They were also both considered to have left home, and in the process took on new names. There was thus, in sum, a natural kinship between the two that frequently made them allies."[74]

Vincent Goossaert has documented the particularly strong affinity that eunuchs felt for Quanzhen Daoism, which fostered a mass conversion of eunuchs in the nineteenth century. These "eunuch clergy" formed their own ritual lineage and founded their own Daoist institutions that survived the fall of the dynasty.[75] Goossaert suggests that this affinity had two sources. First, "in the almost fanatically ascetic milieus of early Quanzhen," some famous practitioners had castrated themselves in order "to reach immediately a state of nondesire"; it seems likely that eunuch converts identified with and felt redeemed by this "self-castration lore." Second, the eunuch experience had "a special resonance with the Daoist vision of the body": "Daoist ascesis is widely said to lead to the disappearance of the sexual organs, male and female. A male Daoist's penis gradually diminishes and eventually disappears, or so say countless manuals and contemporary lore, whereas a female adept's breasts disappear. The male ceases to ejaculate, whereas the female's periods stop. One twentieth-century Peking Daoist, while discussing the natural reduction and disappearance of the penis, compared the physical appearance of advanced Daoist practitioners to that of eunuchs."[76]

This perspective made it possible to reinterpret emasculation in a positive light: instead of a crippling mutilation that betrayed Confucian family ethics, it was an advantage that facilitated Daoist transcendence. This would have been especially true, one imagines, for those castrated early enough to preempt puberty: instead of returning to the primordial, nonbinary condition to which Daoists aspired, such eunuchs would never have left it in the first place.

Several historians have contested what Norman Kutcher calls "the myth of no wives or children," arguing that many eunuchs in fact did create families of their own through marriage and adoption, and that some also retained close ties with birth families.[77] However, almost all of the evidence they cite comes not from the Qing, but from previous dynasties when eunuchs had wielded tremendous political power, and it focuses on notorious individuals who enjoyed extraordinary privileges.[78] As Kutcher himself emphasizes, the Qing dynasty went to great lengths to avoid what its rulers saw as the grave errors of the former Ming, when eunuchs had been allowed to dominate the court: "The Qing would witness absolutely nothing like the Ming, when sons were openly adopted and emperors gave their favorite eunuchs gifts of women."[79] During the Qing, most of the eunuchs who did have wives and children had already formed families before submitting to castration later in life. But such men were viewed as less desirable recruits and were usually assigned to manual labor far away from the inner sanctum of the palace.[80] Some eunuchs did adopt offspring, but they had to be extremely discreet in order to avoid notice; thus, for example, adopted boys would be referred to as "nephews" rather than "sons."[81] It was only in the last decades of the dynasty that these rules were somewhat relaxed, notably in the Empress Dowager Cixi's treatment of her favorites.[82] But the domination of the late Qing court by women and eunuchs has been widely interpreted as a symptom of dynastic decline, and, indeed, of the "emasculation" of the Chinese nation.[83]

Some of these same scholars have cited the evidence of family ties to argue further that eunuchs saw themselves (and were seen by others) as men who sought to live a normative masculine life. For these scholars, eunuchs' gender is not at issue: they were simply men. Most emphatic, perhaps, is Jennifer Jay, who writes that eunuchs "remained unquestionably male in gender and identity and social role while aspiring to a normal Confucian life."[84] It is not my purpose to debate whether eunuchs (or, for that matter, monks) were "really" men—obviously, in some respects they were (as I point out in the introduction, to justify my use of gendered pronouns to refer to them). But the evidence from the Qing, at least, suggests that although some eunuchs regretted their condition and aspired to some approximation of a conventional masculine life, they did so against the odds and against the rules. It seems likely that only the most privileged eunuchs had sufficient means to establish families (and those who submitted to emasculation *after* forming families did so out of desperate poverty). Such evidence actually strikes me as confirmation of the dominant paradigm that, in "leaving the family," eunuchs were understood to have forsaken normative gender roles defined in terms of marriage and procreation. The eunuchs who sought to mitigate their stigmatized condition certainly understood that paradigm: it was what they were trying to escape.

Surely, the most significant and interesting thing about both eunuchs and clergy is not whether they were one thing or the other, but, rather, their very liminality, which derived from having "left the family" in the ways we have discussed. The sheer ambiguity of their status generated a range of distinctive tensions and controversies, to which we shall now turn.

Wolves in Sheep's Clothing?

A pervasive and persistent stereotype held that Buddhist and Daoist clergy were not what they seemed: instead of the celibate, chaste exemplars of piety they pretended to be, they were in fact gluttonous lechers who violated their vows by indulging in sex, meat, and wine. They were not only frauds, but also potentially dangerous predators, whose pretense of piety helped facilitate their evil schemes.

This stereotype is a stock theme in vernacular fiction from the Ming-Qing era, which provides countless examples.[85] In the novel *Plum in the Golden Vase* (*Jinpingmei*), for example, the hero Ximen Qing dies of priapism and excessive semen loss after overdosing on an aphrodisiac given to him by a mysterious "foreign monk." This monk, who also consumes a huge amount of meat and wine, is portrayed as the personification of a set of male genitalia.[86] Elsewhere in the same novel, we encounter the Daoist abbot Jin Zongming, who patronizes female prostitutes but also sodomizes the male novices at his temple.[87] In other texts, Buddhist and Daoist clergy are portrayed as heterodox deviants who kidnap and rape women and practice sexual vampirism—for example, the Qing novel *A Country Codger Puts His Words Out to Sun* (*Yesou puyan*), in which the hero, a sort of "Confucian superman," defeats all manner of demonic forces and succeeds in eradicating Buddhism from the face of the earth.[88] The late Ming collection of con artist tales *The Book of Swindles* (*Pian jing*) includes many anecdotes that portray Buddhist and Daoist clergy in a similar light. In one particularly gruesome tale, a monk murders pregnant women in order to extract their fetuses, which he uses to make magic pills that enable him to survive despite eating nothing else. He consumes these pills while pretending to fast, as part of a confidence scheme to cheat the faithful out of their money.[89] This stereotype did not spare female clergy either, who often appear as lascivious, and as corrupt procuresses who facilitate other people's illicit sexual liaisons.[90] As we shall see in chapter 3, one theme is the seemingly innocent nun who is exposed as a shape-shifting sorcerer who can conceal his penis in order to insinuate himself into a nunnery and seduce the all-too-willing nuns within.

This stereotype of clergy was powerful enough that it may have influenced judicial proceedings. As Karasawa Yasuhiko has shown, the records of court cases involving Buddhist monks suggest systematic bias—specifically, officials seem to have assumed that monks were predatory lechers unless proven otherwise.[91] It also seems to be reflected in the many laws that specifically targeted Buddhist clergy (which, by default, also applied to Daoists, and vice versa). For example, the Qing code imposed heavier penalties for sex offenses if they were committed by clergy.[92] More broadly, the Ming and Qing dynasties both sought to control clergy by requiring them to register at authorized temples, issuing official licenses, and restricting their geographic mobility. As a corollary, both dynasties also sought (largely in vain) to prohibit women from visiting temples and otherwise participating in public religious activities.[93]

In part, at least, the stereotype of lascivious clergy can be attributed to a long-standing anti-Buddhist polemic that began with the introduction of the Indian religion into China.[94] But there seems to be more to it than just that—and it is worth noting that this Chinese literary theme had a close parallel in medieval and early modern Europe, in the cynical portrayal of Catholic clergy by such writers as Bocaccio, Chaucer, Rabelais, and Sade. Simply put, it seems that pious claims of chastity inevitably provoke skepticism. Moreover, I suspect that there was at least a grain of truth to the stereotype of Chinese clergy, just as there is clearly some truth to the stereotype of Catholic priests.[95]

In this connection, a consistent pattern that has been documented for many times and places is the prevalence of same-sex sexual activity in single-sex communities or occupational groups: in prisons, the military, and boarding schools; among sailors, hired laborers, and hoboes; and, of course, among clergy. This pattern of sexual behavior is often attributed to "situational homosexuality"—namely, the (dubious) theory that, in the absence of opposite-sex partners, the libido will compel otherwise heterosexual people to settle for temporary surrogates of the same sex.[96] An alternative explanation is that a same-sex environment simply enables people to discover their true homosexual nature.[97] (Ironically, both explanations seem to assume that everyone is potentially queer, given the right environment.) Moreover, there is no doubt that some people purposely seek out such an environment—for example, choosing to join the clergy or go to sea—precisely because they prefer the company of the same sex.[98] But it is also true that the typically hierarchical structure of such settings increases the likelihood that sexual acts and relations will be coercive and exploitative. At any rate, if Qing legal records are to be believed, the same pattern prevailed in China, and male Buddhist and Daoist clergy feature prominently in the large sample of cases of male-male "sodomy" (jijian, including both consensual acts and rapes) that I have collected in the course of my research. Anti-clerical bias may account for part of this caseload, but presumably not all of it.[99]

With regard to clergy, a significant reason for skepticism was that they retained their sexed bodies, even as they transed gender by leaving the family and vowing celibacy. Clergy themselves were sensitive to this fact, which explains, for example, the rigid sex segregation seen in Buddhist institutions. Eunuchs, of course, present a different picture. But a similarly paranoid scenario involved an intact male being disguised as a eunuch in order to gain access to the women inside the palace. This fraudulent eunuch scenario dates to antiquity: its locus classicus is Sima Qian's third-century BCE account in the *Records of the Grand Historian* (*Shiji*) of how the famous minister of the state of Qin, Lü Buwei, arranged to provide sexual entertainment for the Queen Dowager. Lü recruited a man named Lao Ai, who was endowed with an exceptionally large penis (comparable in girth to the axle of a wheel), and disguised him as a eunuch by having his facial hair plucked. Then the Queen Dowager bribed the official in charge of eunuchs to smuggle Lao Ai into the palace, where he could service her. She became infatuated with Lao Ai and secretly bore him two children before their liaison was finally exposed.[100]

In the Qing dynasty, "imperial anxiety about the eunuch body" found expression in persistent rumors that fake eunuchs had managed to bribe their way into the palace, in the manner of Lao Ai, or that genuine eunuchs had used occult techniques (including cannibalism of young boys) to regenerate their amputated genitals.[101] All eunuchs were subjected to physical examinations twice a year, in order to rule out either kind of fraud.[102] Even so, there persisted a degree of anxiety about whether even genuine eunuchs might be completely free of sexual desire and capacity—therefore, for example, the most intimate services for palace ladies in the bedchamber and bath were provided by maidservants, not eunuchs.[103]

It is striking that concern about the potential wolf in sheep's clothing applied even to the boy actresses of the opera. As Sophie Volpp has documented, moral commentators worried about "fraternization" between literati and actors (which was assumed to include sex), partly because of the low social status of actors, but mainly because as "femmes fatales," they constituted a potential security threat: "Intimacy of association between literati and actors was particularly threatening given the protean malleability of the actor's gender. It was feared that actors would first use their feminine wiles to ingratiate themselves with officials, and then take advantage of these liaisons to enter the world of officialdom themselves, ultimately assuming a masculine and empowered position."[104] The seventeenth-century literatus Shen Defu claimed that actors "worked for the government as spies, eavesdropping in order to gain information about confidential matters, and for this reason should be viewed with mistrust and apprehension"; after all, "they were professionally trained to simulate and deceive." The artifice inherent in the boy actresses' vocation was a focus of both fascination and anxiety: "It was precisely the actor's ability to cast illusion—his power over representation—in which the literati aficionados of the theater delighted. The source of the literatus's pleasure was also the source of danger."[105]

As previously mentioned, the Qing dynasty continued to stigmatize and discriminate against actors, even while acting as an occupation was tolerated. During the Yongzheng era, all prostitution as well as consensual male-male sodomy were explicitly criminalized for the first time; moreover, the Qing dynasty banned officials from "consorting with actors" (*xia you*), conduct that was assumed to include sexual relations.[106] Within the imperial capital of Beijing, the government made repeated efforts to control opera—what was performed, by whom, and where, and who could attend. But these policies were difficult to enforce, given opera's enormous popularity among elites, a popularity that extended even into the palace.[107]

A Transphobic Paradigm

A common theme uniting several of the gender-transing scenarios we have surveyed is fear that benign surface representation is a fraud or masquerade intended to lower people's guard in order to facilitate some nefarious scheme, most likely sexual misconduct. Notably, this fear focused primarily on males who had literally left their families and were living in some kind of context that deviated from Confucian norms. The fear of people who transed gender in these ways therefore reflected a more general anxiety about the threat supposedly posed by single, rogue males outside the family system: the "bare sticks" (*guanggun*), who were a major focus of Qing criminal legislation. "Bare sticks" lacked the socializing "roots" and "branches" of wives and family to keep them in check, and they were stereotyped as rapists and sodomites who threatened the wives, daughters, and young sons of good families.[108]

The idea that male clergy and eunuchs might be sexual predators in disguise bears close resemblance to a final transgender paradigm, which is the one most pertinent to this book: the M–F cross-dressing sexual predator. Ming-Qing officials could imagine only one credible reason for a man to "disguise" himself as a woman: to gain access to "wives and daughters of good family" (*liangjia funü*) in order to seduce or rape them. Thus, when they encountered cases of "a man masquerading in women's attire" (*nan ban nüzhuang*), they would interpret the facts through the lens of this paradigm.

If this paradigm seems familiar, it is because in some ways, the past is not so different from the present after all. Deceit is also one component of modern transphobia, which targets transwomen with special ferocity via the notion that a transwoman is really a man *pretending* to be a woman for some evil purpose. Either he is a gay man trying to lure "normal" men into sexual relations, or he is a deranged sex fiend trying to sneak into women's space (such as public restrooms) in order to commit rape.[109] Much of this would have made perfect sense to a magistrate in a Ming or Qing courtroom.

CHAPTER II

The Paradigm of the Cross-Dressing Predator

We can be sure *without even bothering to ask* (*bu wen ke zhi*) that he must have seduced and raped women on a routine basis!

—JIANG PU, GOVERNOR OF HUNAN, 1744

The Midwife Who Sued Their Brother

In the summer of 1744, Jiang Pu, the governor of Hunan Province,[1] wrote a secret memorial to the Qianlong emperor about a matter of urgent concern.[2] "Since assuming office here," Governor Jiang began, "I have come to realize that the people of Hunan are perverse and treacherous by habit, and prone to bizarre delusions." Therefore, he had worked hard to reform the people's customs: "Whenever I lecture about the Sacred Edict, I strive to enlighten the people; and when I encounter court cases involving deception and fraud, I impose the strictest penalties without fail."[3] But recent intelligence had cast doubt on the efficacy of his efforts.

Two weeks before, Governor Jiang had received a most disturbing report from Magistrate Zhang Jun of Anfu County:

A treacherous scoundrel named Xiong Ersheng, despite being male, has been masquerading in women's attire (*nan ban nüzhuang*). His younger brother turned him in, and Magistrate Zhang, upon examining the culprit, found that the accusation was true. He requested my approval to sentence Xiong Ersheng to a beating with the heavy bamboo. But it seems to me that for a man to masquerade in women's attire shows an extraordinary degree of treachery and cunning, and therefore his behavior must include further acts of extreme evil that remain to be discovered.

Governor Jiang rejected the magistrate's proposed sentence as premature and insufficient. Instead, he turned the prisoner over to the magistrate's superior, the circuit intendant for Northern Hunan and ordered him to make an exhaustive investigation of Xiong Ersheng's history and activities. Now the circuit intendant's report had arrived, and its shocking contents compelled the governor to prepare a memorial for the emperor's eyes only, bypassing the routine channels of communication.

According to the governor, Xiong Ersheng was in their sixties when arrested and had been living as a woman for decades. Xiong was born a peasant in Wuling County, Hunan, in about 1680. They had never taken a wife, and, around 1706, at the age of about twenty-six *sui*, they had left home, whereupon Xiong "grew out his hair, pierced his ears, bound his feet, changed into women's attire" (*xufa chuan'er chanzu, gaizhuang wei nü*), and began "masquerading" as a woman. In this guise, Xiong adopted the appellation "Xiong Mumu," which we might translate as "Elder Sister-in-Law Xiong"—*mumu* being a respectful term of address for the wife of one's older brother. Significantly, *mu* could also mean "nurse" or "governess."

Upon leaving home, Xiong first traveled to Cili County (about seventy-five kilometers to the northwest), and later to Shimen County (about thirty kilometers northeast of home). Then, in 1723, about seventeen years after leaving home, Xiong arrived in Anfu County (about thirty kilometers southeast of home), and settled down, staying there for the next twenty-one years.[4] All of the places visited by Xiong are located in northern Hunan, within roughly seventy-five kilometers of each other. During this time, Xiong also kept in touch with their younger brother Xiong Erliang (the only sibling mentioned in the record), who stayed home on the farm back in Wuling County.

Governor Jiang did not name the community in Anfu County where Xiong Mumu had settled down, but, clearly, it was rural. Upon arriving there, Xiong presented as a woman and told the following story. She was a widow who insisted on remaining chaste and faithful to her dead husband, and she had fled home because her evil in-laws were trying to force her to remarry. To escape, she had shaved her head and become a Buddhist nun, but had recently returned to lay life, growing out her hair and earning a living as a midwife (*wei renjia chanfu shousheng*).[5]

According to the governor, "everyone believed this story" (*ren gong xin zhi*), and Xiong Mumu had no trouble settling down and joining the community. What is more, Xiong became a popular member of the community and a much sought-after midwife, and thereby achieved a substantial measure of prosperity. After just three years, Xiong adopted a youth named Peng Tianruo from their home county of Wuling to serve as a "successor son" (*jizi*) to Xiong's supposed dead husband. Xiong also arranged and paid for Peng to take a wife. Then Peng adopted a "successor son" of his own—for reasons that are not clear, Peng and his wife apparently were unable to produce a son themselves—and that successor son also took a wife in turn. Xiong Mumu covered the expenses for all of these transactions.

Xiong further expanded their kinship network by pledging to adopt three younger women in the community as "dry daughters" (*gan nüer*). "Dry" (*gan*) kinship is a form of pledged kinship based on intimate friendship rather than biological or marital ties, and, unlike sworn brotherhood, it can bind individuals of different generation or sex. The governor's memorial provides no further information about these young women, but their pledge of kinship is further testimony to Xiong's popularity. Thus, without themself marrying or procreating, Xiong Mumu assembled a new family, by formal successor adoption (*liji*), acquisition of women through marriage, and the more informal pledging of dry kinship—a family of eight people in all, including themself. Finally, Xiong also paid for their younger brother Erliang to take a wife back in Wuling County.

Xiong's construction of a network of chosen kin, in a new location completely separate from their natal family, is an example of a pattern I have documented elsewhere, in which marginalized people in Qing society who lacked (or were rejected by) "natural" family would form alliances with other people in similar circumstances that better met their needs. It can also be compared to family formation among queer people today, whose chosen alliances may be far more meaningful and real than those based on the accident of birth, especially if they have been rejected by natal kin.[6] Xiong's continuing relationship with their younger brother Erliang suggests that they had not been rejected, exactly, by their natal family, although we have no detailed information on this point. It seems, however, that to live as a woman required Xiong to relocate and start over in a new place where no one knew them from before.

The foundation of Xiong Mumu's kinship network was land: by the time of their arrest (when Xiong had been living in Anfu County for twenty-one years), they had amassed thirty-two *mu* of paddy land and were living with their adopted son, his wife, *their* adopted son, and *his* wife in a six-room house. In this part of Hunan, by the standards of Communist-era land reform, thirty-two *mu* of paddy land would have qualified Xiong as at least a "rich peasant," if not a landlord.[7] Such an estate represented a remarkable achievement for someone who had arrived in Anfu County a stranger, with no friends or kin, and little more than the clothes on their back. Presumably it was Xiong Mumu's earnings as a midwife that had paid for this land. We have no evidence of any other source of income, and their natal family was far from rich, as indicated by the fact that brother Erliang was able to marry only because Xiong Mumu covered his expenses.

For twenty-one years, then, Xiong Mumu lived as a popular and increasingly prosperous member of their community and had become the matriarch of a substantial household. In 1744, however, this progress narrative came to an end when their brother Erliang "outed" them as an anatomical male by reporting them to the authorities. Erliang knew that his sibling had been assigned male at birth and raised as a boy, but was now living as a woman, and Erliang had kept their secret for decades, while remaining in touch all the while. What prompted him to betray his sibling?

In fact, it was Xiong Mumu who had taken their brother Erliang to court, in an unbelievably brazen act of chutzpah. Back in Wuling County, their father had died (it is not clear when), and, instead of dividing the household property with Mumu, Erliang had kept it all for himself.[8] Mumu insisted that they were owed a full half share of the property, but Erliang refused, and, as the dispute escalated, Xiong Mumu finally filed a lawsuit at the Anfu County yamen, accusing Erliang of plotting "to seize his older sister's property" (*di zhan zi chan*). In their plaint, Mumu used the name "Xiong Shi" (*née* Xiong), which would be the standard appellation for a woman whose natal surname was "Xiong." It was in this context that Erliang, in a counterplaint, "exposed their sibling's masquerade" (*shouchu jia zhuang qingshi*). Magistrate Zhang then ordered "Xiong Shi" to strip and "be examined in court" (*dangtang yanming*) by a midwife, who confirmed that Erliang's accusation "was true" (*shu shi*): "Xiong Shi" had what appeared to be normal male genitalia. Confronted with this fact, Xiong confessed that their "real" name was Xiong Ersheng, and that they had been "masquerading" as a woman for more than thirty years.

Thus the circuit intendant's report, which the governor had confirmed via his own "discreet inquiries." Having summarized the facts for the emperor, he offered his opinion:

> The criminal Xiong Ersheng, despite being male, masqueraded in women's attire (*nan ban nüzhuang*) for more than thirty years, adopting dry daughters and using the alias "Xiong Mumu." On that basis, we can be sure *without even bothering to ask* that he must have seduced and raped women on a routine basis (*ze pingri jianwu zhi shi bu wen ke zhi*). Someone who destroys family relations and injures the public morality in such an egregious manner cannot be tolerated in Your Majesty's sacred realm! (*si ci bailun shanghua zhi ren bu ke gurong yu shengshi*). . . . Xiong Ersheng's crimes largely took place in the obscurity of the female chambers (*duo she guimen aimei*), and an exhaustive investigation would involve countless people and endless trouble—moreover, it is inevitable that some of the implicated women, upon hearing of this, would commit suicide out of shame (*weimian you xiukui qingsheng zhi shi*). The scale of harm is truly great!

Under the circumstances, Governor Jiang opined, the county magistrate's failure to make a thorough investigation, and his premature request to close the case with such a lenient punishment, were "particularly inappropriate" (*shu shu bu he*).

As the governor pointed out, however, the Qing code contained no law explicitly addressing the crime of "a man masquerading in women's attire" (*nan ban nüzhuang*), a matter we shall return to shortly. But that should be no obstacle. Because "this villain's treacherous and evil deeds (*yinjian zuo te*) are simply unforgiveable," the governor begged the emperor to order Xiong beaten to death at once. Beating to death is nowhere prescribed by the Qing code, but it was occasionally inflicted on the emperor's orders in unusually shocking cases.[9] A summary execution of this kind would represent an extraordinary deviation from standard procedure and therefore would provide salutary "warning against treachery and heterodoxy" (*yi jing jianxie*). The governor did add, however, that, aside from Xiong's masquerade as a woman, careful investigation had thus far uncovered no further evidence of "heterodox teachings, sorcery, or bewitching and deceiving people" (*xiejiao, yaoshu, guhuo renxin*).

In addition, the governor recommended that brother Xiong Erliang receive a "severe beating," on the grounds that he was a coconspirator who had "abetted and concealed Ersheng's treachery" (*pengjian rongyin*) for many years. Despite having exposed Ersheng's crimes, Erliang deserved no lenience, because, after all, his only motive had been to grab the family property for himself. As to the kinship network Ersheng had created, the governor recommended that each person be handled individually according to their deserts and then returned to their respective natal lineages. Ersheng's accumulated property in Anfu County should be confiscated by the state, as "there is no one who is entitled to receive it."

The governor's memorial went to the capital by express for the emperor's eyes only. Despite its shocking contents and rather hysterical tone, the emperor reacted calmly: "This culprit's crimes are not yet serious enough to warrant death (*shang bu zhi si*), but he cannot be allowed to remain in place." Instead of having Xiong beaten to death, the emperor ordered the governor to "shave off his hair" (*ti qi fa*)—on the front of the head, to conform to the hairstyle mandated for men by the Qing dynasty—and transfer Xiong to the Board of War, which, in turn, would transport them to Heilongjiang (in the far north of Manchuria), where they would spend the rest of their life in military slavery. Under the circumstances, the emperor's decision counted as lenience. He approved the rest of the governor's recommendations.

More Questions Than Answers

This remarkable story raises more questions than we can answer. Unfortunately, Governor Jiang's memorial is the only source I have been able to find that bears on Xiong Mumu's case. It summarizes the circuit intendant's investigation without quoting any original testimony from the principals involved. As a result, we can make, at best, educated guesses about many matters of interest. Most opaque of all is the subjective perspective of Xiong Mumu themself.

We know that Xiong transitioned and began living as a woman only after leaving home in their mid-twenties, and that up to that point they had never married. This information suggests that Xiong may have left home *in order* to transition—a common theme for people who transed gender in the early modern world and even today. The lack of a wife is intriguing: normally, the oldest son in a peasant family would have married by his mid-twenties, unless the family was very poor, and the fact that younger brother Erliang had not taken a wife either suggests that poverty may have made marriage impossible for both. There is no word at all about Xiong's parents, which suggests that they had died well before the case came to official attention.

Who Knew?

It is not clear who, if anyone, knew the truth about Xiong Mumu—aside from brother Erliang and perhaps other relatives back in Wuling County. One of many remarkable features of this story is that Xiong Mumu had managed to keep in touch with their brother, and that he seems to have known and kept their secret for decades.

According to the governor's memorial, when Xiong settled down in Anfu County, "everyone" there believed their tale that they were a chaste widow and former nun on the run from evil in-laws who sought to force her to remarry. Assuming that Xiong was taken for a woman, this tale was the ideal explanation for a woman to be on her own far from home: she had defied her in-laws and run away in order to defend traditional patriarchal values, not to defy them. (One is reminded of the Mulan trope.)

Did Xiong's family, friends, and neighbors in Anfu County really not know that they had male anatomy? We have no description of Xiong's appearance, but it is hard to believe that in twenty-one years not a single person learned the truth—especially the members of Xiong's household, with whom they were living on intimate terms, not to mention their three "dry daughters." In the cases discussed in chapters 4 and 5, we find that anatomical males who were living as women might have difficulty keeping their assigned sex a secret, because at least some observers thought they looked like men. To be sure, there was a limit to how much an adult could change their gendered appearance, especially before the invention of modern gender-confirming therapies.

According to the governor's memorial, Xiong's transition involved shaving their whole head (supposedly as a nun) and then growing out all their hair at uniform length in the manner of a woman (previously, the front of their head would have been shaved, with the back hair tied into a long queue); piercing their ears and wearing earrings; binding their feet (loosely, one presumes, because Xiong was in their mid-twenties when they transitioned); and wearing women's clothing. These exterior cues were so strongly gendered that they may have outweighed any contrary impression conveyed by Xiong's physique or other characteristics.

Another possibility is that everyone knew the truth, but no one cared. I believe this is actually the most likely scenario, but there is no way to know for sure. Perhaps it was a case of "Don't ask, don't tell," in which other people minded their own business. At any rate, what we do know is that nobody from Xiong's own community reported them to the authorities; on the contrary, over the course of two decades they seem to have become a pillar of the community. Xiong never came to official attention or had any other trouble that we know of until they were outed by their brother—and he did this only after becoming the target of his sibling's lawsuit. Had Xiong Mumu not filed that lawsuit, we would have no record that such a person ever existed.

One implication of Xiong Mumu's decades of quiet, untroubled life is that there may have been other people—perhaps many other people—who transed gender in this way, and who were tolerated or even accepted by their communities. Liu Xing Shi (protagonist of chapter 5) is another example of someone assigned male at birth who lived as a woman for years and played a valuable role in their community, without getting in trouble— and, again, when Liu Xing Shi finally did get arrested, it was not because anyone in their community had complained about them; rather, the local police had heard about their faith-healing, became curious, and then noticed their masculine appearance. How many others lived their lives in relative peace, without leaving any trace in the historical record? There is no reason to assume that ordinary people in the Ming-Qing era shared the official hysteria about gender nonconformism, any more than they embraced the famous elite obsession with female chastity.[10] In cases like this, we catch a glimpse, however imperfect, of a popular culture informed by very different values from those that guided the judiciary.

How Did Xiong Learn Midwifery?

What was Xiong doing for the seventeen years or so between leaving home in Wuling County and arriving in Anfu County? Somehow, during those years, they became a midwife. Moreover, their success shows that this was no con: they must have provided good service. But midwifery was the exclusive practice of women—it was unthinkable for a man to become a midwife in Qing China—and, needless to say, to do it well required specialized skills as well as practical knowledge and experience. It was one of very few lines of work outside the household that was open to women; it was learned through apprenticeship, and, like many skilled crafts, it often ran in families, being passed from mother to daughter.[11] Thus, we must assume that Xiong learned midwifery after transitioning and presumably was understood to be a woman by whoever taught them.

In the world of traditional Chinese medicine, the basic gender division of labor (which also aligned with class) cast elite men as the gentlemen heirs to a highly literate tradition of text-based herbal pharmacology, whereas ordinary women did most of the dirty work that involved manual grappling with the human body, including midwifery.[12] It was no more thinkable for an elite woman to become a midwife than for a male peasant to master the classic pharmacopoeia. A midwife's work included helping pregnant women and delivering their babies, of course; occasionally, midwives also dealt in abortifacients, although, given the toxicity and unreliability of such drugs, it is not clear how often they actually did this.[13] Midwives were on call to help local magistrates examine female rape victims and corpses (when foul play was suspected) and, when necessary, to ascertain the sex of living individuals—as seen, for example, in Xiong Mumu's own case, but also in the "stone maiden" (shinü) cases to be examined in chapter 6. Midwives are nearly invisible in legal case records—we learn nothing about them as individuals or their qualifications—and yet, paradoxically, in these matters their judgment seems to have carried absolute authority. Incidentally, midwives were also responsible for assigning sex to newborns and for interpreting any anomaly they observed—so, ironically, this would have been a basic part of Xiong Mumu's work in delivering babies.[14]

An intriguing possibility suggests itself: if it was known in Xiong Mumu's community that they were transing gender, then, instead of being a problem, it may have been perceived to enhance their qualifications for this line of work. After all, childbirth involves a profound transition or boundary-crossing of its own, from the realm of the unborn into the world of the living. In chapters 4 and 5, we shall encounter two other individuals transing gender in order to live as women who also worked as healers: one would summon a deity for exorcistic faith healing, and the other served as medium to channel a female fox spirit. Such faith healing also involved facilitating a profoundly meaningful (and potentially dangerous) crossing of boundaries, and it also seems possible that transing gender reinforced the numinous talents of these individuals.

Why the Lawsuit?

The lawsuit also raises all sorts of puzzling questions that we can answer only imperfectly. Most basic is why Xiong Mumu chose to pursue what proved to be a disastrous course of action.

The fundamental problem here is that household division and inheritance in both law and custom were governed by the universally known principle that "all sons receive equal shares" (*zhuzi junfen*) of their father's property. In prosperous families, a daughter might take a dowry with her when she married, but daughters were excluded from direct inheritance via household division.[15] In other words, if the Xiong family had two sons, each would receive half. But Xiong Mumu was living as a woman, some distance from home. Erliang's logic seems to have been that if Xiong Mumu wanted to be treated as a woman, then in household division they should receive a daughter's share (i.e., nothing) with Erliang as the "only son" receiving 100 percent. But Xiong Mumu insisted on receiving a son's full share (i.e., 50 percent). This manifest contradiction gave their lawsuit an absurd quality: How could a daughter claim a son's share? It seems that Xiong Mumu wanted to live as a woman without surrendering the privileges of a man.

Why, then, did Xiong Mumu press this quixotic lawsuit, despite the obvious risk of exposure? Perhaps they had become complacent, after more than thirty years of living successfully as a woman. Or perhaps they simply trusted their brother to keep their secret, as he had for so many years. By the time they filed charges, however, I suspect that they were motivated primarily by anger at their brother's callous ingratitude; after all, Erliang had managed to acquire a wife only because Xiong Mumu paid her brideprice. But Erliang may have known of Xiong Mumu's newfound prosperity in Anfu County and genuinely resented their demand that he divide their father's small farm. Erliang's decision to expose his sibling's secret suggests that he, too, was acting out of spite, because he must have understood that once he crossed that Rubicon, there was no going back. (He may not have realized just how dire the consequences would be, however.) It is well known that when parties to a dispute become motivated by anger and a desire for revenge, compromise may become impossible even if compromise would best serve the interests of both parties.[16]

It is also possible that Xiong Mumu never intended to press their case all the way to a formal court hearing. For parties to a dispute, it was a common tactic to file charges as a way of raising the stakes, to try to intimidate one's opponent into capitulating, and many of the people who did so were content to abandon their lawsuits as soon as a compromise could be reached. For this reason, a large percentage of the cases in local court archives from the Qing ended after one or two plaints had been filed—the parties never showed up in court, and yamen runners found it impossible to track them down. Mediated settlements of this kind account for perhaps half of all lawsuits filed in the local courts during the Qing.[17] But, for whatever reason, Xiong Mumu's case did end up in a formal court hearing, and their secret was exposed, with the consequences we have seen.

Sang Chong, the Paradigmatic Cross-Dressing Predator

In his memorial, the governor did not attempt to explain Xiong's own subjective perspective—indeed, he showed no interest in trying to understand it. To the governor, Xiong was a man who had pretended to be a woman. Instead of inquiring about Xiong's own perspective, the governor attributed a criminal motive and history to them for which the bare facts of the case would seem to provide no evidence. The following lines in the memorial are especially telling: "For a man to masquerade in women's attire shows an extraordinary degree of treachery and cunning, and therefore his behavior must include further acts of extreme evil"; "we can be sure *without even bothering to ask* that he must have seduced and raped women on a routine basis"; "Xiong Ersheng's crimes largely took place in the obscurity of the female chambers"; and "some of the implicated women, upon hearing of this, would commit suicide out of shame."

In short, the governor interpreted Xiong's gender transing as a cover for sexual predation against women. But also note the governor's assurance that his investigation had uncovered "no *further* evidence of heterodox teachings, sorcery, or bewitching and deceiving people" (*bie wu xiejiao, yaoshu, guhuo renxin zhi chu*). Evidently, he believed it logical to assume that a man who pretended to be a woman might also engage in these sorts of crimes. How can we explain the governor's reasoning? After all, his summary of the facts includes no mention of any sexual behavior whatsoever, let alone sorcery or heterodoxy. On what grounds, then, did he assert that "we can be sure *without even bothering to ask*" that Xiong had "routinely" debauched women?

The governor's rhetoric and assumptions in this case exemplify how late imperial officials and elites understood M–F crossing: for a man to dress as a woman was to debase himself, and the only plausible reason they could think of for a man to do so was to insinuate himself into the inner female quarters of proper households in order to seduce or rape women. Far from being an "invert" or a homosexual, let alone a real woman, the M–F cross-dresser was a fundamentally masculine, hypersexual predator whose disguise as a woman was intended to facilitate his crimes.

Nonfiction Accounts of Sang Chong

The locus classicus for this paradigm is the Ming dynasty case of Sang Chong, which was well known during the Qing. Most of what we "know" about Sang Chong comes from later fictional accounts. The earliest and most important source—and one of very few that can be considered non-fiction—is a brief summary of the case found in the *Veritable Records of the Ming Dynasty* (*Ming shilu*). According to that summary, Sang Chong was a commoner from Shi Department, Shanxi, who was executed by dismemberment on the emperor's orders in the thirteenth year of the Chenghua reign (i.e., 1477).

> In the beginning, there was a man in Shanyin County, Datong Prefecture, who practiced women's handiwork and disguised himself as a woman (*xi nügong, wei furen zhuang*), in order to seduce and debauch daughters and wives of good families (*yi youyin liangjia nüfu*). If any refused him, he would use black magic (*momei*) to make them submit, so that he could succeed in debauching them.
> Sang Chong learned all this man's techniques, and then recruited seven followers whom he instructed in turn. Sang Chong traveled

through more than forty departments and counties, debauching more than eighty women in all, and no one suspected his disguise. But when he reached Jin Department, a man who tried to rape Sang Chong discovered his fraud and reported him to the authorities for punishment.

When word reached the capital about this case, the Censorate reported it to the emperor, who ordered Sang Chong executed by dismemberment (*lingchi*) in the marketplace, on the grounds that his repulsive, vile crimes had injured the public morality (*you shang feng-hua*). The emperor further ordered that Sang Chong's seven accomplices be hunted down and punished as well.[18]

The *Veritable Records* for a given emperor's reign were compiled under his successor's administration, based on the imperial court's archives.[19] Therefore, we can date this account to early in the Hongzhi reign (1488–1505), about a dozen years after Sang Chong's execution, making it the closest we have to a contemporary account of the case. Even if the story seems far-fetched, its inclusion in the *Veritable Records* shows that at least the court compilers of that chronicle believed it to be true; therefore, we can be confident that someone named Sang Chong was actually executed for these alleged crimes. Assuming that this account accurately summarizes Sang Chong's confession, then it may well be an example of torture-driven confession—what historian Laura Stokes has called "creativity inspired by torment"—that says more about the assumptions and expectations of Sang Chong's interrogators than about their actual conduct.[20]

The only other ostensibly nonfiction sources that I have found on Sang Chong are even briefer summaries that appear in two gazetteers from Shanxi that were published much later in the Ming, during the Wanli reign (1573–1620). These two summaries are identical to each other in nearly every respect. Here is the text from the *Taiyuan Prefectural Gazetteer* of 1612:

During the Zhengde reign, Yuci County had the case of Sang Chong, who, despite being male, masqueraded as a woman (*yi nanzi zhuang nü*). He traveled to more than 78 towns and villages in a total of 45 departments and counties, practicing embroidery and having illicit sexual intercourse with a total of 182 daughters of good families (*liangjia nüzi*). Later on, in Zhending Prefecture, Gao Xuan discovered his fraud and, seizing him, delivered him to the magistrate of Zhao Department. Discovering the truth through interrogation, the magistrate reported the case by memorial to the emperor, and Sang Chong was executed by dismemberment (*zhe*) in the marketplace.[21]

This summary diverges from the *Veritable Records* in certain key details: it dates the case to the Zhengde reign (1506–1521) instead of the earlier Chenghua reign (1465–1487); it inflates considerably the number of women Sang Chong supposedly debauched; and it disagrees on where Sang Chong was arrested. It also adds two pieces of new information: Sang Chong hailed from Yuci County, and the man who turned them in to the authorities (presumably the would-be rapist identified in the *Veritable Records*) was named Gao Xuan. (The likely source of these embellishments is Lu Can's fictional account, to be addressed later in the chapter.) The second summary, found in the *Shanxi Provincial Gazetteer*, adds a single new detail: that Sang Chong was the adopted son of one Sang Mao.[22] The gazetteers say nothing about where Sang Chong learned their black arts, or about their recruitment of followers. On the basic story line, however, all three sources agree: a *man* named Sang Chong had disguised himself as a woman and learned women's handiwork in order to practice sexual predation on a fantastic scale; the targets of his predation were chaste women of good families; and, in the end, he was exposed and put to death for his crimes.

Fictional Accounts of Sang Chong

The notorious story of Sang Chong provided the inspiration for fiction and "notation books" (*biji*) by some of the most famous late-Ming and Qing writers, including Feng Menglong, Huang Wei, Li Yu, Ling Mengchu, Lu Can, Pu Songling, Xie Zhaozhe, and Yuan Mei.[23] All of this literature belongs to the "episodes of the strange" (*zhiguai*) genre, and none of it should be taken at face value as a record of fact. It was highly influential, nevertheless, and, thanks to these authors, Sang Chong's story was well known in the Qing.[24] The paradigm of the cross-dressing sexual predator was so taken for granted that it can be said to have formed part of the "common sense" of Qing elites, including officials like Governor Jiang.

It is worth bearing in mind that even the three ostensibly nonfiction sources from the Ming disagree on such basic issues as the century when Sang Chong's escapades supposedly took place. Moreover, other versions of the story modify and embellish it in all sorts of fanciful ways. In some versions, for example, Sang Chong was raised as a girl and had bound feet since childhood. These texts cannot even agree on how to write the character "Chong" in Sang Chong's name (at least four different characters are used; see character list). Therefore, it may be impossible to identify a coherent set of facts for this case, beyond the basic paradigm of the cross-dressing sexual predator who uses deception and black magic to target chaste women of good family.

The account in the *Veritable Records* contains important hints about the ideological and legal import of Sang Chong's alleged crimes. First of all, Sang Chong is portrayed as part of an evil cult that grew and spread through recruitment, its weird techniques being passed from master to disciples across three generations—and, even with Sang Chong safely eliminated, their master and seven disciples presumably remained at large, free to carry on debauching women and recruiting still more adepts. In other words, Sang Chong's arrest exposed a criminal conspiracy of vast scale.

Second, the description of how Sang Chong's master practiced his debaucheries deserves special attention: he would "seduce" (*you*) women of good family, but, if they resisted, he would "use black magic (*momei*) to make them submit." The implication is that chastely cloistered women, if confronted by a strange man in their bedchamber, would be highly susceptible to seduction, which tells us something of the paranoid anxiety behind the Ming-Qing obsession with female chastity. But, if women resisted seduction, the master had recourse to *momei*, which I translate here as "black magic," but that has connotations of demonic enchantment or possession. In other words, the occult techniques at the center of Sang Chong's conspiracy implied intercourse with demons—it carried a profoundly heterodox character.

This demonic implication is reinforced by the two gazetteer summaries: both carry the title "A Male Sorcerer Harms Public Morality" (*nan yao shang hua*). The character *yao*, which I have translated in this context as "sorcerer," typically means "demon" (as in the term *yaoguai*, "demon" or "monster"). *Yao* has the female radical *nü*, thus implying there is something feminine about these demons. In Ming-Qing legal texts, *yao* is used interchangeably with *xie* (heterodox), as in the terms for "heterodox speech" (yao/xieyan) and "sorcery" (yao/xieshu—literally, "heterodox techniques"). We have already seen the latter term in Governor Jiang's memorial, when he assures the emperor that "no *further* evidence of heterodox teachings, sorcery (yaoshu), or bewitching and deceiving people" has been found—Xiong's "masquerade" already constituting evidence of such matters. The term "renyao" (or "yaoren") has long carried a wide range of meanings associated with gender-crossing, demonic shape-shifting, and black magic.[25] In China today, the term is often used to refer to glamorous transwomen such as the Thai beauty queen and actor Treechada Petcharat, celebrated on Chinese social media as "the empress of *renyao*" (renyao huanghou), but it is also a term of abuse for effeminate gay men (the equivalent of "faggot" or "fairy").[26] In literary texts, Sang Chong is often referred to as a *renyao* or *yaoren*. Judith Zeitlin has translated *renyao* as "human prodigy"; here, I translate it as "cross-dressing sorcerer," which strikes me as more precise.[27] In some fictional versions of the Sang Chong paradigm, the gender-crossing sorcerer is portrayed as a shapeshifter, who is fundamentally male but can manipulate his genitalia (including a retractable penis) to appear either female or male as needed: passing as a woman in order to penetrate the inner chambers, and then assuming male form in order to perpetrate his sexual assault.[28]

Lu Can's "The Case of the Cross-Dressing Sorcerer"

The most important of the fictional accounts, and probably the earliest, appears in Lu Can's *Notes from the Last Two Years of the Zhengde Reign* (*Gengsi bian*), written in the 1510s.[29] Lu Can's account, "The Case of the Cross-Dressing Sorcerer" (renyao gong'an), purports to be a copy of memorials to the emperor and his edicts about the case that Lu Can claims to have transcribed from an old casebook he found at a friend's house, but its informal rhetoric and lurid details indicate that it is a fictionalization. Lu Can's use of the term gong'an ("the case of") in his essay's title places it within the genre of "court case fiction" (gong'an xiaoshuo), which often includes supposedly genuine legal documents written in quasi-official style.[30] One curious detail is that Lu Can's version agrees with the gazetteers on most points where they diverge from the *Veritable Records*, making for an even more sensational story, but the gazetteers postdate Lu Can's essay by many decades. It seems possible, therefore, that Lu Can's fictional elaboration became the basis for the gazetteers' ostensibly non-fictional accounts.

Given that Lu Can's version of the Sang Chong story was so influential and has been taken by at least some readers for a genuine case report, we should attend to some of its more interesting features. For example, Sang Chong's transition is described as a process of being trained by their master to present as a woman:

> Chong pledged Gu Cai as his master (*toubai wei shi*). Gu Cai tweezed and shaved Chong's eyebrows and face to look like a woman (*fen zuo san liu*), rolled his hair up in a topknot (*jiuji*) in the style of a married woman, and then dressed him in women's clothing and jewelry. Then Gu Cai taught Sang Chong how to do women's work: how to draw and cut patterns, how to embroider the tops of shoes, how to cook meals, and so on. Having completed his training, Sang Chong thanked his master and returned home.

In the Ming dynasty, the standard hairstyle for men was to wear the hair long; thus, Sang Chong's transition would have required no radical modification of the hair, beyond fashioning it into the topknot or bun of a married woman. In contrast, since the front of Xiong Mumu's head had been shaved (as required of men by the Qing dynasty), their transition was more complex: they first shaved their entire head (posing as a Buddhist nun) and later grew out their hair at uniform length, in the manner of an ordinary woman.

Here is Lu Can's description of how Sang Chong would perpetrate their crimes:

> Everywhere he went, he would make discreet inquiries to discover good families that had beautiful daughters. . . . First, he would find temporary lodgings with a small, poor family, and would do a day or two of handiwork for them. Then he would ask them to spread the word that he was available to be invited in by families to teach women's work to their daughters. Once invited, at night he would sleep together with the daughters: he would tell lies, tease them, and deceive them into submitting happily to his designs (*kuangyan zuoxi hongshuo xi yun*). Then he would quietly have illicit sex with them.

But, if necessary, Sang Chong had recourse to "black magic" (*momei*—the same term that appears in the *Veritable Records*), by combining a knockout drug with verbal incantations:

> If he encountered a righteous girl who refused to submit, he would wait until the first stroke of the watch, late at night, and then work his petty magic (*xiao fazi*). He would take from his purse the following materials: a chicken egg (using the yolk only), seven parts of peach and of willow; having burned them to ashes, he would add a new needle, and then use an iron mallet to crush and mix everything together in a mouthful of heated wine. When combined, these ingredients made a knockout drug (*miyao*). Then he would spray the drug onto the girl's body while silently chanting a spell to make her pass out (*hunmi zhou*), in order to paralyze her limbs and render her unable to speak. Once he had finished raping her, he would chant a spell to revive her (*jiehun zhou*), and only then would she regain consciousness.

Then Sang Chong would beg the girl to keep their secret, and, in her shame, she would remain silent. "In this way a decade passed," Lu Can reports, "during which he had illicit sex with a total of 182 daughters of good families (*liangjia nüzi*), without ever being caught."

Here, Sang Chong is portrayed as using a knockout drug in conjunction with black magic to render their victims helpless to resist—and the introduction of a drug is an important innovation on the *Veritable Records* account. As we shall see, in real life knockout drugs were sometimes used by sexual predators in the Qing, together with verbal spells, talisman diagrams, special hand gestures, and other occult techniques. Different editions of Lu Can's essay offer slightly different versions of the drug's formula, none of which make sense in terms of traditional Chinese medicine. It is not clear what parts of the peach and willow were to be used. The use of a "new needle" (*xin zhen*) is also strange: it appears to be an ingredient in the drug rather than a device used to prepare it. In some traditional Chinese prescriptions, a new needle (as opposed to one that has been used many times) is added, and it will "melt" into the concoction over time. The strangeness and inconsistency of this formula suggest that it is part of Sang Chong's black magic rather than a description of any genuine drug.

It is Sang's verbal incantations that activate the knockout drug and also that revive their victim after they have finished raping her.[31]

In Lu Can's account, Sang Chong was finally brought to justice in the following way:

> He begged Gao Xuan for lodgings, claiming to be a concubine [who] had run away because her husband beat and cursed her. Gao agreed, and arranged for Sang Chong sleep in the southern room of his house. Late that night, Gao Xuan's son-in-law Zhao Wenju snuck into Sang Chong's room and asked to have illicit sex. Chong pushed Wenju away so that he fell over, but Wenju embraced Chong tightly and pressed him down on the *kang*. Groping Chong's body, Zhao realized that Chong had no breasts, and instead had a scrotum! So he seized Chong and delivered him to the authorities.

Beginning with the *Veritable Records*, most versions of the Sang Chong story agree that Sang was exposed and turned in to the authorities by a man who tried to rape them (either Gao Xuan or Gao's son-in-law), but in no version is that man ever held criminally liable for the attempted rape, nor does any comment on the irony of a serial sexual predator being exposed by their would-be rapist. Like the *Veritable Records*, Lu Can's account ends with the emperor sentencing Sang Chong to death by dismemberment and exhorting his ministers to arrest Sang's seven accomplices, who remain at large (and whose names and home jurisdictions Lu Can helpfully provides).

To my jaundiced eye, these passages read far more like court case fiction than like a genuine legal case report. Lu Can has taken the basic "facts" from the *Veritable Records* (or some other source lost to us) and has enhanced their entertainment value by adding juicy, sensational details and exaggerating even further the scale of Sang Chong's alleged crimes.

Misogyny and Transphobia

It is important to note the profound misogyny of the Sang Chong paradigm: behind this apparent concern for women's safety lay a deep contempt for women. Hypothetically, it might have been understandable to Qing officials why a woman would pose as a man; after all, gender crossing in that direction could be considered an act of upward mobility, reflected, for example, in Buddhist teachings that virtuous women ascended the karmic ladder by being reborn as men, and that the only way for a woman to enter the Pure Land was to be reborn there as a man.[32] (I should point out, however, that I have seen no example of F–M crossing in the Qing legal archives, and I have no evidence of how such behavior would have been treated by the judicial system.) But for a man to pose as a woman would have been understood as a bizarre act of self-abasement. Women were seen as inferior, subordinate creatures, their bodies being deeply polluted in ways specifically threatening to men.[33] As Wilt Idema has observed with regard to cross-dressing in Ming-Qing fiction:

> In a patriarchal society, where there is an unequal division of power between genders, it may be unnatural but still understandable that women aspire to the status of men, but the reverse is both unnatural and scandalous. A woman who wants to be a man underlines the superior position of the male. However, a man who willingly acts the role of a woman denies by this act the normalcy of existing gender relations. A woman may be praised by calling her a man, but a man is effectively damned by calling him a woman.[34]

Therefore, only a powerful ulterior motive could explain a man's choice to pose as a woman, and the only one that Qing authorities could imagine was a desire to gain access to women.

It is intriguing how closely the Ming-Qing paradigm of the cross-dressing sexual predator resembles the paranoid fantasies that inform modern transphobia in the United States and elsewhere. This modern transphobia directs particularly virulent hostility toward transwomen. A classic example is the portrayal of transwomen as insane serial killers in popular Hollywood movies such as *Psycho*, *Dressed to Kill*, and *The Silence of the Lambs*.[35] A more recent example from American politics is the effort to ban trans people from public restrooms that match their gender identity, because of "the supposed danger that transgender women, . . . vilified as deranged male sex predators in drag, would pose to the safety of women and girls."[36] A final example is a subset of feminists—labeled "trans-exclusionary radical feminists" (TERFs) by their critics—who denounce transwomen as "infiltrators of women's space," and as men who are actual or potential rapists in disguise. The TERF embrace of the trope of the "transsexual rapist" represents a strange alliance between activists who, after all, consider themselves feminists, and deeply misogynist and homophobic forces on the right wing of the American political spectrum.[37] Like the Sang Chong paradigm, what all these manifestations of modern transphobia share is the paranoid fantasy of the transwoman as a dangerous, predatory fraud who poses a threat to "real" women.

Forced Disclosure and Identity Enforcement

Let us pause to consider the forced disclosure of genital status that the midwife's examination of Xiong Mumu entailed. Their entire prosecution rested on the outcome of this court-ordered examination. Its premise was that the truth of Xiong's gender could be determined by their genitals: if they had male genitals, then Xiong was "really" a man, and their presentation as a woman was a "masquerade" (*jia zhuang, jia ban*), an act of deception that must have malicious intent. The Chinese terms used in the text emphasize the "falsity" (*jia*) of Xiong's womanly presentation: rather than an expression of their true self, it was a pretense that disguised their genuine identity. For Xiong Mumu, the consequences of exposure were catastrophic.

Today, transgender people—in particular, straight transwomen—find themselves in "a dangerous double bind": they may be punished for either disclosing or not disclosing their trans status, which in practice usually means their genital status. If they disclose, then they may be accused of not "really" being women, but, rather, a fraud; at the same time, paradoxically, they find themselves "vulnerable to sexualization. . . . represented as whores—sexually available and disposable."[38] On the other hand, if they fail to disclose but are discovered, they stand accused of deliberate deceit. The latter scenario may be especially perilous for a transwoman confronted by cisgender men who feel sexually attracted to her.[39] As Janet Mock has written, "The moment of forced disclosure is a hostile one to experience, one in which many trans women, even those who have the conditional privilege of 'passing' that I have, can be victim to violence and exiling."[40] The more convincingly she can "pass," the more likely she is to be blamed for this "deception." She may even find herself accused of being a gay man in disguise who seeks to entrap "normal" men into sex.

This forced disclosure amounts to a kind of identity enforcement, wherein a trans person's genital status is cited as proof of their real identity, and it may be compounded by rape (in the case of trans men or butch lesbians) or even murder to reinforce the point. The horrific cases of Brandon Teena and Gwen Araujo are paradigmatic examples from recent American history: both were murdered after having their genitalia forcibly exposed. After exposure, Teena was immediately gang raped by the men who later murdered him—rape apparently being understood as a way to force Teena to acknowledge that he was a woman.[41] In contrast, the men who had had sex with Araujo prior to exposing and then murdering her claimed that *she* had raped *them*, by "deceiving" them into having sex with "a man." They apparently feared that their sexual attraction to Araujo implied that they were gay, and they felt it was necessary to murder her in order to punish her "deceit," as well as to reassure themselves of their own masculinity and heterosexuality.[42]

For Xiong Mumu, the consequences of exposure by the authorities were more formal but no less disastrous, and coercive regendering was a fundamental part of their punishment. It took the form of being referred to throughout the case record by their deadname, "Ersheng," but also (as the emperor specifically ordered) by being forced to shave the front of their head in conformity with the tonsure mandated for men.[43] Presumably they were also forced to take out their earrings, unbind their feet, and put on men's clothing. This identity enforcement preceded Xiong Mumu's transportation to the frigid far north of Manchuria, where they would spend the rest of their life enslaved to the military. One can only imagine how miserable and short that life must have been.

Sang Chong, too, was "outed" by forcible disclosure. Nearly all versions of Sang Chong's story agree that they were exposed by a man who tried to rape them, and who then, upon discovering their genitals, turned them in to the authorities for prosecution. All versions also agree that Sang Chong was publicly executed by dismemberment—the most extreme and cruel form of capital punishment employed by the Ming dynasty. If, as I suspect, the real, historical Sang Chong (as opposed to the demonic figure of legend) was a gender-transing person not unlike Xiong Mumu, then these details seem to ring true. Sang Chong was supposedly a serial rapist, so, for narrative purposes, it is a satisfying irony that they were exposed by a would-be rapist who turned the tables on them. But I find the grandiosity and scale of Sang Chong's alleged crimes completely incredible. It seems likely that they confessed under torture, which induced them to produce a narrative that would satisfy the expectations of their inquisitors. Sang

Chong's era was obviously very different from China today, let alone the United States, and yet perhaps the most believable part of their unbelievable story is the specter of a transwoman being subjected to sexual harassment and rape, and then, after forcible exposure, being put to death most cruelly for their supposed "deceit."[44]

The Statute Against Heterodoxy

As Governor Jiang correctly pointed out, the Qing code contains no explicit mention of "a man masquerading in women's attire" (*nan ban nüzhuang*). Xiong's case was handled outside the routine judicial system, with the emperor passing judgment in summary manner via vermilion rescript, as was his prerogative; he did not bother citing the Qing code, because he (and through him, his ancestors) was the ultimate source of law. But, as we shall see in chapters 4 and 5, when such offenders were formally sentenced, Qing authorities cited the statute prohibiting "sorcerers, shamans, and heterodox techniques" (*shiwu xieshu*), which appears in the code's section pertaining to the Board of Rites, in the chapter on "sacrifices" (*jisi*). Its main clause reads as follows:

Any sorcerer or shaman who deploys any technique based on deviant ways and heterodox principles (*zuodao yiduan zhi shu*)—for example, falsely pretending to summon heterodox spirits (*jia jiang xieshen*), writing talismans or magically charging water by incantation (*zhoushui*), or performing magic writing on a sand table (*fuluan*) and praying to the divine; or presuming to claim the title of wizard or witch (including such terms as *duangong*, *taibao*, or *shipo*); or outrageously adopting the name of a heterodox sect such as the "Maitreya Buddha Society," the "White Lotus Society" (*bailian she*), the "Enlightened and Respectful Teachings" (*mingzun jiao*), the "White Cloud Lineage," etc.; or who hides pictures of proscribed deities, or gathers a crowd to burn incense, collecting by night and dispersing at dawn, or falsely pretends to engage in benevolent works (*yang xiu shanshi*), in order to incite and deceive the common people (*shanhuo renmin*), shall be punished as follows: the ringleader shall be strangled after the assizes, and accomplices shall receive one hundred blows of the heavy bamboo and be exiled for life at a distance of three thousand li.[45]

This statute is nearly identical to the corresponding statute in the earlier Ming code, most of which was incorporated into the original version of the Qing code in 1646.[46] The statute's key phrases are "deviant ways and heterodox principles" (*zuodao yiduan*) and "to incite and deceive the common people" (*shanhuo renmin*), and this law was often referred to as "the statute against using deviant ways and heterodox principles to incite and deceive the common people" (*zuodao yiduan shanhuo renmin lü*). In this study, I shall refer to it simply as "the statute against heterodoxy."

The term I have translated as "deviant ways"—*zuodao*—literally means "the left way." Its locus classicus is a passage in *The Book of Rites*. Richard von Glahn has translated it as "the sinister way," taking advantage of the parallel nuance in both Chinese and English languages that "left" (as in left-handedness) is somehow insidious, dangerous, and unorthodox. According to von Glahn, by the end of the Han dynasty, *zuodao* had become "synonymous with sorcery."[47] *Zuodao* has a nearly exact parallel in the Western tradition of magic and witchcraft, in which "the left-hand path" is usually taken to mean black magic, or, at least, magical practices that violate social norms and taboos. Adherents of the left-hand path have often incorporated unconventional sexual acts into their rituals.[48] The antonym of *zuodao* is *zhengdao*, "the correct way," which is closely identified with Confucianism. The term I translate as "heterodox principles"—*yiduan*—functions in Ming-Qing legal texts as a synonym of *zuodao*, and they often appear together as a set phrase. *Yiduan* was used by the early Confucians to refer to rival schools of thought and their teachings, which were deemed inferior, and, as Confucianism became orthodoxy, the term *yiduan* came to mean heterodoxy.[49]

Here we should recall Governor Jiang's statement at the very beginning of his memorial that "whenever I lecture about the Sacred Edict, I strive to enlighten the people," in order to combat their "bizarre delusions." The Sacred Edict (*shengyu*) was issued by the Kangxi emperor in 1670 and consists of sixteen pithy maxims that sum up, as Victor Mair has put it, "the bare bones of Confucian orthodoxy as it pertained to the average citizen."[50] Most of these maxims exhort the people to practice filial piety, abstain from quarrels and lawsuits, devote themselves to agriculture, pay their taxes, and so on. But the seventh reads: "Extirpate strange principles, in order to exalt the correct doctrine" (*chu yiduan yi chong zhengxue*).[51] The phrase Mair translates as "strange principles" is *yiduan*, which the maxim juxtaposes to "correct doctrine" (*zhengxue*)—that is, Confucian orthodoxy.

Beginning in 1729, it was decreed that community lectures about the Sacred Edict be given on a regular basis throughout the empire, by local officials and their representatives—hence the governor's comment, which suggests that he delivered such lectures regularly and in person. There is considerable skepticism among historians about the actual scale of the lecture program in practice, not to mention its reception among the people, but, in theory, at least, lectures on the Sacred Edict were to be delivered in every community, in accessible colloquial language, in order to promote orthodox values and respect for the law throughout the empire. Over time, these lectures increasingly focused on the suppression of heterodox sects and ideas and included explicit discussion of the Qing code's relevant provisions, including the present statute.[52] In short, the governor is assuring the emperor that he is personally committed to the extirpation of heterodoxy, and that this commitment informs his handling of the Xiong Mumu case.

The term in the statute that I translate as "to incite and deceive the common people"—*shanhuo renmin*—also deserves attention.[53] *Shan* means to incite or provoke and has a strongly pejorative connotation, whereas *huo* means to deceive, confuse, or bewitch. *Huo* also carries a nuance of black magic, as seen in the compound phrase *guhuo renxin*, which appears in the governor's memorial about Xiong Mumu (I translate it there as "bewitching and deceiving people"). *Guhuo* literally means "to bewitch and deceive using *gu*," which was a notorious (and probably apocryphal) poison supposedly made by sealing scorpions, snakes, and other poisonous creatures together in a jar, waiting until one had eaten all the others, and then fashioning whatever remained into a drug. The concept of *gu* poison dates to antiquity. Among Han Chinese even today, *gu* poison has a strong folkloric connection with women of Miao ethnicity in China's southwest, who supposedly convey it to their unwitting victims (invariably portrayed as sojourning Han men, perhaps the women's lovers) in food as a means of controlling them and compelling their return: if their victims fail to return (and receive the antidote in another meal), they will die.[54] This stereotype of Miao women is an example of the ethnographic fantasy that the territory beyond the bounds of Confucian civilization is inhabited by dangerous, sexually aggressive women—a fantasy also epitomized by the "Kingdom of Women" trope discussed in chapter 1. The use of *gu* poison was classified as one of the "Ten Abominations" (*shi e*) listed at the beginning of the Ming and Qing codes, together with "black magic" (*momei*), the same term used in the *Veritable Records* to characterize Sang Chong's occult techniques. The manufacture of *gu* poison and its use for homicide were to be punished by immediate beheading.[55] *Guhuo* could refer literally to poisoning or bewitching someone, but was more often used figuratively to mean "stirring up public sentiment by false statements."[56]

Deception and fraud are key to the heterodoxy statute, as also seen in its phrases "falsely pretending to summon," "presuming to claim," "outrageously adopting," and "falsely pretends to." The various substatutes appended to it over the course of the Qing dynasty also underscore the theme of deception and the fear that unscrupulous demagogues would use heterodox doctrines and techniques to stir up and delude the masses. The basic position of Ming-Qing authorities on the popular religious sects they condemned as "heterodox teachings" (*xiejiao*) was that their leaders were evil charlatans who deceived the gullible common people in order to exploit them for money, sex, and sedition.[57] Philip Kuhn (citing Qing jurist Shen Zhiqi) argues that the state's main concerns in this statute are "social order and state security," because "simple people, aroused by heterodox teachings, may create disturbances and 'give rise to chaos.'" In Kuhn's view, although Qing officials certainly believed that sorcery existed, their fear focused on the risk that the common people might be deluded into sedition.[58]

Cross-Dressing as Heterodoxy

The heterodoxy statute was usually applied to prosecute proscribed sects and collective sworn brotherhoods. It might also be used to prosecute shamans and faith healers, although such religious practitioners were so ubiquitous that the imperial state never made any systematic effort to suppress them. But the statute nowhere mentions sex offenses, let alone cross-dressing. Why then was it cited to sentence M–F cross-dressing?

As noted, the statute appears in the chapter on "sacrifices" in the Qing code's section of laws pertaining to the Board of Rites. The code also contains a chapter on "offenses of illicit sex" (*fanjian*), which appears under the Board of Punishment. But none of the laws in the "illicit sex" chapter mention cross-dressing either, even though the M–F cross-dresser was imagined to be a sexual predator. Clearly, Qing authorities did not associate cross-dressing with "illicit sex" (*jian*) in any simple way (the basic definition of *jian* being intercourse outside of marriage); rather, their choice of statute indicates that they believed M–F cross-dressing to be somehow fundamentally related to heterodoxy, and especially to sorcery and fraud.

In the case of Sang Chong, the themes of masquerade, black magic, and the initiation of adepts into occult techniques all point to heterodoxy. In that paradigmatic case, disguise as a woman was first and foremost a fraud being perpetrated for malign purposes and facilitated by lies, flattery, drugs, and black magic. The governor's memorial shows without a doubt that he interpreted Xiong's case in terms of the Sang Chong paradigm, even if he never mentions that name. In the first lines, he claims that the people of Hunan are "prone to bizarre delusions," invokes the Sacred Edict, and cites his own record of severely punishing "deception and fraud." Moreover, he is so certain that Xiong Mumu fit the paradigm that he says the facts speak for themselves: "we can be sure without even asking" that Xiong is a sexual predator.

What specific facts did the governor have in mind? Like Sang Chong, Xiong had spent a long time on the road, wandering from place to place over a considerable geographical scale. They had appeared in Anfu County "disguised" as a woman, using a "false" name, and telling a fabricated story to allay any concerns that local people might have felt about this unusual stranger. Xiong's claim of chaste widowhood added an ironic twist to their lies, given that, in the governor's interpretation, Xiong's real goal was to violate women's chastity. Xiong's apparent stint as a Buddhist nun fit the stereotype of the clergy as a refuge for gender deviants rife with promiscuity. But, if Xiong had begun their "masquerade" by pretending to be a nun, that inaugural act of deception confirmed the sexual predator's strategy of using female disguise to gain access to women.

Working as a midwife obviously enabled Xiong to associate with women, to win their trust and learn their secrets, while gaining the most intimate access to their bodies. Pledging "dry daughters" meant further intimacy with young women, and the daughters' act of pledging themselves to Xiong as their "dry mother" must have looked suspiciously similar to a disciple's pledging themself to a master, which was the basic means of recruitment in proscribed sects (including Sang Chong's milieu).[59] In fact, Governor

Jiang singled out the pledging of dry daughters as one of the most damning features of Xiong's case—apparently it was obvious to him that Xiong must be having sex with those women. Overall, Xiong's assiduous effort to build a kinship network must have looked like the recruitment of a cult. Finally, Xiong's success in acquiring so much land must have looked suspicious—where did all that money come from?—given the official conviction that leaders of heterodox sects were charlatans who cheated gullible recruits out of their money.

Sang Chong Strikes Again? A Report from Late-Qing Shanghai

In 1890, the Shanghai newspaper *Shenbao* reported a case that resembles that of Xiong Mumu (and also the fox spirit medium treated in chapter 5) in some striking respects. In its typical sensational way, the newspaper rhetorically packages this case in terms of the sexual predator paradigm. Headlined "A Perverse Nun Is Exposed" (*yaoni bailou*), the report begins by explicitly invoking the specter of Sang Chong: "In the past, there was the case of the sorcerer (*yaoren*) Sang Chong, who, along with his twenty-seven disciples, wore the hairstyle and clothes of a woman, and pretended to be a spirit medium healer (*jiatuo wuyi*) in order to pollute the inner female quarters of other men's households (*wu ren guikun*). Later, they were arrested and executed, one by one. Sang Chong often appears in fiction and anecdotes (*jian yu shuobu*)." This summary of Sang Chong's case is a mashup of its various fictional versions, the clear expectation being that the newspaper's readers would be familiar with the notorious Ming dynasty predator. The article then comments that, "recently, another figure of the same type has appeared," and segues to a news item recounted by "a traveler passing through town":

> In Ren Village near Tianjin, there was a young Buddhist nun who was able to look at incense and serve as a spirit medium in order to ward off disasters and cure illnesses. Apparently, her therapy was effective. Countless numbers of ignorant women worshiped her like a goddess, pledged her as their dry mother (*gan anai*), and became her Buddhist disciples. . . . She circulated through the local villages for about half a year, and no one ever suspected the truth—until

recently, when she was finally exposed. In fact, she was not a female, but a male! (*fei ci er shi xiong ye*)

The newspaper does not explain just how the nun was exposed, but notes that, upon being arrested, they were "kicked and beaten nearly to death," and that they now await judgment in jail.[60]

It is impossible to know what really happened in this case—assuming that the report is based at least to some degree on actual events. But the "facts" appear to be as follows: an individual with male anatomy who lived as a woman and acted as a spirit medium to heal illnesses attracted a sizable clientele of devoted female followers, some of whom pledged dry kinship. *Shenbao* reports no evidence that this person ever harmed anyone or engaged in any sexual activity whatsoever. Nevertheless, the newspaper's characterization of the nun as another Sang Chong makes clear its editorial conviction that anyone who cross-dressed and acted as a spirit medium must be a dangerous, heterodox fraud. (The term *yao* applies to both: the nun is characterized as *yaoni*—that is, "a perverse nun," whereas Sang is a *yaoren*.) That the nun's faith-healing served to recruit a network of women bound to them by chosen kinship would only have reinforced that conviction. As with Xiong Mumu, the only plausible explanation for such activity was to gain access to women for illicit purposes. The fact that the same paradigm informed both the judicial opinion of an eighteenth-century governor and a newspaper report published in fin de siècle Shanghai is striking testimony to the tenacity and power of that paradigm.

The Case of Zengliang

Although he appreciated Governor Jiang's zeal, the "lenient" sentence imposed on Xiong Mumu by the Qianlong emperor suggests that, in his view, "masquerading in women's attire" in and of itself did not necessarily deserve death, as long as there was no solid evidence of sexual offenses or other heinous crimes. This perspective is confirmed by a case prosecuted in Beijing in 1819, in which a young monk named Zengliang was arrested for the crime of "masquerading in woman's attire." The only record I have of this case is a brief summary in the nineteenth-century casebook *Conspectus of Penal Cases* (*Xing'an huilan*), which provides little detail. According to that summary, Zengliang had had two successive sexual relationships in which he was sodomized, first by an older monk named Jiekuan, and later by a layman named Lü Yushan. After Zengliang began his new relationship with Lü, he had a confrontation with his previous sexual partner, Jiekuan, that escalated into a fight, and Zengliang ended up beating Jiekuan severely. Because Jiekuan was injured, Zengliang feared retribution, so, at the urging of Lü Yushan, he attempted to disguise himself by "changing into woman's attire" (*gaiban nüzhuang*) and fled. When arrested, Zengliang falsely accused Jiekuan of having raped him when he was only twelve *sui* (i.e., ten or eleven years old), which would have been a capital offense; this false accusation was also the idea of Lü Yushan, who told Zengliang that this way he could avoid punishment for having beaten up the other monk.

In considering Zengliang's case, the Board of Punishment observed: "We find that in previous cases of men masquerading in women's attire (*nan ban nüzhuang*), if the perpetrators had debauched women (*jianyin funü*) or deceived the masses in order to cheat them out of their money (*huozhong hanqian*), then they would be sentenced to strangulation according to the statute against 'deviant ways and heterodox doctrines' (*zuodao yiduan lü*)." In contrast, Zengliang's sole motive for dressing as a woman had been to evade justice. He did not "scheme to seduce or rape women," nor did he "deceive the masses in order to cheat them out of their money." Nevertheless, "for a monk to be willingly polluted and debased in this manner (*gan shou wuru*) was itself weird and perverse (*guiyi*). Therefore, he should be sentenced to one hundred blows of the heavy bamboo and life exile at a distance of three thousand *li*, which is a reduction of one degree below the sentence of strangulation prescribed by the statute against 'using deviant ways to deceive the masses' (*zuodao huozhong*); in addition, he should serve two months in the cangue as prescribed by the statute, and also be laicized." Lü Yushan received a penalty nearly as severe—one hundred blows of the heavy bamboo and life exile at a distance of three thousand *li*—for having instigated Zengliang's crimes.[61]

Zengliang was spared death (as was Xiong Mumu), but he nevertheless received a remarkably severe punishment for his "willingness" to be "polluted and debased" by disguising himself as a woman. Zengliang had committed other crimes: consensual sodomy, beating and injuring Jiekuan, and false accusation. But these were all deemed "lesser offenses" (*qing zui*), and none of them would have triggered application of the statute against heterodoxy seen here. The penalty for consensual sodomy was a mere one hundred blows of the heavy bamboo and one month in the cangue—a relatively light penalty in the Qing penal hierarchy.[62]

As Governor Jiang's rhetoric demonstrates, Qing officials were predisposed to believe that M–F cross-dressers were sexual predators in disguise. But Zengliang's sentence (like Xiong Mumu's) leaves no doubt that, even in the absence of sex offenses, for a man "to masquerade in women's attire" in and of itself constituted a grave offense, "weird and perverse" (*guiyi*) in nature, that they associated with sorcery and heterodoxy.

CHAPTER III

Clergy as Wolves in Sheep's Clothing

In the Ming dynasty there was the case of Sang Chong, who taught heterodox methods to his disciples and traveled to various places, debauching countless women. In the end, he was exposed and put to death. The present case of this perverse Daoist priest is very similar. The two differ only in that the first masqueraded in *women's* attire (*zuo nüzi zhuang*) and pretended to teach embroidery and to cure illnesses in order to sneak into the female quarters of proper households; whereas the second masqueraded in *Daoist* attire (*zuo daoshi zhuang*) and pretended to write charms and quell demons in order to seduce women at his temple. That is the only difference between them!

— "ON THE DANGERS OF HETERODOXY"
(*LUN ZUODAO ZHI HAI*), *SHENBAO*, 1891

In the final case cited in the last chapter, it hardly seems coincidental that the culprit Zengliang was a monk, and the Board of Punishment singled out this fact in emphasizing the "weirdness" and "perversion" of his cross-dressing. On the one hand, it was even worse for a monk to commit such an act than for a member of the laity to do so. In fact, for clergy simply to dress in lay attire was itself a crime, not to mention adopting the attire of the opposite sex.[1] On the other hand, being a monk seems automatically to have made one an object of suspicion. As noted, a pervasive and persistent stereotype envisioned Buddhist and Daoist clergy as lecherous predators hiding behind clerical disguise. According to that vision, they were precisely the opposite of what they pretended to be: the pious pretense of "leaving the family" was a masquerade designed to facilitate their nefarious schemes. This cynical stereotype has been noted by others, but what has not received attention is its gendered, or, to be precise, transgendered aspect.[2] The stereotype of clergy closely resembles the Sang Chong paradigm of the cross-dressing predator—in fact, they should be understood as two variations of a common theme.

This chapter explores the theme of predatory clergy in three basic scenarios as depicted in a variety of sources. The first scenario concerns fraudulent male clergy who, without dressing as women, allegedly used black magic and knockout drugs to perpetrate a variety of offenses, including seduction, kidnapping, and rape. I present two examples of this scenario from the legal archives and one from the late Qing newspaper *Shenbao*. The second scenario concerns shape-shifting sorcerers who posed as Buddhist nuns in order to penetrate female space and seduce women. It is exemplified by a pair of fictional tales from the subgenre of "the strange" that derived from the case of Sang Chong. The third scenario concerns male clergy who "masqueraded" as women, supposedly for similar reasons, as depicted in *Shenbao* and *Dianshizhai Pictorial*. All of the sources cited in this chapter recount the exposure of predatory clergy and their prosecution by the authorities, and, aside from the two tales of shape-shifting fraudulent nuns, all are ostensibly nonfictional accounts. But, as we shall see, even the archival legal cases and newspaper reports should not be taken at face value as empirical records of events. To one degree or another, all of these narratives reveal the prejudicial influence of the predatory paradigm.

The close parallels between the Sang Chong paradigm and the stereotype of clergy as wolves in sheep's clothing highlight the fact that "leaving the family" was understood to be a transgender maneuver not unlike adopting the attire of the opposite sex. Indeed, the tales of fraudulent nuns and cross-dressing clergy combine the two scenarios into a single paranoid fantasy of predatory deviance.

Predators Masquerading as Clergy

The Qing archives contain many examples of felonious monks and Daoists being prosecuted in ways that strongly confirm this stereotype. They may not have attired themselves as women, but their alleged crimes include much the same repertoire found in accounts of Sang Chong. Another crucial similarity is that these predators are typically exposed as frauds—as *fake* clergy—just as Sang was supposedly exposed as a fake woman.

The Defrocked Daoist, the Spiked Tobacco, and the Runaway Eunuch

In a case prosecuted in Beijing in 1741, an itinerant defrocked Daoist priest named Jiao Laiyi (38 *sui*) was arrested for using knockout drugs (*menghanyao, miyao*) on a livestock dealer at the donkey market just inside the capital's Fucheng Gate.[3] According to the dealer, Jiao tried to sell him a donkey, and, when the dealer insisted that Jiao provide a guarantor (to confirm that the donkey was his to sell), Jiao rendered him unconscious by giving him drugged tobacco to smoke and then took off with the dealer's money. Jiao was arrested at a nearby inn, where he was staying with a boy, Liu Jinxi (15 *sui*), who turned out to be a runaway eunuch from the palace of Prince Zhuang.[4] The boy had been drugged, kidnapped, and repeatedly raped by Jiao.

Under interrogation by the gendarmerie, Jiao Laiyi confessed to the following.[5] Born in Lingqiu County, Shanxi, from early childhood Jiao and his father (a landless, homeless peasant) wandered from place to place, surviving by begging. Then his father placed him at a temple to the Jade Emperor, and Jiao then "left the family to become a Daoist priest" (*chujia zuo daoshi*). But, in 1738, just after the New Year, he was disowned and kicked out of the temple because he "habitually drank liquor and gambled" and otherwise "violated the rules of the Daoist vocation" (*bu shou dao gui*). Still attired as a Daoist, he resumed his homeless wandering, joining the flotsam of rogue males without family or legitimate station that comprised the underclass of Qing society.[6]

Shortly thereafter, Jiao fell in with an itinerant monk named Li Er, from Xianning County, Shaanxi, who peddled medicines for a living. Li confided that he knew how to use a knockout drug to kidnap children and rob adults, and he suggested that he and Jiao join forces in this enterprise. Jiao enthusiastically agreed, so Li mixed up a quantity of the drug and shared it with him. The drug's ingredients included human brains (*ren naozi*) and Chinese azalea (*naoyanghua*). The latter is a well-known herb in Chinese medicine that has powerful analgesic and anesthetic properties and can induce dizziness, hallucinations, and impaired consciousness.[7] This compound could be mixed into food or tobacco, and, when the mark had eaten or smoked the drug, Li would strike them on the abdomen with his hand; at once, they would be rendered mute, senseless, and obedient to commands. The technique was known as "striking flowers with the hand" (*pai hua*). Much later, when his interrogators asked how he had obtained the "human brain" used to prepare the drug, Jiao explained—after much evasion and equivocation—that he had extracted it from the skull of a dead child found lying on the road.

Over the next year, sometimes working with Li and sometimes alone, Jiao used this technique to rob at least seven different men he encountered on the road. He stole cash, clothing, farm tools, and, on one occasion, two horses; he spent the money and sold the goods. During this time, his wanderings took him all over northern Zhili, the administrative region surrounding Beijing. He would offer his victims a smoke of his spiked tobacco and then strike them on the abdomen, rendering them incoherent and disoriented, and then make off with their belongings. He stripped some victims of their clothes and bedding, leaving them naked by the road.

In the spring of 1741, Jiao was on his own just outside Beijing, where he encountered the runaway eunuch Liu Jinxi. Born in Weinan County, Zhili, Liu's original name was Liu Ba'er ("eighth son"). At the age of thirteen *sui* (i.e., eleven or twelve years old), his father had had him castrated and, after he recovered from the procedure, had brought him to Beijing and sold him into imperial service as a eunuch (*taijian*) for a "body price" (*shen jia*) of five taels of silver (the fact that he was the eighth son in a peasant family helps explain why his father considered him expendable). The supervising eunuch who arranged his purchase renamed him "Jinxi" (i.e. "promotes happiness"), which was a very common eunuch name.[8] Liu Jinxi later ran away, because he broke a teapot and feared punishment.

By the time he encountered Jiao, Jinxi had found work as a casual laborer and was grazing his employer's donkey. Jiao used the spiked tobacco to kidnap the boy, leading him and the donkey to an inn, where they found lodgings. Jinxi later testified that after a couple of puffs on Jiao's pipe, he felt dizzy and could neither speak nor control his movements. That night, Jiao made the boy smoke more of the drug, and then sodomized him; over the next few days, Jiao repeatedly raped the boy, using the drug to keep him docile. Jiao was finally arrested when he attempted to sell the stolen donkey and was reported by the livestock dealer he had drugged. When taken into custody, Jinxi was still intoxicated and unable to speak, but the police revived him by having him drink cold water.

The gendarmerie sent Liu Jinxi back to the princely estate from which he had run away. Since Jiao had been arrested within the jurisdiction of the imperial capital, he was transferred directly to the Board of Punishment for prosecution. The board sentenced Jiao to immediate beheading, according to the statute against "using drugs to stupefy or render someone unconscious in order to steal their property" (*yong yao miren tucai*), a sentence that was approved by the imperial vermilion.[9] But an extensive manhunt failed to locate Li Er, so the rogue monk remained at large with his knockout drugs.

The Fake Daoist, the Spiked Wheat Cakes, and the Girl who Saw a Tiger

In the summer of 1749, soldiers on patrol in Fucheng County, Zhili, became suspicious when they saw an apparent Daoist priest on the road leading a young girl by the hand.[10] She had a handkerchief tied around her head to cover her eyes. When confronted, the Daoist tried to run away, but was quickly caught. Strangely, the girl could not talk, and the officer in charge later reported to the magistrate that "it was obvious she had been stupefied by some sort of drug and kidnapped" (*ming xi yaoshu miguai*). The soldiers made her drink cold water, and only then did she recover her power of speech (*yong liangshui guanjiu shi neng kaikou*). As they suspected, she had been drugged and kidnapped.

Under interrogation, the Daoist identified himself as He Yunliang, aged forty-four *sui*, from Wan Department in faraway Hainan, which was then part of Guangdong Province. In fact, he was an imposter: he had no training or credentials as a Daoist priest. He had been very poor, with no wife or family, so, in 1748, he decided to pose as a Daoist and walk to the imperial capital to find a temple that would take him in. He assumed the ritual name "Yangxiu" ("sunlight efflorescence"), and, acquiring the appropriate clothing, he "falsely masqueraded as a Daoist priest" (*jiaban daoren*) and hit the road.

After five months, he reached Nanchang, the provincial capital of Jiangxi, where he encountered an itinerant Daoist named Sun Tanzhang at a temple, where they shared a charity meal. According to He, Sun quickly saw through his disguise and realized he was a "fake Daoist priest" (*jia daoren*). But, since they got along well, He begged Sun to instruct him in genuine Daoist practices. Finally, Sun agreed to teach him two techniques for stupefying and gaining control over another person: a "spell to bewitch and cast a net over people" (*miren sawang zhou*), which was to be chanted, and a "talisman of the Lord of the Cloudy Sky" (*yintian jun fu*), which was to be drawn on a piece of cloth and used to cover the mark's eyes. After that, the two men parted ways, and He Yunliang continued his journey north.

A couple of months later, in Yanzhou Prefecture, Shandong, He Yun-liang joined company with another itinerant Daoist named Hu De, who was also heading for Beijing. Hoping to impress the other man, He confided that he knew "a magic spell for stupefying people" (*miren zhouyu*), but Hu retorted that a spoken spell by itself had little use—to gain effective control over another person, it was necessary to use drugs. He begged Hu for instruction, so Hu revealed the secret formula for "a drug for intoxicating and bewitching people" (*zui miren zhi yao*). Hu had the ingredients on hand and mixed up a batch and gave it to He Yunliang. The drug's ingredients included Chinese azalea, which we have already encountered, and several other herbs. Hu told He that the antidote for the drug was cold water.

The men continued on their journey, all the while looking for opportunities to try out their portfolio of occult techniques, and, one day in En County, Shandong, they kidnapped two adolescent peasant girls. They encountered the first girl, named Xiaolongjie, cutting grass by the road, and Hu De offered her a wheat cake in which he had secreted the drug. She ate it and immediately became incoherent, and Hu led her away by the hand. When they encountered a second girl, later identified as Liu Xiaoyoujie (thirteen *sui*), He Yunliang decided it was his turn to try. He used another spiked wheat cake to drug the girl, but in addition he chanted the "spell for casting a net," and, on a handkerchief, he drew the talisman of the Lord of the Cloudy Sky and used it to bind the girl's eyes. She "fell into a stupor and followed" (*hunmi gensui*) He Yunliang, who led her away by the hand.

Hu De became nervous that the spectacle of two Daoist priests leading adolescent girls by the hand on the road might provoke suspicion, so he took the first girl and parted company with He Yunliang, who kept the second one, Xiaoyoujie, with him. Walking and begging by day, He and Xiaoyoujie spent nights in deserted temples and in the sorghum fields that lined the road. He Yunliang coerced the girl's submission by threatening violence, and every night he raped her. His plan to take her to Beijing and sell her was foiled by his arrest in Fucheng County.

The magistrate questioned the girl closely about the means He Yunliang had used to control her. She testified:

That day, I remember that I saw this He Yunliang and a Daoist priest whose name I don't know together on the road. They had a young girl with them. He Yunliang approached me and offered me a wheat cake. I was hungry, and since I didn't know any better (*bu zhi haodai*), I ate it. Then he used a handkerchief of patterned cloth to cover my head (*meng xiaode toushang*), and he struck me once with his hand (*ba xiaode pai le yi xia*). I don't know why but I felt faint and confused (*mihu qilai*): on both sides I saw water and fire, and behind me I saw a tiger and a dog! (*liangpang you shui you huo, houtou you hu you gou*) I was afraid, so I followed him. Later when I came to my senses, we were in an empty temple. He Yunliang gave me cold water to drink. I didn't know where we were, and the other Daoist and the girl were gone.

During the day, when they walked on the road, "he would cover my head with that handkerchief, and I would follow him in a daze (*mimi huhu de genzhe ta zou*)."

When interrogated about the black magic he had used on the girl, He Yunliang explained that he was illiterate and could only recite the spell, not write it. But he could draw the talisman. So the magistrate summoned the girl and ordered He to demonstrate his technique in the courtroom (without using the drug). He recited the incantation and applied the talisman-handkerchief, and afterward the girl testified "at first I felt cold in the pit of my stomach, and then I felt dazed and confused" (*xinkou chu jue fa leng, hou jue mihu*). When the handkerchief was removed from her head, the spell was lifted.

Xiaoyoujie's description of being drugged and bewitched bears close resemblance to clinical descriptions of the symptoms of intoxication with Chinese azalea, which include hallucinations. But it is also clear from He Yunliang's courtroom demonstration (which did not involve the drug) that his black magic in itself was to some extent efficacious in subduing the girl—even if, we might guess, that effect may have stemmed more from the power of suggestion and from her sheer terror at being blindfolded again by her kidnapper-rapist than from "magic" per se.

He Yunliang received a sentence of immediate strangulation, according to the substatute against "using a drug concealed in food, or any technique of sorcery, to stupefy or render unconscious a child in order to kidnap them" (*yi yaobing ji yiqie xieshu miguai youxiao zinü*).[11] A massive manhunt was launched to track down Hu De and the second kidnapped girl, but they had not been found by the time He Yunliang's case was closed.

Neither of these cases of predatory clergy involved cross-dressing per se. But if we take seriously the gendered implications of "leaving the family" (*chujia*), then both protagonists represented a paradigmatic transgender persona. But also, both were imposters whose masquerade as clergy paralleled Sang Chong's as a woman. One was a defrocked Daoist, having been kicked out of his temple because of incorrigibly bad behavior, and the other was simply a fraud who had "falsely masqueraded as a Daoist" (*jiaban daoren*). Jiao Laiyi and He Yunliang were not sentenced for heterodoxy, but the crimes they confessed certainly flirted with that category, and the penalties they ultimately received were even more severe than those prescribed by the statute against heterodoxy.

As Philip Kuhn and others have shown, the eighteenth century witnessed growing anxiety in official circles about the burgeoning, mobile underclass of single, landless men at the bottom of Qing society. These men were characterized as *guanggun*—literally "bare sticks"—who lacked the "roots" and "branches" of family ties that, in the Confucian scheme, were supposed to socialize individuals into behaving properly and acting as loyal subjects.[12] A particular focus of suspicion was "the clerical underclass," which included countless Buddhist and Daoist practitioners who lacked the requisite licenses and were attached to no authorized temple or monastery. Qing officials believed that many of these rootless mendicants were simply criminals masquerading as priests and monks in order to evade the law, propagate heterodoxy, and prey upon the gullible common people.[13] This belief drew on and reinforced the longstanding suspicion that many clergy were not really what they seemed.

Jiao Laiyi and He Yunliang fit this description perfectly. Both had roamed across a wide geographical scale, joining forces and conspiring with like-minded confederates in the commission of crime. Their encounters on the road demonstrate vividly the process by which evildoers supposedly recruited new disciples to their occult techniques, fostering crime on a widening scale. The spirit summoned by He Yunliang to bewitch and entrap his victims, "The Lord of the Cloudy (*yin*) Sky," sounds more like a demon than a benign protective deity, given that (in Overmyer's words) "demons are manifestations of *yin* force, which can be driven away by symbols of *yang*."[14] Their use of potent *materia medica* also represented a perversion of the good. Every medicine has potentially toxic properties, as well as curative ones, depending on how it is used, and their abuse of these drugs' toxicity—not to mention the brain of a dead child—represented a ghoulish betrayal of the Daoist tradition of medical innovation in pursuit of health and longevity.[15]

In fact, we should hesitate before accepting the confessions of these two fake Daoists entirely at face value. The corroborating evidence seems vivid and convincing—especially the testimony of their victims—and to be sure, kidnappers and child molesters do exist in the real world. But the fact that these narratives conform so closely to standard tropes and official prejudices indicates that caution may be warranted. Here it is well to remember Karasawa Yasuhiko's observation that legal proceedings were sometimes tainted by prejudice against male clergy.[16] Some specific details of these cases provoke doubt, if not skepticism. It seems odd, for example, that in neither case did the authorities manage to obtain a sample of the knockout drugs the culprits confessed to using.

But also, consider once again the testimony of Xiaoyoujie, the young girl who had been kidnapped by He Yunliang. Her description of being drugged may sound clinically correct, but it also bears uncanny resemblance to an episode in the late Ming collection of con artist tales, *The Book of Swindles*, in which a monk uses "sorcery" (*yaofa*) to kidnap and rape young boys. One of the monk's victims gives the following testimony in court: "The monk touched my eyes, and then on both sides and behind me I saw fierce tigers and poisonous snakes (*liang bian beihou dou shi menghu dushe*) that were going to bite me. Only the path ahead of me was bright and clear, and I had no choice but to walk forward."[17]

What are we to make of this resemblance? For one thing, we can be sure that a peasant girl had not read *The Book of Swindles*. But the magistrate and his clerks may well have read it. Conceivably, this scenario derived from some broader cultural trope or common knowledge that informed both the fictional tale and the illiterate girl's narration of her experience. But it may be another example of the feedback loop between court cases and literature that we have already noted with regard to Sang Chong, which had the effect of "scripting" legal proceedings according to fixed preconceptions.

We also know that Jiao Laiyi's story changed a number of times over a series of interrogation sessions, until he was finally threatened with torture: the magistrate ordered the guards to strap the ankle press (*jiagun*) onto his legs, although the record states that it was not necessary to tighten its cords because the prisoner immediately became cooperative. (The ankle press was the authorized means of judicial torture for male prisoners. It consisted of a set of wooden slats that were strapped onto the lower legs and tightened with cords, sometimes to the point of breaking the bones.)[18] We do not know what other kinds of pressure were exerted on Jiao or on He Yunliang—the laconic accounts in the official record leave much to the imagination—but there can be no doubt that they were treated severely.

There is no way to know the exact truth of these individuals' crimes, but it would seem unwise to accept every detail of the official account without at least a grain of salt. Most likely, their confessions were shaped at least in part by a process of interrogation that tended to confirm the expectations and biases of the interrogators.[19] That process is even more obvious in the following case, which involved the heavy use of torture. It can also be clearly seen in the cases of "men masquerading in women's attire" to be explored in subsequent chapters, when magistrates pressured defendants to produce satisfactory confessions.

The Case of the "Perverse Daoist Priest"

In the spring of 1891, the Shanghai newspaper *Shenbao* covered a shocking story from Beijing of a "perverse Daoist priest" (*yaodao*) surnamed Wang who had supposedly "used heterodox methods to deceive the common people and to pollute women with illicit sex" (*xieshu huozhong, jianwu funü*).[20] In a series of seven articles over two months, the paper reported the gendarmerie's arrest of both the Daoist and more than a dozen of his followers (including several women), his extended interrogation under torture, and his final sentencing.

According to *Shenbao*, Wang had first "joined the White Lotus Teachings (*bailianjiao*) and learned their various methods for talismans and spells." He then began "masquerading as a Daoist priest" (*zhuang wei daoshi*), treating illnesses and spreading his heterodox teachings among the grateful people whom he miraculously cured. His closest confederate was a woman who "masqueraded in the attire of a Daoist nun" (*banzuo daogu zhuangshu*).[21] Wang performed his rituals only at night, visiting the homes of the sick: "His routine was to pretend to quell evil forces and cure illnesses in order to incite and deceive people's hearts" (*shanhuo renxin*)." As word spread of the Daoist's efficacious therapies, "ignorant people" flocked to his temple to pray to him, and the "incense money" he collected "piled up in mountains."[22] Finally, the uncle of one of Wang's followers became worried and reported him to the Beijing Gendarmerie, which was the military police force charged with security in the imperial capital.

Under interrogation by the gendarmerie, Wang "refused to say a word, even under torture." Annoyed, the presiding officer ordered "manure poured onto the Daoist's head," which induced Wang to break his silence and declare that he had been falsely accused and had violated no laws. Finally, after getting no further, the gendarmerie handed Wang over to the Board of Punishment, along with fourteen of his followers.[23]

At the board, Wang continued to insist on his innocence, but the judges were "infuriated by his heterodoxy and licentiousness and subjected him to daily rounds of interrogation while beating him and making him kneel on chains."[24] After several days of such treatment, Wang confessed that he had "regularly had illicit sexual relations with four women at the temple, who were widows or unmarried daughters." But, as *Shenbao* editorialized, "if he has already confessed this much, then there must be many more women whom he has secretly violated!"[25] Pressed further, Wang admitted to using drugs and sorcery to facilitate his debaucheries:

> When he encounters attractive women, either he uses tea and incense to court them, or he uses heterodox drugs to befuddle and control them (*yong xieyao milong*). The women who take these drugs will feel faint and confused, allowing him to pollute them with illicit sex (*zi xing hunhun, ren qi jianwu*). In addition, he has black magic techniques (*huanshu*) that render women happily willing to be polluted by him, and afterwards they do not dare to report him (*ling funü gan ren wuru er bu gan yanzhe*).[26]

In sum, *Shenbao* reported, "the perverse Daoist" Wang's crimes consisted of "using heterodox words to deceive the masses" (*yaoyan huozhong*), "recruiting disciples, gathering crowds, and collecting their money" (*shou mentu juzhong liancai*), and "using sorcery to confuse and debauch the wives and daughters of good families" (*yi xieshu mi yin liangjia funü*).[27]

From its very first article on this case, *Shenbao*'s breathless reportage echoed the statute on heterodoxy, even accusing Wang of having joined the proscribed "White Lotus Teachings" (*bailianjiao*).[28] It is interesting to note that, as late as 1891, that paradigm with all its florid tropes was alive and well, even in ultramodern Shanghai.[29] In the end, the Board of Punishment sentenced Wang to strangulation after the assizes, presumably by applying the same statute (the specific law is not cited in the newspaper). Wang's followers were deemed less culpable, but all had willingly joined his sect, and the women had "allowed" him to commit illicit sex with them. Therefore, the men were ordered beaten and deported to their home districts, while the women were permitted to redeem their beatings with cash fines and then returned to the custody of their natal families.[30]

The *Shenbao* editorial quoted in this chapter's epigraph draws an explicit comparison between the "perverse Daoist priest" of the present case and the notorious Sang Chong. The newspaper repeatedly refers to the former as *yaodao*, whereas the standard label applied to Sang was *yaoren* or *renyao*. As the editorial's title suggests, these two figures constituted complementary, parallel examples of "the dangers of heterodoxy." The Daoist did not pretend to be a woman, but his "masquerade" as a Daoist amounted to much the same thing, insofar as it enabled him to deceive his victims in much the same way that Sang Chong had deceived his. "The only difference between them," according to *Shenbao*, was their respective choice of disguise.[31]

To be clear, *Shenbao*'s account of this case is useful mainly as a vivid example of the *discourse* of predatory clergy—and, although presumably such a case was actually prosecuted in Beijing, it would be naive to accept the newspaper reportage as an accurate record of this Daoist's activities. For one thing, *Shenbao* prioritized lurid stories that would sell copy, and its editorial policy seems to have condoned a fair amount of exaggeration and distortion if it served that end.[32] But, even if the newspaper reported the Beijing proceedings accurately, we should not accept the Board of Punishment's conclusions at face value, because the distorting influence of judicial torture is simply too blatant. As soon as the Daoist attracted the attention of the authorities, they decided that he must be a heterodox predator, and they proceeded to torture him (forcing him to kneel on chains, beating him, and even dousing him with manure) until he confessed accordingly. Even so, the Daoist insisted that he had coerced nobody to do anything. Moreover, the board reluctantly concluded from his followers' testimony that they had really believed in the Daoist's cures: they followed him out of gratitude and faith because he had miraculously cured their illnesses. In fact, when the gendarmerie first arrested the Daoist, eight of his male followers confronted them, declaring that, "if our master is in trouble, we are all willing to share his fate," and so they were arrested as well.[33] Finally, the board decided that, despite all the gruesome rhetoric about drugs and sorcery, the Daoist had not actually *raped* anyone (at least not by the dubious standards of Qing rape law)—rather, the women had submitted more or less willingly and therefore should be considered accomplices rather than victims of his crimes.[34]

All we can say for sure is that a charismatic preacher whose successful healing activities attracted a large following became an object of suspicion on the part of the authorities, who were ever vigilant to detect threats to security in the heavily policed imperial capital. His torture-driven confessions only partly confirmed their biases; nevertheless, they had enough evidence to sentence him to death for heterodoxy. Under the circumstances, it seems possible that this Daoist was a victim of paranoid fantasy who had never harmed anyone at all.

Shape-Shifting Nuns in Ming-Qing Fiction

Perhaps the most bizarre variation of the Sang Chong paradigm found in Ming-Qing fiction involves shape-shifting sorcerers or monsters whose masquerade extends to their physical anatomy: although essentially male, they are able to retract their external genitalia within their bodies in order to appear female.[35] Typically, these individuals pose as Buddhist nuns but eventually are exposed as deviant male clergy who have mastered occult arts in order to further their heterodox and lecherous designs.

One inspiration for this scenario may have been the famous catalog of "human prodigies" (*renkui*) found in Li Shizhen's sixteenth-century pharmacopoeia *Compendium of Materia Medica* (*Bencao gangmu*), which included a shape-shifting figure known as the "changeling" (*bian*), to be discussed in chapter 6.[36] Another possible source of inspiration is the tradition that the historical Buddha's penis was sheathed or retracted within his body but could be produced when needed. It was prehensile and, like his tongue, could extend to extraordinary length for the performance of miracles. But it had no sexual function, and its distinctive qualities are attributed to the Buddha's vast accumulated merit and absolute renunciation of sex. In other words, the shape-shifting predator represents a perverse mirror image of the Buddha's sacred body.[37]

The most famous example of this fraudulent nun scenario appears in the first volume of Ling Mengchu's late Ming collection *Slapping the Table in*

Amazement (Pai an jing qi).[38] Ling's tale concerns a young nun surnamed Wang who became the abbess of a nunnery in Suzhou. Aged about twenty *sui*, she is described as beautiful, charming, and exceptionally skilled at embroidery and other women's work. She became enormously popular with the other nuns and the local gentry women, who flocked to the nunnery to enjoy her company.

Finally, the abbess aroused the suspicions of an official who was on tour of inspection. While viewing the nunnery, he caught sight of her drinking wine with a group of young women and embracing them, so he ordered them all arrested and examined by a midwife. The midwife reported that they all appeared to have female anatomy, but that the abbess struck her as somehow strange: "Although she does not exhibit male form, there's something about her that is not quite like a woman (*yu nüren you xie liang yang*)." Convinced that the abbess must be a man who was somehow concealing his anatomy, the inspector ordered her genitals exposed and painted with oil, and then had a dog brought in to lick off the oil: "The fact is, a dog's tongue is very warm, and when it had licked about ten times, the young nun felt unbearably hot and itchy. She gave a tremendous shudder, and suddenly a stiff pole popped out, standing up hard and erect (*teng de yi tiao gunzi zhi tong chulai, qie shi jianying bu dao*)."

Under torture, the "nun" made the following confession. In fact, he was a monk, but since childhood had resembled a girl. He had been trained by a master sorcerer in the dark arts of "supplementing his own vital force by extracting the bodily fluids of others (*caizhan*) and extending and shrinking his penis (*shen suo zhi shu*)."[39] He learned to disguise his anatomy as a woman's and developed an extraordinary sexual prowess, being able to have sex with up to ten women in a single night. Masquerading as a nun, the monk traveled about, practicing the heterodox White Lotus Teachings in order to "delude the masses and gather women together for illicit sex." Settling down at the nunnery in Suzhou, he had exploited his position there to seduce the nuns as well as countless young ladies of good family. Most eagerly yielded to his seduction, but if one resisted, he would use black magic to render her helpless and rape her. He kept a detailed record of his exploits, along with a collection of white cloths stained with the hymen blood of the virgins he had deflowered (*nüzi yuanhong*). A search of the abbess's quarters discovered these grisly trophies. After confessing, the monk was put to death and his naked corpse exposed. Onlookers observed that his penis was as large as a donkey's or horse's, and they laughed, saying, "No wonder all those women liked him so much!"[40]

This story was clearly inspired by the Sang Chong case: the hero's youthful apprenticeship to a gender-crossing sorcerer, his mastery of women's work and disguise, and his combination of seduction with black magic all derive from that basic plotline. To that topos, Ling has added some interesting novelties. By making his protagonist a Buddhist monk who masquerades as a nun, Ling invokes the stereotype of supposedly celibate clergy being licentious predators. By making his protagonist an adherent of the proscribed White Lotus, Ling plays on the Ming dynasty's notorious obsession with heterodoxy, confirming the official conviction that the leaders of such sects were con artists who exploited the common people's gullibility.[41] With the shocking details of sexual vampirism, genital gymnastics, and the blood of virgins, Ling exposes the monstrous nature of heterodoxy. Also, by emphasizing the hero's popularity with his female "victims," Ling underscores (while parodying) the paranoid assumption that female chastity cannot be entrusted to women.

A similar pair of nuns appear in a late-seventeenth century collection by Chen Fangsheng, who no doubt had read Ling Mengchu's earlier tale.[42] Chen's story is entitled "A Two-Formed Person" (*erxing*), a term that, depending on context, might refer either to a stone maiden or to someone with the genitals of both sexes (also known in the Ming-Qing era as a "yin-yang person"). This story, too, follows the form of a legal case, in which a clever magistrate uses a dog to expose a shape-shifter's true identity.

Chen's tale relates a case within a case, set in the Song dynasty. It concerns a family that hired a nun to teach their daughter embroidery. The daughter became pregnant and claimed that it was the nun who had impregnated her. The nun often spoke of "conjugal matters" (*fufu shi*); having aroused the daughter's desire, the nun confided that "I have two forms (*erxing*), so that when I encounter male I am female, and when I encounter female, I am male (*feng yang ze nü, feng yin ze nan*)." (This language closely resembles Li Shizhen's description of the "changeling," which Chen Fangsheng must have read.)[43] The daughter groped the nun's crotch and discovered that indeed the nun was equipped "exactly like a male" (*yanran nanzi ye*). They had sexual intercourse several times, leading to the daughter's pregnancy. The nun was interrogated at the yamen, but refused to confess, and, when examined, "there was no evidence" (*wu zhuang*) that the nun had male anatomy. The authorities were stymied.

Then, one official recalled a similar case, which had involved a beautiful young nun named Dong Shixiu. In that previous case, a man had tried to rape Dong, but, upon groping her genitals, discovered that the nun "was a man" (*nanzi ye*). The would-be rapist reported the matter to the authorities, but the midwife who examined the nun found what appeared to be female anatomy. So the midwife suggested applying "salty meat juice" to the suspect's naked crotch and having a dog lick it off. This maneuver revealed a phallus, "like a turtle's head emerging from its shell" (*ru guitou chu ke*). The judgment concluded: "The Way of Heaven has *yin* and *yang*, and the Way of humankind has male and female (*zai tian zhi dao yue yin yu yang, zai ren zhi dao yue nan yu nü*). But Dong Shixiu's body takes two forms, being neither exclusively male nor female: that is, what is known as *yaowu*, a monster (*shen dai erxing, bu nan bu nü, shi wei yaowu*)." A novel penalty was imposed: Dong Shixiu received twenty blows, was tattooed on the forehead with the characters *erxing* ("two-formed") and publicly exposed for ten days in the cangue and finally ordered held in chains at an army camp indefinitely. Inspired by this precedent, the presiding magistrate in the present case used the dog-licking maneuver with the same remarkable results. Exposed, the culprit was put to death.[44]

Chen Fangsheng's tale departs from Ling Mengchu's in one key respect. Whereas Ling's hero is a man who (like Sang Chong) has mastered the dark arts, Chen's Dong Shixiu appears to be a sort of congenital monster: able to assume opportunistically the physical form of either sex, and yet fundamentally a male predator, as seen in its single-minded pursuit of women, which is the purpose of its shape-shifting. To underscore the difference, Chen's story collection also includes a version of the Sang Chong case, but locates it in a separate chapter.[45] Whereas the chapter that includes the shapeshifting nuns is entitled "Renyao," that which includes Sang Chong is entitled "Yaoren." Elsewhere, the two terms are often used interchangeably, but where they are clearly distinguished, as in Chen's collection, the former means something like "monster"—suggesting a natural but monstrous phenomenon—while the latter means "sorcerer."

The choice of fake nuns for shape-shifting predators tells us something of how nuns were popularly viewed (at least by literati), and specifically about their association with gender transgression and sexual deviance. As with other gender-transing categories—including male clergy, eunuchs, and even the young actors who played female roles—an undercurrent of cynical skepticism questioned whether nuns were really what they claimed to be. Similar suspicions attached to chaste widows, and it is no accident that one way for a widow to resist family pressure to remarry was to become a nun, in effect using Buddhist celibacy to safeguard Confucian chastity. Moreover, it appears that the most common solution for the social problems posed by a stone maiden was to have her "leave the family" and become a nun, a practice that may have fed fantasies that nunneries were a refuge for deviants and monsters, as well as hotbeds of promiscuity.[46] In this connection, we should recall from chapter 2 that Xiong Mumu first transitioned by shaving their head and posing as a chaste widow who had resolved to become a nun. No doubt the governor who prosecuted Xiong envisioned that episode much as Ling Mengchu or Chen Fangsheng would have.

Cross-Dressing Clergy in Shanghai's Popular Press

We have already noted *Shenbao*'s penchant for sensationalism and its regular reporting on people who transed gender in one way or another. Some of this reportage concerns the prosecution of cross-dressing monks and Daoist priests. By dressing male clergy as women, it pushes the gender-transing implications of "leaving the family" a step further into the realm of "the strange."

Hairy Legs Expose a Daoist Imposter

In 1887, *Shenbao* published a brief report about the arrest of a cross-dressing Daoist predator in Fuzhou, the capital of Fujian province to the south.[47] The report includes no names; it is allegedly based on a story "translated from the Western press." Apparently, a certain man who had just married was required to go away on business, leaving his beautiful bride at home alone. One day, an old woman knocked on her door and introduced herself as the husband's aunt, who had come for a visit. Believing her story to be true, the young wife invited her in and entertained her with the respect due a senior in-law, and, when evening came, and the old woman showed no sign of departing, the young wife prepared a room she could spend the night.

As the old woman prepared for bed, she happened to open her gown, and the young wife caught a glimpse of her legs, which were "thickly covered with hair" (*haomao rongrong ran*). Realizing that she had been tricked, the young wife stepped outside, pretending to fetch laundry that had been drying in the sun, and alerted her neighbors. They burst into the house and seized the imposter, who, upon interrogation, was exposed as "a male Daoist falsely masquerading as an old woman" (*daoshi wei zhuang wei yu*) in hope of raping the young wife. The county magistrate ordered that the Daoist be put to death in the standing cangue (*lijia*) on public display. The report closes by informing interested readers that the standing cangue has not yet been taken down, so it should still be possible to view the imposter's remains.[48]

This brief report is supplemented by an illustration in the *Dianshizhai Pictorial*, which was published by the same company as *Shenbao* and provided engraved illustrations to help the paper's readers visualize particularly exciting stories. The dramatic illustration (fig. 3.1) shows the Daoist imposter at the moment he has been seized, with his gown pulled open to expose a hairy chest and legs. The affronted woman is denouncing him before an indignant crowd of onlookers.

Baozhen's First Trial: Monk, Nun, or Yin-yang Person?

Shenbao's coverage is far more detailed for the case of a young, enigmatic, cross-dressing monk named Li Baozhen, who was prosecuted twice in the Mixed Court of Shanghai's French Concession, first in 1888 and again the following year.[49] (For most of the Treaty Port era, Shanghai had one Mixed Court in the French Concession and one in the International Concession. Foreign consular officials and specially appointed Chinese magistrates would preside together over "mixed" cases that involved foreign nationals and Chinese, as well as cases involving only Chinese that occurred within the foreign concessions. In the latter, the Chinese magistrate would have jurisdiction, but a foreign official would observe the proceedings.)[50] *Shenbao* rhetorically frames Baozhen's story within the old paradigm of the cross-dressing sexual predator, even though the "facts" of the case, as reported by the press, do not seem to fit that paradigm very well.[51]

Shenbao's reports on Baozhen's first trial in 1888 emphasize the gender ambiguity of this "perverse monk" (*yaoseng*), a term that parallels the term

Figure 3.1 "An Elderly Daoist Masquerades as a Woman," *Dianshizhai Huabao*: 1887, zi/2:13.

"perverse Daoist" (*yaodao*) used to characterize the protagonists of the cases from Beijing and Fuzhou. The first article opens by observing that "for a woman to masquerade in men's attire, and for a man to masquerade in women's attire, are both strictly prohibited by law (*nü ban nanzhuang, nan ban nüzhuang, jun gan lijin*). But it is even worse for a monk to render it impossible to determine whether his purified dharma body (*qingjing zhi fashen*) is male or female (*ci xiong zhi mo bian*)!"[52] The same article's headline, "A Case of 'Confusion and Ambiguity'" (*mili pushuo zhi an*), is a direct reference to the woman warrior Hua Mulan. In the last lines of "The Poem of Mulan," she asks a famous rhetorical question: "The male hare wildly kicks its feet (*pushuo*), the female hare has shifty eyes (*mili*). But when a pair of hares runs side by side, who can distinguish whether I in fact am male or female (*an neng bian wo shi xiong ci*)?"[53] This image of hares running side by side is a classic metaphor for gender ambiguity and category crisis, and its use by *Shenbao* in this context is an example of the feedback loop between fiction and legal cases within which late-Qing newspapers came to occupy a sort of intermediate position.

According to the paper, Baozhen had been seized and taken to a police station in the French Concession by one Deng Lan, a small merchant from Hunan who had stopped in Shanghai en route to Yantai. Deng Lan accused the monk of borrowing twenty-four foreign dollars and then absconding; Deng managed to track them down and went to the police for help recovering his money. Deng and the monk had both been staying at an inn, and Deng brought the innkeeper and a fellow guest named Li Changlai to court as witnesses.

At first, Deng reported only the matter of the loans, provoking some skepticism on the Chinese magistrate's part: "You were on your own, far from home, and you had never met that monk before. Why on earth were willing to lend him so much money? . . . Are you hiding something from me?" Finally, Deng declared that "they are not a monk, they're a nun!" (*yi bu shi heshang, shi nigu*). When the magistrate asked how Deng knew this, Li Changlai testified that "they whispered to me themself that they are a female nun" (*qingshuo yun shi nüni*). According to Li, in the middle of the night Baozhen had come to his bed "to proposition me" (*tiaoxi*). Li had been startled awake and asked the monk what they were doing. Baozhen then tried to seduce him, whispering that they "are really a nun." Li cried out in shock, arousing the other guests at the inn.[54]

Note that, throughout this summary of their testimony, Deng and Li are using the gender-neutral third person pronoun in classical Chinese *yi*, which I have rendered as "they" (their oral testimony presumably would have used its colloquial equivalent *ta*). Given the pronoun's gender neutrality, Deng and Li could use it to describe Baozhen both when portraying them as a monk and after revealing their belief that Baozhen was really a nun: there was no need in Chinese for an awkward shift from "he" to "she."

The magistrate confronted the monk: "Tell the truth, are you male or female?" (*jiujing shi nan shi nü*). Baozhen insisted that they were not a nun, but a monk. They reported that they were aged twenty *sui* and were from Hefei County, Anhui; they had "left the family" in early childhood. In response, Deng and Li changed their testimony: in fact, they declared, Baozhen was neither a man nor a woman, but "a person of two sexes" (using an idiomatic term in Wu dialect, *ci bu xiong*).[55] But Baozhen denied this claim as well. Finally, the magistrate ordered Baozhen to strip to the waist in the courtroom, exposing their breasts, which turned out to be small and flat, "not at all like a woman's." Convinced that Li Changlai must be lying, the magistrate ordered him slapped and held in custody, along with Baozhen.[56]

But, the next day, a French constable who escorted Baozhen back to the inn to recover their belongings reported that all the people at the inn insisted that Baozhen was really a woman. Therefore, the constable had taken Baozhen to the police station and had them examined there (it is not clear by whom), where it turned out that, "in fact, they are a *yin-yang* person" (*shi xi yinyang ren*); perhaps the constable actually used the French word "hermaphrodite."[57] Curiously, the magistrate does not seem to have followed up on this report, so we do not know what it was about Baozhen's anatomy that prompted this diagnosis.

The case ended inconclusively: the police failed to recover Deng's money, and the magistrate established no consensus about what had actually happened or even about Baozhen's anatomical sex. Because this was the Mixed Court, not a Qing yamen, the magistrate could not resort to torture, so there was no way to force the witnesses to agree. Therefore, he told Deng Lan to give up on his money and get on his way to Yantai. Baozhen was given a beating (the newspaper does not say for what crime) and deported to their home jurisdiction.[58]

Despite the magistrate's repeated questions, Deng never clearly explained why he had "lent" Baozhen so much money, or how he, the monk, and Li Changlai had all ended up staying together at the inn. There is a certain innuendo in the way *Shenbao* emphasizes the magistrate's skepticism on this point. In light of what happened the following year, it seems likely that the ambiguous monk was actually engaged in sex work, and that was why Deng had paid them.

Baozhen's Second Trial: A "Perverse Monk" Masquerades as a Woman

Baozhen reappeared in the French Concession's Mixed Court and in *Shenbao* just over a year later, in November 1889. *Shenbao*'s coverage of their second trial begins with an article entitled "A Man Masquerading in Women's Attire" (*nan ban nüzhuang*); it opens by summarizing the events of the previous year:

Last winter there was a monk named Li Baozhen who masqueraded as a Buddhist nun (*banzuo nigu*) in the French Concession. He was exposed and arrested when he rented lodgings at an inn and fell into a dispute with one Mr. Deng. Interrogation and examination by the Chinese magistrate established that Li was male (*xi nanzi*). He received forty slaps on the cheek and was expelled from the jurisdiction. All this was previously reported in this paper.[59]

In fact, this summary conflicts with *Shenbao*'s own previous reporting: at no point in 1888 did the newspaper claim that Baozhen had cross-dressed. In the account of Baozhen's first trial, their only attempt to "masquerade," if it can be called that, was their alleged statement that they were really a nun. Also, the bald assertion that Baozhen was found to be male elides the unresolved ambiguity about their sex.

In the meantime, however, it appears that Baozhen had indeed adopted women's attire and in that guise had violated the terms of their release by returning to Shanghai:

Baozhen changed his name to Li Huizhen, and he put on women's clothing, grew out his hair and combed it like a woman's, pierced his ears and put on earrings, so that in all respects he appears exactly like a woman. Together with a local barber named Shen Yunting, he rented a room for the night at an inn just outside the Small East Gate, which is managed by Zhu Akun. Suddenly in the night the two began loudly quarrelling. The proprietor heard the commotion and rushed to investigate—only then did Zhu realize that Baozhen was a man masquerading in women's attire.[60]

This scenario sounds strikingly similar to what had happened the previous year, in all its ambiguity.

How had the barber Shen Yunting met Baozhen, and why were they together at the inn? According to Shen:

At first, all I knew was that Baozhen was a Buddhist nun—I first met them when they came to our barbershop one time to beg for alms. Yesterday, I bumped into Baozhen on the street, and saw that they had changed into a woman's lay clothing. . . . They told me that they had decided to quit being a nun and return to the laity, so that's why they had changed clothes. Now they were hoping to meet a man in order to get married (*jiaren*). . . . The hour was already late, and Li begged me to get them a room for the night, so I took them to Zhu Akun's inn. They went to bed first, and then I saw that they are actually a man (*jian shi nanzi*)—that is why we quarreled.[61]

Baozhen's testimony agreed that Shen had not realized that Baozhen had male anatomy until the night of their quarrel at the inn—in other words, according this version, Baozhen had already begun presenting as a woman before they met and kept their sex secret. But Baozhen also claimed that they and Shen had been engaged in a sexual relationship, despite the latter's ignorance of Baozhen's anatomy: "The truth is that because I suffered from hunger and cold, I was terribly anxious to the point of losing my wits (*chidian*). I think this must be karmic retribution for the sins of my past lives (*qian shen zuo nie, jin shen shou bao*). I had illicit sex with Shen twice. The night before last at the inn, I had already gone to sleep, so I don't know how he discovered [that I am a man] (*bu zhi ruhe shi po*)."[62]

This account suggests that Shen may have experienced something like what is now called "trans panic": the shock supposedly suffered by a cisgendered straight man who discovers that his female-presenting sexual partner has male anatomy.[63] Shen himself admitted more or less the same thing. He denied most of Baozhen's accusations, but eventually he did concede that, on that final evening, he had taken Baozhen to the inn expecting to have sex. However, he insisted that he had believed his companion to be a woman: "When I first encountered Baozhen, they were already disguised as a woman (*yi banzuo nüzhuang*). . . . They told me that they were willing to be my companion (*qingyuan gencong xiaode*), and so that night we stayed together at a small inn. At first I assumed they were a woman (*chu dao yi shi nü*), but later, when they took off their clothes to go to bed, they gave themself away (*lou chu pozhan*)."[64]

This scenario was also affirmed by the *Dianshizhai Pictorial*. The text accompanying its illustration of this case (fig. 3.2) refers to Baozhen as a "perverted monk" (*yaoseng*) who "dresses in women's clothes and earrings, has grown out his hair and combed it into a bun, wears flowery embroidered shoes, and altogether looks exactly like a wife from the countryside." Shen Yunting "mistook the monk for a nun who had returned to the laity, and together they took lodgings for the night at an inn outside the small Eastern Gate. But when the moment of truth came, it turned out that 'a square peg doesn't fit into a round hole' (*rui zao*), and the two quarreled."[65] In other words, Shen's discovery that his sexual partner had male anatomy meant that they would not "fit" together in the way he had expected.

In the other three hearings, however, Baozhen told a different story. They had never cross-dressed until they met Shen: it was all Shen's idea: "My master at the monastery died, so I came to Shanghai alone. Three months ago, I encountered Shen Yunting, who urged me to pawn my monk's robes, and arranged for me to change into women's clothing (*dai wo gai ban nüzhuang*). Then he had relations with me (*laiwang*). Now he is hoping to take me out to the countryside and sell me off (*jiamai*)—that is why we quarreled." (Nota bene: the term I have translated as "relations"— *laiwang*—was a euphemism for sexual relations.) After finishing this testimony, according to the news report, Baozhen wept and added that they "had been harmed by Shen" (*bei Shen suo hai*). But Shen denied this account, insisting: "I have never had any relations with them! But I should not have stayed with them at the inn, I only did that because I was temporarily confused (*yishi hutu suo zhi*)."[66]

In a total of four hearings, the magistrate was unable to induce Baozhen and Shen to agree; both stuck to their respective stories. Baozhen: "Shen chatted me up and then I slept with him in a bedroom inside the barbershop. Then, on the seventh day of the sixth month, I had illicit sex with him again, but the proprietor found out and wouldn't let Shen stay there anymore. So after that we would stay together at inns. As to my dressing as a woman, that was Shen's idea, he told me to do it."[67] And again: "Shen and I got along well together. He told me to dress as a woman (*zhu xiaode ban zuo nüren*), and all of my women's clothing I bought together with Shen. We had illicit sex many times (*fanjian duo ci*). . . . Shen won't tell the truth because he is afraid of being shamed." In contrast, Shen testified that, "at the police station, Baozhen said that their getting arrested this time was all my fault, so now they have falsely accused me of sodomy in order to pay me back."[68]

The magistrate expressed deep skepticism at Baozhen's testimony: "Last year you were already punished for being a monk who masqueraded as a nun, but now you have once again changed clothes to masquerade as a woman! What, after all, were your true intentions in doing this? (*jiujing yiyu he wei*)"[69] And again: "You left the family to become a monk—how dare you behave in such an immoral (*bu duan*) way? Don't you know that for a man to masquerade in women's attire is prohibited by law (*you gan xiandian*)?"[70] But Baozhen offered no further explanation. The magistrate even asked, "Are you a female or a male?" (*er shi ci ye xiong ye*), but *Shenbao* does not report how Baozhen answered.[71]

The magistrate could not resort to torture, and finally he sentenced Baozhen and Shen Yunting to spend a month "wearing a conjoined cangue together and being paraded in the streets on display to the people" (*heshuang lianjia youjie shizhong*), after which they were to be beaten and then deported to their respective home jurisdictions.[72] (*Shenbao* reports this same punishment being imposed on several other individuals arrested in Shanghai for M–F cross dressing.)[73] The accompanying illustration in *Dianshizhai Pictorial* (fig. 3.2) shows Baozhen and Shen being paraded through the streets wearing a cangue designed for two people: Baozhen (on the left) is dressed as a woman and has a woman's hair style, whereas Shen (on the right) is attired and tonsured as a man. They are accompanied by a foreign police officer and Chinese yamen runners, one beating a drum and another carrying a sign that says: "A man masquerading in woman's attire, paraded

Figure 3.2: "A Table Set for Two," *Dianshizhai Huabao:* 1889, wei/8:62.

through the streets to be displayed to the people" (*nan zhuang nü ban, you-jie shizhong*).[74]

Note that, in Baozhen's second trial, there is no record that they were subjected to any physical examination. Instead, the consensus held that Baozhen was a "man masquerading in women's attire." Moreover, despite lacking evidence that Baozhen had engaged in any predatory behavior or was even interested in women, both the Chinese magistrate's and the newspapers' editorial comments defaulted to the Sang Chong paradigm in describing the supposed danger posed by their "masquerade." Thus, the magistrate observed that "when Baozhen changed attire to masquerade as a nun, it is likely that the women of other households were seduced by him into illicit sex (*nanbao renjia nüzi bu bei yi jianyou*)—such conduct is truly despicable!"[75] *Dianshizhai Pictorial* opined that the "perverse monk" Baozhen was lucky to have encountered such a "lenient" magistrate in the Mixed Court, who imposed only the cangue and a beating. In a Qing court, "he would have faced the severe penalties prescribed by law for a cross-dressing sorcerer (*renyao*), and no one would have protested!"[76] Finally, *Shenbao* editorialized that "if men are allowed to masquerade as women, then all manner of criminality will arise":

> Take Baozhen: first he's a monk, but then suddenly he's a nun; first he's a man, but then suddenly he's a woman. Who can say what evil intentions he harbored, to behave in such a way? (*hu seng hu ni, hu nan hu nü, qi ju xin shu bu ke wen*) For his part, Shen Yunting's lust was aroused by the sight of Baozhen's charms (*jian se qi yi*), so that he ended up being made to look like a fool. But if it hadn't been for their quarrel, who knows what evil deeds Baozhen might have committed before finally being caught?[77]

Two Variations on a Theme

It is well known that a popular stereotype portrayed male clergy as wine-swilling, meat-gorging lechers. What past studies have overlooked, I believe, is the specifically transgendered dimension of this stereotype. Predatory clergy and the cross-dressing predator represent two variations on a common theme—namely, that the renunciation of assigned gender was a fraud designed to lower people's guard and render them vulnerable to seduction, rape, and other abuse. The tales of shape-shifting nuns and news-paper reports of cross-dressing clergy combine the two into a single para-noid fantasy of transgender predation.

Given the sensational nature of late Qing journalism, we must approach *Shenbao*'s reports with caution. As Rania Huntington has argued, *Shenbao*'s stories about ghosts, monstrous births, and the like should be considered an extension of the fictional genre of "the strange," and her observation surely applies to the paper's stories about cross-dressing clergy, yin-yang people, and the like as well.[78] These stories' many references to Sang Chong, Hua Mulan, Li Yu, Pu Songling's *Liaozhi zhiyi*, and related literary tropes strongly reinforce this impression. At the same time, however, it appears that *Shenbao*'s reports of the prosecution of gender-transing people, how-ever embellished and sensationalized, were probably based on actual legal cases. That seems especially likely for the cases that are reported as having occurred in Shanghai, some of which were covered in multiple articles that include detailed accounts of specific people and places and name the actual magistrates who judged the cases.

If I am correct, then such reporting might be considered an extension not only of *zhiguai* fiction, but also of the narrative genre of court records, such as the archival cases of fraudulent clergy cited in the first section of this chapter. In other words, late Qing newspapers seem to have occupied an intermediate place within the long-standing feedback loop whereby actual court cases and fictional accounts informed each other and together produced and reinforced the paradigm of the gender-transing predator.

CHAPTER IV

Creativity Inspired by Torment?

My motive to change into women's attire was that I hoped to seduce women to have illicit sex with me. But when young ladies from proper families saw that I was covered with filth, they would steer clear of me and pay me no attention.

—ZHANG YAOGUNIANG, 1818

The "Facts" of the Case

In 1818, a homeless beggar couple from Hubei, husband Wang Shixian (thirty-one *sui*) and wife Zhang Yaoguniang ("youngest daughter Zhang," thirty-eight *sui*), were arrested in Queshan County in southern Henan.[1] It is not clear exactly why they came to the attention of the authorities, but suspicion focused on the wife Zhang Yaoguniang, and examination by a midwife at the yamen revealed that this individual had male anatomy. They were, in fact, "a man masquerading in women's attire" who, upon exposure, confessed their "real" name to be Peng Ziren.

The pair were deported back to their home province of Hubei and handed over to the magistrate of Hanyang County, which was the seat of the provincial capital. The county magistrate interrogated the defendants, issued preliminary sentences for their crimes, and reported his findings up the chain of command. But the provincial judge rejected his report on the grounds that "the facts of the case have not been accurately established" (*anqing wei que*) and ordered him to redouble his efforts. The magistrate's second attempt satisfied the provincial judge but was rejected in turn by their superior the provincial governor, who expressed concern that "these criminals may well have committed other crimes as yet undiscovered" (*gai fan deng kong ling you bufa bie an*). The governor took the case out of the county magistrate's hands and ordered an extraordinary joint investigation by the prefects of Hanyang and Wuchang Prefectures. Once they had finished, the governor interrogated Zhang Yaoguniang in person to confirm their findings.

Everything we know about this case comes from this third, joint investigation, as summarized by the governor in a memorial approving and forwarding the prefects' report to the imperial capital for review. The prefects' findings are the product of repeated interrogation sessions over eighteen months during which local authorities came under increasing pressure to "discover the truth," and presumably transferred that pressure to the defendants. It comes as no great surprise, then, that the final account accepted by the governor and his superiors in Beijing largely conforms to the sexual predator paradigm discussed in chapter 2. As a result, this case presents an especially challenging example of the difficulty of discerning the truth from confessions extracted under duress that conform to official expectations. In fact, Zhang Yaoguniang's confession may reveal more about the expectations of their interrogators than about Zhang's actual record of conduct.

"Masquerading in Women's Attire"

According to their confession, "Peng Ziren" was born in 1781—the year *xinchou*, according to the traditional calendrical system of stems and branches—and therefore was also known as "Peng Xinchou'er" ("child of the *xinchou* year"). They were from Tianmen County, located about one hundred kilometers west of Hanyang. According to two lineage relatives later interviewed by yamen runners, the Peng family had been poor, landless peasants, one of more than ten households of that surname in their village; orphaned at a young age, and with no immediate family to care for them, "Ziren" had survived by begging and not been seen in their home village for many years. The representatives of the Peng lineage had no idea when or why he (to them they would have been "he") had started presenting as a woman.

According to Zhang Yaoguniang's confession, this transition occurred in the spring of 1816, when, at the age of thirty-five *sui*, in Yingshan County, they decided to start dressing as a woman. They gave two reasons for this decision: "Because I could not beg enough food, my life was very hard, and I often went hungry. So I got the idea to change into women's dress, hoping that people would pity me more and give me more cash and rice (*qiyi gaizuo nüzhuang, yi ren lianmin duo gei qian mi*). I also hoped to become intimate with women and seize opportunities to have illicit sex with them and kidnap them (*tu yu funü xiangjin, chengji jianguai*)." Growing out their hair and piercing their ears, they bought a tattered second-hand women's blue cloth gown (*po lanbu nügua*) and a pair of tin earrings at a used clothing stall. They "changed attire by putting on the gown and earrings" (*chuan dai gai zhuang*), and thereupon assumed the name "Zhang Yaoguniang" ("youngest daughter Zhang") and began presenting as a woman. "Youngest daughter" implies that they had had older siblings.

The two motives confessed by Zhang in this passage seem oddly out of sync with each other. On the one hand, we have desperate hunger and the hope that, by presenting as a woman, they might receive more pity and alms and thereby manage to survive; that motive at least seems to reflect the grim reality of life for a beggar. But does it really make sense that a man in his mid-thirties would pretend to be a woman in order to attract pity? Chinese beggars certainly employed a variety of creative strategies in collecting alms (faking an injury or illness being perhaps the most common), and there is some evidence that—in 1930s Shanghai, at least—women (especially mothers with children) were able to collect more than men, although the difference does not seem very great.[2] I have read dozens of Qing legal cases involving beggars, and, for what it is worth, I have found no other evidence of M–F cross-dressing as a strategy for collecting alms, either in those cases or in any other source.

On the other hand, we have a grandiose ambition to seduce and kidnap women. It seems unlikely that a hungry beggar worried about survival would have ranked that a high priority, let alone a realistic one. Moreover, presenting as a woman might well have increased Zhang's vulnerability to the dangers encountered on the road—not to mention the risk of exposure and prosecution, which, in the end, proved all too real. Therefore, I suspect the two motives cited for Zhang to present as a woman reflect Zhang's genuine subjective perspective *less* than the investigators' demand for purely instrumental motives that would fit the procrustean bed of the sexual predator paradigm.

An intriguing detail ignored by the authorities suggests something more meaningful: the new surname our protagonist adopted, "Zhang," was their mother's natal surname. In transitioning to live as a woman, therefore, they symbolically abandoned not only the social role of a man but also their patrilineal ancestry (as a scion of the Peng lineage) and the duties of a son to that ancestry. This change of surname underscores the fact that gender roles, fundamentally, were family roles defined in terms of marriage and procreation. Therefore, for "Peng Ziren" to become "Zhang Yaoguniang" was not simply a change in gender, but a willful rejection of filial duty, a profound betrayal of Confucian values. Here is one reason why, to Qing officials, M–F cross-dressing in and of itself must have smacked of heterodoxy, even in the absence of sexual predation; it reminds us of the connection between the separation of the sexes and the priority of the father-son axis emphasized by *The Book of Rites* (see the epigraph to the introduction). Also, this detail seems to reveal something deeper and more genuine of Zhang Yaoguniang's persona: a connection to their dead mother that they wished to honor and preserve, as they transitioned into living as a woman. They did not reject family altogether, but they chose the mother over the father, the matrilineal connection over the mandated patrilineal one.

The detail of "growing out the hair" also begs further consideration. As a man, Peng Ziren would have been expected to shave the front of the head—and growing out one's hair, if the head has been shaved, is not something that can be accomplished on short notice. But maintaining the tonsure properly required frequent shaving, and typically this was done by barbers, who were paid for their service. Male beggars, who could not afford to be shaved regularly, were known for their shaggy unkempt hair, which went along with the rest of their filthy and ragged appearance and helped mark them as polluted creatures outside the bounds of decent society to whom norms and rules did not really apply.[3] Therefore, it seems likely that Zhang Yaoguniang already had some hair on the front of their head when they decided to transition, and the key to changing their appearance was probably making the length of the hair in front match that in back.

"Performing Cures and Cheating People Out of Their Money"

Having begun presenting as a woman, Zhang Yaoguniang continued on the road, begging to get by. About a month later, at a noodle shop in Huanggang County, they encountered a former acquaintance, one Zhu Da, who was an itinerant "smallpox doctor" (*douke yisheng*) from Chen

Department, Hubei. Later, under interrogation, Zhang Yaoguniang testified that Zhu had known them before they began to live as a woman, but Zhang provided no information about Zhu's reaction to their transformation. Zhu was eating a bowl of noodles with meat, and Zhang begged him for the dregs. But a bone that Zhang was sucking got stuck in their throat, and they began to choke. Zhu Da saved their life by speaking an incantation over a bowl of water, drawing a magic design in the water with two fingers, and giving it to Zhang to drink. According to Zhang Yaoguniang's testimony, the cure was miraculous: the bone simply "melted away" in their throat. Zhu Da explained that this method enabled him to summon "a divine spirit to descend and rescue" a sick person (*you shendao jianglin youhu*).

Impressed and grateful, Zhang begged Zhu to teach them how to effect this magical cure, and, when Zhu agreed, Zhang "pledged him as master to learn how to make talismans and incantations" (*bai ta wei shi xuexi fuzhou*). Zhu then showed Zhang how to draw the talisman in water with their fingers and taught them the incantation, which translates roughly as follows: "Princely Heaven, command and bestow your numinous perception in abundance! Command and decree! Command and decree! I beseech the Great General to descend into this talisman and provide protection! (*wangzi zhi tian chi ci you ling you gan you yu, chi chi ling ling, you qing dajiangjun lingfu yi dao jianglin baohu*)". After two days together, Zhang and Zhu parted company.

The ritual that Zhang Yaoguniang learned from Zhu Da appears to be a simplified version of an exorcism to cure illness, which was (and remains) an extremely common category of ritual in Chinese popular religion, usually being performed by spirit mediums and Daoist priests. As Daniel Overmyer explains, exorcism involves "the use of dramatic words and gestures to drive out demons believed to be causing problems. . . . Gods represent order and demons disorder, so exorcism consisted essentially of the priest asking for an order from the gods, which he in turn communicated to the demons, commanding them to leave. The commands could be oral, written, or both."[4] A typical Daoist exorcism to treat illness would begin with the practitioner summoning the spirits at their command; drawing a magic talisman on paper; reciting "an exorcistic mantra, or conjuration" commanding all demons to depart; divination using specially shaped wooden blocks, to make sure the correct demon has been exorcised; and, finally, burning the paper talisman, mixing its ashes in water, and having the patient drink it as an exorcistic cure.[5] An alternative was to charge the water magically by drawing the talisman in it with the fingers, as seen in Zhu Da's ritual.

Thenceforth, Zhang Yaoguniang wandered from place to place, supplementing their begging by treating illnesses and injuries for a modest fee. In their confession, Zhang recalled two specific instances when they had provided treatment for snakebites. One was for a sedan chair carrier named Wang San who had been bitten on the foot. For a fee of 800 cash, Zhang treated Wang's snakebite by performing the incantation, charging water with the magic talisman and then spitting the water onto the wound. They then applied a plaster made of incense ashes and sesame oil. Several months later, in Wuchang County, Zhang treated a peasant named Xiong Gui, who had been bitten on the finger, in the same manner for a fee of 1200 cash. After Zhang Yaoguniang had been arrested, the Wuchang County magistrate was ordered to track down this peasant and get his story. Xiong Gui testified that he had indeed been cured of snakebite by a "beggar woman" (*gaifu*) named Zhang Yaoguniang, whom he had encountered on the road. Xiong further testified that he had had no idea that Zhang was actually "a man masquerading in woman's attire" (*nan ban nüzhuang*).

In their confession, Zhang Yaoguniang characterized these treatments using the formulaic phrase "performing cures and cheating people out of their money" (*xing yi kuangpian qianwen* or *xing yi pian qian*)—in other words, intentional quackery. Deception, fraud, and cheating people out of their money were part of the official package of wicked behaviors associated with heterodoxy, so, in this respect, Zhang's confession fit the predatory paradigm. But, in their description of what actually happened, Zhang testified first of all that they themself had been cured by Zhu Da of a dangerous choking fit and had been inspired to pledge Zhu as master and learn his healing ritual in part out of gratitude. Zhang's description of the two episodes of treating snakebite seem like straightforward acts of exorcistic faith healing, without any hint of deception; moreover, the peasant Xiong Gui himself testified that his snakebite had been "cured" by Zhang—he did not claim to have been cheated. For these reasons, I suspect that the phrase "performing cures and cheating people out of their money" is another artifact of Zhang's interrogation, in which they were induced to conform to their interrogators' expectations.

We should also note that Chinese beggars were traditionally credited with special expertise about snakes. Many beggars added snake handling and charming to their begging routine, sometimes to entertain observers and at other times to intimidate them into providing alms. Others augmented their incomes by capturing and selling snakes: their meat for food, organs for medicine, and skins for making purses and other useful things. Live snakes were sold to the Buddhist faithful, who earned merit by releasing them. Beggars were hired for pest control, when a venomous snake had been sighted in a dwelling. Most striking, however, is the fact that beggars were regularly consulted to treat snakebites, which was seen as their special "calling."[6] The fact that Zhang Yaoguniang's specific examples of faith healing both involved the treatment of snakebites adds verisimilitude to this aspect of their story.

"Illicit Sex and Kidnapping"

In the autumn of 1816, Zhang Yaoguniang was back in Tianmen County (although they apparently did not visit their home village), where, according to their confession, they encountered two widowed beggar women, Wang Hu Shi and Wang Lu Shi, who were mother-in-law and daughter-in-law, respectively. The two women decided to keep company with Zhang and beg together; at night the three slept together in "empty" temples (*kong miao*), as beggars commonly did (there seems to have been no shortage of such buildings). Finally, according to their confession, Zhang Yaoguniang had a chance to "become intimate with women and seize opportunities to have illicit sex with them and kidnap them." One night, Zhang revealed their male anatomy to the younger woman, Wang Lu Shi, and seduced her. After that, they frequently had sex, but took care to conceal this activity from the older woman. After a month, Zhang persuaded Wang Lu Shi to abandon her mother-in-law and run away. But before they could get away, Wang Hu Shi caught them. Zhang fled the scene, and only then did Wang Hu Shi learn the truth about Zhang Yaoguniang.

After Zhang Yaoguniang's arrest and confession, the magistrate of Tianmen County was ordered to find the two beggar women and verify Zhang's story with them. The older woman, Wang Hu Shi, was somehow tracked down, but she reported that her daughter-in-law had died. In his report to the two prefects running the joint investigation, the magistrate of Tianmen County summarized Wang Hu Shi's testimony as follows:

Her husband, Wang Qi, and his son, Wang Hei, both died, so, because of poverty, she and her daughter-in-law, Wang Lu Shi, had to beg to survive. In JQ 21.9 they encountered a beggar woman named "Zhang Yaoguniang." At first she didn't realize that this was a man masquerading in women's attire (*nan ban nüzhuang*), so they went along on the road begging together, and at night they all slept together in empty temples. She does not know when her daughter-in-law began having illicit sex with Zhang Yaoguniang. After one month, her daughter-in-law and Zhang Yaoguniang ran away together, but she managed to find her daughter-in-law and bring her back. Zhang Yaoguniang fled. She questioned her daughter-in-law and only then learned that Zhang Yaoguniang was a man masquerading in women's attire (*nan ban nüzhuang*), and that her daughter-in-law had been seduced into illicit sex and running away (*bei jian you tao*). Because her daughter-in-law was willing to reform her ways and begged to be forgiven, and because she herself was an old woman and feared being left alone, in the end she did not report the incident to the authorities. Later her daughter-in-law died of illness. Now she is old and ill and begs to be spared having to testify in person.

Soon thereafter, according to Zhang Yaoguniang's confession, they had a second opportunity to act according to the paradigm of the sexual predator, when, in Jiayu County, they found employment doing household chores at the home of a villager named Chen Yao. At night Zhang would sleep with Chen Jia Shi, who was the widow of Chen's younger brother. According to Zhang Yaoguniang, "Chen Jia Shi could tell that I had a male body, and so I had illicit sex with her (*kanchu nan shen, xiaode jiu yu xing jian*). I can't remember how many times we did it." At the New Year, Chen Yao and his wife visited relatives, leaving Zhang and Chen Jia Shi alone, and so the two engaged in sex "in broad daylight," only to be interrupted and discovered by Chen Yao, who had returned to the house. Once again, Zhang Yaoguniang fled the scene.

Upon hearing this tale, the investigating prefects ordered the magistrate of Jiayu County to summon Chen Yao and his sister-in-law Chen Jia Shi, and, if Zhang's story proved to be true, to prosecute Chen Jia Shi for adultery. Chen Yao was interrogated, but he reported that he had already married off his sister-in-law to a man surnamed Feng, who had taken her home with him to Henan. Chen did not know where in Henan Mr. Feng was from and could not remember his full name, so the magistrate concluded that Chen Jia Shi could not be located. Still, the magistrate did report that Chen Yao had confirmed Zhang Yaoguniang's story:

> According to Chen Yao's testimony, when he returned to the house, he found the two of them right in the middle of having illicit sex, and it was only when he walked in on them that he realized that Zhang Yaoguniang was actually a man masquerading in women's attire (*nan ban nüzhuang*). Chen Yao wanted to seize him and deliver him to the authorities for prosecution, but he managed to escape. Chen Yao questioned Chen Jia Shi, and she confessed that because she was sleeping with Zhang Yaoguniang she had figured out that Zhang had a male body, and so she had illicit sex with him (*kanchu nan shen, yu zhi chengjian*). After that Chen Yao married Chen Jia Shi off to a man named Feng from Henan, and did not bother to report the incident. . . . Now Chen Yao is very ill with dysentery and begs to be spared having to testify in person.

Thus, in addition to two instances of "performing cures and cheating people out of their money," Zhang Yaoguniang had confessed to two instances of "having illicit sex with other men's wives and daughters" (*jian ren funü*), plus one instance of "unsuccessful abduction" (*youguai wei cheng*) of a woman. These were the critical features of their confession (in addition to cross dressing) that conformed to the sexual predator paradigm and justified their legal treatment.

Several aspects of this tale provoke skepticism. First, there is the apparent alacrity with which both women allegedly agreed to have sex as soon as Zhang was revealed as an imposter. That strikes me as an echo of the Sang Chong story, which reflects the official and elite anxiety over female chastity for which the Ming and Qing dynasties are so famous (i.e., that women could not really be trusted to guard their own chastity, because otherwise there would be no need to make such a fuss about it).[7] Second, neither of the women whom Zhang Yaoguniang had allegedly seduced was available to testify: Wang Lu Shi had died, and Chen Jia Shi had disappeared into Henan with the elusive Mr. Feng. Zhang's confession was confirmed by Wang Hu Shi and Chen Yao, but both of those key witnesses were reportedly too ill to testify in person, either in their home counties or in Hanyang. Instead, it appears, they were tracked down and interviewed by yamen runners deputed by their respective county magistrates. Therefore, we are hearing the testimony of Zhang's alleged sexual partners only fifth hand: the two women confessed to Wang Hu Shi and Chen Yao, respectively, who repeated what the women had said to the yamen runners, who then reported it to their magistrates, who summarized it for the investigating prefects in Hanyang, who finally included abbreviated summaries in their report to the governor. These final summaries, which are quoted in the governor's memorial that we have before us, effectively put official terms for crimes into the mouths of witnesses—notably the phrase "a man masquerading in women's attire" (*nan ban nüzhuang*), which appears repeatedly. All of this testimony has been highly processed by intermediate parties. In fact, as far as I can tell, only two witnesses actually testified in person in Hanyang before the county magistrate, the prefects, or the provincial governor: Zhang Yaoguniang themself, and the man identified as their husband, Wang Shixian.

The Role of "Accomplice" Wang Shixian

Some four months after fleeing the Chen residence, Zhang Yaoguniang met fellow beggar Wang Shixian in Macheng County, Hubei. Wang Shixian was from Yunmeng County, Hubei; like Zhang, he had been orphaned at an early age, and, with no family to look after him, he found himself begging on the road to survive. As Wang later testified:

Zhang Yaoguniang and I decided to keep company while begging, and that night we slept together in an empty temple. I could tell that he was a man masquerading in women's attire (*bei xiaode kanchu nan ban nüzhuang*), so I questioned him, and he told me that his name is Peng Ziren, and that he had changed his attire in hope of seducing and having illicit sex with women (*yin tu youjian funü shi yi gai zhuang*). But when young ladies saw how filthy he was, few were willing to come near him (*nianshao funü jian ta huiwu duo bu jin shen*). So he had managed to have illicit sex with only two women so far. He also told me that he had pledged Zhu Da as master to learn how to use spells and talismans, and had twice treated men for snakebite. I was going to tell everyone what he had told me, and he became very anxious—so he offered to let me sodomize him and to acknowledge me as his husband and himself as my wife (*qingyuan ting xiaode jijian, ren wei fufu*), and to stay together thereafter, begging together.

In Zhang Yaoguniang's words, "I was afraid, so I let him sodomize me, and agreed to acknowledge him as my husband and myself as his wife" (*xiaode haipa, ting ta jijian, ren wei fufu*). Wang Shixian accepted this offer, and they sexually consummated their union that night. Just a couple of weeks later, however, the couple were arrested in Queshan County, Henan, and then deported back to Hubei for prosecution.

In their confessions, Zhang and Wang both portray the decision to begin a sexual relationship and to unite as husband and wife as being the result of blackmail: Zhang suggested this arrangement supposedly in order to prevent Wang from spreading the word (to unidentified other parties) that Zhang was "a man masquerading in women's attire." But does that explanation really make sense?

The first thing to note is that male same-sex acts and relationships were both extremely common and quite open among beggars in Qing-dynasty China. In that milieu, at least, there seems to have been no particular cause for shame or embarrassment. Long-term relationships would often be framed by chosen kinship: occasionally sworn brotherhood, but more often "dry kinship" adoption (*ganqin*), with the younger partner pledging to be the older one's "dry son" (*gan erzi*), in exchange for the older partner's promise of protection and support. In that context, chosen kinship was not a way to conceal a sexual relationship so much as a way to understand and talk about it—so, among beggars, if an older beggar introduced a younger beggar as his "dry son," everyone would understand that they were committed sexual partners.

Therefore, if Wang and Zhang had simply wanted a sexual relationship, it would not have been necessary for Zhang to "masquerade" as a woman, much less to pose as Wang's wife. If Zhang was worried about exposure "as a man," why didn't they simply switch back to presenting as a man? If Wang was blackmailing them, why did Zhang agree to partner with him? Why didn't they simply leave? The fact that Zhang offered not only to let Wang sodomize them but also to acknowledge themself as Wang's wife, while continuing to live as a woman, suggests that these decisions were not motivated simply by fear. More likely, it seems that for Zhang to live as a woman reflected some deeply felt need, and also, perhaps, that

Wang's attraction to Zhang may have derived from the fact that Zhang was transing gender as a woman.

It is important to note that the forms of chosen kinship that framed male same-sex relationships were limited to *ganqin* adoption and (far less often) sworn brotherhood, and in both forms age hierarchy seems to have been the key organizing factor. There was no model based on marriage, probably because the purpose of marriage was understood to be procreation to continue the patrilineal family, and marriages were arranged by patriarchal elders, whereas the long-term male same-sex relationships found in Qing legal cases were usually formed by consensual agreement between two individuals who were abstracted from family context. In the hundreds of cases I have read, the sole exceptions are the relationship between Zhang Yaoguniang and Wang Shixian discussed in this chapter, and the relationships between Liu Xing Shi and their two husbands to be discussed in the next. But their very uniqueness underscores the fact that they are best understood *not* as "male same-sex relationships," but rather as what the couples themselves called them: marriages between husband and wife that were based on Zhang and Xing's personae as women. The fact that these couples chose to pledge as husband and wife (instead of either male-male option) points to the fundamentally different nature of these individuals' identities and their relationships to their partners.[8]

The second thing to note is the inverted age hierarchy in this relationship: Wang (thirty-one *sui*) was seven years younger than Zhang (thirty-eight *sui*). In male same-sex acts and relationships as described in Qing legal cases, sexual roles were nearly always keyed to age hierarchy, with an older dominant partner penetrating a younger subordinate partner. This age hierarchy generally aligned with other axes of hierarchy as well, when relevant, such as class, status, wealth, power, and a gendered division of labor between long-term partners. Younger partners were feminized as objects of possessive desire, for whom older males competed and sometimes fought. The underlying assumption here was that sexual penetration constituted a performance of gendered hierarchy, the template being a stereotyped act of heterosexual intercourse. A closely related notion was that normative adult gender roles were defined by the marital roles of husband/father and wife/mother and were enacted through conjugal intercourse. Thus, if we consider Zhang and Wang to be a male homosexual couple, then it was highly unusual for Zhang to submit to being penetrated by the much younger Wang, especially in a committed relationship (in the event, they spent only a couple of weeks together, but their apparent intent was to stay together indefinitely).

In sum, Zhang and Wang's relationship makes no sense, in their own contemporary terms, as a same-sex relationship between two men. It makes far more sense, I submit, to understand them as husband and wife—in short, to take Zhang's self-presentation at face value, instead of following the Qing judiciary in seeing it as a masquerade and attributing it to some set of instrumental ulterior motives. For this couple, the gendered hierarchy between man/husband and woman/wife seems to have trumped the age hierarchy that typically would have structured a male-same sex relationship.

But this interpretation was beyond the ken of the couple's interrogators, whose conceptual portfolio included nothing usefully similar to the concept of transgender that is familiar today, and who understood Wang Shixian simply as an accomplice to "Peng Ziren's" evil masquerade. I suspect that the blackmail story was simply a way to make their relationship comprehensible to Qing officialdom and may even have been suggested by interrogators who found it the only plausible explanation for Zhang's submission to a younger man.[9]

It is possible, however, that the blackmail aspect of the story is true—in other words, that Zhang submitted to Wang out of fear of exposure of their assigned sex. If so, it would fit a trope seen in some Chinese fiction (e.g., Li Yu's "The Human Prodigy," to be discussed in the next chapter) and also in some non-Chinese cases, of a gender-transing individual desperate to keep their assigned sex secret who submits to sex in order to avoid being exposed. For example, in his classic study of "transvestites," first published in Germany in 1910, Magnus Hirschfeld recorded the case of an M–F crosser who ran away from home as an adolescent, adopted female guise, and found work as a nanny and a seamstress. They were repeatedly subjected to sexual harassment and rape attempts by men who discovered their genital status, including one who blackmailed them into a sexual relationship: "I became acquainted with an embroiderer who found out I was no young woman. He threatened to call the police and tell them I was playing a masquerade. He forced me into sodomy and fellatio and a few months passed during which I got more miserable each day." Eventually, they managed to run away.[10] This account underscores the tendency for trans-women to be objects of both fetishization and violence, as well as the dangerous consequences of forced disclosure of their genital status.

But, if Zhang Yaoguniang did submit to Wang because of blackmail, it is hard to reconcile that fact with Zhang's supposedly insatiable desire to seduce *women*, which was their confessed motive for cross-dressing in the first place. On the contrary, it would seem to confirm that Zhang was committed to living as a woman, at great risk to themselves, for other than purely instrumental reasons.

Summing Up

In the governor's memorial, Zhang Yaoguniang's confession ends with the following summary of their crimes:

> My original motive to change into women's attire was that I hoped to seduce women to have illicit sex (*yuantu youjian funü*). But when young ladies from proper families saw that I was covered with filth, they would steer clear of me and pay me no attention (*zhengjing renjia shaonian funü jian xiaode shenshang huiwu duo, jie zoubi buli*). So I could not get close to them, and had no way to seduce and take advantage of them (*bude jinshen, wu cong youpian*). The truth is that I had illicit sex with only two women, Wang Lu Shi and Chen Jia Shi. I did try to kidnap Wang Lu Shi, but I failed. I learned how to use talismans and incantations in order to provide cures and cheat people out of their money, and I did that twice. Also, I was sodomized by the beggar Wang Shixian.

Note how, by this point in the proceedings, Zhang's other alleged motive for transing gender—namely, to gain more sympathy and alms—has disappeared from the case record in favor of the expected desire to prey upon women: it is almost as if the script is tightening up and focusing. Note also that Zhang's sexual relations with Wang appear in this summary as an afterthought: among Zhang's many crimes, this one held the least interest for their interrogators. Zhang denied having committed any other crimes: "Nobody else was deceived or harmed by me (*ciwai bing wu bei huo shouhai de ren*), nor did I transmit my methods to any disciples (*chuan tu*), nor did I practice any other heterodox teachings or sorcery, or commit any other crimes (*xi jiao xieshu wei fei bu fa de shi*)." This last statement appears to be a response to questions guided by the wording of the statute against heterodoxy.

Zhang was also questioned closely about Zhu Da, the itinerant small-pox doctor who had taught them faith healing, but Zhang denied having seen their "master" since they parted ways back in Huanggang County and insisted that they did not know where Zhu Da could be found. Did Zhu Da have any heterodox books or paraphernalia? "He had with him only a small medicine chest. I never saw that he had any books or images of any kind." A major manhunt was ordered in Huanggang County but failed to apprehend Zhu Da.

Wang Shixian's confession confirmed Zhang's on all points since they had become companions. When pressed, he insisted: "I am just a beggar, I survive by begging. I was with Peng Ziren for only about two weeks before we were arrested in Queshan County. I have never learned to use talismans or incantations, nor have I committed any other crimes. As far as I know, Peng Ziren does not know any other heterodox techniques or sorcery, but I have no idea whether he committed any crimes in the past before I met him. This is the truth."

The Prefects' Judgment

The revelation that Zhang Yaoguniang was "a man masquerading in women's attire" and their subsequent confession had triggered a logistically massive investigation. From the provincial capital of Hanyang, orders had gone out to Huanggang County to find Zhang's "master" Zhu Da (this effort was not successful); to Huanggang and Wuchang counties to find the men who had been "cheated" with bogus faith healing; and to Tian-men, Jiayu, and Yunmeng counties to find the women Zhang had seduced and their relatives, along with the representatives of the Peng lineage and other witnesses implicated by Zhang. Each county's magistrate had mobilized yamen runners across the countryside to track down these individuals and take their testimony, and, over time, their reports arrived back in Hanyang for the two prefects to peruse, while their interrogation of the defendants continued. The entire investigation took nearly a year and a half to complete.

Finally, the prefects decided they had enough:

The criminal Peng Ziren masqueraded in women's attire for well over a year and trekked all across the provinces of Henan and Hubei in this disguise, so it seems impossible that the accomplices he recruited into his cabal and the people who were deceived and harmed by him would be so few in number. Therefore, we have repeatedly subjected him to the strictest interrogation, but he steadfastly maintains the following: that his motive for masquerading in women's attire was his hope of debauching women, but young ladies of proper families would always avoid him because of his filthy beggar's appearance, so he could not approach them and had no way to seduce and take advantage of them; therefore, in fact he had illicit sex with only two women, Wang Lu Shi and Chen Jia Shi; he did try to abduct Wang Lu Shi, but failed; in addition he submitted himself to Zhu Da as his disciple to learn how to use talismans and incantations in order to offer cures and cheat people out of their money, which he actually did a total of two times; but he truly never recruited disciples in order to deceive and bewitch the masses, nor did he use any other heterodox methods, or practice proscribed teachings, or commit any other crimes (*shi wei chuan tu huozhong, yi wu ling you xieshu feiwei ji xi jiao bu fa qingshi*). Despite repeated and strict interrogation, he insists this is the truth. It appears that he is hiding nothing.

One of the most striking things about this summary is that the prefects do not bother to mention Wang Shixian at all, much less Zhang Yaoguniang's sexual relationship with him. "Consensual sodomy" (*hetong jijian*) between males was prohibited and would be listed as one of Zhang's "lesser crimes" (*qing zui*). But Zhang's sexual role as the penetrated partner did not fit the paradigm of the cross-dressing sexual predator (who was an aggressive penetrator, obsessed with pursuing women), and same-sex acts had no bearing on the statute against heterodoxy, so Zhang's sexual relations with Wang were not a priority for the investigators in this case. In the minds of Qing officials, M–F crossing clearly had nothing to do with male same-sex attraction, let alone "homosexuality" as an orientation or social type—a concept that did not exist in the Qing.

As to Zhang's sentence, the prefects reasoned as follows:

For Peng Ziren to masquerade in women's attire was already in itself weird and perverse (*yi shu yaoyi*). But then he employed this scheme in order to have illicit sex with women and abduct them; moreover, he falsely claimed to cause spirits to descend (*shendao jianglin*), writing talismans and using incantations to charge water with magic, in order to offer fake cures and cheat people out of their money. Without question, his crimes meet the statutory definition of "using deviant ways to deceive the masses" (*zuodao huozhong*), and so he must be judged severely.

The first sentence of this passage confirms what we saw in the cases of Xiong Mumu and Zengliang in chapter 2—namely, that M–F cross-dressing in and of itself constituted a grave offense that Qing officials closely associated with sorcery and heterodoxy. (The term I have translated as "weird and perverse"—*yaoyi*—includes the character *yao*, with its connotations of sorcery, demonic possession, and the Sang Chong paradigm.) In this case, however, the defendant's crimes also included illicit sex with women and bogus faith healing. The prefects sentenced "Peng Ziren" to strangulation after the assizes, according to the statute against heterodoxy.

As to Wang Shixian,

interrogation has produced no evidence that he abetted Peng Ziren in "inciting and deceiving" (*shanhuo*) the people or other crimes. Nevertheless, even though he realized that Peng Ziren had a male body (*xi shu nanshen*), he did not report him to the authorities for masquerading in women's attire. On the contrary, he engaged in sodomy with Peng Ziren and joined him as travel companions, pretending to be husband and wife, and this conduct also violated the law.

Therefore, Wang Shixian was sentenced as an "accomplice" (*wei cong*) in "Peng Ziren's" crime. According to the original statute, accomplices should be sentenced to one hundred blows of the heavy bamboo and life exile at a distance of 3000 *li*, but a recent substatute had modified that sentence: now they should be "deported to the Muslim cities" (*hui cheng*) of Xinjiang "and given as slaves to the greater or lesser begs, or to Muslims who are able to supervise them properly" (*gei daxiao boke ji li neng guanshu zhi huizi wei nu*).[11] In addition, Wang Shixian was ordered tattooed on the face so that if he tried to escape, he could be readily identified.[12]

The governor approved the prefects' recommendations and forwarded them to Beijing in a "routine memorial on criminal matters" (*xingke tiben*). The case was then referred to the Three High Courts (*sanfasi*) for review, as was standard practice—an ad hoc committee of senior officials representing the Board of Punishment, the Censorate, and the Court of Judicial Review. The Three High Courts endorsed the governor's memorial but added one further recommendation: that Zhang Yaoguniang's penalty of strangulation be changed from "after the assizes" (*jiao jianhou*) to "immediate" (*jiao li jue*). In the Qing dynasty, most death sentences were provisional, being subject to a final stage of review and possible commutation at the annual "autumn assizes" (*qiushen*). In other words, a death sentence to be carried out "after the assizes" left open the real possibility of a reprieve, and in practice most such sentences do seem to have been commuted. The alternative was "immediate execution," which meant exactly what it sounds like: as soon as the emperor had approved the recommendation of the Three High Courts (which seems to have been routine), the defendant would be put to death without further ado.[13] Therefore, the Three High Courts' recommendation of "immediate" strangulation, which the Jiaqing emperor approved, consigned Zhang to certain and immediate death. It was a mark of what the presiding officials saw as the extremely heinous nature of their crimes.[14]

The Demonization of Faith Healing

Three crimes triggered the application of the statute against heterodoxy in Zhang Yaoguniang's case: "masquerading in women's attire," cheating people by using heterodox techniques to pretend to treat illnesses, and seducing and attempting to abduct women ("consensual sodomy," cited as a "lesser crime," did not count for this purpose). As we saw in the case of Zengliang in chapter 2, cross-dressing by itself would have been sentenced according to the statute against heterodoxy, but with reduced penalties. In the absence of cross-dressing, the illicit sex and attempted abduction would have been covered by other laws, and, as we will discuss, probably the faith healing as well. It was the combination of the three that determined Zhang's sentence of strangulation and then, on review, its increase from "after the assizes" to "immediate."

In chapter 2, we examined the paradigm of the cross-dressing sexual predator epitomized by Sang Chong, which explains why Governor Jiang interpreted Xiong Mumu's M–F transition the way he did. The case of Zhang Yaoguniang adds spirit-summoning and exorcistic faith healing to the picture. Ming-Qing officials associated such activities with heterodoxy not only because of the occult techniques they involved, whether real or fake, but also because of their implicit reliance on deception: for officials, the default assumption was that such practitioners were con artists who had no intention of actually treating illnesses, and were simply out to cheat people.

Faith Healing in Qing Law

Qing law addressed the crime of bogus faith healing from two closely related, overlapping perspectives: heterodoxy and medical malpractice. The statute against heterodoxy lists a number of examples of techniques based on "deviant ways and heterodox principles" (*zuodao yiduan*): "falsely pretending to summon heterodox spirits (*jia jiang xieshen*)," "writing talismans or magically charging water by incantation (*zhoushui*)," and "performing magic writing on a sand table (*fuluan*) and praying to the divine."[15] Zhang Yaoguniang confessed to several of these acts. In fact, all of the supposedly heterodox acts enumerated by the statute were basic parts of the ritual repertoire of Chinese popular religion.[16]

As to medical malpractice, a substatute promulgated in 1725 provided that "any shaman or Daoist priest (*duangong daoshi*) who uses heterodox magic (*yiduan fashu*) to treat someone's illness, resulting in death, shall be sentenced according to the statute on 'homicide in a fight.'" This substatute was originally attached to the statute against heterodoxy.[17] In 1801, it was revised into the following form:

> Any shaman, Daoist priest, or other sort of person (*ji yiqie ren deng*) who uses heterodox magic [such as drawing "halo" talismans, etc.] (*yuanguang huafu*) to treat illness, resulting in death, shall be sentenced to strangulation after the assizes, according to the statute against "homicide in a fight."[18] If the victim does not die, then the perpetrator shall receive one hundred blows of the heavy bamboo and be sentenced to life exile at a distance of three thousand *li*. In either instance, any accomplices shall receive a penalty one degree lower than that of the principal offender.[19]

The revised substatute was relocated to the homicide chapter and attached to the statute against "incompetent physicians killing or injuring others" (*yongyi sha shang ren*). This statute covers dangerous incompetence in prescribing drugs and acupuncture, fraudulent medical treatment to cheat people out of their money, and the malicious misuse of medicines to harm others. The substatute added heterodox magic to the list, and, in nineteenth-century texts, it is referred to as "the substatute against using heterodox methods to treat illness" (*xieshu yi ren li*). The prohibited conduct sounds similar to that prohibited by the statute against heterodoxy, and both laws prescribe identical sentences for both principal offenders and accomplices.

The deep paranoia of the imperial state about popular religion during the Ming and Qing dynasties is well documented.[20] Both dynasties required temples and monasteries to register with the Board of Rites and receive official approval to operate; both also sought to license all Daoist and Buddhist clergy, to attach them to authorized establishments, and to restrict their movements.[21] Unauthorized religious practitioners and their activities were viewed with deep suspicion and were targets of sporadic persecution, even though complete suppression was beyond the powers of the imperial state. Collective sworn brotherhoods ("triads") and local millenarian Buddhist sects that coalesced around charismatic individuals were imagined to be inherently subversive and were persecuted with special ruthlessness.[22] On a less grandiose scale, spirit mediums were objects of contempt and suspicion for Ming-Qing elites, who saw them as "an inversion of the Confucian paragon"—"exploitative, insincere, depraved, or vulgar in their ritual movements, and . . . completely ineffective in curing their patients."[23] The basic assumption was that mediums were charlatans. In fact, this assumption has persisted even in the post-Mao era, when spirit mediums have routinely been accused of "charlatanry for cheating people out of their money" (*pianqian shouduan*).[24]

It is worth noting, however, that Daoist adepts believed that much of their ritual repertoire could be used either to help people or to harm them, and that the difference between white and black magic might depend simply on the end to which it was directed. According to Michael Saso, within Daoism "orthodoxy" is defined simply by the use of magic "only for man's good, not to his detriment," whereas "heterodoxy" is the opposite.[25] As chapter 2's cases involving knockout drugs suggest, all such rituals and therapies, however benign, seem to have had a malignant mirror image. Perhaps this ambivalent aspect of popular religion helps explain some of the deep official suspicion directed at it—especially at spirit-channeling, exorcism, and faith healing.

The Bogus "Ghost Masters" of Guangxi

A bizarre case reported in 1767 by the governor of Guangxi illustrates how the specter of bogus faith healing brought together this full range of fears and associations, including flirtation with heterodoxy.[26] The governor begins by explaining the lamentable state of popular customs in his province: "In Guangxi, by custom people deeply believe in ghosts and spirits (*yue su zui xin guishen*), so that when someone falls ill they usually do not call a doctor, but instead engage in prayer. There are practitioners known as 'ghost masters' (*guishi*), who vulgarly recite incantations and dance, in order to drive illnesses out of sick people. This ritual is called 'dancing the ghosts' (*tiao gui*)." The magistrate of Liucheng County had uncovered a conspiracy to exploit these superstitions of gullible peasants in order to cheat them of money. A "ghost master" named Wu Huguo, who also practiced herbal medicine and fortune-telling, had noticed that peasants would treat skin diseases such as scabies and ringworm by washing the sores with an infusion of Chinese azalea (*naoyanghua*, which we encountered in the last chapter) and another herb with similar properties, Hindu datura (*mantuoluo*, i.e., "mandala" plant).[27] Apparently Wu Huguo was literate, and, by consulting the classic Ming-dynasty pharmacopoeia *Systematic Materia Medica* (*Bencao gangmu*), he learned that wine infused with these herbs "can make people laugh wildly and fall into a deep stupor (*kuang xiao hun chen*)."[28] He obtained the herbs, infused them in water, and then surreptitiously tested this potion on two small children of his neighborhood. Both children "went crazy" (*fakuang*), but after some time they recovered their senses.

His experiments a success, Wu Huguo began using this potion to drug children and then arranging to be hired by their parents to "cure" them by "dancing the ghosts" away. He would charge anywhere from a few hundred to a couple thousand cash for each "cure." Eventually, Wu expanded his operation by recruiting a second ghost master, Chen Mingzhang, to assist him, and then several other men to help with drugging the children and advertising his profound ritual mastery. The drug was infused in tea or wine, as well as made into rice candy, and distributed to the accomplices to use as the opportunity arose. This operation continued for several months, during which a large number of children were drugged. Most recovered, apparently without lasting harm, but three children overdosed and died. The local people were fooled by this con and had no idea that the gang was actually drugging the afflicted children. But, eventually, this epidemic of temporary madness among children, along with the supposedly marvelous ability of Wu Huguo to drive out the responsible ghosts, came to the attention of the local magistrate, who had Wu and his accomplices arrested.

Wu Huguo and his accomplices were sentenced to immediate beheading followed by public exposure of their heads (*xiaoshou*), according to the clause of the statute against robbery (*qiangdao*) that states: "If drugs are used to stupefy or render someone unconscious (*yi yao miren*) in order to steal their property, then the perpetrator(s) shall be punished in the same manner" as if they had used violent coercion to commit robbery.[29] Immediate beheading with exposure of the head was the severest penalty available to the Qing judiciary, short of the extreme penalty of dismemberment (*lingchi*). In addition, the governor issued a proclamation throughout the province banning the profession of "ghost master" and the ritual of "dancing the ghosts." The sentences and the governor's initiative were approved on review in Beijing.[30]

This case illustrates a number of the themes familiar from the crossdressing sexual predator paradigm and from the prosecution of Zhang Yaoguniang: the vulnerability of naive and gullible commoners to exploitation; the use of weird, occult techniques including magic and knockout drugs in the commission of crime; the recruitment of accomplices into a widening criminal conspiracy; and fraudulent faith healing to cheat people out of their money.

The Persecution of Popular Religion

It appears, however, that the vast majority of the faith healing actually prosecuted by Qing authorities consisted of commonplace religious practices. In published casebooks such as *Conspectus of Penal Cases*, one can find many examples of the crime of "treating illness to cheat people out of their money" (*kan bing pianqian*) that involve faith healing. Some are listed under the statute against heterodoxy, and others appear under that against "incompetent physicians killing or injuring others."[31] But most of the "crimes" of this kind that are summarized in these casebooks seem perfectly innocuous, and some closely resemble the faith healing for which Zhang Yaoguniang was condemned. The following six examples are typical.

1. In a case from Shaanxi prosecuted in 1800, a medical practitioner named Yang Shengchun used the "halo method" of divination and healing (that was proscribed by the substatute against medical malpractice), in combination with medicines, to treat his patients. Yang would recite an incantation over a bowl of water, draw the talisman in the water, and use the magically charged water to draw a circle on the palm of his left hand. Then he would have a small child look at the circle and describe whether he saw a "black shadow" inside the circle, and, on the basis of the child's description, Yang would judge the severity of the illness. Then he would prescribe medicine and give the patient a paper talisman to burn and swallow with each dose. Yang came to the attention of local authorities because of his evident success and popularity. At first the magistrate applied the statute against heterodoxy, but he was overruled on review and told to apply instead the substatute against "using heterodox magic to treat illness, when the victim does not die." Since Yang's teacher (who had died some time before) had been the original "ringleader" in this heterodox practice, Yang was sentenced as an "accomplice," to one hundred blows of the heavy bamboo and three years of penal servitude.

2. In an 1813 case from Shandong, a man named Zhao Bing earned money doing divination and treating illnesses; his ritual involved bowing to heaven and singing magical songs for several days, during which his patients would recover.[32] None of his patients had died, so he was sentenced to one hundred blows of the heavy bamboo and life exile at a distance of three thousand *li*, according to the same substatute.

3, In an 1819 case from Jiangxi, a man named Wu Dongzhou earned a living by drawing healing talismans for sick people. He copied the talismans out of a popular daily-use encyclopedia. He, too, was sentenced to one hundred blows of the heavy bamboo and life exile at a distance of three thousand *li*, according to the same substatute.

4. In an 1819 case from Zhili, a woman named Ding Sha Shi acted as a medium for a snake deity (*shejing*) and treated illnesses by burning incense and preparing tea for her patients to drink.[33] In the governor's opinion, although this conduct resembled the prohibited "using heterodox magic to treat people's illnesses," since Ding Da Shi had used no talismans or incantations (*fuzhou*), it was not a very serious case. Therefore, she could

be sentenced to a reduced penalty of a beating and penal servitude and, as a woman, would be permitted to redeem that penalty with a cash fine.

5. In an 1817 case from Henan, a woman named Feng Zhang Shi had inherited from her aunt a paper image of a heterodox deity affiliated with martial arts to whom she would pray and may have served as medium. She treated sick people by burning incense, giving them a medicine made from tea leaves and a popular stomach remedy, and providing them with hand-drawn copies of her deity's image and with talismans on paper. She, too, was sentenced to a beating and penal servitude, but not permitted to redeem her penalties.

6. In an 1821 case from Zhejiang, a woman named Wang Li Shi treated illnesses by channeling a female deity known as the Lady of Yaji Mountain (Yaji Shan Niangniang).[34] When possessed by the goddess, she would burn incense, chant "Amitabha" over water to charge it with power, and then have the sick person drink the water. However, she did not draw talismans or recite incantations, and therefore she, too, was sentenced to a beating and penal servitude, but permitted to redeem her penalties with a cash fine.

As many have pointed out before, "heterodoxy" is very much in the eye of the beholder. None of the rituals described in these brief case summaries seem unusual in the context of popular religious practice in China, and there is no evidence that these six practitioners ever harmed anyone. On the contrary, at least one of them seems to have been a notable success in helping his patients. But, in every case summary, the practitioner is described as a con artist, "falsely pretending" to treat illnesses, in order to cheat people out of their money. Most likely this motive was ascribed to the defendants by their interrogators, who encouraged them to confess accordingly. It is clear that the presiding officials judged these particular acts of "heterodox magic" to be relatively benign, however, given the reduced penalties they imposed (no one was sentenced to death). But the defendants still suffered beatings and either penal servitude or life exile to the frontier—and it is an open question whether the two women allowed to redeem their penalties with cash fines could afford to do so.[35]

Note how closely some of the rituals described in these case summaries resemble that which Zhu Da used to save Zhang Yaoguniang from choking, and that Zhang in turn used to treat snakebite. Zhang's faith healing activity was right in line with the mainstream of popular religious practice, and, as we have seen, there was a striking disconnect between the reality of such practices and the official ideology that demonized them. It is also striking how prominently women featured in faith healing. In many parts of China, the role of shaman or spirit medium has traditionally been open to both women and men, which is one reason why elites and officials viewed such ritual practices with suspicion and distaste.

Confession Under Duress

To understand the meaning of Zhang Yaoguniang and Wang Shixian's confessions, we must consider how they came to exist in the form we have seen. To the uninitiated eye, confessions of this kind may read as if they were spontaneous statements that have simply been transcribed, but they were nothing of the kind. Instead, they were answers to series of specific questions and have been edited and strung together, usually leaving out the questions, as if they were a monologue. For this reason, such confessions typically include only information that magistrates solicited and deemed directly pertinent to their duty of proving and sentencing criminal acts. In fact, this is true of all courtroom testimony, as it was summarized in official case reports during the Qing.[36]

When Zhang was arrested in Queshan County, nobody had yet accused them of seducing women, attempted kidnapping, or bogus faith healing, and one can hardly imagine the defendants volunteering this sort of information spontaneously. Therefore, regardless of what Zhang had actually done, these issues must have been introduced by their interrogators, who (like Governor Jiang Pu in chapter 2) believed they *already knew* what M–F cross-dressing signified and questioned the defendants accordingly.

In other words, something like the following must have happened. Zhang Yaoguniang came under suspicion for cross-dressing—evidently someone thought they looked like a man in drag and reported them—and the couple were arrested. This suspicion was confirmed by the midwife's examination of Zhang at the yamen, and her confirmation that Zhang was "a man masquerading in women's attire" triggered an interrogation that followed a "script" derived from the Sang Chong paradigm. "You decided to masquerade in women's attire so that you could seduce and rape women, isn't that so? How many women have you seduced and raped? How many have you kidnapped? Give us the details! What other crimes have you committed—what about black magic?" As the interrogators considered how to apply the statute against heterodoxy, they would have added questions based on that statute's list of specific crimes: "Have you ever summoned or channeled spirits? Have you ever practiced bogus faith healing in order to cheat people out of their money? Who taught you how to do these things? Have you pledged anyone as master, in order to learn these dark arts? Have you recruited any disciples yourself?" The confessions from Zhang and Wang that we have before us were produced through this sort of process: a coercive dialogue in which the interrogators' leading questions helped the defendants understand what they were supposed to confess.

This process was not fast: it unfolded over a period of eighteen months. It must have begun in Queshan County, Henan, when the couple were first arrested, and Zhang's anatomy was exposed. It then would have continued in Hanyang County, to which the couple had been deported under escort. Since the two preliminary judgments by the Hanyang magistrate were rejected as insufficient, his investigations must not have produced this full confession—or, at least, not all of its elements. But since his second judgment did satisfy the provincial judge, who had rejected his first, it must have contained new information absent from the first judgment—new information that had been developed through more intensive interrogation. We also know that the county magistrate recommended sentencing Zhang and Wang according to a "substatute" (*li*); we do not know which one, but clearly the final sentence applying the statute (*lü*) against heterodoxy was a product of the very last stage of investigation, after the prefects had extracted the full confession that we have seen and had fashioned it into a satisfactory and reasonably coherent narrative.

In other words, this confession was developed over time, in stages, as the defendants came under increasing—and no doubt increasingly unpleasant—pressure to satisfy the expectations of their interrogators, who themselves faced increasing pressure from their superiors to discover "the truth." Although the case record does not say explicitly whether Zhang and Wang were tortured with the ankle press, it seems likely that they were. But, even if they were not, there were plenty of other less formal—but also cruel—methods available to the authorities and their minions (methods that would not have been officially classified as "judicial torture") to induce the defendants' cooperation.[37] In the end, as we have seen, their cooperation was secured.

Unfortunately, this sort of process is far from rare, especially when political and ideological crimes are under investigation. An excellent example comes from Laura Stokes's study of witchcraft trials in late medieval and early modern Switzerland. Through repeated sessions of torture, interrogators would assist defendants in crafting elaborate confessions that conformed to the popular understanding of witchcraft—a process Stokes characterizes as "creativity inspired by torment" (a phrase I have borrowed for the title of this chapter).[38] Judges "were guided by common sense in the process of torture and interrogation, and this arrangement powerfully confirmed any prejudices they might hold against the accused." The resulting confessions reveal more about how interrogators imagined witchcraft than about the actions of the defendants.[39] In his masterful study of religious persecution in China during the Ming-Qing era, Barend ter Haar documents how a very similar process created a narrative of pervasive heterodox sedition that confirmed what interrogators already believed they knew about the White Lotus Teachings (*bailianjiao*) and their adherents. Interrogators convinced of suspects' guilt would use leading questions to elicit confessions that they were members of the White Lotus conspiracy (turning that label into what ter Haar calls a "pseudo-autonym"), even though the name "White Lotus" was entirely alien to their own religious beliefs. One result has been the unwitting perpetuation of Qing officials' paranoid fantasy of the White Lotus by modern historians who have relied uncritically on the confessions of tortured rebels to study popular religion and peasant rebellion.[40]

The 1768 "soul-stealing" panic so memorably analyzed by historian Philip Kuhn provides a spectacular example of how pressure from superiors (including the Qianlong Emperor himself) might induce local officials to resort to ever more desperate measures in order to secure satisfactory confessions. In that episode, a series of torture-driven confessions fueled a widening dragnet for soul-stealing sorcerers, of whose existence the emperor was convinced. Ultimately, it turned out that there were no soul-stealers after all, but that conclusion was reached only after dozens of hapless beggars and monks had been arrested, several had been crippled by the ankle press, and at least two had died in custody.[41]

As these examples suggest, the investigation of political and ideological crimes such as heresy, witchcraft, heterodoxy, and sedition is especially susceptible to distortion through this kind of confirmation bias. Such crimes are understood as the manifestation of terrifying evil forces that pose a vital threat to social, political, and moral order. In such cases, the conviction that the crime has been committed, and that the stakes are high, may be intensified by the attention of senior officials who demand results. At the same time, investigators may be frustrated by a lack of tangible evidence to confirm their suspicions—how does one prove "heterodoxy," anyway? In such circumstances, there can be overwhelming temptation to use coercive measures to elicit a confession that conforms to a script already existing in the minds of the interrogators.[42]

As Europe's notorious witchcraft trials demonstrate, people enduring torture (especially over a sustained period of time) will confess practically anything that can be imagined, including human sacrifice, cannibalism, sexual intercourse with demons and animals, the ability to fly, and the power to manipulate the weather.[43] Moreover, as ter Haar warns, a similar dynamic may occur even without actual physical torture: "Modern research on interrogation techniques has made it abundantly clear that psychological pressure, physical exhaustion and apprehension in anticipation of the potential application of torture, are in themselves sufficient to influence confessions to a large extent. Confessions made under duress are, therefore, subject to conscious manipulation and unconscious influences."[44] In fact, it was not uncommon for Qing magistrates investigating major cases to threaten suspects with torture while ordering the ankle press (or, for women, the finger press) strapped onto their limbs. Sometimes this maneuver elicited sufficient cooperation that there was no need actually to tighten the device.[45]

The Fate of Zhang Yaoguniang

I believe that something of this nature must have transpired in Zhang Yaoguniang's case. As I have tried to show, evidence internal to the case report suggests that the final version of the defendants' confessions that satisfied the governor and his superiors in Beijing was the product of "creativity inspired by torment." There is no way to know for sure what parts of the confessions are true, and what parts are creative additions, but I find the accounts of seducing women especially hard to believe: they fit too awkwardly with the rest of the narrative, and they conform too neatly to the paradigm of the cross-dressing predator; moreover, it seems suspicious that none of the witnesses to those alleged crimes were available to testify in person. More credible, it seems to me, is Zhang's response to the interrogators' skepticism that they had managed to seduce only two women: "When young ladies from proper families saw that I was covered with filth (*huiwu*), they would steer clear of me."

I suppose we should consider the possibility that Zhang Yaoguniang's confession may have been completely truthful. It seems conceivable—if not very likely—that the cultural script of the cross-dressing sexual predator was so prevalent and influential that it could have inspired an exceptionally lecherous sociopath to emulate Sang Chong by cross-dressing in order to pursue chaste women (although that hypothesis begs the question of how an illiterate beggar like "Peng Ziren" would have learned about that paradigm). As we have seen, that hypothesis is hard to square with the claim that Zhang submitted to blackmail by Wang Shixian. But, even if Zhang really did seduce two women, in addition to committing at least two acts of exorcistic faith healing, there seems to be a bizarre mismatch in both ambition and achievement between such a petty record and the dynasty's grandiose fantasies about heterodox conspiracy. In the end, Zhang Yaoguniang was a pathetic, homeless beggar who met a horrible death. Moreover, "accomplice" Wang Shixian spent no more than two weeks in Zhang's company, and there is no evidence that he ever harmed anyone (aside from the alleged blackmail, which held no particular interest for the authorities); nevertheless, he received a life sentence of slavery in Xinjiang. The official response seems grossly out of proportion to the couple's alleged crimes.

Incidentally, the case of Xiong Mumu discussed in chapter 2 could easily have turned out the same way, I believe, had its adjudication not been short-circuited by the emperor's peremptory judgment sparing Xiong's life. In that case, Governor Jiang was ready to launch a much more intensive investigation to uncover Xiong's alleged further "crimes" and "accomplices." If left to his own devices—and especially if encouraged by the emperor—the governor might well have used torture to extract a more elaborate confession that would have more fully confirmed his own paranoid fantasies.

CHAPTER V

The Fox Spirit Medium

I have often treated women's illnesses, but I never had illicit sex with any of them.

—XING SHI, 1807

The Arrest

In the spring of 1807, three Manchu commanders of the Beijing gendarmerie memorialized the emperor to report their arrest of a "man masquerading in women's attire" (*nan ban nüzhuang*).[1] Local constables (*fanyi*) in the Taojiawan area just east of the city had learned of a woman named Liu Xing Shi (thirty-four *sui*) who "worshiped an image of a fox spirit in her home, acting as a medium to burn incense and cure illnesses" (*jianei gongfeng huxian tuxiang, dingxiang zhibing*). Suspecting heterodoxy and a possible confidence scheme, they had placed the medium and her husband, Liu Liu (thirty-two *sui*), under surveillance. But then the constable who was deputed to tail the couple reported his suspicion that the woman might actually be a man: "Although she wears women's clothing and her hair and facial features are the same as a woman's, there seems to be something suspicious about her manner and comportment (*guan qi juzhi xingji, si you keyi*)."[2]

The constables ordered a neighbor woman to pretend to engage Liu Xing Shi to treat an illness, and to observe the medium closely and find out whether she was in fact a man in disguise. When this woman confirmed that the medium "really does not appear to be a woman" (*shi fei furen xingzhuang*), the constables arrested the couple and handed them over to the gendarmerie. The officer in command ordered Liu Xing Shi examined by a midwife, who reported that the medium "is in fact a male" (*shi xi nanzi*). The medium's husband Liu Liu expressed astonishment at this revelation: he claimed that he had had no idea that his wife of five years had male anatomy.[3]

Two Sets of Confessions

In the previous chapter, we saw how "creativity inspired by torment" over a period of some eighteen months eventually produced confessions that satisfied the inquisitors by largely confirming their preconception of what M–F transing signified. But, since we have only the final record of that case, we were able to deduce this process only indirectly, from hindsight. For Liu Xing Shi and Liu Liu, however, we are fortunate to have two separate sets of confessions, made before and after the application of torture, that show exactly how the authorities produced a satisfactory narrative of the case. Upon arresting the suspects, the gendarmerie interrogated them and prepared a preliminary report to the Board of Punishment, which would take over the case. As we shall see, the presiding judges at the board gave short shrift to the prisoners' initial confessions, and quickly resorted to torture in order to extract "the truth."

The First Interrogation, by the Gendarmerie

Under interrogation, Liu Xing Shi confessed that their original name had been "Xing Da" (*Da* meaning "eldest son"), and they were originally from rural Renqiu County, about 140 kilometers south of Beijing. "Liu Xing Shi" would be the normal term of address for a woman whose natal surname was "Xing" and who had married a man surnamed "Liu" (i.e., the equivalent of "Mrs. Liu née Xing").[4] I shall refer to them here as "Xing Shi" (née Xing) or simply "Xing." In 1781, when Xing Shi was eight *sui*, their father had died and their mother, Xing Du Shi, brought them to Beijing to seek a livelihood. For three years, Xing Du Shi eked out a living as a seamstress mending clothes, but in 1784 she died, leaving Xing Shi an orphan at the age of eleven *sui*.

At this point, an acquaintance named Hong Da arranged for Xing Shi's employment helping out at a bootmaker's shop, through the intercession of a friend named Li Si, who worked there as a cook. The shop was located on Dongzhi Street, in the northeast quarter of Beijing's Inner City. "Then," according to Xing's confession, "Li Si sodomized me," in what appears to have been a quid pro quo for taking Xing off the street. Xing Shi kept in touch with Hong Da during this time, and, in 1790, when Xing was seventeen *sui*, "Hong Da called me back to live with him, and he, too, sodomized me. Then he told me to grow out my hair and count myself his wife (*jiao wo liule toufa, suan ta nüren*)." In their initial confession as reported by the gendarmerie, Xing gave no other explanation for their transition, but from that point on they presented not only as a woman but also as Hong's wife. In this capacity, they would have been known as "Hong Xing Shi" (i.e., Mrs. Hong née Xing).

Over the next dozen years, the couple lived in and around Beijing. In 1802, however, Hong Da came down with "blood spitting disease" (*tuxiebing*—tuberculosis perhaps?) and could no longer work or support Xing Shi. At this point, the couple moved to a location just east of Beijing's Drum Tower, at Nanxiawa, near a huge nightsoil drying yard (*fenchang*).[5] We do not know what Hong Da had done for a living, but this location gives us some idea of the poverty to which the couple had been reduced, because Beijing's nightsoil yards were notorious for their ghastly stench, and no one would live nearby unless they had no other choice. The couple talked over their options and finally agreed that Hong should sell Xing Shi in marriage; that way, Xing Shi would have means of support, and Hong would get some money to pay for medical care.[6]

Hong Da engaged an acquaintance named Zhang Er to act as matchmaker, telling him that Xing Shi was his widowed younger sister, and that she needed to remarry in order to survive. The case record does not say explicitly what name Xing Shi used in this transaction, but presumably they were presented to the matchmaker and prospective buyers simply as "Hong Shi" (née Hong). In other words, this transaction involved a double deception: not only was Xing Shi's anatomical sex concealed from their prospective husband and in-laws but also, by pretending they were Hong's widowed sister, the couple was perpetrating what amounted to a fraudulent wife sale. Since most wife sales were illegal, and "a wife with a living husband" (*you fu zhi fu*) came with potentially risky strings attached, it was easier to secure a buyer and also to get a higher bride-price if the wife to be sold were posed as a widow. This tactic was very common. Since widow remarriage was structured as a form of wife sale (with the in-laws acting in place of the dead husband to negotiate the terms and receive the bride-price), there was no way for a prospective buyer to learn the truth, as long as the woman kept the secret.[7]

Matchmaker Zhang Er believed this tale, and, working with a second intermediary, he found a man named Liu Liu who had never previously married and was willing to pay a bride-price of twenty-five strings of capital cash to take "Hong Shi" in marriage.[8] Liu was from Tong Department (immediately southeast of Beijing) and he lived with his parents and older brother in the semirural environs of Beijing, in Daxing County, where he worked as a laborer hauling grain. The two matchmakers, Liu Liu's parents ("Old" Liu Liu and Zhang Shi), and brother Liu Wu were all convinced that Xing Shi was a woman; according to their later testimony, they never suspected that Xing Shi was "a man masquerading as a woman." Nor did they suspect that Xing Shi was actually Hong Da's wife, rather than his sister.

What happened on the wedding night? Xing Shi later gave the following account: "When it came time to consummate our marriage, I covered up my inconvenient place and said that I was ill and could not have intercourse, but I was willing to let him sodomize me instead (*chengqin shi wo jiang bu bian chu zheyan, zhi shuo you bing bu neng xingfang, qingyuan jiao ta jijian*). Liu Liu believed me and so he sodomized me (*Liu Liu xin yi wei shi, jiu jiang wo jijian le*)." According to Liu's own testimony before the Gendarmerie, for five years this subterfuge worked: "I really didn't know that Xing Shi is a man" (*shi bu zhi Xing Shi shi nanren*).

In the second lunar month of 1805, Xing Shi was visited in a dream by a "fox spirit" (*huxian*) and realized that they could serve the spirit as a medium (*dingxiang*). So they talked it over with Liu Liu and came up with a plan to augment their income by "treating illnesses and cheating people out of their money." They had someone write a spirit tablet (*paiwei*) for the fox spirit for them to worship. In the tenth lunar month, Xing Shi cured a boy of an illness, and his grateful father painted a picture of a female fox spirit (*nü huxian*) on a scroll and gave it to them, along with five ceremonial dishes (for food offerings), to go on their altar with the spirit tablet.

Xing Shi's healing practice focused on women. As they later testified:

When men's wives fell ill they would invite me to their homes to treat them. First I would set up an incense stand and light the incense, then I would hold the incense and move it three times around the sick person's head, and then place the incense stick in the incense burner. Then I would sit beside the table and close my eyes, pretending that the fox spirit had descended into me (*jiazhuang huxian jiangxia*), and try to guess the sick person's condition. I would randomly say a few crazy words (*suikou hunbian kuangyan*) and then pretend the fox spirit had left. Then I would ask the sick person some vague questions, and say, "It's like that, isn't it?" (*hanhu chawen shuo de shi bu shi*). Then I mixed some stuff like ginger, lotus root, lampwick grass, white sugar, and tea leaves together in yellow wine and gave it to the sick person as medicine. For each treatment, I would get one or two hundred cash in incense money.

When Xing Shi began channeling the fox spirit, this new role transformed their relationship with both husband and in-laws. At that time, they and Liu Liu were living with Liu's parents and brother. The in-laws all opposed Xing Shi's plan to act as a fox spirit medium and cure people's illnesses, so Xing Shi "pretended to be mad and possessed by a demon, and made a wild scene in order to scare them" (*jiazhuang fengmo sapo xiahu*). Liu Liu's parents "had no choice" but to make the couple move out and live separately, disowning them. Moreover, according to Xing Shi's testimony (which Liu confirmed): "After I began worshiping the fox spirit's image I never again had sexual relations with Liu Liu. I just focused all my effort on looking at incense and curing illnesses" (*wo cong gong le huxian de xiang zong wei yu Liu Liu xingfang, zhuanyi kan xiang zhi bing*).

Incidentally, it is not clear when Liu Liu realized that Xing Shi had been Hong Da's "wife," instead of widowed sister. At any rate, by the time they were arrested, Xing Shi was identified not as "Liu Hong Shi" (Mrs. Liu née Hong), but rather as "Liu Xing Shi" (Mrs. Liu née Xing). This detail suggests that, at some point, Xing Shi must have told Liu Liu that they had been Hong's wife, and that their own surname was "Xing." Of course, the credibility of that story depended on Liu Liu continuing to believe that Xing Shi was a woman.

After separating from Liu Liu's family, Xing Shi and their husband were living in the semirural suburbs of Beijing, outside the Chaoyang Gate. One day, a neighbor woman named Wang Du Shi, who lived in the same courtyard, was plucking Xing Shi's facial hair (*lianshang de hanmao*) for them as a favor. Suddenly, Wang Du Shi reached out and groped Xing Shi in the crotch: "Her hand bumped into my inconvenient place" (*peng zhao wo bu bian chu*). Evidently, Wang Du Shi was suspicious about Xing Shi's sex and decided to find out for herself what was there. Xing Shi was frightened "that there would be trouble," so they and their husband moved away to the neighborhood of Taojiawan, further to the east. This episode suggests that Xing was aware of the risk and possible consequences of exposure. It was there, a year later, that Xing Shi came under suspicion and the couple were finally arrested. As we would expect, the gendarmerie pressed Xing Shi specifically about how many women they had raped or seduced, but Xing Shi adamantly denied ever doing any such thing: "I have often treated women's illnesses, but I never had illicit sex with any of them" (*sui shichang yu funü yizhi, bing wu jianwu qingshi*).

Having reported this testimony, the memorialists summarized their preliminary understanding of the case. Paraphrasing the statute against heterodoxy, they observed that "for a sorcerer or shaman to pretend falsely to summon a heterodox spirit, to conceal a picture of a proscribed deity, and to burn incense, in order to incite and deceive the people's minds (*shanhuo ren xin*) is a grave violation of the law":

> In the present case, the civilian Xing Da, despite being a man, grew his hair out long, masqueraded falsely as a woman, was married to Liu Liu as wife, worshiped a picture of a fox spirit, and burned incense to treat people's illnesses in order to cheat them out of their money. He is truly lawless in the extreme (*mu wu faji*)! Moreover, it seems entirely likely that he has committed other acts of heterodoxy and licentiousness (*qie nanbao wu xie yin qingshi*). As to the matter of Liu Liu taking Xing Da as his wife, how is it possible that for five years he never realized that Xing Da had a man's body (*he yi wu nian zhi jiu jing bu zhi xi nanshen*)? It is obvious that Liu Liu colluded with Xing Da to conceal the truth and perpetuate this fraud (*xian you tongtong zhuangshi qingbi*)! The testimony of both criminals is slippery and evasive (*shanshuo*), and many aspects of the case are suspicious (*an duo yidou*).

The gendarmerie commanders requested an edict from the emperor ordering the transfer of Xing Shi and Liu Liu to the Board of Punishment, where they could be thoroughly interrogated and sentenced appropriately for their crimes. In closing, they noted that "a case like this, in which a criminal has masqueraded as a woman, pretended to channel a heterodox spirit, and treated illnesses to cheat people out of their money, may very easily stir up further incidents and trouble. . . . We have exhorted the local constables to redouble their vigilance. If they encounter any other individuals of weird appearance or behavior (*xingji guiyi zhi ren*), they should immediately seize them and deliver them for interrogation."

The Second Interrogation, by the Board of Punishment

In response to this memorial, an imperial edict ordered Xing Da and Liu Liu transferred to the Board of Punishment for "strict interrogation" (*yanshen*). Based on the suspicions raised by the Gendarmerie, the board's interrogation of the couple focused on two questions.[9] Had Liu Liu known all along that Xing Da was really a man and therefore had colluded in Xing's nefarious masquerade? Had Xing Da employed his disguise as a woman in order to seduce or rape women?

When first questioned, Xing Shi and Liu Liu simply repeated their previous testimony. In their later report, the investigators at the Board of Punishment observed: "We find that for Xing Da to pretend to be a fox spirit, to make a prohibited picture of that spirit, and to look at incense and treat illnesses, already constitutes conduct that is strictly prohibited by law. On top of that, he shockingly dared to grow out his hair and wear women's clothing and accessories! It is obvious that he has committed crimes of debauching women by illicit sex (*xian you jianyin funü bu fa qingshi*)." Here we have strong confirmation of the paradigm of the cross-dressing sexual predator: if Xing masqueraded as a woman, then he must have seduced or raped women. Therefore, the investigators ordered both suspects tortured with the ankle press, and started over again.

Under torture, their story changed. As the board later summarized,

on the wedding night when they went to bed, Xing Da used various means to conceal his sex (*duo fang yanshi*) and seductively persuaded (*youling*) Liu Liu to sodomize him. Even after they had been together for several days, Liu Liu surprisingly failed to see through Xing Da's deception (*jing wei kuipo dili*). But eventually, as they gradually became familiar with each other and more intimate, he finally realized that Xing Da had a male body (*shi bei Liu Liu kanchu xi shu nanshen*). At first, Liu Liu was very unhappy and wanted to reject him. But Xing Da earnestly begged him to swallow his anger and to accept him, promising to work hard at sewing and embroidery and to serve him for the rest of their lives. He also told Liu Liu that he could earn money to augment their income by looking at incense and treating illnesses. Liu Liu realized that there was no way to get back the bride-price he had paid, and he was persuaded and fooled by Xing Da's sweet words, so he decided to restrain himself and accept the situation, and did not tell his parents what had happened.

Moreover, in the days that followed, "Liu Liu was seduced by Xing Da into taking turns sodomizing each other, and their mutual illicit sexual relations became passionate (*hongyou huxiang jijian, bici lian jian*). But they were very discreet and concealed the truth from everyone else."

According to this new confession, then, Liu Liu had been a knowing coconspirator after all, having been seduced by "Xing Da" with the joys of reciprocal anal intercourse and the promise of lucrative earnings from faith healing (we shall further explore the significance of this change and others). But on the second question—sexual predation targeting women—Xing stuck to their original testimony, even under torture:

> This criminal claims that he began masquerading as a woman only because as a youth he was seduced into sodomy by Hong Da—this was not something he had planned on doing himself as part of some scheme or plot. He also claims that he got the idea to look at incense and treat illnesses only because after remarrying his deception was discovered by Liu Liu. Xing Da begged Liu Liu not to reject him, and to persuade Liu Liu, he offered to earn incense money by pretending to be a fox spirit and cheating ignorant people (*hongpian yumin*). Later, Xing Da and Liu Liu became passionate in taking turns sodomizing each other and could not bear to be apart, so for these last several years they have spent every single night together. Xing Da used every possible means to conceal the truth, so that Liu Liu's parents and brothers were all deceived. He insists that truly, he has never had illicit sex with any woman (*shi wu ling you jianyin funü zhi shi*). . . . He asks why he would endure torture in order to lie about this one thing, after having confessed everything else?

Note that, since Xing had never married a woman, *any* sex they might have had with a woman would have counted as "illicit sex" (*jian*) in legal terms.

Hence, the import of their testimony is that they had never had sex with any woman at all; their entire sexual experience had been with men.

The investigators "repeatedly subjected Xing Da to severe interrogation, but he insists he is telling the truth." Liu Liu, also under torture, confirmed Xing's testimony. So the Board of Punishment summoned Liu Liu's parents and older brother for interrogation. According to investigators, "the three of them prostrated themselves and kowtowed and testified that, although they lived with Xing Da for several years, they were all deceived and truly never realized that he is a man." After that, the board decided that the confessions and witness testimony were all consistent, and that, therefore, it had enough evidence to close the case.

The board recommended that Xing Shi be sentenced to strangulation according to the statute against heterodoxy, as a ringleader, and further requested the emperor's approval to increase the penalty from "after the assizes" to "immediate," in order to demonstrate clearly the heinousness of Xing's crimes. As to Liu Liu, "he knew that Xing Da was a man masquerading as a woman, but he did not report his crime to the authorities. Instead, he dared to harbor Xing Da and engage in mutual sodomy with him (*shouliu huxiang jijian*); he also allowed Xing Da to pretend to worship a fox spirit picture in order to cheat people out of their money, and relied on this income for his livelihood (*lian qian hu kou*). Therefore, he is clearly an accomplice to Xing Da's crimes." A recent substatute had modified the sentence for "accomplices" (*wei cong*) in heterodoxy; on that basis, and setting aside his "lesser crime" of consensual sodomy, Liu Liu was sentenced to "life exile in Heilongjiang, where he shall be given as a slave to the Oroqen or Daur (*Suolun, Dahu'er*) banner troops."[10] He was ordered tattooed on the face and transferred to the Board of War for deportation to Manchuria. In addition, Liu's father, "Old" Liu Liu, was sentenced to eighty blows of the heavy bamboo according to the catch-all statute against "doing things that ought not to be done—severe cases" (*bu ying zhong*), because he had failed to report Xing Shi to the authorities when they announced their intention of acting as a spirit medium and "cheating people out of their money." The other parties implicated in Xing Shi's story were judged innocent of any crime or could not be located. The emperor approved all of the board's recommendations, and Xing Shi was strangled forthwith.[11]

Here we have another example of how a confession developed under duress, which in this instance explicitly included torture. But note the relatively short duration of the investigation in Xing Shi's case, in contrast with that of Zhang Yaoguniang, which lasted some eighteen months. Xing Shi and Liu Liu were arrested in the middle of the third lunar month of Jiaqing 12 (i.e., 1807—we do not know the exact day of their arrest); the gendarmerie's memorial is dated the seventeenth, and the emperor's edict ordering the prisoners' transfer to the Board of Punishment was issued the same day; that transfer occurred in the next day or two, and the emperor's second edict approving the Board of Punishment's recommendations is dated the twenty-seventh. Since Xing Shi's crimes had been committed in Beijing and its immediate environs, it would not have been necessary to transport them elsewhere for execution, and, since their execution was to be "immediate," it would have been carried out within days of the emperor's approval.[12] In sum, the entire process from arrest to execution probably took less than a month.

The relative speed of this process stemmed in part from the fact that it took place in Beijing, was reported directly to the throne by secret palace memorial, and was judged at the apex of the imperial system. That speed may explain why Xing Shi did not end up confessing to illicit sex with women. Had the board (or the emperor) refused to accept their confession, interrogation would have continued and eventually Xing might have been induced to capitulate on this point as well.

We shall explore the discrepancies between the two sets of confessions further later in the chapter. But, first, we must consider foxes: both the literati discourse of fox spirits and their role in popular religious practice.

Fox Spirits and Spirit Mediums

What are we to make of Xing Shi's confession that they decided to "pretend" to act as fox spirit medium and treat illnesses "in order to cheat people out of their money"? Xing Shi's activity as medium played a central role in the last few years of their life and also in their ultimate fate at the hands of the Qing state, having been a key factor in their death sentence for heterodoxy. To make sense of this story, we must explore two separate issues. The first is the literati discourse of foxes in late imperial China, especially the fictional genre of "the strange" (zhiguai), in which foxes and ghosts feature prominently. The second is the role of foxes and other animal spirits in the actual religious beliefs and practices of ordinary people, especially in north China.

Supernatural foxes play a lively role in Ming-Qing literature, most famously in the short fiction and essays of Ji Yun and Pu Songling.[13] These foxes are understood to have been ordinary animals that through centuries of self-cultivation and a quasi-Daoist "internal alchemy" have acquired "transcendent" (*xian*) powers and the ability to intervene in human affairs. Progress toward transcendence may involve the accumulation of merit through good works in the human world (such as healing illnesses), but most often is portrayed in fiction as a parasitical acquisition of "vital force" (*jing* or *qi*) from human beings. Foxes typically appear as shape-shifting seducers and sexual vampires: they may target humans of either sex, but most famously they take the form of alluring young women in order to prey upon naive young men who are susceptible to seduction. There are also tales of benign foxes who pursue transcendence by other means, or even virtuous ones who act as faithful concubines to male human partners, promoting their prosperity and good fortune. But, in *zhiguai* literature, the main way foxes pursue transcendence is by robbing men of their "vital force" through compulsive sexual intercourse, so that their victims waste away of exhaustion and even die. In the West, vampires want blood, but in China they want semen.

In the religious fox cult as portrayed in literati discourse, fox spirits are a capricious, disturbing force that must be pacified and contained. Foxes are liminal, marginal figures who move between worlds, "betwixt and between," as Xiaofei Kang puts it: "Fox spirits might appear as women or men and transform themselves into youths or elders; they are just as variable as human beings themselves. At certain times they act like ghosts, haunting and bewitching people, causing sickness or death; at others they assume the role of ancestors, granting wealth and prosperity."[14] In Ming-Qing literature, fox spirits are associated with marginal figures within the household and in society at large, who (like mediums and shamans elsewhere in the world) would draw on the power of such spirits to challenge normative power structures: "Feared yet worshipped, the fox embodied popular perceptions of marginal groups, ranging from daughters and daughters-in-law in family life to courtesans, entertainers, spirit mediums, migrants, and outlaws in society at large. The cult of the fox harbored morally ambiguous pursuits, such as trading sex for money or stealing from one family to enrich another. It also symbolized politically dubious activities, for fox spirits were believed to preach sectarian teachings, instigate rebellions, and take up residence in government offices."[15]

Literary discourse aside, fox spirits had a reputation for creating a nuisance by invading and colonizing government offices, and, over the Ming-Qing era, many yamens established shrines on their grounds to propitiate these foxes. By the late Qing, foxes were actually being worshiped by local officials as guardians of their seals of office, and one of the first acts of a newly appointed official arriving at his post would be to pay his respects to its guardian fox. Regardless of whether those officials actually believed in fox spirits, they clearly felt it best to carry on the local traditions of the yamen.[16] An example of such a shrine can be seen at the well-preserved yamen of Pingyao County, Shanxi, which contains a two-story structure called Tower of the Great Transcendent (*Daxian Lou*)—the English-language label on the tower translates *daxian* as "the Fox Immortal."[17]

The literati discourse of "the strange" would seem to be a poor guide for understanding the actual religious beliefs and practices of ordinary people, the vast majority of whom were illiterate. But it may help us understand how Qing officials would have perceived the activities of a medium like Xing Shi. In general, elites looked down on such popular religious cults and viewed spirit mediums especially with suspicion and contempt.[18] Animal cults were broadly deemed heterodox, despite the fact that many officials found it necessary to honor foxes inside their yamens. The most famous incident that explicitly linked a fox spirit to heterodox sedition is the 1622 White Lotus uprising led by the followers of lay Buddhist preacher Wang Sen, who had already died in prison in 1619. According to the confessions of Wang Sen and his son (as summarized by various Ming officials), a fox whom Wang had assisted in time of need rewarded him by teaching him an occult technique of empowerment. The details of this technique are unclear, but, among other things, Wang allegedly used knockout drugs to gain control over women so that he could rape them. Over time, he recruited a gang of adherents whom he initiated into his heterodox cult, and who later rebelled against the imperial state. Barend ter Haar's analysis indicates that Wang Sen and his son were interrogated over a period of time, almost certainly under torture, eventually producing confessions that confirmed a "stereotyped perception of the adherents of the White Lotus Teachings as 'dangerous and rebellious magicians.'"[19] Wang Sen was not accused of cross-dressing, but his case shares some key elements with the Sang Chong paradigm, adding foxes, heterodox religion, and rebellion to the mix, and, like Sang Chong's case, that of Wang Sen later became popular in fictionalized form, being the subject of stories by Pu Songling and at least one novel.

Elite suspicion and contempt notwithstanding, fox cults do not seem to have been targeted for suppression in any systematic way during the Ming-Qing era. The subsequent Republican and Maoist regimes did attempt to suppress animal cults, which they denigrated as "feudal superstition," although their efforts seem to have failed.

Foxes and Spirit Mediums in Popular Religious Practice

Foxes have long been worshiped in a variety of local cults throughout China, but they are associated most strongly with the North China plain. For helping us understand Xing Shi's vocation as a fox spirit medium, the most directly relevant information comes from early twentieth-century ethnographic surveys of rural North China. They include, most importantly, the work of Li Weizu, who conducted his research in the 1930s on animal cults in villages just outside Beijing,[20] but also the work of several Japanese ethnographers who were active in Hebei, Shandong, and Manchuria (where most of the population is descended from peasants who migrated there from the North China plain).[21] Further research conducted in the post-Mao era shows strong continuities in beliefs and ritual practices, and, today, there is a lively commerce online in images and statues of sacred animals, including the fox, so this tradition appears to be thriving and to have spread well beyond its village roots.[22]

The fox is considered the most important of the "four great households" (*sidamen*): "lineages" of sacred animals or "transcendents" (*xian*) that continue to be worshiped widely in rural North China. The other three are the weasel, the hedgehog, and the snake.[23] In some communities, a fifth animal is added, with the rat and the rabbit both being common. As in literary discourse, these spirits are understood to be ordinary animals that have acquired transcendent powers over a long period of self-cultivation, but the sexual vampire trope appears to be a literati fantasy that does not feature in actual religious beliefs and rituals. Fox spirits can certainly cause mischief and especially illnesses, but they also can become patrons who protect and assure the prosperity of their beneficiaries. All are shape-shifters, being able to appear in either animal or human form, as either men or women, and it is considered polite never to refer to them directly as animals. Instead, they are to be addressed by their human surnames, the fox's surname being "Hu," which is a homonym for the word for fox, *hu*: polite terms of address include "Elder Grandfather Hu" (*Hu Laotaiye*), "Transcendent Great Aunt Hu" (*Hu Erxiangu*), and the like.[24] In the painted images used for worship, they are usually depicted as elderly men or women and are dressed in a manner similar to imperial officials.[25]

Regarding fox worship in practice, the ethnographers distinguish several different dimensions: organized cults based in temples, where foxes and other animal deities were worshiped primarily as gods of wealth (often in a secondary capacity to other, dominant deities); small shrines maintained by individual households in order to propitiate a local fox who will bring good fortune to the family but might otherwise cause trouble; and the channeling of fox spirits by mediums to provide healing and other services to people in need. The same basic patterns were found for the other principal animal deities in North China.

In Hebei, mediums who channeled animal spirits were (and continue to be) known as *xiangtou* ("incense masters"), *dingxiang de* ("those who serve as a medium with incense"), or *kan xiang de* ("those who look at incense"). Nobody *chose* to become a medium—rather, the animal spirits selected their own mediums, usually one for each, with whom they developed an intense, personal relationship. As Li Weizu puts it, "The incense master is the servant of the animal spirit."[26] This relationship had to be directly negotiated by the animal spirit with the medium and, significantly, with their family as well: the spirit would possess the prospective medium and speak through their mouth directly to the family. Some fox spirits insisted on securing the approval of the patriarchal head of household before they would proceed further. If the prospective medium's family opposed the spirit's wishes, the result might be harassment, conflict, and misfortune.[27]

According to the ethnographers, most mediums for animal spirits were women, although men of low social status might also be chosen. Sometimes an individual would be chosen because of a slight mental or physical disability, which provided an opening for the spirit to gain access, and mediums are often described as unusual individuals. Thomas Dubois notes that, in the rural Hebei communities where he conducted his fieldwork, mediums exhibited a range of personality types, but that "each is noticeably different from other villagers": "Whether kindly or intimidating, *xiangtou* are recognized by others as having a particular power that makes them extraordinary. This difference is precisely the source of *xiangtou* power—and this link to the spirit world, particularly to fox spirits, is innate to that person."[28] The process of being chosen or initiated by the fox spirit often involved an illness, hallucinations, or other disturbing experience—an ordeal of some sort—which would resolve only after the chosen person yielded to the fox's will and agreed to serve it (this seems to be a universal feature of the medium or shaman experience throughout the world). The medium would then set up a simple altar in their home to worship, consisting of an image of the fox spirit and a spirit tablet, before which incense was burned and other offerings provided.[29]

The main service provided to their communities by mediums, through channeling the fox, was healing illnesses. They also performed rituals to exorcise evil forces or other animal spirits that were causing trouble, as well as divination. The fox's motivation for doing these good deeds was to accumulate merit in order to make further progress in transcendence. To engage their services, a client would visit the medium's home or invite the medium to their own home. In spirit possession and healing, there was much variation in practice both by locale and by individual mediums, but burning and "looking at" incense played a central role for all. In a typical healing ritual, a medium would burn incense to invite the spirit "to descend" (*jiangxia*) and then, once possession had taken place (literally, the spirit had "attached itself to the medium's body," *futi*), she would diagnose the problem, often while looking at incense—hence the set phrase "looking at incense and treating illnesses" (*kan xiang zhi bing*). Then the medium would provide advice and prepare medicine for the patient, with incense ashes and tea leaves being common ingredients. Sometimes the provision of advice took the form of a dialogue with the patient, in which the medium would describe the symptoms and then ask for confirmation; after the patient confirmed the accuracy of the description, the medium would proceed with further description, again asking for confirmation, and so on.[30] Some mediums, after being released from possession, could not remember what they had said or done while possessed, but others could. The medium would never explicitly ask for payment, but those who had been helped were expected to provide some sort of compensation ("incense money"), nominally to pay for offerings to the spirit.

The spectacle of a medium undergoing possession by an animal spirit could be deeply unsettling. In 1932, Ishibashi Ushio recorded his experience of consulting a male medium in Beijing for a headache. Possessed by a female weasel spirit, the medium prostrated himself and then danced about in a wild, frenzied manner, and, upon being released by the spirit, he provided Ishibashi with advice that revealed an alarmingly accurate knowledge of the ethnographer's activities over the previous several weeks.[31] More recently, Thomas Dubois has described his encounter with a fox spirit medium in rural Hebei, a woman in her forties: "Four times during our interview, she rolled her eyes back into her head and made a growling noise that we were told was the sign that she was entering a trance. For the author this was an unnerving enough sight, but for our host, an illiterate peasant woman, it was absolutely frightening."[32] Dubois observes that the medium had "a disturbing manner": "Villagers are clearly intimidated and uncomfortable" in her presence and "maintain a distance from her."[33]

Becoming a spirit medium would considerably enhance a woman's influence and status in her community, but also vis-à-vis patriarchal authority within her own household. A wife who became a medium would likely become the dominant figure in her household, with her husband being relegated to a supporting role and perhaps serving as her assistant during rituals; moreover, her services might generate significant income. According to Li Weizu, a medium "has a powerful position in his family, even if she is a female, as in fact most of them are. In ordinary rural families the wife is subordinated to her husband. A female medium however is superior to her husband."[34] This pattern is well documented for female mediums in both northern and southern China.[35] Xiaofei Kang suggests that, "in resolving conflicts and restoring order in family and community life," fox mediums actually became "an alternative source of authority in villages of North China."[36] It is unlikely that any other vocation or social role would have empowered a peasant woman to such a degree.

Xing Shi's Vocation as a Fox Spirit Medium

How, then, should we understand Xing Shi's vocation as a medium, in light of the evidence we have surveyed? First of all, I believe we should disregard the formulaic language of "pretending" and "cheating," which was routinely included in confessions of faith healing and, as we have seen, appeared in Zhang Yaoguniang's case as well. I consider it an artifact of interrogation rather than an honest expression of these healers' own motives and understanding of their religious practices.

Here we should note some important discrepancies between the two sets of confessions. According to their first confession (at the gendarmerie), Xing Shi was visited in a dream by a fox spirit in 1805, three years after they had been sold in marriage to Liu Liu. It is only then that they began serving as a medium, and, once they began, they stopped having sexual relations with Liu Liu. Liu confirmed this account in his own first confession. But, according to the second set of confessions (extracted under torture at the Board of Punishment), Xing Shi's offer to "pretend" to act as a medium was a desperate measure taken as soon as Liu Liu discovered their sex, in order to persuade Liu not to reject them. This supposedly happened shortly after they were married, within a couple of weeks at most. Of course, in their first confessions, both Xing and Liu maintained that Liu had never realized that Xing had male anatomy until they were exposed by the midwife at the gendarmerie, a full five years after they married. At the Board of Punishment, in contrast, Xing confessed (and Liu confirmed) that they had persuaded Liu not to reject them by, first, promising to serve them faithfully for the rest of their lives; second, offering to augment their income by "pretending" to act as a spirit medium; and, third, seducing Liu Liu into the joys of reciprocal anal intercourse, in which the two took turns penetrating each other.

If we set aside the confessions that were extracted under torture (to be discussed further), the original account of Xing Shi's role as a spirit medium given to the gendarmerie conforms closely to the actual religious beliefs and practices of ordinary people in North China as documented by the ethnographers a little over a century later. Xing did not choose to be a medium; rather, they were visited in a dream by a female fox spirit that had chosen them. When Xing explained this to their husband and in-laws, Liu Liu acquiesced, but his parents and brother opposed the fox spirit. Thereupon, Xing Shi "pretended to be mad and possessed by a demon, and made a wild scene in order to scare them." The upshot was *not* that Xing Shi submitted to patriarchal authority like a good daughter-in-law should; on the contrary, newly empowered by the fox, they and Liu Liu separated from the in-laws altogether and embraced their new vocation.

This account sounds very much like the confrontation between a fox spirit and their newly chosen medium's family described by ethnographer Li Weizu, in which the fox would possess the medium and speak through her to her family, to persuade them to allow her to serve. Usually, according to Li, the family would submit, but, if they refused, then conflict would ensue—and it certainly sounds like Xing Shi provoked a conflict with their in-laws. Note also the role reversal between spouses that took place: upon being chosen by the fox, Xing dominated their husband, Liu Liu, who meekly obeyed and followed them in rejecting his own parents and older brother. The end of their sexual relationship also seems to fit: for the first time since adolescence, Xing Shi took command of their own life and put an end to the pattern of being sexually used by one man after another, all through the empowering agency of the fox. As Xing Shi testified, once they began serving the fox spirit, "I just focused all my effort on looking at incense and curing illnesses."[37]

The other details related by Xing Shi also fit what we know from the ethnographers: the use of a spirit tablet and a painted image to create an altar for the fox spirit; the ritual of possession for healing illnesses, including the use of incense, the fox spirit speaking through Xing Shi, and the specific nature of the dialogue between Xing Shi and their patient ("then I would ask the sick person some vague questions, and say 'it's like that, isn't it?'"); the medicine made with tea leaves and other ingredients; and the modest amounts of "incense money" they collected in remuneration. Taking into account the fact that ritual practice varied to some degree from place to place and even between mediums, all of this rings true.[38] Note also the grateful father whose son had been cured of illness by Xing Shi, and who donated the painting and bowls for the fox spirit's altar: clearly, he did not believe that had been conned.

An obvious question is whether Xing Shi's M–F transing of gender facilitated their role as a spirit medium. There are clear parallels between the two practices. To serve as a medium is to coordinate a profound crossing of boundaries between sacred and mundane realms, as the spirit "descends" and possesses the medium, and through the medium's body communicates and acts in the human world. In various parts of China, male mediums have been known to channel female spirits or deities, and female mediums to channel male ones, and some wear the clothing of the opposite gender while conducting these rituals. In effect, these mediums undergo a temporary change of gender, as they adopt the mannerisms and speak in the voice of the possessing spirit.[39] It also seems significant that the four sacred animals were especially venerated as protective deities by three categories of gender nonconformists in North China: the eunuchs in the imperial palace, who made offerings to them twice a month (in hope of preventing cruel treatment by their masters); actors, whose profession also involved what we might consider a sort of shape-shifting, and an important subset of whom transed gender by performing female roles; and prostitutes, who worshipped fox spirits in their capacity as gods of wealth.[40]

In many other societies, gender variant individuals have played special ritual roles and may be credited with sacred qualities, although, paradoxically, they may also be stigmatized. Famous examples include the hijras of South Asia, many of whom today identify either as transgender or as members of a third gender. In India, most hijras are "phenotypic men who wear female clothing and, ideally, renounce sexual desire and practice by undergoing a sacrificial emasculation—that is, an excision of the penis and testicles—dedicated to the goddess Bedhraj Mata. Subsequently they are believed to be endowed with the power to confer fertility on newlyweds or newborn children."[41] Hijras often live in groups at Hindu temples, and one of their most important traditional roles is to dance and perform music at private homes to bless the birth of a son. But many other hijras live in poverty and survive through sex work. Another example is the people in some Native American cultures who identify as "two-spirit." This term refers broadly to those who adopt the social and/or sexual roles usually associated with the opposite sex, as well as some who might now be considered intersex. In some Native American cultures, people with these special qualities may become shamans or healers.[42]

It is an open question, however, whether Xing Shi's transing of gender explicitly informed how their community and patients saw their role as spirit medium, because it is clear that Xing Shi sought to keep their anatomy secret and feared exposure. We know this because, in Xing Shi's first confession, they explained their move from a location outside the Chaoyang Gate to Taojiawan as having been motivated by fear that a neighbor woman Wang Du Shi had discovered their male genitals while plucking their facial hair. It seems unlikely, therefore, that Xing Shi would have openly advertised their transing of gender. On the other hand, we also know that by the time of their arrest, at least some observers believed that Xing Shi looked like a man dressed as a woman—after all, that is why they were arrested (although no one from their community turned them in). Generally speaking, mediums were perceived as unusual and even strange people whose distinctive affect and behavior denoted special powers. It is conceivable then that Xing Shi's androgynous or masculine quality was understood in these terms and was perceived as enhancing their ritual efficacy.

More likely, for Xing Shi themself, their role in channeling a female fox spirit aligned in a meaningful way with their transing of gender, as two extraordinary abilities that paralleled and confirmed each other. Xing Shi's (male) body already served as a vessel for a woman's persona; it seems a logical next step for it to serve as the vehicle for a female spirit to become manifest in the world. Possession by the fox would in turn have confirmed Xing Shi in their role as a woman. We can speculate that becoming a medium "completed" Xing Shi and helped give them the confidence to take command of their own life for the first time.

How the Confessions Changed

In Xing Shi's initial confession at the Gendarmerie, they provided only a bare-bones account of how they came to present as a woman: "Hong Da called me back to live with him, and he, too, sodomized me. Then he told me to grow out my hair and count myself as his wife (*jiao wo liule toufa, suan ta nüren*)."[43] This most laconic of statements—it is not really an explanation—raises more questions than it answers. Why did Xing agree to move in with Hong Da? Was their relationship mutual or exploitative? Above all, why did Hong "tell" Xing to adopt women's attire and pose as his wife? Did this momentous transition in any way reflect Xing's own identity or agency?

The implication of the first confession is that Xing was simply following Hong Da's instructions, perhaps because they had no choice. It may be that for Xing to move out of the boot shop and into Hong Da's home represented an improvement in their condition: they exchanged a precarious livelihood that depended on submitting to an exploitative sexual relationship (being sodomized by Li Si) for a more secure and possibly less distasteful situation. We cannot be sure. The statement provides no rationale for what is represented as Hong's decision that Xing change into women's attire and act as his wife. What we do know is that the couple stayed together for twelve more years, during which time Xing Shi presented as a woman. Moreover, by the time Hong sold Xing in marriage, the couple were concealing the fact that Xing had male anatomy and simply presenting them as a woman.

Xing Shi's second confession at the Board of Punishment presents a far more detailed account that is strikingly different in emphasis and tone. Here is the board's summary:

> Hong Da persuaded Xing Da to move in with him and have illicit sex, promising in exchange to take care of his food and support him for the rest of their life (*yangshan zhongshen*). So Xing Da rejected Li Si. Then, when Xing Da turned seventeen *sui* [i.e., fifteen or sixteen years old], Hong Da saw how pretty and charming he looked (*jian qi rongmao junqiao*) and told him to grow out his hair, pierce his ears, and dress as a woman (*xufa chuan'er banzuo furen*), in order to act as Hong's wife (*zuowei qishi*), so as to facilitate their living together forever in an illicit sexual relationship (*yi bian yongyuan jiansu*), by preventing other people from finding out what was going on (*ke mian pangren kanpo*). Xing Da was young and dissolute, and infatuated with their illicit sexual relations and intimacy, and so he happily agreed (*shaonian kuangdang, lianjian qingmi, yi ji xinyuan yingyun*). Once his hair had grown out, Hong Da no longer let him go outside. So he stayed at home learning to do women's work such as sewing and embroidering, and dressed in women's clothing and accessories (*xue zuo nügong zhenzhi, chuanyong furen yishi*).[44]

According to this account—in which the board officials have used their own words to summarize Xing's confession—the proposal for Xing to adopt women's attire was a strategic act of deception, motivated by lust: Hong judged that Xing was sufficiently "pretty and charming" that they could pass, and that, if outsiders believed Xing to be both a woman and Hong's wife, then the couple would be left alone and could enjoy their illicit lust "forever." Xing is portrayed as eagerly agreeing to this proposal, because of their passionate devotion to what is portrayed as their entirely mutual sexual relationship. Again, the board: "This criminal claims that he began masquerading as a woman only because as a youth he was seduced into sodomy by Hong Da—this was not something he had planned on doing himself."[45] Presenting as a woman was a disguise, rather than a reflection of Xing's true persona: it was meant to facilitate an otherwise easily comprehensible male same-sex relationship.

Turning to Xing Shi's relationship with husband Liu Liu, the key change from the first set of confessions to the second is that Liu Liu's assertion of ignorance about Xing's male anatomy was replaced by a confession that he had known the truth all along and was a witting accomplice to Xing's masquerade. But the second set of confessions also portrays their sexual relationship in dramatically different terms from the first. In Xing Shi's initial confession, they portrayed themself as an object of the desires and actions of others: "Li Si sodomized me"; "Hong Da called me back to live with him, and he, too, sodomized me"; "Liu Liu believed me, and so he sodomized me."[46] According to the first confessions, since Liu had never discovered Xing's sex, it is clear that Xing's sexual role (while it lasted) was entirely receptive: far from penetrating Liu, Xing did everything they could to prevent Liu from learning that they had a penis.

In contrast, the second set of confessions reveals what I believe to be the interrogators' systematic effort to cast Xing in an active role as a lecherous seducer and deceiver vis-à-vis Liu Liu. This is what the board had to settle for in lieu of Xing confessing that they had debauched women. According to this scenario, Xing's relationship with Hong Da was effectively that of disciple to master, who initiated them into a passionate sexual relationship and into masquerading in women's attire. This disguise enabled Xing to marry Liu Liu, insinuating themself into Liu's home and bed, and then, in effect, Xing debauched Liu by first persuading him to substitute anal for vaginal intercourse, and next, after revealing their anatomy, by seducing Liu into submitting to anal penetration himself. Xing's relationship with Liu Liu (as portrayed by the board) was highly unconventional for its sexual reciprocity and therefore would have been viewed as bizarre. As discussed in chapter 4, sexual roles in male-male relations were heavily gendered according to a stereotyped hierarchy of penetrator versus penetrated, so the alternation between sexual roles by male partners would have implied a switching or even transing of gender roles as well.[47]

Here, I believe, we can discern an echo of the sexual predator paradigm as well as the topos of the fox as a vampiric shape-shifter. At first, Liu was understandably shocked to discover that his bride was really "a man." But Xing bewitched Liu with the taboo pleasures of being penetrated and thus suborned him into accepting Xing as "wife" and hiding the truth from his parents and older brother. As Xing came to dominate Liu and to set the agenda for their relationship, it is as if the spouses traded genders, with Xing casting themself in the man's social and sexual role. The logical conclusion of this corrupting seduction was to reduce Liu to the role of wife, passively acquiescing to Xing's scheme to act as a spirit medium and meekly obeying Xing in defying and abandoning his own parents.

There is no way to ascertain the exact truth of this case, except for the fact that we have two very different sets of confessions, with the second set having been extracted under torture. Even under torture, Xing Shi denied having had sex with women, and Liu Liu backed them up. But on many other points their confessions did change—and all of these changes conveniently tended to confirm the biases and preconceptions of the judiciary, as we have already seen with regard to Xing Shi's vocation as spirit medium. In short, the second set of confessions represents the Board of Punishment's effort to coax from the tortured defendants a narrative that would make sense according to what the interrogators already believed about M–F cross-dressing and spirit mediums.

It may seem hard to believe that, for five years, Liu never discovered that Xing had male anatomy, given the fact of their sexual intimacy. Certainly, the Gendarmerie and the Board of Punishment refused to believe it, and in the end the board managed to secure confessions that confirmed their skepticism. On the other hand, Xing Shi seems to have presented very persuasively as a woman, at least when they first married Liu. The matchmakers who arranged the wife sale apparently never suspected the truth, nor did Liu Liu's parents and brother, who lived with Xing for over two years. Also, if Liu accepted Xing Shi's story that they could not engage in vaginal intercourse and was willing to perform anal intercourse instead, then it seems plausible that Xing might have been able, in the dark, to conceal their genitalia.

If that is what happened, then the case is not unique. Take the example of the disgraced French diplomat Bernard Boursicot (immortalized by David Henry Hwang's play *M. Butterfly*), who over a period of nearly twenty years carried on a romantic and sexual relationship with the male actor of Peking opera Shi Peipu, who was actually working for the Chinese intelligence service. Shi persuaded Boursicot that he was in fact a woman who had been raised as a boy to satisfy his father's wish for a son. Boursicot believed his lover to be a woman—even though Shi generally dressed and presented as a man—and their lovemaking over many years did nothing to dispel this belief. Apparently, this activity took place in the dark, while Shi remained partly clothed, and Shi always took the initiative in guiding the placement of Boursicot's penis. During this time, Boursicot was induced to convey classified documents to Chinese agents, and it was only after both men's arrest on espionage charges in 1983 that he finally learned that Shi Peipu was a man—and he refused to believe it until being allowed to examine Shi's body himself, evidently for the first time.[48]

One also recalls the horrific murder of the young Californian transwoman Gwen Araujo in 2002 by four men whom she believed to be her friends, and to whom she had not divulged her transgender identity. According to their trial testimony, two of these men had had sex with Araujo multiple times, but it was only after several weeks that they began to suspect she might not be a cisgender woman. When her partners wanted to have vaginal intercourse, she claimed to be menstruating and would offer anal intercourse or fellatio instead, and when they tried to touch her genitals, she covered them and pushed their hands away. In the end, they discovered the truth by forcibly examining her, and then they murdered her.[49]

Although all of the newspaper *Shenbao*'s reporting must be taken with a healthy dose of salt, it includes many stories of gender-transing for the purpose of marriage fraud that suggest a similar degree of gullibility on the part of naive husbands. Some of these stories, although presented as unembellished news, read very much like tales from the genre of the strange. Many report a version of marriage fraud that resembles the practice of "falconing," in which a man would arrange a marriage for his "widowed sister-in-law" (often, in fact, his own wife), receiving a substantial brideprice for her, after which the woman would abscond, leaving the groom with "neither wife nor money" (*ren cai liang kong*). In *Shenbao*'s transgender variation on this theme, the "bride" turned out to be a man masquerading as a woman, and he would rob the groom's house when running away.[50] In at least one example (which closely resembles Sang Chong's tale), the imposter supposedly was caught while attempting to rape the head of household's wife.[51]

An especially pertinent example from *Shenbao* is a 1911 report from Zhenjiang, Jiangsu, about a *renyao* in his early twenties named Zhu Daguan who grew out his hair and masqueraded in women's attire, "scheming to seduce wives and daughters of good family (*xitu hongyou liangjia funü*)." He married an unwitting soldier named Wang.

> On the day of their wedding Zhu told Wang, "I am possessed by a messenger from the court of the underworld, so I cannot engage in intercourse (*qie yin yinsi you chaishi zai shen bu neng tongfang*). If we pollute the chthonic messenger by having intercourse, then you and

I cannot live a long life!" Wang replied, "But if this messenger never leaves you, will we have to live our entire lives without ever having intercourse (*qi wo fuqi yisheng bu neng tongfang hu*)?" Zhu assured Wang, "If it doesn't go away within a year, then I will get you a concubine."

The newspaper reports that Wang felt suspicious, but his bride was otherwise devoted to his happiness, and it turned out that being possessed by the chthonic messenger enabled Zhu to make a lot of money "telling fortunes" (*mai bu*), all of which they turned over to Wang. Later, an observant official who was checking household registrations became suspicious of Zhu, who was examined and found to have male anatomy. According to *Shenbao*, the police gave Zhu a severe beating and paraded them in a cangue to the four gates of the county seat, "as a warning to shameless people." Then Zhu was turned over to the county magistrate, who ordered them put to death, "in order to uphold public morality." The newspaper closes by reporting that husband Wang was inconsolable and refused to face "the truth" that his wife had been a man:

> This pair of male mandarin ducks could not "share the pleasure of fish in water" (*yu shui zhi huan* [i.e., conjugal intercourse]); nevertheless they were affectionately "stuck together like glue on lacquer" (*jiao qi zhi tou*). But now that the truth is out, Wang is so shocked that he can neither sleep nor eat—it is as if his beautiful wife had died and he is in mourning, to the point of losing his senses! His commanding officer has both scolded and consoled him, but without effect—he remains trapped in his own delusions. As the saying goes, "A fool fools himself" (*yuren zi yu*)—but Wang can also be pitied.

Wang bears more than a little resemblance to the hapless diplomat Bouriscot.

To reiterate, given *Shenbao*'s freewheeling approach to "the news," there is no way to know what really happened in this case. But it seems at least possible that the bare bones of the *Shenbao* story are true—that a gender-transing medium who presented as a woman married a husband who did not realize they had male anatomy. Of course, both the Zhenjiang authorities and *Shenbao* interpreted that scenario in terms of the Sang Chong paradigm: Zhu's sole purpose in "masquerading as a woman" must have been to seduce "wives and daughters of good family."[52]

Returning to Xing Shi's case: all things considered, I am inclined to believe their first set of confessions, which were produced before they endured torture. I believe that Liu Liu probably never realized that Xing Shi was an anatomical male, until they were exposed by the midwife at the Gendarmerie, and that the most plausible way to understand their relationship is through Xing Shi's successful transing of gender, which culminated in their role as a genuine fox spirit medium.[53]

Xing Shi's Fictional Afterlife

Xing Shi was put to death in 1807. But, like Sang Chong and Wang Sen before them, they, too, had a fictional afterlife. In 1850, the writer Wu Chichang published a tale entitled "The Cross-Dressing sorcerer Xing Da (*Yaoren Xing Da*).[54] The tale appeared in a sequel to Wu's earlier miscellany, *Gossip at the Inn* (*Chuanghu xianhua*, 1839), which belongs to the genre of "the strange." Wu Chichang claims to have based his tale on a record of the actual legal case, which was shared by a friend who "works in the judiciary" (*ren xingcao zhe*). This claim may be true, as Wu's tale does reveal a familiarity with the Board of Punishment's ruling, although it also diverges from the board's account in significant ways.[55] But note that this claim echoes that made by Lu Can three centuries before, that his account of Sang Chong was transcribed from an actual record of the case that he saw at a friend's house. As we shall see, Wu's rendering of Xing Shi's case echoes the fictional treatments of Sang Chong in other interesting respects—but it also draws on the topos of the fox.

Wu Chichang's title regenders Xing Shi as masculine by using their original name, "Xing Da" (as is standard in the case reports, too), but Wu also identifies Xing as a *yaoren*, which I translate as "cross-dressing sorcerer." This term (and its variant, *renyao*) was often applied to Sang Chong; it implies a quasi-demonic, feminine power to bewitch and seduce. This characterization of Xing sets the tone for the tale as a whole.

Wu's account begins as follows: "At the age of seventeen *sui*, Xing Da of Beijing, who had been orphaned in childhood, possessed an extraordinary beauty surpassing that of the finest girl (*yanli guo hao nü*). Having no employment, he lived in great poverty." Hong Da is described as "modestly prosperous," living on his own without parents or wife, and having "the obsession of Longyang" (*Longyang zhi pi*)—a literary reference to male homoerotic desire. One day, Hong happens to catch sight of Xing on the road and is dumbstruck: "This is the most bewitching beauty under Heaven! I cannot miss this rare opportunity!" So he follows Xing back to their home and sees "a run-down ruin with collapsing walls, lonely and completely deserted." Hong accosts Xing, who is demure, shy, and embarrassed, "like a young girl who meets her husband for the first time" (*ruo nüzi chu jian liangren*). Seeing Xing's poverty, Hong invites them back to his house: "If younger brother is willing to follow me home, then you can dress warmly and eat your fill." Blushing, Xing agrees and accompanies Hong to his home.

Hong adorns Xing with fresh clothes, feeds them a sumptuous meal, and in all ways shows the most attentive hospitality. As they drink wine together, Xing becomes tipsy, and their cheeks flush in the most alluring way. As a result, "Hong could no longer control his desire, and, embracing Xing, he begged him to make love." Xing answers him thus: "Older brother's generosity is limitless! I am not made of wood, so how could I not feel affection for you? I am willing to repay you with my body. My only fear is that in the future, 'after I've lost my looks your affection will wane' (*se shuai ai shi*), and I will be abandoned once again, alone and in poverty, with nothing to show for it except the scorn of having lost my virtue. It would be better to stop before we go too far!"[56] But Hong has a plan: "I lust after beauty, and I make no distinction between male and female. If younger brother is willing to grow your hair long and do it up in a woman's hairstyle, and agrees to follow me until the end of our days, then I will make you my wife. I swear I will never marry any other or change my mind!" Xing moves in with Hong, and when they grow out their hair, pierce their ears, and dress as a woman, "the result was on par with the greatest beauty in the realm" (*yanran guose*). Then Xing practices women's work, demonstrating "extraordinary skill" at sewing and embroidery. Xing obeys all of Hong's desires, and Hong's passion for them grows by the day.

By this point in Wu Chichang's narrative, any reader familiar with the genre of the strange should be on the alert, for the portrayal of Xing Da hints at a vampiric fox or similar demon. Xing has no history or context, aside from the bare statement that they were orphaned in childhood. There is no mention of Xing's mother bringing them to Beijing or working as a seamstress, or of Xing's employment at the boot-making shop, where Li Si had sodomized them. Instead, Xing suddenly appears on the scene, as if out of nowhere, at the age of seventeen *sui*, ready for their "random" encounter with Hong Da. With no occupation or livelihood, how have they survived all this time? The lonely tumble-down ruin where Xing lives alone also provokes suspicion: it is exactly the kind of place frequented by foxes and ghosts in *zhiguai* tales.[57] But foxes also seek to encroach on and take up residence in dwellings occupied by humans, which, of course, is what Xing ends up doing by moving in with Hong Da.[58] Xing's beauty is described in such excessive terms as to suggest something superhuman. At the same time, Xing is depicted as shyly demure, but that image hardly accords with their alacrity in accepting a strange man's hospitality—not to mention agreeing to submit to sodomy and then to switch gender and pledge lifelong fidelity as this man's wife, all within just a few hours of meeting him for the first time! Then there is Xing's seemingly magic ability not only to pass as a woman but also to become the most beautiful woman of all and to master the classic skills of women's work effortlessly. Hong's behavior, in turn, exceeds anything that might reasonably be explained by lust: he is simply bewitched at the sight of this beautiful boy, and his subsequent actions suggest a degree of infatuation verging on madness.

Readers of Ming-Qing fiction know that men must beware of unattached beauties who are encountered by chance in public spaces, and who seem open to their advances. By the conventions of "the strange," Hong Da has walked into a trap with his eyes wide shut. On the other hand, Xing's apparent devotion to Hong Da suggests the fictional scenario of the virtuous fox spirit who becomes a faithful concubine to their human companion.[59] Perhaps this tale has a happy ending after all? Alas, no: "Those who are passionate for male love (*hao nanse zhe*), inevitably suffer illness of the limbs and eyes, and if they damage themselves through daily indulgence, an early death is inevitable." Within three years, Hong's business fails, his eyesight dims, and he becomes half paralyzed. According to the actual case record, Hong Da had fallen ill with a "blood spitting disease" that was not connected to Xing Shi. In contrast, the fictional account blames Hong's compulsive overindulgence in sex with Xing for the collapse of both his finances and his health—again, calling to mind the topos of the vampiric fox.

Enter Liu Liu, who is described as a handsome man and Hong Da's sworn brother, to whom Hong has introduced Xing Shi as his "younger sister." Liu lusts after Xing, and Hong is actually willing to share, but Xing Shi refuses to cooperate and chastely avoids Liu's company, retiring to an inner room whenever he visits. When Hong Da's illness worsens, however, Liu proposes to marry Hong's "sister," and Hong urges Xing Shi to agree:

> I cannot recover from this illness. You are already attired as a woman, and your voice, appearance, and gestures are all those of a fine young girl. Originally, we pledged to spend our lives together, but now I must abandon you halfway. You may pine for me, but there is no such thing as a man preserving his chastity; you could return to dressing as a man, but the fact is, you have already lost your original character (*benlai mianmu*), and, anyway, you have never learned to do any work appropriate for a man. In that case, you would starve to death, and it would all be my fault! Even if you were to bear me no grudge, I would never be able to rest in peace, even in death. All things considered, it would be best for you to take advantage of Liu's affection and marry him. I will be able to use your bride-price to pay for my funeral, and you will secure a place for yourself.

Xing protests: "But I am not a real woman (*wo fei zhennü*), and if he takes me as his wife but then discovers the truth, will he ever accept me?" Hong: "Every man lusts after beauty! If he discovers the truth, you must handle it skillfully. Since he adores you, there's no way he will ruin the situation. Anyway, Liu is just like me, and that's the only reason I'm willing to entrust you to him." Xing agrees, the marriage is set, and Liu's parents are delighted at his lovely, demure bride.

Xing Shi prepares for the wedding night "by binding up his scrotum and penis" (*jiang shennang qianyang baoqi*) to conceal them, and, when it is time to consummate the marriage, "he contorted his buttocks to put his anus in position to be penetrated" (*quju qi gu yi tunqiao shou yin*). Liu is deceived. But, as the days go by, he becomes ever more passionate and finally insists on stripping his bride naked in order to enjoy her body completely—". . . and the thing was revealed." Liu reacts with predictable shock, but Xing embraces him and, "using all his charm," declares: "If you let me go, you will never find a woman who surpasses me!" Liu raises the obvious objection: "But the purpose of taking a wife is to have sons—can you give birth? (*qu qi wei zi ye, ru neng shengyu hu*) My family has only enough to get by, I can't afford to marry again. If I keep you, won't I be cutting off my line of descent?" Xing: "Fear not! I have a magic technique passed down from my ancestors, that enables me to look at incense and cure illnesses. If you hire someone to paint a picture of a female spirit (*nüxian*) for me to make offerings to, then the spirit will possess me as her medium (*xianren futi*), and my cures for illnesses will be miraculously effective. As word spreads, our business will prosper, and when we earn enough money, you can take a concubine—I won't stop you."[60] Liu agrees. But then he asks, "You have a man's body—how can you stand to play this sexual role?" Xing "turned on all his charm" and said,

> If only men knew the taste of this ecstasy [i.e., of being penetrated anally], they would all seek to marry themselves as wives to husbands (*kong tianxia nanzi zhi ci wei, renren yu jia zhangfu*)! In fact, I am not the only male who takes pleasure in doing this. If you don't believe me, why not try it and see? Anyway, what happens in the bedchamber is unknown to outsiders—what's to stop us from giving each other pleasure (*guizhong shi wairen bu zhi, hefang huxiang wei le ye*)?

Enchanted, Liu follows Xing's suggestion, and, from then on, they take turns "acting as husband to husband and then wife to husband, acting as wife to wife and then husband to wife: the two pleasures blended together, and their marital passion became ever more intense."

Meanwhile, Xing's practice as a medium prospers, as word spreads that "a beautiful woman was acting as a doctor," and each day they earn "many strings of cash." But a local constable who "drooled with lust for women" (*chuixian fuse*) hears about this beautiful spirit medium and, feigning illness, summons Xing Shi to treat him. As soon as Xing enters the room, the constable, intent on rape, grabs them and gropes their crotch: "To his astonishment, Xing was a fully equipped male!" Xing begs for mercy and offers to let the constable sodomize them and also to pay a hefty bribe. But the constable refuses, saying that "my reward for arresting a cross-dressing sorcerer (*yaoren*) will be much greater than whatever you offer!" But also, "in this village there is no shortage of young and beautiful women, and they are all either my relatives or my friends. If I allow you to remain here, none of them will be able to preserve their virtue (*jie bude zuo wanren yi*)!" The constable arrests Xing and Liu and turns them in, and their punishments in the story are the same as those actually meted out to them.

Here, we can discern a number of parallels with Sang Chong and further hints of the supernatural. Liu's discovery of Xing's sex can be compared to the moment of revelation in the Sang Chong story, when he has managed to insinuate himself into the female quarters and is sleeping with the daughter of the house, to whom he reveals his sex. At this point, she either yields to seduction or is subdued with drugs and black magic, and, after Sang has had his way with her, she keeps his secret out of shame. The parallel is that Xing also gets their way: instead of being resisted, Xing overcomes Liu's objections and seduces him into keeping their secret and accepting them as a wife, and then they turn the tables by inducing Liu to submit to penetration. In this respect, the fictional version follows the spirit if not the letter of the second set of confessions found in the board's report on the case.

Xing's exposure by the constable is an obvious reference to Sang Chong, who was also exposed and turned in to the authorities by a would-be rapist. But the constable's declaration that he cannot allow Xing to remain at large because the young women of the community will be at risk indicates that he assumes Xing to be a paradigmatic cross-dressing sexual predator—in fact, he characterizes Xing as a *yaoren*, echoing the story's title. Neither of these details appear in the actual case record.

Finally, according to Xing Shi's first confession, they were chosen as medium by a fox spirit who visited in a dream, and this took place after three years of marriage to Liu Liu. The fictional portrayal instead follows the basic story line of the second confession, except that here Xing claims to have inherited "a magic technique passed down from my ancestors, that enables me to look at incense and cure illnesses." This statement only adds to their mystery. What "ancestors" are these? Will Xing channel a spirit, as they also say, or is Xing themself perhaps such a spirit?

Wu Chichang may have had another fictional scenario in mind when he refashioned Xing Shi's case into this story. One of the best-known works of fiction inspired by Sang Chong is Pu Songling's tale "Renyao," which Judith Zeitlin has translated as "The Human Prodigy."[61] This tale traces the fate of one of Sang Chong's many disciples. An attractive young woman who claims to have fled her in-laws' abuse (not unlike Xiong Mumu discussed in chapter 2) arrives in a community, takes lodgings with an older widow, and makes herself available to provide nighttime massages to cure ladies' ailments. A neighbor man named Ma Wanbao lusts after her and has his wife engage the young woman for a massage. In the dark, Ma trades places with his wife, intending to rape the masseuse, and, when she makes a pass at him, Ma seizes her, and they simultaneously discover that they both have male genitalia! Ma seizes the imposter and forces him to confess: it turns out that he is a disciple of Sang Chong's named Wang Erxi ("Double Joy"), who has already debauched a total of sixteen women (he explains this "low" number by saying that he is just getting started). Ma considers turning Erxi in for prosecution, but is aroused by his beauty, so Ma castrates him instead and promises to conceal him from the authorities as long as he serves Ma as a concubine until the end of his days. Erxi agrees, and, after he recovers from his wound, he sleeps with Ma every night and faithfully serves Ma's wife by day. Later, after Sang Chong is apprehended, a manhunt is launched for his disciples who are still at large, but, because everyone believes Erxi to be a woman, he evades justice. He and the couple live happily ever after.[62] In this way, the predator Wang Erxi is trapped by a more powerful predator, Ma Wanbao, in an echo of how Sang Chong himself was caught by his would-be rapist. But Ma rationalizes the situation by castrating Erxi: in effect, castration "disarms" Erxi, and he is domesticated both figuratively and literally, being transformed from a sexual predator into a model concubine.

An even more literal sex change takes place in Li Yu's tale "Nan Meng mu jiaohe san qian" (A male Mencius's mother), when the faithful youth You Ruilang castrates himself in order to serve his older lover, the widower Xu Jifang, as his concubine. The castration wound miraculously heals in the form of a vagina, making conventional intercourse possible, and Xu encourages the youth to begin dressing as a woman.[63] In addition, Ruilang binds his feet and changes his name to "Ruiniang" (*lang* meaning "young man," *niang* meaning "daughter") so that it sounds like a woman's name. As Sophie Volpp explains, "You then begins to play the role of the paradigmatic virtuous woman, supporting Xu in his studies by his needlework and raising Xu's child."[64] Emulating the famous tale of Mencius's mother, Ruiniang moves house three times in order to defend himself and Xu's son from sexual predators.

In both tales, male anatomy is posed as an obstacle to the fulfillment of a woman's sexual and social roles. The solution is what amounts to gender confirmation surgery, which realigns the problematic bodies appropriately. For Erxi, who is already masquerading very convincingly as a woman for the purpose of rape and seduction, castration neutralizes that predatory threat and relegates him to a penetrated sexual role. As Judith Zeitlin explains, Erxi's castration can be seen as "a perverse Confucian 'rectification of names.' "[65] His M–F transition is completed when he seamlessly adapts to the social role of concubine. For Ruilang/niang, castration arrests the development of masculine secondary sexual characteristics and underscores his renunciation of a man's sexual and social roles in order to serve his lover for life; changing into women's clothes and developing a vagina simply complete that transition. Despite their different starting points, both Erxi and Ruilang end up as exemplary women.

No such neat surgical resolution occurs in Wu Chichang's fictional rendering of Xing Shi, but it is similarly preoccupied with the problem of sexed bodies that do not properly align with gendered sexual and social roles. The tale ends with the author's editorial comment in the form of a mock "judgment" (*pan*), in which he expresses his shock at the couple's behavior and his approval of their punishment. He begins with a series of hackneyed classical allusions to male love, comparing Xing to famous male favorites of yore. The import of these allusions is that male love is nothing new and, indeed, has had famous devotees ever since ancient times. But then the author changes tone: "For a man to exchange his attire for a woman's *temporarily* is something known to happen on occasion; but for a man to do so *permanently* is something rarely seen in all of history! For this mad youth to indulge in such deviance was truly deserving of death (*ying zao ming ji*)." Wu Chichang then zeroes in on Liu Liu's role in the tale:

> As soon as Liu Liu realized that Xing was male not female (*ming bian cixiong*), he should have exploded with anger. How could he instead agree to alternate between male and female sexual roles (*hu wei pinmu*)? . . . If they take turns playing husband, then there is no distinction in rank between *yin* and *yang* (*bi zhangfu, wo zhangfu, yinyang diti*). "Do unto others as you would have them do unto you," as the saying goes, so they "compensate" each other, one after the other (*chu hu er, fan hu er, qianhou xiang chang*). If such behavior is concealed in the bedchamber, then you may be able to get away with it and evade the law. But daring to show it off before the community is unforgivable! The law treats such deviants as *yaoren*, and they should be strangled; their accomplices should be sentenced to military slavery.

Here, Wu Chichang emphasizes that gender roles are supposed to align with sexed bodies in a way that confirms and supports normative social hierarchies. Anatomical males are supposed to dress and present themselves as men. But, also, the sexual roles of penetrator and penetrated are reserved to male and female, respectively—and, by extension, even for same-sex couples, that division of sexual labor should conform to a clearly gendered hierarchy between a dominant masculine partner and a subordinate feminine one. The classical tales of male love alluded to in Wu Chichang's "judgment" all certainly conform in this way: they all concern the passion of male rulers for their young male concubines, so that sexual roles conformed to status hierarchy.

In his "judgment," Wu Chichang says nothing about Xing Shi's vocation as spirit medium and healer. Moreover, Wu's condemnation of the couple (however tongue-in-cheek it may be) focuses not on male same-sex love per se, although his attribution of Hong Da's illness to sexual exhaustion suggests that he does not exactly approve of it. Instead, he zeroes in on the two greater taboos that this couple have violated: Xing's permanent adoption of a woman's attire, and Liu's agreement to alternate sexual roles. In both instances, it is the couple's willful blurring of gender roles that attracts Wu's condemnation. It would have been bad enough for the couple to indulge in such deviance in the secrecy of their bedchamber, but to pose publicly and interact with their community as husband and wife was simply going too far.

Making Sense of Xing Shi

The purpose of Wu Chichang's fictionalization was to entertain his readers, but at the same time—and, in part, for the same purpose—it represents an attempt to make sense of Xing Shi's life story. It does so by modifying and embellishing the story in ways that conform to the conventions of the *zhiguai* genre. Similarly, I have argued, the second set of confessions extracted with torture represents the Board of Punishment's effort to make sense of Xing Shi's story, by making it conform to the conventions of the cross-dressing predator paradigm that informed judicial thinking. Behind these efforts lay the reality, which can be glimpsed only imperfectly through the filtering screen of the surviving sources, of Xing Shi's transgender life. Neither the Board of Punishment nor Wu Chichang was capable of understanding that reality on its own terms. Therefore, their efforts to make sense of it required the narrative distortions we have seen.

Xing Shi certainly transed gender—that is, they were a transgender person according to Susan Stryker's expansive definition, which favors practice over identity and emphasizes movement away from the gender assigned at birth without assuming any particular motive or endpoint for that movement.[66] But the question of Xing Shi's own subjective identity remains open and cannot be answered with any certainty. Two possibilities occur to me, and, to be clear, they are not mutually exclusive. First, if Xing Shi were alive today, they might well identify as a transwoman according to our current understanding of that concept. But Xing Shi's account of their upbringing—if it can be called that—suggests a second scenario that must also be considered.

By their own testimony, Xing Shi's entire sexual experience had been with men. Beginning in adolescence, they had three consecutive sexual partners that we know of: from age fourteen to seventeen *sui*, Li Si; from age seventeen to twenty-nine *sui*, Hong Da; and from age twenty-nine until their arrest at thirty-four *sui*, Liu Liu. The relationship with Li Si appears to have been a straightforward quid pro quo: Li secured employment for the child and in exchange used them for sex—and, by definition, any sexual relationship between an adult man and a child of that age is abusive, at least by modern standards. (To be clear, fourteen *sui* is the equivalent of twelve or thirteen years old.) Xing Shi's relationship with Hong Da may have been based on a similar quid pro quo: Xing was already in Hong's debt for his having interceded with Li Si to take them off the street, and, later, Hong provided Xing with a home and support (and escape from Li Si) in exchange for sex. Finally, Hong Da told them to start presenting as a woman in order to pass as his wife and thenceforth confined them indoors. This momentous decision is described in both confessions as having been Hong Da's initiative, which was (according to the second confession) motivated by a desire to disguise their same-sex relationship as a marriage of husband and wife, in order to facilitate its indefinite continuance.

Was it also an expression of Xing Shi's own identity and agency? Given the limitations of the surviving evidence, we cannot be sure. But Hong's entire treatment of Xing Shi up to that moment might be interpreted as the grooming of an abused child by their molester. (Note that seventeen *sui*, the age at which Xing Shi transitioned, is the equivalent of fifteen or sixteen years old.) From this point of view, Hong Da's mandate for Xing Shi to present as a woman and remain at home doing women's work may be interpreted as a way to limit their movements and restrict their contact with other people—a well-known strategy of abusive partners to control their victims.

By the time Hong Da sold Xing Shi in marriage to Liu Liu, Xing had been living as a woman and as Hong's wife for twelve years; moreover, Hong had what was likely a fatal illness, and, with no other means of support, Xing would have had little choice but to cooperate in the fraudulent wife sale. Xing Shi must have been desperate to convince Liu Liu that they were a woman, at least at first, in order to avoid being thrown out on the street or even prosecuted for cross-dressing and marriage fraud.

But, regardless of which set of confessions one believes, it is clear that serving as a medium for the fox spirit transformed Xing Shi's life and their relations with others. It was a liberation of sorts. According to the first set of confessions, from that moment on, Xing Shi ceased having sexual relations with their husband, Liu Liu, and, according to both confessions, when their in-laws refused to accept their role as a medium, Xing Shi and Liu Liu cut off relations with them and moved out. Xing's healing vocation gave them unprecedented mobility, free from patriarchal scrutiny, as they visited and treated their patients. This centrifugal movement was the opposite of the cloistering that had attended their transition under the supervision of Hong Da.

From then on, Xing Shi seems to have dominated their marital relationship with Liu Liu, becoming its chief earner and decision-maker. Serving the fox spirit was an empowering move that reversed the hierarchy of their marriage and finally brought an end to the sexual objectification and abuse that had been a constant theme in their life since early adolescence. Moreover, serving as a medium seems to have been the moment when Xing Shi finally took control of their own gender identity, as they transed gender by channeling a female fox deity in order to treat women's illnesses.

CHAPTER VI

The Truth of the Body

The masculine principle of Heaven (*qian*) makes fathers, and the feminine principle (*kun*) makes mothers. But there are five kinds of deformed males (*feinan*) who cannot become fathers, and five kinds of deformed females (*feinü*) who cannot become mothers. So what are they?

—LI SHIZHEN, "ON HUMAN PRODIGIES" (*RENKUI*)

Reading the Gendered Body

Chapters 2, 4, and 5 focused on individuals who took deliberate measures to move away from the gender they had been assigned at birth. Our protagonists adopted women's names, grew out their hair and dressed it in the manner of women, and began wearing women's clothes and earrings. Xiong Mumu bound their feet, Xing Shi plucked their facial hair, and both took up healing work that was exclusive to women. For all three, the end of the road came when they were stripped and examined by court-ordered midwives, with the catastrophic consequences we have seen.

For Qing authorities, "men masquerading in women's attire" posed the fundamental problem of what to do when bodies did not align with gender roles in the expected way. In these cases, judicial attention focused on anomalous behavior, given that these people all possessed what the midwives judged to be normal male genitalia. In effect, they did not behave in the manner dictated by their sexed bodies.

This chapter expands our inquiry to explore a wider range of scenarios in which midwives and magistrates scrutinized the body in the interest of securing an orthodox order of gender and sexual relations.[1] Sometimes it was the body itself that posed problems, by failing to fulfill the duties of the assigned gender. How did the authorities make sense of anomalous

[173]

anatomy that prevented the appropriate performance of gender roles? How did they try to solve the social problems that such bodies posed? And how did they read the body for evidence of sexual history and capacity?

The Sexed Body and Social Gender

For some time now, it has been conventional to posit a clear distinction between sex and gender—sex being transcultural, biologically and genetically determined, and grounded in the body, whereas gender is socially and culturally constructed and therefore learned and performed according to varying scripts. As convenient as this sex/gender distinction may be, it has provoked intense debate about exactly where to draw the line between them, or whether it is even possible to discern a stable, unmediated category of sex (or the body) apart from discourse. The pose of extreme skepticism is exemplified by a typical comment from feminist theorist Judith Butler: "Is there a 'physical' body prior to the perceptually perceived body? An impossible question to decide."[2] Moreover, attempts to draw a simple distinction between sex and gender—let alone to link them in any sort of fixed causal relationship—tend to be confounded by the facts of transgender and intersex existence.

It seems, however, that a tentative consensus has emerged, at least among historians of gender and sexuality: while there does exist a real, physical body, it is difficult, if not impossible, to observe that body in any purely empirical or unmediated way. Thomas Laqueur's history of the shift in Western science from a one-sex model of the body to a two-sex model is foundational for this perspective.[3] The old one-sex model interpreted female reproductive organs as inverted and inferior male organs, on a vertical scale of more or less realized versions of an ideal male body. In contrast, the new two-sex model clearly identified female anatomical difference, and to our modern eyes it seems far more objective than its predecessor. Nevertheless, the scientists and doctors who articulated the new model argued that the female organs were the sources of feminine weakness, thereby establishing a new biological rationale for the social subordination of women. In this way, Laqueur shows that the shift in paradigms masked deeper continuities in the shaping of perception by gender ideology and in the use of scientific observation to rationalize social hierarchy. Although he does concede the existence of "the real, transcultural body," Laqueur concludes that "sex, like being human, is contextual. Attempts to isolate it from its discursive, socially determined milieu are as doomed to failure as the *philosophe*'s search for a truly wild child or the modern anthropologist's efforts to filter out the cultural so as to leave a residue of essential humanity."[4] Therefore, as Jeffrey Weeks has observed, it would be a mistake to treat the body as "a biological given which emits its own meaning. It must be understood instead as an ensemble of potentialities which are given meaning only in society."[5]

That socially given meaning has a strong performative dimension, since, typically, the body is judged in terms of what it is expected—or forbidden—to do. This perspective is closely associated with Butler, who has famously argued that gender comes into existence only through its performance, and to persist it must be repeatedly performed. In Butler's view, all gender performance is a kind of "drag," because there is no real gender grounded in nature. Furthermore, the need for gender to be constituted through "incessant and repeated action" opens up the possibility of incorrect performances, as well as purposeful subversion of the dominant script through parody and invention. She envisions a world of radical self-determination, in which there come into being as many genders as there are individuals to perform.[6] But her theory also implies that correct performance might be reinforced and rewarded, while incorrect performance might have to be corrected and punished. Law comes into the picture as a codifier and enforcer of correct standards.[7]

The Marital Imperative

In late imperial China, the expectation that all women marry and produce sons was the organizing principle and stable reference point for gender discourses that made the female body legible. Rates of marriage and fertility vary in different societies and historical periods, but in China, marriage at an early age (shortly after menarche, in the late teens) was a nearly universal experience for women.[8] For the vast majority, conjugal intercourse, pregnancy, and child-rearing were simply fate; these bodily constraints were real, even if imposed by society rather than nature. For women, compulsory marriage and reproduction were something like the equivalent of modern "compulsory heterosexuality," and a woman's body acquired social meaning within this circumscribed frame of reference.[9]

Thus, for example, Charlotte Furth has shown that discourses of *fuke* (women's medicine) in late imperial China simultaneously articulated two different paradigms of the body: the androgynous body of *generation* versus the specifically female body of *gestation*. The body of generation was an ideal type in which male and female principles complemented one another in a shifting balance, so that difference was a matter of degree. The body of gestation, on the other hand, emphasized female difference and materiality as sources of impurity and weakness that caused medical problems specific to women. The latter paradigm clearly reflects gender hierarchy in society, whereas the former seems to suggest timeless complementarity and equivalence. Nevertheless, even within the apparently androgynous generative body, the female essence Blood was "encompassed" by the male essence qi, in a process that consistently reestablished gender hierarchy at "ever-ascending levels"[10]; the underlying theme was the "necessary subordination of women to men in society."[11] Moreover, what linked both paradigms was the common mission of marital procreation: medical discourse treated women "primarily as childbearers," and the "primary agenda" of medicine was to "safeguard female primary vitalities and to make sure that other illnesses in fertile, pregnant and postpartum women were not prescribed for in a way that might damage their reproductive health."[12] In sum, it was women's vital role in reproducing the family that organized and motivated *fuke*.

Like medicine, law required the scrutiny of bodies for evidence, and, as we have seen, the regulation of gender roles and sexual behavior according to the Confucian family scheme was a fundamental priority for the Qing judiciary. All of the legal cases presented in this chapter somehow challenged the marital frame of reference, straining the legibility of the gendered body and the coherence of the normative categories that informed judicial reasoning. In some of these cases, it seems as if a *real* body that defies simple categorization is struggling to tear through the veil of discourse that stretches to encompass it.

We begin with "stone maidens" (*shinü*), whose anatomy rendered them incapable of conjugal intercourse; having been rejected by their husbands, they had to be placed somewhere in society. Second, we consider husbands who were rejected by their wives because problems with their penises similarly rendered them unable to consummate their marriages. A third category of anomaly was the "two-formed person" (*erxing ren*), whose apparent shape-shifting inspired some remarkable fiction in the genre of "the strange." At least some of the people in these categories would probably identify as intersex, were they alive today.

Moving beyond physical anomaly, we further explore how magistrates understood the relationship between bodies and gender roles, using the prosecution of rape as an example. The case of a Buddhist nun who was raped helps to clarify how jurists conceptualized the category of woman to include individuals outside the family who had renounced normative gender roles by eschewing marriage and procreation. I also revisit what I have written elsewhere about the plausible male rape victim.

These case studies probe the complex interweaving of bodily sex and social gender in the Qing: they provide insight into how the authorities would interpret the body in terms of what society demanded of it. Each legal judgment represents an effort to make sense of anatomy or behavior that defied the normative framework for gender performance. These cases are artifacts of normative discourse, but the body does not appear in them as a blank surface to be filled arbitrarily with words. Rather, we find midwives, magistrates, and others working to contain a disorderly world of physical anomaly and transgressive behavior within a contingent yet surprisingly elastic set of norms.

Stone Maidens

The Stone Maiden Who Became a Chaste Widow

A homicide case from Tianmen County, Hubei, memorialized in 1739, involves a poor widow named Xie Shi (nineteen *sui*) who remarried following the death of her first husband, He Hanzhang.[13] After He's death, Xie Shi had depended on relatives for support, and with their help had negotiated her second marriage, to a peasant from her husband's village named Dong Xianzhao. Problems arose when this new husband tried to consummate their marriage: as Xie Shi later testified, "Five or six days after I joined him in marriage, Dong Xianzhao tried to have intercourse with me (*jin xiaofuren de shen* [literally, 'get close to my body']), but he couldn't (*bu neng jin*), and he told me that I am a stone maiden (*shinü*). He was so unhappy that he couldn't even eat." A couple of days later, Dong went in search of one of the matchmakers, Dai Luzhi, with the intention of canceling the marriage and demanding a refund of Xie Shi's bride-price. The matchmaker was not at home, so Dong confronted his son, Dai Zhenxia (twenty *sui*). As Zhenxia later confessed, "Dong Xianzhao came over and told me that my father as matchmaker had swindled him with a stone maiden, so he wanted to cancel the marriage. I said, 'Xie Shi was married into the He family for several years, and I never heard anyone say she was a stone maiden then. Now she's been married into *your* family for only a few days—how come she's suddenly a stone maiden?'" This implied insult to Dong's masculinity—that if there were any problem in consummating the marriage, then something must be wrong with the groom, not the bride—provoked him to attack Zhenxia. In the fight that followed, Zhenxia killed Dong Xianzhao.

When this homicide came before the county magistrate, one of his first priorities was to interrogate Xie Shi. Was she really a "stone maiden"? If so, then what sort of conjugal relations had she had with her *first* husband? Xie Shi testified, "I am a stone maiden. My first husband and I were married for several years, but he didn't have intercourse with me even a single time (*meiyou jinshen yi ci* [literally, 'get close to my body'])." Note the ambiguity of her testimony: she does not say explicitly whether he even tried. The magistrate then ordered the yamen midwife to examine Xie Shi in a "private room" (*mishi*). The midwife reported: "Even a finger can't penetrate (*zhitou dou jin bu qu*) Xie Shi's lower body (*xiashen*). She is definitely a stone maiden. On her upper body, her breasts are collapsed flat (*pingta de*), like a man's breasts (*yu nanren de ru yiban*). Your Honor can see for himself."[14] Thereupon, as the magistrate wrote in his case report, "this humble official ordered Xie Shi to expose her bosom, and he personally examined her breasts, finding them exactly as described by the midwife."

The magistrate summarized this physical evidence as follows: "Xie Shi's body is that of a stone maiden (*shen xi shinü*), so she cannot engage in sexual intercourse (*bu neng renshi*)." His precise wording is significant: what he wrote, literally, is that Xie Shi "cannot engage in human activity." "Human activity" (*ren shi*) is a polite term for sexual intercourse, similar to *ren dao*—literally, "the way of being human." In this context, the term would seem to imply that conjugal relations are a definitively human activity: if one becomes human, in part, through conjugal intercourse, then Xie Shi's disability might suggest some incompleteness of her personhood.

The magistrate sentenced Dai Zhenxia to strangulation after the assizes (for "homicide in a fight") and forwarded his case up the judicial hierarchy for review (as required in all capital punishment cases). Upon reinterrogation at the provincial capital, however, Dai recanted his confession; among other things, he denied that Xie Shi was a stone maiden. For this reason, the governor ordered the case retried by the magistrate of nearby Qian-jiang County, who ordered his own midwife to "take Xie Shi to a private place where there are no other people (*wuren mi chu*) and make a careful and detailed examination of her body to find out the exact truth." She confirmed the testimony of the first midwife: "Even the tip of a finger cannot penetrate Xie Shi's lower body (*zhitouding ye bu neng ru*): she's defi-nitely a stone maiden. Both breasts are collapsed flat (*liang ru pingta*), in no way different from a male's (*yu nanzi wu yi*)."[15] In the end, Dai confessed again, and his sentence was confirmed.

Aside from solving the homicide itself, a key priority in this adjudica-tion was to determine whether the crime of marriage fraud had been com-mitted. This priority helps to explain the careful attention paid to Xie Shi's anatomy. The very first statute of the Qing code's chapter on mar-riage provides that "when male and female are betrothed, if either party has some crippling defect (*canfei*) or disease (*jibing*) . . . then the other fam-ily must be clearly informed of the facts." In such circumstances, if a bride's family committed fraud by passing her off (*wangmao*) as normal and healthy, then those responsible were liable for eighty blows of the heavy bamboo, and the bride-price would be returned; if the groom's family committed this kind of fraud, then the penalty would be increased by one degree, and they would forfeit the bride-piece they had paid; and, in either instance, the marriage would be canceled.[16]

The question, therefore, was whether those who arranged Xie Shi's mar-riage to Dong Xianzhao had known that she was a stone maiden. When the magistrate pressed Xie Shi on this point, she testified, "I knew about this secret illness (*anbing*) myself, but I never told anyone else about it." The matchmaker was pressed even harder: "Xie Shi is a stone maiden; how could you, in your capacity as matchmaker, dare to use her to swindle Dong Xianzhao?" The matchmaker answered, "This is a secret illness of a wom-an's body (*nüren shenshang de anbing*)—why on earth would I have known anything about it? If I'd known she was a stone maiden, I never would have dared to act as matchmaker and arrange for Dong Xianzhao to take her in marriage!" The magistrate also interrogated relatives of Xie Shi's first hus-band, but they had been unaware of any problem and described the cou-ple's marriage as harmonious. Thus, the magistrate concluded, "with regard to Xie Shi: her body is that of a stone maiden, but her relatives were all ignorant of this fact, and they definitely did not commit the crime of fraudulently representing a crippled person as a healthy one in order to marry her off (*yi canfei wangmao jiaren*). Therefore, the bride-price and matchmakers' fees need not be returned, and Xie Shi should be entrusted to the custody of her brother-in-law, Dong Yinzhao, to be taken home." This time, the judgment was approved on review.

In other words, Xie Shi's marriage was legal, and so she should return to her rightful place in her husband's family. What made this judgment tenable was the convenient fact that this stone maiden was now a widow, which solved the social problem raised by her vaginal impenetrability. Everyone involved clearly saw Xie Shi's condition as a disability that made it impossible for her to perform the sexual and reproductive roles of a wife. But the death of her husband had opened a place within the family system for a woman that did not require sexual intercourse or reproduction—namely, widowhood, a role that required only the ritual and social dimensions of wifehood and depended on the widow's complete abstention from sexual intercourse. Impenetrability certainly guaranteed a sort of chastity, although it seems an odd legerdemain to equate physical disability with virtuous self-restraint. From a judicial point of view, however, nothing further needed to be done. As a widow, Xie Shi enjoyed the rights to remain unmarried in her husband's lineage, to gain custody of her husband's estate, and to have an appropriate nephew appointed as her husband's heir (to perform ancestor worship, inherit his property, and care for her in old age).[17] Of course, this solution ignores the fact that her relationship with her in-laws was likely to be awkward at best.

I have no interest in trying to diagnose Xie Shi's condition in modern biomedical terms—a wide range of causes could produce the symptoms described.[18] But it seems significant that no one involved in Xie Shi's case doubted she was a woman. She had been raised as a daughter, and she had already been married and widowed once before being exposed and rejected as a stone maiden.[19] All parties in the case record referred to her as "Xie Shi" (i.e., née Xie), the form appropriate for an adult woman. As to judicial treatment, we find that the magistrate ordered her examined by a midwife, rather than by the male coroner (whose duties included the examination of male victims of rape). The choice of midwife reveals the magistrate's a priori categorization of Xie Shi as a woman. Also telling is the way the magistrate ruled out marriage fraud. He interrogated the matchmaker and Xie Shi's male relatives closely about whether they had known of her disability, and it is clear that they would have been punished (and the marriage canceled) if they had been shown to have deceived the other party to the marriage. But Xie Shi's own knowledge of her "secret illness" was deemed irrelevant—or so we can infer, since she was not punished for having failed to reveal it when either of her marriages was being arranged. Apparently modesty and passivity were expected of her, confirming that the magistrate (and everyone else) had cast her in a woman's role.

What Is a Body For?

But what sort of woman was a stone maiden like Xie Shi? In a famous passage of his *Systematic Materia Medica* (*Bencao gangmu*), the sixteenth-century medical authority Li Shizhen organized sex-related anomalies in two categories, *fei nan* and *fei nü*, listing five of each. This categorization takes for granted that anomaly can be comprehended within the male/female (*nan/nü*) binary division of the sexes. Less obvious is what Li Shizhen means by the prefix *fei*.[20] *Fei ren*, which might literally translate as "nonhuman" or "not a human," is a venerable classical term for a crippled or deformed person, but it can also mean an evildoer or traitor, and there may be a connection between these meanings, given the variety of mutilating punishments that were inflicted on criminals in early China (including castration).[21] The most straightforward rendering of Li Shizhen's terms may be "deformed males and females." This translation resonates with the language used in the case report to characterize Xie Shi's condition: "crippled" (*canfei*) or "ill" (*bing*).[22]

The individuals that make up Li Shizhen's taxonomy all suffer from some crippling defect or deformity related to sex, but they are still considered male or female. Li explains that "the five kinds of deformed males cannot become fathers, and the five kinds of deformed females cannot become mothers" (*wu zhong fei nan bu ke wei fu, wu zhong fei nü bu ke wei mu*), implying a sort of arrested development that precludes the full realization of adult gender roles. Therefore, he concludes, "their bodies are useless (*wuyong*)."[23] As Charlotte Furth observes, "Four of the five terms applied to women refer to genital abnormalities of the sort that would make sexual penetration impossible" (including the stone maiden, also known as the "drum," *gu*); the fifth term refers to highly erratic menses, which were associated with infertility. Similarly, four of the terms in the category of "deformed males" refer to "the functionally impotent."[24] (The fifth is the "changeling," *bian*, to be discussed in a separate section.) Normalcy, therefore, depended on an ability to play the role appropriate to one's sex in conjugal intercourse and reproduction: the "deformed" male and female were anomalies that defined normalcy by contrast.

In an important paper, Tani Barlow has invoked Li Shizhen's taxonomy to support her thesis that gender in late imperial China derived exclusively from family roles, and not from bodies: "The foundational or categorical figure is mother/father, not woman/man."[25] She is certainly correct, insofar as Li Shizhen takes for granted that the defining purpose of anatomy is to fulfill normative sexual and reproductive roles. Indeed, the perspective of "crip theory" would suggest that reigning heteronormative assumptions about the proper use of bodies are what actually *create* such anomalies or disabilities, in the sense of giving them social meaning.[26] But it seems significant that Li Shizhen does not cite the binary of mother/father: he nowhere speaks of "deformed mothers" versus "deformed fathers." Instead, he chooses the binary of females versus males, implying broader categories grounded in anatomy that are somehow prior to specific social roles, and that include individuals whose disabilities prevent them from completely fulfilling those roles.

As I have argued elsewhere, in late imperial China the sexual consummation of marriage constituted a key rite of passage into social adulthood, in which male and female took up their respective roles in the division of sexual labor (penetrator/penetrated) and in the division of gendered social labor (husband/wife).[27] From this perspective, the stone maiden's disability arrested her development into a mature woman: it prevented her from taking up the sexual and gender roles within marriage that defined gendered maturity and trapped her in the permanently juvenile condition of a virgin daughter.[28]

All of this helps us to interpret the midwives' testimony about their pelvic examination of Xie Shi. First, both the midwives and their magistrates believed that a penetrable vagina and full breasts were definitive of normal female anatomy; they were necessary "props" for the correct performance of the wifely role. Second, the purpose of that anatomy was heterosexual intercourse and reproduction. The midwife's finger stood in for a husband's penis, implying a prior judgment about the purpose of the anatomy being tested ("even the *tip* of a finger cannot penetrate"). Third, Xie Shi was not a male, but a female with a problem—a deficient female (to borrow

Charlotte Furth's term). It is important to note what the midwives who searched Xie Shi's body did *not* report: they found nothing recognizable as a penis or scrotum. In the absence of those organs, they categorized her as a female, albeit a deficient one.[29]

The contrast between Xie Shi's two marriages raises the question of when exactly she can be said to have become "disabled" and highlights the degree to which disability in this context was a product of normative social expectations rather than an objective physical condition. We do not know exactly what went on between Xie Shi and her first husband, aside from her euphemistic testimony that he did not *jinshen*—literally, "get close to my body," by which she apparently meant vaginal penetration. But, since her first husband did not insist on vaginal intercourse—in fact, we cannot tell from her testimony whether he even attempted it—she seems to have had no trouble acting as his wife: he accepted her without complaint, and her in-laws, who testified that the couple got along well, were unaware of any problem. The fact that they had a harmonious relationship suggests that her disability derived as much from what others expected to do with her body as from her body itself: a vagina can be considered "impenetrable" only if someone expects to penetrate it. Her anatomy acquired social and legal significance *as a disability* only when her *second* husband made her condition public ("outing" her, in effect) and cited it as grounds for divorce. In short, the disability of the stone maiden was not simply an anatomical fact: it was a social problem "in anatomical disguise."[30]

The Stone Maiden Who Remained a Wife

In Xie Shi's case, the problem of where to place a stone maiden achieved solution through a separation of the different dimensions of the wifely role. A widow was not expected to have sexual intercourse or to reproduce; indeed, she was forbidden to do so. Xie Shi's condition in no way disqualified her from the role of widow.

An 1865 case from Nanbu County, Sichuan, resulted in a different solution to the problem of placing a stone maiden, but one that shared the same logic of separating the biological and social dimensions of the wifely role.[31] In this case, as the groom Wang Guicai (sixteen *sui*) explained in his petition, "it was only when I slept with [my bride] Zou Shi that I discovered she is a two-formed cripple and cannot bear children (*erxing fei* ren, bu neng shengyu)." The term *erxing* or *erxingzi*, which I translate as "two-formed," was sometimes used as a synonym for "stone maiden" (as seen in this example) but could also mean something like "hermaphrodite" (of which more later).[32] The groom's statement was confirmed by the bride Zou Shi: "My body has a crippling illness and I cannot bear children (*shen you canji, bu neng shengyu*), so my husband and I are not happy together." After this discovery, Wang and his father demanded that Zou Shi's natal family pay them thirty strings of cash in compensation. When her father, Zou Shaopan, refused to pay, the Wangs insisted on divorcing her and getting a refund of her bride-price (amount unspecified). But her father also refused to take her back. Finally, the groom and his father filed charges in the Nanbu County court.

Since the facts were not in dispute, the magistrate did not bother to order a pelvic examination of Zou Shi. Instead, he simply ordered her father to pay the Wangs the 30 strings of cash they had demanded, so that they could buy a concubine for Wang Guicai, "to secure his line of descent;" in exchange, the Wangs would agree to keep Zou Shi as Wang Guicai's main wife. Zou Shaopan was not happy with this decision, so the magistrate scolded him and told him to consider what was best for his daughter:

> Since Zou Shaopan's daughter has a "crippling disability" (*canfei*), it would be appropriate according to law to return her to her natal family. But for her sake, this judgment is a better solution: this way, your daughter will have sons even though she cannot bear them herself (*wu zi er you zi*), she will have successors and her incense fire will continue—that is what is most important! You should not begrudge this small payment, because if you fail to pay you will force your daughter to bear a lifelong burden of pain (*shi nü bao zhongshen zhi tong*).

Zou Shaopan pledged to pay the required amount, but later he dragged his heels, provoking the Wangs to file a complaint. In response, the magistrate ordered Zou to take custody of his daughter until he saw fit to pay up—in other words, if he wanted to secure a place for her in the Wang family, he would have to compensate them.

The magistrate's decision in this case confirms Francesca Bray's insights into the politics of the polygynous elite household. Bray argues that polygyny was based on the performance of different aspects of the wife-mother role by different women within a single family: the main wife (*qi*), who came from the same elite background as her husband, and who was the titular mother (*dimu*) of all her husband's children, would perform the *social* and *ritual* aspects of motherhood. Meanwhile, she could displace much of the *biological* aspect of motherhood (e.g., sexual intercourse, pregnancy) onto the subordinate women of the household: the concubines (*qie*) and maidservants (*binü*), who were also sexually available to her husband (these women had been purchased through brokers from poor families). In this way, an elite wife could enjoy the prestige and authority conferred by the social-ritual aspects of motherhood, without the burden of the risky and possibly distasteful biological duties of that role. Bray's analysis lays bare the class exploitation at the heart of the elite family and shows how polygyny might serve the interests of the elite women who cooperated in its perpetuation.[33]

In the present case, we are not discussing members of the elite, although the magistrate's decision did assume a certain level of prosperity. (The magistrate must have believed that Zou Shupan could afford thirty strings of cash, or he would not have ordered him to pay that much.)[34] If Wang Guicai acquired a concubine, then—as the magistrate explicitly pointed out—that second woman could perform the biological role to secure his line of descent, leaving Zou Shi, as main wife, to play the social-ritual role only. The ability to separate the social from the biological through polygyny created a space within marriage that could accommodate a stone maiden.[35]

We find the same solution in a case judged by the famous writer Yuan Mei, when he was serving as magistrate of Jiangning County, Jiangsu, during the 1740s. A man named Pang Feiji had married a woman named You Shi, but on their wedding night he discovered that he had "mistakenly taken a stone maiden for his wife" (*wu qu shinü*), so he filed suit to cancel the marriage. Yuan Mei found that You Shi's father had known about her condition and concealed it from the groom's family, and therefore he was liable for the crime of marriage fraud. But Yuan took pity on You Shi, whom he describes as beautiful and talented. Instead of canceling the marriage, he ordered her father, in lieu of punishment, to refund her entire bride-price so that Pang Feiji could "also take a concubine" (*ling qu xiaoxing*), thereby securing his line of descent while allowing You Shi "to retain her position as main wife" (*reng wei zhengshi*). The wisdom and compassion that Yuan Mei displayed in this "marvelous judgment" (*miao pan*) attracted the praise of the local gentry.[36]

Other cases involving stone maidens ended with a very different solution. In 1851, Liao Ronghua of Ba County, Sichuan, married his eldest daughter Zhanggu (thirteen *sui*) to Tan Xinxi, the son of Tan Tianyuan.[37] The two families were already connected by marriage, as Liao Ronghua's uncle Liao Yongtai was Tan Tianyuan's father-in-law, and this man served as matchmaker for the marriage. At first all appeared to go well, but, after six months, the groom reported to his father and maternal grandfather (the matchmaker) that the bride's "vagina is solid" (*yin shi*); as Liao Ronghua later explained in his plaint to the Ba County magistrate, this condition made it "impossible to use her as a wife" (*nan yi wei qi*). "Solid vagina" is another expression for the impenetrability of a stone maiden: in Chinese, "solid maiden" and "stone maiden" are homonyms as well as synonyms.[38] The Tan family sought to cancel the marriage, and the matchmaker helped negotiate a settlement.

The settlement was that Zhanggu would leave both families and become a Buddhist nun. The groom's family was expected to pay some amount in order to gain her natal family's agreement to take her back and place her in a temple. That money would help establish her in her new life (apparently an endowment was necessary for the temple to accept her as a novice). The matter ended up in court because of a dispute over how much the groom's family should pay. At first, they paid eight strings of cash, and Liao Ronghua wrote out a "receipt" (*lingyue*) and took his daughter home. Later, however, Ronghua pressed the Tans for a larger sum, and, when he failed to get it, he sued Tan Tianyuan for canceling the marriage (without mentioning the girl's disability in his plaint). Tan Tianyuan then filed a counterplaint frankly explaining the situation and suggesting that his son may have been the victim of marriage fraud. After this exchange of plaints, the dispute was mediated by neighbors and settled out of court. The mediators reported to the magistrate that the marriage indeed had to be canceled because the bride's "womb is afflicted with solidity of the vagina" (*tai huan yin shi*). Therefore, the groom's father, Tan Tianyuan, had agreed to pay fifteen strings of cash, in exchange for Liao Ronghua's agreement that his daughter be divorced and "shave her head to enter a temple as a nun" (*pi ti ru miao wei ni*). The magistrate approved this settlement and ordered both parties to come to the county yamen to file affidavits confirming its terms.[39]

In the previous cases, the problem of the stone maiden's placement was solved by finding places inside the family that did not require sexual intercourse or reproduction from a woman. In the present case, the problem was solved by finding a corresponding place outside the family, in the celibate clergy—a gender-transing maneuver that would obviate the stone maiden's disability.

In social practice, clerical celibacy seems to have been the solution of choice to the problems posed by a stone maiden, since widowhood and purchase of a concubine were not always practical options (disabled sons were sometimes donated to become clergy, too.)[40] Ming-Qing fiction usually depicts stone maidens as Buddhist or Daoist nuns. As Furth has pointed out,[41] the most famous example is the character "Sister Stone" (Shi Daogu, i.e., "Daoist Nun Shi") in the sixteenth-century drama *Peony Pavilion* (*Mudanting*), who explains, "Driven by yin and yang, people rush pell-mell in pursuit of marriage, but Heaven denied me woman's proper parts and so my sole recourse was to the Way, to don the shaman's robe."[42] She recounts that she did originally marry, but her husband was unable to consummate their marriage in the usual way, although he did temporarily substitute anal for vaginal intercourse (a theme to which we shall return). Finally, her husband acquired a concubine and "abandoned" (*qi*) Sister Stone, who then became a Daoist nun.[43] Another stone maiden turned nun can be found in the Qing novel *Plum in the Golden Vase: The Sequel* (*Xu Jinpingmei*). She is the reborn Pan Jinlian, notorious heroine of the Ming novel *Plum in the Golden Vase*, and her disability is karmic retribution for the excessive licentiousness of her previous life.[44]

The stone maiden posed a practical problem: somewhere in society a place had to be found that would obviate her disability by making sexual intercourse and reproduction unnecessary. My sources document two basic solutions to this problem. The first was to separate the social and ritual requirements of the wife/mother role from the biological requirements of that role; the second was for a stone maiden simply to "leave the family" by joining the celibate clergy. We can find a hybrid solution in a tale from the early Qing collection *Laughter of Cloud Fairies* (*Yunxian xiao*), similar to that of Sister Stone in *Peony Pavilion*. The hero's wife turns out to be a stone maiden. After he acquires a second woman (who can bear sons), the stone maiden becomes a Buddhist nun, which she asserts is her fate, and the hero provides a cash endowment at a temple to support her. This resolution combines the two solutions found in our legal cases: the second wife performs the biological role, freeing the stone maiden to "exit the family." Eventually, the hero's son wins top honors on the civil service examination, and everyone lives happily ever after.[45]

It is striking that the normative gender system could accommodate such anomalous individuals, for whom magistrates seem to have felt considerable sympathy, in striking contrast with how they treated "men masquerading in women's attire." Stone maidens are consistently represented in legal cases and fiction as unfortunate women who suffer from an illness or disability for which they are not to be blamed, whereas M–F crossers are portrayed as actual or potential sexual predators caught perpetrating a nefarious fraud. Every effort was made to find a place for the stone maidens, but the normative gender system furnished no place for M–F crossers; no official suggested, for example, that they be allowed to join the celibate clergy. All of our stone maidens had been assigned female at birth, but were prevented by their condition from fulfilling the adult gender role associated with their sex, and no law prescribed penalties for abnormal anatomy. In contrast, the M–F crossers had been assigned male at birth based on what midwives (then and later) judged to be normal male anatomy, and yet they had willfully adopted the gender presentation and performance appropriate to the opposite sex. In other words, the focus of official opprobrium was transgressive behavior, rather than anatomy.

A third "solution" to the stone maiden problem, which hardly bears contemplation, appears in yet another legal case (from Shunyang County, Henan, dated 1743). When peasant Liu Cao'er (twenty-three *sui*) discovered that his bride Jiang Shi (seventeen *sui*) was a stone maiden, he tried to return her to her natal family to be sold off, so that he could marry someone else with the proceeds. But her natal family refused to cooperate. The protagonists in this case were far too poor to consider buying a concubine or endowing a place for Jiang Shi at a temple, and Liu Cao'er saw his wife as a useless burden. He became frustrated and irate, and finally he murdered the unfortunate young woman, attempting to pass off her death as a suicide. As extreme as this scenario is, it seems a logical result of the fundamental difficulty of finding a place in Qing society for a woman who could not perform the biological role of wife. Jiang Shi's life chances were constrained by her body—but it was society that imposed those constraints.[46]

Problems with Penises

The Husband Whose Penis Was Too Small

I have yet to find a clear example of one of Li Shizhen's "deformed males" (*fei nan*) in the Qing legal archives, but a 1748 case from Licheng County, Shandong, comes close.[47] In this case, the peasant Ren Mei (thirty-two *sui*) killed his new wife, Zheng Shi (eighteen *sui*), one night after less than two months of marriage. In his confession, Ren explained that his wife had been very unhappy with his attempts to consummate their marriage: "She resented me because she thought my penis was too small (*zeng xian xiaode xiashen xiao*), and she wasn't willing to sleep with me. . . . Every night Zhang Shi was annoyed at me, because I performed unsuccessfully (*bu ji shi*), and she refused to sleep with me." He would kowtow to her and beg her to let him try again, and usually she would eventually give in. But, on that fatal night, she adamantly refused and demanded that he divorce her: "She cursed me, saying: 'A guy like you shouldn't expect to get married, because you only harm someone else by doing so! I'm not willing to be married to you any longer. The sooner you divorce me, the better (*ni zhey-ang yi ge ren jiu bu gai qi xin tao laopo kenghai bieren, wo rujin bu ken tong ni zuo liang kouzi de le, ni zaoxie ba wo xiu le ba*)!" Then she pushed him off the bed, and he fell over backward on the floor. This was too much, he testi-fied: he threatened to kill her if she did not submit, but she continued curs-ing him, so he hacked her to death with a cleaver.

After hearing this confession, the magistrate ordered Ren Mei to expose himself for inspection: "This humble official then examined Ren Mei's penis (*xiati*): it appears impotent and small (*wei xiao*)." Aside from this brief-est of statements, the magistrate made no comment on the genitals that played such a pivotal role in this homicide. His report summarizes the couple's conjugal difficulties without going into detail: "After they mar-ried, Ren Mei failed to satisfy Zhang Shi in bed, so that whenever he wanted to sleep with her she would curse and scold him; this had hap-pened many times."[48] Ren Mei was sentenced to strangulation after the assizes, according to the statute against "purposeful killing of one's wife." The magistrate charged no one else with any crime.

The whole matter of just what was wrong with Ren Mei is left a bit vague. From his own testimony, it would appear that Ren's problem involved both size and performance, and the magistrate's two-character opinion—*wei xiao*, itself the epitome of brevity—seems to confirm that impression. This language echoes Li Shizhen's description of the deformed male known as the "natural eunuch" (*tianhuan*), whose "penis is impotent and useless" (*yang wei buyong*).[49] But we have no way of knowing what standard the magistrate was using to judge either size or performance (nor can we answer the interesting question of what standard Ren's wife was using). In medieval and early modern Europe, when a woman sued her husband for divorce on grounds of impotence, the court might delegate a group of matrons or prostitutes to attempt to arouse the man by exposing their breasts, kissing and masturbating him, and so on, and to report their findings. But I find no evidence of such heroic investigative zeal on the part of Qing courts, at least with regard to male potency. Male impotence in and of itself seems to have carried no legal significance during the Qing; it was certainly not grounds for a wife to seek divorce—that innovation was first introduced into Chinese law by the Republican Civil Code of 1931.[50]

The vagueness about Ren Mei's problems seems remarkable in contrast with the graphic precision of the midwives' testimony about the stone maiden Xie Shi (in the first case recounted). What explains this reticence? The likely explanation is Ren Mei's lack of any visible physical anomaly severe enough to trigger charges of marriage fraud. Presumably the magistrate's purpose in examining Ren Mei's penis was to check for such deformity. Since no one was charged with or even questioned about marriage fraud, the magistrate evidently judged that Ren Mei's penis fell within acceptable range. Apparently Ren Mei's problems did not meet the standard of "crippling deformity" (*canfei*) or "disease" (*jibing*) specified by the statute against fraud. Therefore, his marriage was valid, and Zhang Shi was his legal wife.

With fraud ruled out, why include so much testimony about Zhang Shi's sexual dissatisfaction in the case report? The answer is that, aside from justifying the provisional sentence imposed on Ren Mei (by proving that he had killed his wife and explaining his motive), this report was designed to inform the review process undertaken at the annual autumn assizes. The Qing code mandates death for some scenarios of wife-killing, but in every instance with the qualification that "execution should take place after the Autumn Assizes" (*qiu hou chu jue*), and published regulations for the Autumn Assizes specify that any husband who killed his wife because she had been "defiant" (*bu shun*) or "unfilial" (*bu xiao*) should have his sentence commuted significantly.[51]

There can be little doubt that Ren Mei's sentence of strangulation was commuted: the way his wife had defied, cursed, and pushed him would have been interpreted as mitigating circumstances, any one of which justified a certain amount of violence on his part (Qing law permitted a husband to beat his wife, as long as he broke no bones or inflicted worse injury).[52] This is the main reason why Ren's testimony about his wife's sexual dissatisfaction was included in the case report. In this respect, the report follows the standard pattern for cases of wife-killing: if the wife had provoked her husband's violence through some egregious failure of gender duty (e.g., defying, cursing, or striking him; disobeying or abusing his parents; leaving home without permission; committing adultery), then her misbehavior would be recorded in detail, so that his sentence could be commuted appropriately.[53]

We should note that, in contrast with the stone maidens, Ren found himself in court only because he had killed his wife. If he had simply failed to satisfy her sexually, or to sire descendants for his ancestors, then he might have been unhappy, but he would have suffered no formal consequences. In other words, he would not have been forced to divorce his wife or to become a monk, let alone to provide her with a second husband capable of sexual intercourse.

The Husband Who Had No Penis

The anomalies described by Li Shizhen all appear to be congenital, and were understood to be the result of peculiar imbalances in natural forces at the time of conception. But illness or injury could also deform the anatomy so as to generate equally difficult social problems. A case from Jia County, Henan, concerns the murder of peasant Chen Erchuan (thirty-three *sui*).[54] In 1864, Erchuan had fallen ill "with an ulcerating sore on his penis, which rotted away, leaving him a deformed cripple" (*jingwu huan chuang kuilan, zhi cheng canfei*). With medical treatment, he eventually "recovered," but he kept his lack of a penis secret.

In late 1865, Erchuan's older brother Chen Erda arranged for him to marry Yue Shi (eighteen *sui*), the daughter of an acquaintance in a neighboring village. Before arranging the marriage, Erda had questioned Erchuan closely about his illness, and Erchuan assured him that he had made a full recovery. But, on the wedding night, "he was unable to engage in conjugal intercourse" (*bu neng xingfang*), and when his young bride discovered his condition she was shocked and upset. Yue Shi complained to her brother- and sister-in-law and also to her own natal family, demanding that they cancel the marriage. But they counseled her to accept the situation, because the marriage had already taken place, and there was nothing to be done about it. Erchuan, in turn, became abusive and violent, venting his shame and frustration on Yue Shi by frequently beating her. She retaliated by refusing to share his bed at all, and, finally, she murdered him by cutting his throat while he slept.

Yue Shi later explained her deed as follows: "Chen Erchuan was crippled and could never have children, so in the future I would have no one to support me at the end of my life (*cheng fei bu neng shengyu, jianglai zhongshen wu kao*). So I decided to vent my anger by killing him." Her choice of words is significant: *zhongshen* refers to the vital role of adult sons in securing their parents' comfort in old age (by working the farm and providing their livelihood), but also in seeing to their proper burial and commemoration after death. Achieving this security was arguably the single most important reason for marriage.

The facts were not in dispute—Yue Shi was caught literally "red-handed"—so the key legal question was how she should be sentenced. Three possibilities suggested themselves. First, she could be sentenced as a wife who had committed the "premeditated murder" (*mousha*) of her husband, in which case her penalty would be dismemberment. But this sentence seemed inappropriate, because Erchuan's concealment of his disability had constituted the crime of marriage fraud, which rendered their union invalid. As the magistrate commented (echoing Yue Shi's testimony), Erchuan's deception had "ruined Yue Shi's hopes for her marriage and for support at the end of her life (*yi zhi wu ren zhongshen*). This marriage was not legitimate, and the couple should have been divorced."

Following this logic, a more likely option was to deny Chen Erchuan the legal status of husband and to sentence Yue Shi instead for premeditated murder of an "unrelated party," for which the penalty would be beheading after the assizes (which left open the possibility of a reprieve). Going a step further, a final possibility was to sentence her for the "unauthorized killing of a criminal" (*shansha zuiren*), given that Erchuan's prior crime of marriage fraud is what had ultimately provoked his murder. This law assumed that the homicide victim bore at least some blame for their own fate; its original form envisioned a fugitive killed while resisting arrest, but the concept was later extended to cover a variety of scenarios.[55]

Since no law covered the precise scenario in Yue Shi's case, the governor of Henan appealed to the Board of Punishment for a ruling. The board struck a balance: they sentenced Yue Shi to beheading after the assizes for the premeditated murder of an unrelated party, but stipulated that, because of the mitigating circumstance of fraud, her execution should be "delayed" (*huanjue*) when her case was considered at the annual autumn assizes. This stipulation strongly suggests that Yue Shi's sentence would be commuted.

Perhaps the most striking feature of this case is the degree of sympathy shown for the murderess, whom the authorities believed to have been profoundly wronged by the fraud perpetrated against her. Whereas no one seems to have held stone maidens responsible for failing to divulge their condition, the clear expectation in this case was that Chen Erchuan should have reported his disability to those arranging his marriage. Also, Yue Shi's testimony, and the Board of Punishment's ruling, shows that, like husbands, wives were entitled to expect sexual intercourse and procreation from marriage. Although patrilineal descent per se may have carried less ritual importance for women than for men, wives, too, needed sons for security in old age as well as a proper burial and commemoration after death. The resentment and despair expressed by Yue Shi confirms that, as we would expect, women too cared deeply about these matters.[56] The previous case—in which Ren Mei killed his wife Zhang Shi after she ridiculed his sexual inadequacy and demanded a divorce—tells us much the same thing: that Zhang Shi, like Yue Shi, understood conjugal intercourse and a chance for children as a requirement of marriage and that she, too, refused to accept a husband who could not meet this most basic of conditions. In fact, both women accused the men of having *harmed* them by their inadequacy.

The difference in how the authorities handled these two homicides rests on the specific mitigating circumstances in each. In the first case, Ren Mei was judged to suffer no physical defect severe enough to have invalidated his marriage. Therefore, Zhang Shi was Ren's legal wife, and her disobedience and defiance were circumstances (potentially criminal in themselves) that mitigated his crime against her. In the second case, there was no question that Chen Erchuan's failure to disclose that his penis had "rotted away" invalidated his marriage. That circumstance—compounded by Erchuan's violent abuse of a woman who was not, after all, legally his wife—mitigated Yue Shi's crime against him. As a result, both defendants could expect to be spared at the autumn assizes.

The Two-Formed Person

An 1807 edition of the official forensic manual *The Washing Away of Wrongs* (*Xi yuan lu*) includes the following remarkable account, which I have translated in full:

> There was a case in Wu County, [Jiangsu,] in which Ma Yunsheng's wife Wang Shi had illicit sex and spent the night (*jiansu*) with Jin Sanguan's wife Zhou Sijie ("Fourth Elder Sister Zhou"). Examination and interrogation of Zhou Sijie revealed that inside her vagina (*chanmen*) there was a soft, fleshy protuberance (*ruan rouzhuang yitiao*), which she had had since childhood. It did not create any obstacle when her husband had intercourse with her, but when aroused (*jufa*) it would extend about two or three *cun* in length [i.e., about six to nine centimeters], and was about as thick as a thumb. She could use it to have illicit sex with women (*ke yu furen tongjian*).

This summary of Zhou Sijie's case appears in the forensic manual's section on "Examining the Corpses of Women" (*yan funü shi*). Most of this section concerns how to tell whether a woman was a virgin; how to determine cause of death in women who died while pregnant or in childbirth; how to distinguish death caused by the ingestion of toxic abortifacients from that related to spontaneous miscarriage or injury; and so on. Zhou Sijie's case summary appears in an appendix entitled "A Two-Formed Person" (*erxing ren*).[57]

Unfortunately, I have found no other information about this case, so we cannot tell what the presiding magistrate decided to do with Zhou Sijie, beyond his judgment that their behavior constituted the crime of "illicit sex" (*jian*). Nor do we know exactly when the case occurred, although we can guess it was fairly recent, because it does not appear in earlier Qing editions of *The Washing Away of Wrongs*.

After summarizing Zhou Sijie's case, the forensic manual cites Li Shizhen's taxonomy of sexual anomalies. First, it considers the five types of "deformed females," of which the first four were incapable of vaginal intercourse and the fifth was rendered infertile by highly erratic menses. But none of these conditions accounted for Zhou Sijie's anatomy, which evidently posed no "obstacle" to intercourse with her husband (although we have no information about her menstruation or fertility history). Next, the text considers Li Shizhen's five "deformed males," skipping the first four (the functionally impotent, which seem irrelevant to Zhou Sijie's case) and focusing on the fifth, known as "the changeling" (*bian*):

> The changeling's body is both male and female (*ti jian nan nü*)—this is what is colloquially known as a "two-formed person" (*erxing*). . . . There are three kinds of changeling. The first kind, upon encountering a male, becomes female; and upon encountering a female, becomes male (*zhi nan ji nü, zhi nü ji nan*). The second is female (*yin*) for half a month, and then male (*yang*) for the other half. The third can serve as a wife, but cannot play the part of a husband (*ke qi bu ke fu*).[58]

Since the summary of Zhou Sijie's case is entitled "A Two-Formed Person," which Li Shizhen identifies as a colloquial synonym for "changeling," it seems clear that the editor of the forensic manual decided to classify them as an example of that category of "deformed male"—most likely the first kind listed by Li, who could adapt both anatomy and sexual role to complement their partner and therefore was capable of intercourse with both sexes. Note that the term "two-formed person" was also used in fictional sources to characterize the shape-shifting nuns described in chapter 3.

But this classification raises more questions than it answers. First of all, in Li Shizhen's taxonomy, the changeling is a category of "deformed *male*," which the forensic manual's editor evidently chose after considering and rejecting all five female options. Was Zhou Sijie therefore a man? From the language of the summary, we know that Zhou was found to have committed the crime of "illicit sex" (*jian*) with Ma Yunsheng's wife, Wang Shi. In law, *jian* was defined fundamentally as phallic penetration of the vagina, with the subject of action being assumed male—and I have seen not a single reference to *jian* between women in any other legal text from China's imperial era.[59] Therefore, the magistrate's judgment that Zhou Sijie had committed *jian* with a woman might be considered prima facie evidence that he considered Zhou to be a man.

In other respects, however, the text genders Zhou Sijie as a woman. Zhou had a woman's name ("Fourth Elder Sister Zhou") and a husband,

Jin Sanguan, and their case appears in the forensic manual's section on examining the corpses of women, not men. This evidence shows that, unlike the protagonists of chapters 2, 4, and 5, Zhou had been assigned female at birth and assumed to be a woman throughout their life; they never transitioned, one way or the other. Moreover, the text also seems to *sex* Zhou as a woman, in that it describes their anatomy as fundamentally female: it is the phallic appendage to their vagina that is judged anomalous, not the vagina itself, and it seems significant that the text never labels that phallus a penis, nor does it express any doubt about whether Zhou's vagina was really a vagina. Although their phallus could enlarge and become erect, it posed no obstacle whatsoever to intercourse with their husband. That conjugal intercourse, in which Zhou played the normative role of wife, may be the fundamental ground on which they were judged to be female: by perceiving the sexed body through the gendered sexual/social role. In other words, despite labeling Zhou Sijie a "two-formed person," which in Li Shizhen's authoritative scheme is a fundamentally male classification, the forensic manual also seems to represent Zhou as a woman, albeit an anomalous woman.

Zhou Sijie's phallus is not a characterized as penis, and, although it could be used for penetration, there evidently was no perceived risk of pregnancy, and, hence, pollution of blood lines, the classic harm threatened by the crime of *jian*.[60] In Ming-Qing fiction, love and sex between women are generally portrayed as a titillating curiosity safely contained within polygyny, with the classic trope being an affair between a main wife and her husband's concubine.[61] Thus contained and trivialized, this activity poses no threat to the sexual and reproductive prerogatives of men. Of course, such texts were written by men with a male readership in mind, so they are probably a better guide to male fantasies than to women's actual feelings and behavior.[62] Still, the absence of any other mention (let alone prohibition) of sex between women in any legal code or casebook from the imperial era, or the use of the legal term *jian* to refer to sex between women in any other text I have seen, suggests that such behavior was not considered dangerous or even particularly significant by the male jurists responsible for codifying a Confucian moral order. For those jurists, the focus of concern was the threat that male predators posed to chaste "wives and daughters of good family."[63] It was the early twentieth-century specter of the New Woman, whose social and economic independence freed her from male custody, that introduced into discourse the pathologized figure of the lesbian: a woman who could act on her own desires and did not need men and therefore directly threatened male privilege and dominance.[64] On the other hand, Zhou Sijie's sexual activity with Wang Shi must have been reported to the authorities by their husbands—who else would have done so?—suggesting that at least one of those men felt deeply threatened by it.[65]

Zhou Sijie defied categorization, embodying ambiguity and paradox. In this text, at least, they are not explicitly accused of being a man in disguise, or of practicing sorcery. But the implications of labeling Zhou Sijie a "two-formed person" remain unclear, because we do not know their fate.

That fate may have been grim. For comparison, in 1912 *Shenbao* reported a case from Suzhou that also closely resembles Li Shizhen's description of "the changeling" as a shape-shifter whose anatomy can be adapted for intercourse with either sex. According to this report, a person of ambiguous gender presentation was arrested and examined by a midwife, who reported that they had the overall appearance of a woman, but also possessed a tiny phallus through which they could urinate while standing. The magistrate had this individual detained in the women's jail, but later it turned out that they were having sexual intercourse with the women inmates. Examined once again, their phallus was found to have grown large and erect, and they confessed that "during the daytime (the period of *yang*) their body assumed female form, but upon nightfall (the period of *yin*), it would become male" (*yang fen shi wei nüshen, yi jiao yinfen ze hua wei nan yi*). The magistrate labeled this individual a *renyao* and condemned them to death in the standing cangue.[66]

Sex Versus Gender in the Judicial Imagination

We know that in late imperial China, the dominant ideology linked gender norms very closely to the archetypal roles of husband/father and wife/mother. As I have shown elsewhere, legal reforms of the Yongzheng and early Qianlong reigns further tightened this link.[67] Nevertheless, we also know that Qing society contained many individuals—including an increasing number and probably proportion of single men—who lived outside the family system. If such individuals failed to perform family roles, did they constitute a category outside gender? If they failed to conform to kinship-based gender roles, how were their sexed bodies understood?

Clergy provide obvious material for pursuing this inquiry: since they transed gender by "leaving the family," it might be appropriate to regard them as a category beyond gender (indeed, this was a Buddhist ideal), or perhaps as some sort of third gender—and it would logically follow that a nun should not be considered a woman, even if she had a female body. In fact, this logic would help to explain our cases in which stone maidens became nuns: such a solution placed them outside the family and therefore, in effect, outside womanhood altogether. But even if this analysis is correct, it leaves open the question of how Qing authorities understood the sexed bodies of such individuals.

The Buddhist Nun Who Was Raped

Some clarity is provided by legal judgments concerning nuns who were raped. For example, in a 1745 case from Huaining County, Henan, the young Buddhist nun Zhao Wan (twenty-three *sui*) was raped by three men who lived near her temple.[68] Zhao Wan lived with her elderly mother in a small rural temple. She had been in the temple since childhood (when her widowed mother had moved there with her) and had never married; the nun who had been her teacher had recently died, leaving her in charge of the temple. The ringleader in the gang rape, an unmarried barber named Chen Yuan (twenty-six *sui*), got the idea to rape her one day when she thanked him politely for helping to catch her runaway mule. Chen noticed that no one else was at the temple, so he took the nun by the hand; she pulled back her hand and scolded him, so he ran away. But he was consumed by desire, and he persuaded two friends (single, landless peasants who worked as casual laborers) to help him rape her. Late that night, the three men broke into the temple and took turns raping her in her bed at knifepoint.

The next day, Zhao Wan reported the rape to the county magistrate, bringing along her bedding, soiled with the men's semen and her own blood, as evidence. The magistrate inspected the scene of the crime, noting evidence of the break-in, and then ordered the yamen midwife to perform a pelvic examination on the nun. The midwife testified that the nun was "definitely a virgin who has just been penetrated for the first time" (*shi xi chuzi chu poshen*). The rapists testified to the nun's chastity by confirming that she had resisted Chen Yuan's initial advance, and that they had used "violent coercion" (*qiangbao*) to rape her, threatening to kill her if she cried out. Chen, as ringleader, was sentenced to immediate beheading, and his two accomplices to strangulation after the assizes, according to the substatute against "gang rape" (*lunjian*); this sentence was upheld upon review and confirmed by imperial edict.[69]

The significance of this case for our discussion is that it was handled in exactly the same manner as the rape of a chaste wife or daughter. The fact that the rape victim was a nun seems to have made no difference whatsoever.[70] The law cited and the penalties imposed were the same that would apply in any other gang rape case. One interesting detail is the pelvic examination: performing such examinations in rape cases was the most important forensic duty of midwives, but they were ordered to do so only when the alleged victim was unmarried and presumed to have been a virgin prior to being raped. Midwives were expected to read female genitalia for evidence of penetration: had the alleged victim indeed been penetrated— literally, had her "body been broken" (*poshen*)? Pelvic examinations were never performed on married women who claimed to have been raped, presumably because any readable evidence might be the result of their husbands' legitimate actions. In such cases, conviction for rape depended on other kinds of proof.[71] Usually a woman of Zhao Wan's age would have been married. But, since this nun had lived a celibate life since childhood, having never married, her body could be read for evidence in the same manner as that of an unmarried virgin daughter.

In other words, for purposes of rape prosecution, eighteenth-century jurists equated a nun's celibacy with the virginity and chastity of the classic rape victim defined by law—"a wife or daughter of good/commoner family" (*liangjia funü*). She shared the same anatomy as females within the family system and, for that reason, shared the same vulnerability to rape. This conclusion is confirmed by evidence from the system for canonization of chastity martyrs: in 1747, a Daoist nun who "preserved her purity (*quan zhen*) in the face of violent attack" (i.e., was murdered while resisting rape, without yielding to penetration) was canonized by imperial edict, "even though she does not fall within the ranks of wives and daughters of military personnel or civilians" (*bu zai bing min funü zhi lie*).[72] With this precedent established, celibate female clergy became eligible for canonization if they died resisting rape.

This evidence shows that legal authorities during the High Qing defined a broad category of woman in terms of shared anatomy and "rapability" that included females outside the Confucian family system.[73] They understood female sexuality fundamentally in terms of penetrability and viewed male sexual predators (stereotyped as rogue "bare sticks" outside the family system) as a constant and ubiquitous threat; female virtue they defined in terms of how much a woman was willing to suffer in order to defend that penetrability, to reserve it exclusively for her husband. Chastity and rapability were two sides of the same coin.

The stone maiden fits into this picture, albeit imperfectly, in that she was deficient or incomplete according to a standard that equated normalcy (of both anatomy and gender role) with penetrability. From this perspective, the stone maiden was an exception that proved the rule: her disability prevented her from fully realizing a standard of womanhood that applied generally, just as unchaste women confirmed by negative example the standard of virtue to which all women were held.

The Male Rape Victim

What then made the rape of a *male* comprehensible to Qing jurists?[74] The first laws in imperial China explicitly prohibiting male-male rape were promulgated by the Qing dynasty. These laws, and the procedure that Qing jurists developed for dealing with male-male rape, were based by analogy on preexisting laws and procedures for prosecuting male-female rape. This analogy extended to the male rape victim himself, who in various ways was put in a female position.

For example, when a male alleged that he had been raped, the magistrate would order the yamen's forensic examiner to inspect his anus for evidence of penetration, much the way midwives examined female rape victims who were presumed to have been virgins. The logic for such examination is outlined in a 1788 statement from the Board of Punishment reprimanding the Guangdong authorities for mishandling the investigation of a homicide involving sodomy. The coroner in this case had failed to examine the anus of the homicide victim, with whom the killer claimed to have had a long-term sexual relationship:

> It is true that the code contains no explicit measure providing for examination of the anus of a male who has been sodomized. Nevertheless, the code *does* contain a substatute mandating the examination

of the vagina of a female virgin (*chunü*) who has been raped, in order to ascertain whether she was really a virgin, and that logic can certainly be extended by analogy (*yi ke tuilei*) to sodomy cases. Especially in cases where the victim has provided no testimony before death, it is absolutely necessary to examine his anus to determine whether it is stretched out (*kuansong*). Only then is it possible to establish proof of a prior illicit sexual relationship.[75]

Qing editions of *The Washing Away of Wrongs* explain that the anus of a male who "has been sodomized over a long period of time" (*jiu bei jijian*) will be "stretched out, not tight at all" (*kuansong, bing bu jincou*), whereas the anus of a virgin male who has been raped will be "open, with the inside red and swollen" and possibly bleeding.[76] The stakes were high in such examinations, because if a homicide took place in the context of a rape attempt it was supposed to receive penalties of even greater severity. Therefore, it was necessary to ascertain whether the killer had indeed had consensual sodomy with his victim or had instead raped him. Moreover, the penetrated anus was evaluated strictly as evidence of crime, since Qing law allowed no legitimate context for homosexual penetration: the point of forensic examination was to distinguish between *victims* of crime and habitual sodomites who were *themselves* criminals. Thus, males who had been used in the "female" sexual role would be examined for evidence in the female way.[77] To pursue this logic further: If rapability defined the category woman, then were male rape victims considered in some sense to be women?

The key here is not anatomy per se, but age. Men, as a category, were defined not by penetrability, but by its opposite, the "active" sexual role of penetrator. A male could be imagined as vulnerable to rape, like a woman, only by being imagined as powerless, like a woman. What made this possible was the physical weakness of childhood. Therefore, Qing jurists imagined the plausible male victim as an adolescent or even younger boy, assaulted by a powerful, mature man. This image is clearly expressed by the language of the Qing code, which (for example) characterized the male rape victim as "a son or younger brother of good/commoner family" (*liangjia zi di*), and it is confirmed by the records of cases where male-male rape was actually prosecuted, which invariably concern children or youths assaulted by significantly older and more powerful men. Moreover, it is clear that male youth was feminized and eroticized as an object of masculine possessive desire. In this way, the weakness of a young boy corresponded to the gendered vulnerability of women generally, and male vulnerability to rape (like male erotic appeal as a sex object) was considered a temporary transitional phase that ended with the empowered masculinity of adulthood (the "boy actress" of the opera represents an extreme elaboration of this theme). In a sense, this androgynous ambiguity of the adolescent male corresponded to the arrested development of the permanently juvenile stone maiden: both conditions make sense when we understand that normative gender identity was fully realized only with adulthood, marked above all by marriage and procreation.

A related question is whether rape law can shed light on how jurists conceptualized male clergy. Just as the rape of a Buddhist nun was handled in the same manner as the rape of a "wife or daughter of good/commoner family," case records show that the rape of a male novice in the Buddhist or Daoist clergy was punished exactly like the rape of "a son or younger brother of good/commoner family." Therefore, for purposes of rape prosecution, Qing jurists recognized a broad category of males, whose immaturity made them temporarily vulnerable to rape, that included individuals both inside and outside the family system.

Moreover, from the limited evidence I have seen, it seems we can extend this logic to eunuchs as well. For example, in chapter 1, we discussed a case involving the use of knockout drugs to kidnap and rape a runaway eunuch who was just fifteen *sui*. The rape counted as a "lesser crime," nevertheless it appears to have been handled in exactly the same way as the rape of an intact male youth.[78]

Fictional Solutions to Social Problems

As we have seen, Ming-Qing fiction is rich with fanciful episodes that call into question the links between anatomical sex and gender performance. Such fiction provides both complement and antidote to our grim legal narratives. Whereas the legal cases show that anomalous bodies imposed constraints on the performance of normative gender, this fiction brings to mind Judith Butler's utopian vision of radical self-determination, in which there may come into being as many genders as there are individuals who perform gender. Its category-defying phantasmagoria suggest the alternative scripts and subversive performances that a world without laws and norms might generate. But, paradoxically, such fiction also represents an attempt to make sense of anomaly and to solve social problems based on some of the same assumptions and priorities that informed the judicial agenda.

A Miraculous Cure

A typically fantastic story by the seventeenth-century author Li Yu draws together many of the themes of this chapter.[79] The young hero marries one of three sisters. She is exceptionally beautiful, and he looks forward eagerly to their wedding night, but upon attempting sexual intercourse he discovers, to his shock, that she is a stone maiden. She begs him not to reject her, but instead to acquire concubines who can bear sons in her place. Her beauty and charm inflame his desire, they embrace passionately, and after some fumbling he finally satisfies himself by penetrating her anus: "When it came time to vent his passion, he gave up on the front and rushed to the rear (*she qian qu hou*)—under the circumstances, it was the only reasonable thing to do!"

The next day, however, his parents learn about her disability, and without telling the groom they exchange her for one of her sisters. Late that night, the groom returns from a party, drunk, to find his new bride waiting in the dark. Groping her, he is pleased—though startled—to discover that her disability has magically disappeared, and he manages to consummate their marriage in the conventional manner. When it grows light, however, he discovers that, instead of his beautiful stone maiden, he is in bed with her ugly, coarse sister, who has a disgusting bladder condition that makes her wet the bed constantly.

Horrified, he prevails on his parents to exchange her so that he can get back the beautiful stone maiden. Instead, they swap her for the *third* sister. This one turns out to be just as beautiful as the first, but, upon having her naked in bed, he discovers that she is no virgin: her vagina is open and slack, unlike that of the bed-wetting sister, who at least was a virgin. (The hero can read female anatomy like a midwife!) To make matters worse, she is six months pregnant. Alas, she, too, must be rejected.

After this Goldilocks-like series of failures, the hero works through several other brides, but in every instance the woman either proves unacceptable, or dies shortly after their wedding. In the meantime, his first bride, the beautiful stone maiden, has been circulating through the marriage market:

more than twenty grooms have tried her out and in turn rejected her upon discovering her disability. Finally, she and the hero end up back together; through a broker, the hero marries her again, without realizing until the wedding night that his latest bride is she. They recognize that they are fated to be together and resolve to make the best of the situation. At first, they engage in anal intercourse, but this act leaves the bride unsatisfied, and eventually her unrequited desire causes an ulcerated sore to develop between her legs where a vagina should be. The hero discovers that he can penetrate this sore, instead of her anus, and, eventually, this makeshift intercourse cures the bride's condition: in place of the ulcer, she develops a normal vagina and is able to bear him sons! They live happily ever after.[80]

Like much of Li Yu's fiction, this tale interweaves a number of lines of subversive parody. The comic series of wedding night disasters recalls Butler's idea of gender as a repeated performance susceptible to failure or subversion. If the consummation of marriage was supposed to signal the adoption of adult gender roles, then these repeated failures undermine the coherence of normative gender and highlight its contingent and fragile nature. Instead, the hero's makeshift intercourse with his stone maiden bride suggests the possibility of alternative forms of sexual satisfaction that are not linked to procreation; it also brings to mind the relationship that the stone maiden Xie Shi was able to have with her first husband, who did not require vaginal intercourse as a prerequisite for harmonious marriage. Moreover, Li Yu's pairing of a penetrable anus with an impenetrable vagina—each taboo being the mirror image of the other—reminds us of the unstable parallel that Qing law drew between male and female rape victims. Qing jurists understood the male anus as a sexual organ only for the limited purpose of proving crime. But this maneuver seems simultaneously to deny while tacitly acknowledging the ubiquitous phenomenon in their society of the young male as object of possessive desire.

Finally, the stone maiden's preservation of her "purity," despite trial by ordeal with more than twenty other grooms, is a hilarious parody of the female chastity so fetishized by Ming-Qing elites. It echoes the absurdity of equating the disability of a stone maiden with the chastity of a faithful widow or a celibate nun. After all, as Li Yu shows, a stone maiden was not disabled from *all* forms of sexual activity, let alone passion and desire, any more than a widow or nun was incapable of fornication.

What can we learn from the case studies presented in this chapter? Each illustrates how Qing magistrates interpreted bodily evidence in order to enforce orthodox norms of gendered behavior. Each supports the insight that perception of the body is shaped by the prior influence of gender ideology, revealing the body as "an ensemble of potentialities" that acquires meaning largely through social expectations.[81] In particular, these cases highlight the performative aspect of embodied gender, blurring the distinction between the physical and social dimensions of being. As many scholars have argued, the body acquires meaning primarily through what it is expected (or forbidden) to do.

These cases all involve anomalous anatomy or transgressive behavior that defied such expectations and therefore subverted the normative script of gender. Qing jurists sought to enforce conformity to Confucian family roles, but there were always some individuals whose bodies or behavior defied category and somehow had to be accounted for. As the stone maiden cases show, to perform normative gender required normal anatomy. Without that "prop," a woman could not fulfill the procreative mission of a wife, and to place such a woman in society required some complex discursive and financial maneuvering. The purpose of Qing rape law was to defend the chastity of "wives and daughters of good family," but cases involving nuns show that jurists in practice defined a broader category of woman in terms of a shared anatomical vulnerability to rape, a category that included individuals who transed gender by "leaving the family." As a corollary, rape prosecution required the peculiar legerdemain of stretching Confucian wifely chastity to include Buddhist celibacy.

Even odder, perhaps, is the unstable analogy that Qing jurists drew between woman (defined in terms of rapability) and the plausibly rapable male. Like the impenetrable stone maiden, the taboo of the penetrable male is an example of reading the body in performative terms. Women, of course, were legitimately penetrable within the context of marriage, procreation being what gave their bodies social purpose and meaning. For males, however, feminine vulnerability to penetration was a transient and aberrant condition that they were expected to outgrow, and the law allowed no space for legitimate sexual acts between males. Nevertheless, Qing jurists tacitly acknowledged that some boys *welcomed* penetration, as shown by laws that made thirteen *sui* (i.e., eleven or twelve years old) the age of liability for consent to sodomy.[82] Moreover, the open secret of elite men was an intense erotic fascination with the young male—and, of course, it was erotic objectification that made youths vulnerable to rape in the first place. It is as if the young male were simultaneously expected and forbidden to submit to sodomy.

In the legal cases recounted in this chapter, magistrates restored order by interpreting the material evidence of bodies according to cultural and legal norms and, on that basis, assigning people to their proper places. In contrast, Li Yu appears to transcend the limits of official imagination: he mocks the linkage between physical bodies and social roles that legal and medical authorities strove to maintain. But his story works only because he, his protagonists, and his readers take for granted those very norms and standards. They all assume that only a fertile virgin would make a suitable bride (hence the problem that the story must solve), and by the end of his tale Li Yu, too, manages to restore order, through the proper alignment of reproductive capacities and duties. The stone maiden's fidelity to the hero is rewarded by a karmic cure that transforms her into the penetrable and fertile wife he needs—and, although this happy end rewards the hero's willingness to accept her as she is, his rejection of her sisters reveals the limits of his tolerance. Ultimately, the story follows a normative trajectory: its happy ending is a marriage in which vaginal intercourse produces sons. Thus, in an ironic dovetailing with the judicial imagination, Li Yu ends by restoring the same sexual order that magistrates worked so hard to defend. One's lingering impression is of both the elasticity and the tenacity of empowered values.

CHAPTER VII

The Hustler

To my surprise, Xinxiang told me that he is actually a woman, and he behaved wildly and without regard for propriety.

—GOVERNMENT STUDENT WANG XU, YONGJI COUNTY, 1746

The culture of con men is no more than a superficial veneer which, combined with attractive personalities and a ready mother-wit, gives the illusion of polish.

—DAVID MAURER, *THE BIG CON*

We conclude this book with the enigmatic Xinxiang, an incorrigible hustler who adopted at least eight different names or personae, while practicing at least three different kinds of drag. Xinxiang defied category, and the term "transgender" seems almost inadequate to encompass their protean behavior. They transed gender, to be sure, both as cross-dressing actor and as novice monk, and on at least one occasion even claimed to be a woman. But they devoted at least as much effort to transing *class*, through a series of increasingly grandiose confidence schemes involving impersonation and identity theft. This latter activity, which put an end to Xinxiang's brief career, provides our entry point into their story.[1]

An Imperial Censor Proposes Marriage

In the spring of 1748, on the twelfth day of the New Year, the magistrate of Yangcheng County, Shanxi, received an unusual petition:

A young monk is currently staying at the Guanyin Temple in our village. He claims to be the "Imperial Censor (*yushi*) Zhang Chun" and to have come to Shanxi to inspect local affairs. He also claims that he wants to marry his fourth younger sister to Zhao Sipu (who is the nephew of petitioner Zhao Yuqi) to be his wife. We hereby present in evidence the marriage contract stamped in red ink with his seal. It seems appropriate for us to make a secret report of this matter to Your Honor.

The petitioners were Zhao Yuqi (forty-seven *sui*), a minor member of one of the leading merchant families in the county, plus two young men named Xu Lun (thirty-two *sui*) and Lu Lie (twenty). The latter two were close friends of Zhao's son, Zhao Silun (twenty-five *sui*), and nephew, Zhao Sipu (who was named in the petition as the potential groom). These four young men were students preparing for the civil service examinations, and both Xu Lun and Zhao Silun had already achieved the status of "licentiate" (*shengyuan*), qualifying them for government stipends and the triennial provincial examinations.[2] The petitioners hailed from the village of Shangfo Cun, which was home to the Zhao merchant lineage and their extensive living quarters, the "Zhao family mansion" (*Zhao jia dayuan*), along with many associated businesses.[3]

The contract that the petitioners submitted in evidence was very strange indeed:

I, Zhang Chun, the Imperially Delegated Investigating Censor for the Shanxi Circuit and concurrent Vice Minister of the Right in the Board of War, have received imperial orders to manage official affairs. On my travels through Shanxi I came to Shangfo Cun Village in Yangcheng County. There I happened to encounter Zhao Yuqi's nephew Sipu, who is filial to his parents and deferential to his brothers, faithful and modest, loyal and generous, and has a bright future. Respectfully obeying the imperial mandate, I am willing to offer my fourth younger sister, who is now aged nineteen *sui*, in marriage to him in accordance with the tradition of intermarriage between the Chen and Zhu lineages and between the states of Qin and Jin. Fearing that afterwards there will be no proof, I affix my seal as Imperial Delegate here [for Zhao Yuqi] to save as guarantee.

Done, on the fifth day of the first month of thirteenth year of the Qianlong reign.

Upon examining this document, the magistrate declared that "its wording is absurd, and the calligraphy of the seal's characters is a mess—it is obviously a fraud" (*yuyan huangtang, yin wenzi hua hutu, mingxi jianie*).

The young men testified that, in the ninth month of the previous lunar year (i.e., late 1747), they and their friend Zhao Silun had visited Kaiming Temple (*Kaiming Si*) to see the sights. The temple had just completed major renovations and was holding three months of special rituals and public festivities to celebrate. At the temple, they had encountered a young monk from Xiangling County, who gave his Buddhist name as "Xinxiang" (Auspicious Mind). The men exchanged courtesies and names with Xinxiang, who then confided that he was actually the "adopted son and heir" (*guoji erzi*) of a prominent member of the Xiangling County gentry (*xiangshen*) named Lu Bingchun. But, because Lu Bingchun had "gotten in trouble and been dismissed from office" (*huai le guan*), this son of his had been forced to "leave the family" and become a monk and to "wander abroad from place to place" (*zai wai yunyou*) living on charity. Seeing that Xinxiang "was the son of an established family and seemed to be an educated person" (*shi ge jiujia zidi, you xiang shi wenmozhong ren*), the three young men began socializing with him, and over the next three months they often visited him at the temple, sometimes together and sometimes singly.

According to their testimony, two weeks before the New Year Xinxiang appeared in the young men's home village of Shangfo Cun, taking up residence at the small Guanyin Temple and calling on his new friends at their homes. In the process, the monk met Zhao Silun's father, Zhao Yuqi (the chief petitioner), and cousin, Zhao Sipu. Then, on New Year's day, Lu Lie visited Xu Lun's home to pay his respects and to share some extraordinary news about their new friend. Xinxiang had confided to Lu that he was not really a monk, or Lu Bingchun's son, or even from Shanxi. In fact, he was an imperial censor dispatched by the emperor himself on a secret mission to investigate local conditions in Shanxi. His real name was "Zhang Chun," and he hailed from the Yangzi Delta. He had shaved his head and dressed as a monk, adopting the alias "Xinxiang," in order to travel incognito. Xu Lun reacted skeptically: "So what if he's an Imperial Censor— what does that have to do with us?" Lu Lie replied that there was more news. Upon visiting Zhao Silun's home, Xinxiang had been impressed by Silun's cousin Sipu, whose serious, studious demeanor promised a bright future. Xinxiang had a younger sister back home who had not yet married, and he proposed to betroth her to Zhao Sipu, asking that Lu Lie and Xu Lun represent him as matchmakers. Lu Lie persuaded Xu Lun to agree.

The two young men visited Zhao Silun's home to make their New Year's greeting and informed Silun's father, Zhao Yuqi, of Xinxiang's true identity and his marriage proposal (it appears that Sipu's father was dead, so Zhao Yuqi was the senior patriarch responsible for his affairs). Yuqi rejected Xinxiang's story as incredible—"I've heard nothing about any imperial censor inspecting Shanxi!"—but Lu Lie argued, "Never mind for now whether he's true or false, just wait until he has written the marriage contract and then we can talk it over again." Yuqi sent the pair back to the temple to question Xinxiang further: Was his story true? Was he serious about this marriage? "How could I possibly lie about such a serious matter?" Xinxiang retorted. Still skeptical, Yuqi agreed to let negotiations proceed, so, on the fifth day of the New Year, the young matchmakers invited Xinxiang to the Zhao home. The three men convened with Zhao Silun in the Zhao family's study, and Xinxiang apparently asked for the bride-price for his sister. It is not clear whether he demanded any particular sum, but Silun's response was to suggest that Xinxiang draw up a marriage contract to make his proposal concrete; the Zhao family would provide the bride-price if they were satisfied with the contract. Xinxiang turned to Lu Lie and said, "Since you are the matchmaker, it's only right that you take the brush and write it for me. I'll dictate what you should write." Once the contract was written, Xinxiang took it back to the temple to stamp it with his official seal in private. The next day he returned it to Lu Lie, who promptly delivered it to Zhao Yuqi.

Zhao Yuqi's suspicions were confirmed: "I picked up the contract and looked at it. With a glance, I could see that the seal looked wrong, but also even his official title didn't seem quite correct (*budan yinxin buxiang, jiushi na ge guanxian ye you xie bu shen dique*)." Keeping the contract, he gave Lu Lie the following message for the bogus imperial censor: his marriage proposal was rejected absolutely, and he should leave their village immediately, or he would find himself in trouble. Lu Lie complied, but after a week Zhao Yuqi learned that Xinxiang remained at the Guanyin Temple; so he ordered the two would-be matchmakers to accompany him in reporting the monk to the county magistrate.

Thus, the petitioners' testimony . . .

The Monk's Confession

The potential political implications of this matter prompted the magistrate to accompany his runners to Shangfo Cun and supervise Xinxiang's arrest in person. Who was this apparent monk, who had so far claimed three separate names? No doubt to the magistrate's relief, Xinxiang offered their confession freely, and apparently without torture, since the magistrate made a point of reporting to his superiors that none had been used in this case.

Xinxiang gave their age as twenty-three *sui*, meaning that they were twenty-one or twenty-two years old, by a Western reckoning. Their original name was Zhao Jianlin, and they had been born in Dongfu Village in Xiangling County, which lies about 250 kilometers northwest of Yangcheng County (both counties are located in southern Shanxi).[4] They provided no information about their parents; they had one brother, Zhao Jianye, who was thirteen years older. In the spring of 1739, when they would have been no more than thirteen years old, Xinxiang had "left the family" to become a Buddhist monk at nearby Chaoyang Dong Temple, under the supervision of the senior monk Tongzhi ("Penetrating Intention"), who shaved Xinxiang's head and chose their Buddhist name. Xinxiang offered no explanation as to why their parents had given them away to become a monk, but it was an unusual thing to do, when they had only one other son.

After just a year at the temple, however, the novice monk ran away— Xinxiang did not explain why—and made their way to the imperial capital Beijing.

Xinxiang testified that, upon arriving in Beijing, they "returned to the laity" (*huan le su*) and "studied to become an actor" (*xue zuo xizi*). They then "sang for three to four years as a performer of female roles in opera" (*chang le san si nian xidan*). In 1744, at the age of seventeen or eighteen years old, they quit the opera, walked back home to Shanxi, returned to the temple, reshaved their head, and once again dressed as a monk. But, after a few months, Xinxiang again ran away from the temple and resumed lay attire.

There are many gaps in the record; unfortunately, all we have is whatever portion of Xinxiang's testimony the magistrate saw fit to include in his report up the chain of command. At any rate, in the spring of 1745, Xinxiang was arrested in Hongtong County, which lies on the Fen River about thirty kilometers north of Xinxiang's home. As Xinxiang frankly

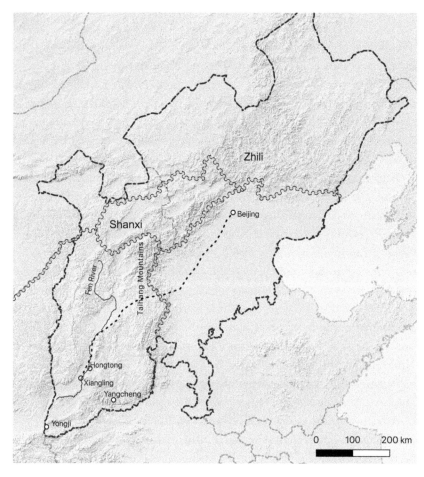

Figure 7.1 The Travels of Xinxiang.

confessed, "I put on lay clothing and casually wandered from place to place, as the spirit took me (*chuan le sujia yifu, zai ge chu xian zou*). . . . In Hongtong County, I was pretending to be the son of Mr. Cui, a member of the gentry in Yongji County, when the yamen runners arrested me. Then I was sent back home to Xiangling County under escort and beaten." After Xinxiang reported this episode, the Yangcheng County magistrate sent runners to Hongtong County to request information about Xinxiang's prior arrest. The Hongtong County magistrate reported:

On Qianlong 10.4.10, Xinxiang was arrested by runners on patrol in the county seat. They reported that although he is a monk, he was caught wearing lay clothing, and was going around claiming to be the son of one Mr. Cui, a member of the gentry in Yongji County (*kou cheng yi xi Yongji Xian Cui xiangshen zhi zi*). This humble official interrogated him and determined that he is a shameless young mendicant monk (*wuchi nianshao youseng*). I ordered him deported to his home jurisdiction of Xiangling County, where he was to be beaten with the heavy bamboo and released under guarantee so that he would keep the peace.

Xinxiang was surrendered into the custody of their older brother, who returned them to the temple.

We have no specific explanation why Xinxiang chose to impersonate the son of a member of the gentry from a different county, but no doubt this false identity was part of a confidence scheme. For Qing dynasty con artists, a favorite scam was to pretend to be someone important who had encountered bad luck and needed to borrow money (or lodgings, transportation, and the like). Perhaps this unfortunate young man had lost his money and baggage when the ferry capsized in the river, in which case the promise of a handsome reward from his wealthy father "Mr. Cui" might persuade gullible people to help him by providing a place to spend the night, a new outfit, travel expenses. . . . After expressing his gratitude, the con artist would abscond, only to try his scam somewhere else.[5] In this instance, however, someone had smelled a rat and reported Xinxiang to the local authorities. The stated reason for Xinxiang's punishment was that "he wore lay attire despite being a monk" (*yi sengren er chuandai sujia yimao*).[6] But clearly the authorities understood Xinxiang's masquerade as a member of the laity to be part of a fraudulent scheme.

Five months after being deported home and beaten, Xinxiang again ran away from the temple and made their way south to Yongji County, where they continued "aimless wandering" (*xianzou*). This time Xinxiang maintained clerical attire and passed their time hanging out with young men who were studying for the civil examinations (a preview of his later modus operandi in Yangcheng County). But also, Xinxiang later confessed, "I decided to sell illicit sex (*maijian*)," and, after some eight months of this activity, they were arrested for prostitution. Xinxiang had been reported to the Yongji County magistrate by a government student named Wang Xu, whom they had tried to seduce.

Hearing Xinxiang's confession of this *second* prior arrest, the Yangcheng County magistrate sent to Yongji County for the details, and received the following report:

> On QL 11.r3.13, the local government student Wang Xu came to the yamen and reported: "There is a monk from Pingyang Prefecture named Xinxiang, whose lay surname is Zhao. I saw that he had some education (*shao shi zhi hu*) and so I socialized with him. To my surprise, Xinxiang told me that he is actually a woman (*kou cheng xi nüren*), and he behaved wildly and without regard for propriety (*sixing wuji*). It is my duty to report him and request that he be arrested and punished." This humble official sent runners to arrest Zhao Xinxiang and bring him to the yamen. Upon interrogation, he confessed that it was true he had intended to sell illicit sex (*yitu maijian shu shi*). I ordered him deported to his home jurisdiction of Xiangling County, where he was to be beaten with the heavy bamboo and released under guarantee.

Six months after being arrested in Yongji County, however, the peripatetic Xinxiang was back on the road. Making a second visit to Beijing, they spent nearly a year in the capital and its environs staying at various temples, including the famous Wofo ("Reclining Buddha") Temple (*Wofo Si*) in the western hills outside the city. Evidently, they maintained their guise as a monk in order to secure these temples' charity; their testimony makes no mention of returning to the stage. By the autumn of 1747, Xinxiang was back in southern Shanxi. In Fengtai County, they heard about the ritual festivities being held to celebrate the renovation of Kaiming Temple, so they made their way there to enjoy the scene and seek out likely targets for confidence schemes. The elderly head monk agreed to give them lodgings, and it is at Kaiming Temple, as we have seen, that Xinxiang met the three young examination students. Xinxiang also bought a piece of beeswax and a small knife for carving seals and used them to make the fake seal they would later affix to the bogus marriage contract (beeswax was a favorite medium for forging seals).[7] Xinxiang also bought some red cloth and an oil they used to extract its color in order to make ink, which they hoped would resemble that used for official seals. Having prepared these items, Xinxiang concealed them in a tin box that they kept hidden in their clothing, intending to wait for an opportunity to use the forged seal "to cheat people out of money" (*kuangpian caiwu*). Then they decided to deepen their acquaintance with their new friends by following them home to Shangfo Cun Village.[8]

At this point in their confession, Xinxiang related an episode involving Lu Lie that the latter had not bothered to mention in his initial testimony or to his fellow petitioners. On the evening of the last day of the old lunar year (i.e., the twenty-ninth day of the twelfth month), Lu Lie had bought a flagon of wine and paid a visit to Xinxiang at the Guanyin Temple, where they had secured lodgings. Lu had already become very friendly with the young monk and had exchanged visits several times over the previous two months; of the four young men who befriended Xinxiang, Lu Lie seems to have been by far the most enthusiastic in seeking their company. As Lu later admitted, "because the monk at that temple, Guomi, is a vulgar, uneducated person, he would not be proper company to celebrate the New Year with Xinxiang (*shi ge suren, bu shi Xinxiang de banr*) and I was afraid that Xinxiang would feel lonely being all by himself on New Year's Eve (*kong ta yi ge ren lengjing bu hao guo*). So I bought some wine and went over to drink with him." As the evening progressed, Lu Lie became tipsy and fell asleep on the kang where they were sitting, and, seeing that he was in no condition to get home, Xinxiang went to sleep next to him without disrobing.

It seems, however, that Lu Lie had a particular idea of how best to assuage Xinxiang's loneliness. He woke up in the night and groped Xinxiang, waking them up, too. "Why haven't you taken off your clothes to sleep?" Lu asked. Xinxiang replied, "I have to get up early in the morning." Then Lu Lie embraced Xinxiang, holding them close, and whispered, "I'll help you take off your clothes, and we can sleep together naked, OK?" (*wo ti ni tuo le yifu, zanmen dahuo guangzhe shenzi shui ba*). Xinxiang later testified that they worried Lu Lie's groping fingers would expose the tin box with the fake seal, but they were also not interested in having sex with Lu, so Xinxiang pushed him away, saying, "Do you have any idea who I really am? Watch your manners! I'll tell you frankly—my surname is not really 'Lu,' and I'm not from Shanxi. In fact, I am an imperial censor currently on duty, my surname is Zhang and my given name Chun, and I am from the Yangzi Delta. The reason I am disguised as a monk is that I have come to Shanxi to make a secret investigation of local affairs!" As Xinxiang later testified, this statement struck Lu Lie dumb, and he did not dare make any further moves, and finally Lu went back to sleep. But Xinxiang lay on the kang pondering their next move: "I thought to myself, now that I've claimed to be a censor, this Lu Lie will no doubt tell everyone else, and if I am arrested I'll end up getting beaten and deported back home again (*fan le chulai you yao da banzi dijie*)." Xinxiang needed to make themself scarce, but were short on cash—how could they raise some in a hurry? They had already been wondering how best to use the fake seal in a scam, and it was now that they came up with the hare-brained idea of marriage fraud: "I had seen that Zhao Sipu was young and rich, and he wasn't yet married. So I decided to cheat the Zhao family out of the brideprice in order to cover my travel expenses, and then run away."

The next morning, Xinxiang said to Lu Lie:

Last night I ended up telling you the truth, so now I can't stay in this region for long, because word might get around and my identity would be exposed to all. But before I leave, there is one matter I want to settle. The other day, I noticed that Zhao Sipu is a studious, serious young man, and he definitely has a bright future. I heard that he has not yet married. At home, I have a younger sister who is not yet betrothed. I would like to ask you and Xu Lun to act as matchmakers to arrange their marriage for me. I have to leave here in a few days, but today is the first day of the New Year, which is the most auspicious day of all to make a match. You must go negotiate this match for me! And make sure to tell nobody else about my real identity.

The credulous Lu Lie agreed to act as matchmaker, with the results we have seen.

But there was a sequel to that eventful New Year's Eve on the *kang*. Once Zhao Yuqi had seen through Xinxiang's fraud, Lu Lie returned to the temple to tell Xinxiang that the marriage proposal was rejected, and that they should depart the premises immediately. Hearing this news, Xinxiang panicked, and, in an attempt to secure Lu Lie's help and support, they seduced the younger man into spending the night and let Lu sodomize them. (By this time, even the gullible Lu Lie had seen through Xinxiang's lies: "When he panicked and invited me to sodomize him, I realized that he must really be a fraud.") Two days later, Lu returned to the temple for a second night of sex. Despite granting these favors, Xinxiang soon found themself under arrest, with Lu Lie among the petitioners who had denounced them to the authorities. But Xinxiang got revenge: by testifying about these sexual escapades, they made sure that Lu Lie would be disgraced and punished—and, in the process, no doubt ruined whatever prospects Lu may have had of examination success and an official career.

Xinxiang's Sentence

Their confession complete, Xinxiang was provisionally sentenced to beheading after the assizes, for the crime of impersonating a senior official. (Their other crimes, including forging a seal and consensual sodomy, constituted "lesser offenses" because their mandated penalties were lighter.) The Yangcheng County magistrate reported Xinxiang's case up the chain of command and his recommendations were approved on review, ultimately by imperial edict. The applicable statute in the Qing code reads as follows:

> Whoever fraudulently claims without any basis (*pingkong zhacheng*) to be a minister in close attendance on the Emperor, or a member of the Grand Secretariat, the Six Offices of Scrutiny, the Six Boards, or the Censorate, or an Investigating Censor or Provincial Judge, and pretends to investigate matters in the provinces, deceiving and cheating the local officials, and thereby incites and deceives the common people (*shanhuo renmin*), shall be beheaded after the assizes, even if he has not forged identification papers.[9]

This statute appears in the code's chapter on "fraud and forgery" (*zhawei*), which falls into the category of laws pertaining to the Board of Punishment. As Mark McNicholas explains, the offenses punished in this chapter all involve some kind of "misappropriation of official authority," including counterfeiting an imperial order, forging official seals, impersonating an official or a yamen runner, and minting counterfeit coins.[10]

The political implications of these crimes link them closely to heterodoxy, as does the overarching concept of deception or fraud. Significantly, the phrase *shanhuo renmin* ("incites and deceives the common people") also appears in the statute against heterodoxy discussed in chapter 2. Recall that

Ming and Qing officials imagined heterodoxy to be a malicious fraud perpetrated on the gullible masses by a handful of cynical ringleaders; they gave no credit whatsoever to the content of "heterodox" teachings, nor did they allow that "heterodox" leaders might be sincere in their beliefs. From this standpoint, the most dangerous sort of fraud was precisely the misappropriation of official authority covered by the "fraud and forgery" chapter of the code, and the basic penalty for most of these crimes was beheading after the assizes (which was more severe than even the strangulation mandated for heterodoxy).

Motive mattered, of course, and close attention was paid to the ambitions and actual achievements of the perpetrators of forgery and fraud. For example, a con artist like Xinxiang might forge an official seal in order to cheat people out of money, and, by the same token, the usual motive for counterfeiting (which involved debasing the metal content of coins) was profit. But individuals of far greater ambition also committed these crimes: it was common for rebels against the imperial state to claim official titles and to prepare corresponding seals, and those attempting to found new dynasties would also mint coinage inscribed with their own invented reign periods.[11] Moreover, other statutes in the "fraud and forgery" chapter of the code prohibit forging an official almanac or fraudulently inventing a good omen. These were explicitly ideological crimes, because establishing the calendar and predicting and interpreting omens (such as eclipses) were imperial prerogatives, such cosmic matters being closely tied to the fortunes of the ruling dynasty. Manipulation of the calendar and of omens was precisely the sort of heterodox scam that rebel leaders might use "to incite and deceive the common people."

Aside from Xinxiang, the Yangcheng County magistrate closely interrogated the three young men who had befriended the monk: Zhao Silun, Xu Lun, and especially Lu Lie. He was particularly concerned to find out whether they or anyone else had abetted Xinxiang's impersonation of an imperial official. At first the magistrate rejected out of hand the idea that the young men might have actually believed Xinxiang's lies:

> First he said his name was Lu, then he said it was Zhang! Not only that, he's a monk! How could you possibly believe that he was a censor on an official tour of inspection? On top of that, how could you be so stupid as to do what he told you and act as matchmakers to negotiate the marriage of his supposed younger sister to Zhao Sipu?

It's obvious that all three of you had sodomy with him and abetted his carving of the fake seal and impersonation of a censor in hope of cheating people! Quickly, confess!

In the end, the three succeeded in persuading the magistrate that they were not coconspirators—after all, had they not joined Zhao Yuqi in reporting Xinxiang to the authorities? But Lu Lie could not escape the consequences of his own behavior: he was sentenced to one month in the cangue and one hundred blows of the heavy bamboo for consensual sodomy. In addition, the monk Guomi was sentenced to eighty blows of the heavy bamboo according to the catch-all statute against "doing things that ought not to be done—severe cases" and ordered to return to the laity, because he was an unlicensed monk, but also, by allowing Xinxiang to stay at his temple, he had unwittingly facilitated the monk's crimes. Finally, administrative sanctions were recommended for the local officials whose negligence had allowed both Xinxiang and Guomi to shave their heads and become monks without receiving official licenses.

In certain respects, Xinxiang's case received special handling not seen in a routine death penalty case, such as a homicide involving ordinary people. For example, the Yangcheng County magistrate made a point of reporting to his superiors that he had used no torture when interrogating Xinxiang, who had confessed freely. When Xinxiang fell ill in custody, the prefect of Pingyang Prefecture (which had jurisdiction over Yangcheng County) ordered the magistrate of a neighboring county to travel to Yangcheng County and personally examine Xinxiang at the jail to make sure they had not been abused and were receiving appropriate care (it was important to keep the prisoner alive until the possibility of a wider conspiracy had been ruled out). When Xinxiang's case was forwarded to the provincial capital, it was reviewed jointly by the provincial judge and the provincial treasurer, whereas only the judge would have been involved in a routine case. When they were finished, the provincial governor interrogated Xinxiang in person to confirm that their oral confession matched that recorded in the file (governors were expected to review major cases, but in this instance the governor of Shanxi made an explicit report).

This special handling can be compared to that seen in the three cases of "men masquerading in women's attire" addressed in chapters 2, 4, and 5. Xiong Mumu's case was taken over from the county magistrate by the provincial governor, who entrusted it to a circuit intendant and then reported his findings directly to the emperor in a secret palace memorial. In Zhang Yaoguniang's case, preliminary judgments were twice overruled, after which the provincial governor ordered a special joint investigation by two prefects, whom he personally supervised. Xing Shi's case was handled with extraordinary speed by senior ministers in the Board of Punishment, who interrogated the suspects under torture until they provided a satisfactory confession and then reported their findings directly to the emperor. Details vary from case to case, but the special care taken in all reflects the ideological and political significance attributed to them by senior officials.

Making Sense of Xinxiang

As with our other case studies, the surviving record of Xinxiang's life contains many gaps, and it raises more questions than we can definitively answer based on the available evidence. But educated guesses can help fill in the gaps, however tentatively.

Xinxiang's Career in Beijing

Take, for example, Xinxiang's first sojourn in the imperial capital, where they would abandon their vocation as a monk in order to become an actor of female roles—a "boy actress," to borrow Andrea Goldman's felicitous phrase.[12] The case record provides no information about Xinxiang's journey from Shanxi to Beijing, but as far as we can tell they traveled alone and on foot. They would have been thirteen or fourteen years old. The most direct route from Xiangling County would have taken Xinxiang north along the Fen River as far as Pingyao County, where they would have left the river and headed northeast via Yuci County (the home of the notorious Sang Chong), Shouyang County, and Pingding Department to cross the Taihang mountains (and pass through a southern extension of the Great Wall) at Jingxingkou. Entering Zhili Province, their route would have continued directly northeast to the capital, via Zhengding Prefecture, Baoding Prefecture, and Zhuo Department. The entire trip of approximately eight hundred kilometers might have taken the runaway novice monk six to eight weeks, assuming all went well. Today, one can drive almost exactly the same route in about eight hours.[13]

This route was an important postal artery as well as a key link in the Shanxi merchants' transportation network, which connected south-central Shanxi with the imperial capital and Mongolia. It would have been well traveled, with plenty of restaurants, taverns, inns, and (most important for our story) temples along the way. Presumably, Xinxiang survived by receiving free board and room at Buddhist temples, as we know they later did on their second trip to Beijing and also in Yangcheng County; it seems to have been routine for mendicant monks and other travelers to receive this kind of hospitality.[14] It is also possible that Xinxiang began doing sex work on the road: we know that is one of the ways they made ends meet later on, and their interactions with Lu Lie also suggest experience in using sex as a means to an end.

Upon arriving in the capital, how did Xinxiang switch from being a novice monk to an actor? All the information we have about this key episode is contained in their brief statement that "I went up to the capital and trained as an actor, and then I sang female roles for three to four years" (*shang jing xue zuo xizi, chang le san si nian xidan*). Fortunately, we know enough about the opera scene in eighteenth-century Beijing to posit a couple of plausible scenarios.

First, it is important to note the strong overlap between the temple and the theater throughout North China, where opera performances played a fundamental role in local religion and were a regular feature of festivals and temple fairs. Operas were performed to celebrate the New Year and other major holidays, including the birthdays of various deities throughout the year. Many temples had permanent stages where traveling troupes of players would perform. Shanxi was particularly well known for its local traditions of ritual opera, which David Johnson has documented in remarkable detail. As Johnson observes, "Southern Shanxi and the rest of north China was saturated with temples, and large-scale sacrifices to the gods who occupied those temples took place constantly throughout the year."[15] It is safe to assume, therefore, that anyone growing up in rural Shanxi in the eighteenth century would have had considerable exposure to local opera.

In Beijing, too, the temple was one of the three main venues for opera performance, the others being purpose-built theaters (usually referred to as "teahouses") and private homes of the wealthy, who might maintain their own private troupes. The temple fair was the most lowbrow of these venues, and it witnessed the most promiscuous mixing of social classes and of the sexes among its spectators.[16] In both Shanxi and Beijing, therefore, the temple was a setting where clergy and actors would have regularly encountered each other.

What we now know as "Peking opera" (*jingju*) was a hybrid of regional theatrical forms brought to the capital by merchants and other sojourners from various parts of China. It achieved mature form in the late eighteenth century, and its golden age lasted from then until the end of the dynasty. One of its four main sources was "clapper opera" (*bangzi qiang* or *Qin qiang*), which originated in eastern Shaanxi and southern Shanxi during the Ming and became the dominant theatrical form in the capital during the eighteenth century. Clapper opera got its name from a wooden device used to strike a loud beat, accompanied by string instruments. This style of opera was brought to Beijing by Shanxi merchants (who included grain and vegetable oil dealers from Xinxiang's native Xiangling County) and was well established in the capital by the time the novice monk arrived in 1740. Clapper troupes were exclusively male, and in the eighteenth century many of Beijing's best-known actors were the boys who performed female roles, the *dan*, in those troupes. Celebrated for its acting more than its singing, clapper opera was notorious for lively, bawdy, and controversial content and hence was denigrated as vulgar by some literati. It was also closely associated with prostitution (of which more later in this chapter), and many prominent "boy actresses" were known to be the sexual partners of wealthy male patrons. If anything, the overlap between "actor" and "prostitute" became even more blatant during the nineteenth-century golden age of the Peking opera.[17]

Against this background, the following scenario seems plausible. When Xinxiang arrived in the capital, they stayed at a temple, where they encountered an opera troupe—perhaps a clapper troupe that included players from their home province—and they managed to get themself recruited. We know from Xinxiang's testimony that they sang female parts, and, given their youth and other qualities, they would no doubt have trained to perform as a *huadan*: the role of a young, lively, flirtatious girl. Whoever recruited Xinxiang must have perceived some aptitude for the stage and for female impersonation in particular, and, since Xinxiang performed for three to four years, we can surmise that they must have had some talent. Most important, however, Xinxiang must have been pretty; "in line with aesthetic taste in Qing Beijing, an effeminate, pale and delicate looking boy became the first choice for *dan* training," and much of the training regimen endured by boy actresses was designed to enhance these qualities.[18]

All of this seems to fit the rest of what we know about Xinxiang: they were a charming raconteur and liar who could switch roles and adopt new identities with apparent ease; moreover, at least some men found them sexually attractive. Given that so many of the "boy actresses" moonlighted as high-end prostitutes and escorts, Xinxiang's sex appeal would have been an important qualification.[19]

Another plausible scenario is that Xinxiang was kidnapped and sold to an opera troupe. Qing dynasty Beijing was the site of an extensive, multi-faceted traffic in young boys that supplied the imperial household's eunuch establishment, the boy brothels ("barbershops") located along with the teahouse theaters just outside the southern gates of the Manchu "inner city" and, of course, the opera.[20] Most of the boys who entered this traffic were initially sold by their own parents (especially to the eunuch establishment, which was tightly regulated), but, in the theater world at least, such boys might be resold again and again. Others were kidnapping victims, and some of the most famous *dan* actors in eighteenth-century Beijing started out as homeless orphans who were simply picked up on the street. The opera drew most of its supply of boys from the southern provinces Jiangsu and Anhui, but some, like Xinxiang, were recruited locally.[21]

Occasionally, this traffic in boys—and the sexual exploitation with which it was closely linked—surfaces in the legal case records that survive from Beijing. For example, a case from 1834 involved a boy named Xu Sanxi, who at the age of thirteen *sui* (i.e., eleven or twelve years old) had been brought to Beijing from his home in Jiangsu by his maternal uncle, who hired him out as a servant to the household of a senior official in the Board of Works named Zhang Shichen. After less than a month, however, Xu Sanxi's uncle took him away and "conditionally sold" (*dianmai*) him to Xiao Rong, the leader of the Sanqing Opera Troupe (*Sanqing xiban*), for training as an actor. Conditional sale (as opposed to "irrevocable sale," *jue mai*) meant that, in theory, the boy could be "redeemed" (*shu*) after a fixed period of time, as long as his uncle could refund his original sale price.[22] But, in reality, it is unlikely that most boys trafficked in this manner were able to keep in touch with their families. Xu Sanxi showed little promise for the stage, so after two years Xiao Rong "conditionally resold" (*zhuandian*) him to Hao Juqing of the Hechun Opera Troupe (*Hechun xiban*). Hao Juqing repeatedly raped the boy (who was then thirteen or fourteen years old), but otherwise found no use for him, because he clearly had no talent for opera, and, finally, Hao told Xu Sanxi to find himself a new situation.

In desperation, the boy returned to Zhang Shichen's household and begged his former master to take him back in service. Out of pity for a former servant who had fallen on hard times, Zhang agreed to "conditionally buy" him for a price of fifty strings of capital cash, paid to Hao in order to secure the boy's release from the Hechun troupe. Later, however, the boy felt unhappy at being scolded and beaten, so he robbed his master and ran away. The case record concerns the boy's prosecution for these acts and also Zhang Shichen's punishment for having hired an actor into his service (which violated the prohibition against officials consorting with actors, a law that seems to have been honored mainly in the breach).[23]

In a second example, from 1837, Imai, Prince Zhuang, was punished for having established a private opera troupe for his own pleasure at his mansion. Through brokers, he had "conditionally purchased" more than twenty local boys from their parents and was having them trained to sing *dan* roles. He was also sexually exploiting these boys as a sort of harem: he personally inspected each boy before agreeing to purchase him and had them take turns in pairs waiting on him at night in his bedchamber, where he would rape them. The boys were all Han Chinese from poor families who had migrated to the capital from the surrounding countryside, and their ages were around thirteen or fourteen *sui* (i.e., eleven to thirteen years old). Their parents sold them out of poverty, for prices ranging from fifteen to twenty strings of "capital cash" each. After a trial supervised by the emperor's brother, Prince Zhuang was fined five years' worth of his official stipend, and his troupe-cum-harem was disbanded.[24]

These two cases illustrate the way impoverished parents supplied both the commercial and private troupes with their fledgling actors, as well as how even boys who had been "conditionally" sold, with the theoretical hope of eventually being redeemed, might continue to circulate in the market. What also stands out is the systematic sexual exploitation that pervaded the opera scene, in addition to the fact that everyone knew about it. These were by no means marginal phenomena: the Sanqing and Hechun troupes to which Xu Sanxi was sold happen to have been two of the most famous Peking opera troupes in nineteenth-century Beijing.[25] These two cases postdate Xinxiang's arrival in the imperial capital by nearly a century, but there is no reason to believe that the traffic in boys that fueled the theater industry would have operated any differently in their day.

The involvement of a first-ranked Manchu prince in such a case also exposes the sordid social realities that framed certain episodes in the eighteenth-century novel *Dream of the Red Chamber* (*Hongloumeng*)—specifically, the story of actor Jiang Yuhan, who is avidly pursued by two infatuated fictional princes and also has an intimate, if ambiguous, relationship with the novel's hero, Jia Baoyu. One of Jiang Yuhan's patrons, the prince of Zhongshun, actually installs him in his palace, presumably to serve as his catamite, and, when the actor runs away, the prince sends his minions to hunt him down. Although the sexual dimension of these relationships is never spelled out, it would have been obvious to any Qing dynasty reader.[26]

Between "leaving the family" to become a monk in 1739 and their arrest in Yangcheng County for impersonating an imperial censor in 1748, the longest time Xinxiang spent in any one place was these four years in Beijing. In 1744, they returned home to Shanxi and briefly resumed the monastic life in Xiangling County. Why did they quit the opera and leave the capital? Xinxiang does not seem to have felt any profound commitment to a monastic vocation; after all, within a few months they would once again run away from the temple and resume lay attire, only to be arrested in Hongtong County. The case record provides no explanation for this decision, but there are a couple of possibilities. When they first arrived in Beijing, they were fifteen *sui* (i.e., thirteen or fourteen years old), and when they quit the opera they were nineteen *sui* (seventeen or eighteen years old). In other words, during their time onstage they were in the prime age range for an actor of young female roles. According to Colin Mackerras, *dan* actors were nearly all adolescent or teenage boys, and they had short careers, because "their appeal as actors depended to some extent on physical attraction." They began performing as young as twelve *sui*, and most "lost their appeal" and left the profession by the age of twenty. Those who stayed on past that age usually stopped performing themselves and instead focused on training their successors.[27] Wu Cuncun's estimates are similar: "The career of a *dan* was short, commencing around thirteen and lasting until around eighteen years of age. As soon as signs of masculinity began to show on their faces and bodies customers began to fall away and their careers soon came to an end. This was the case for the stars as well as run-of-the-mill actors."[28] Therefore, it is likely that Xinxiang was forced to retire because of their age.

Another possibility is that Xinxiang was unhappy and ran away. One can understand why that might have been the case, especially if they were a victim of trafficking and sexual exploitation. It seems unlikely that the arduous training and discipline of an opera troupe would have appealed to Xinxiang, given their chronic refusal to submit to authority.[29] Whatever the reason, it seems more surprising that they stayed put for four years, given their incorrigible wanderlust, than that they finally moved on. If anything, that uncharacteristic perseverance suggests that Xinxiang may have found some kind of fulfillment or even self-revelation in the theatrical life.

Xinxiang's Confidence Schemes

Xinxiang's scams (at least the ones we know about) involved posing either as the son of an important member of the regional gentry or as an imperial official, and in either capacity as an educated man of superior pedigree. In 1745, they were arrested in Hongtong County for wearing lay attire (despite being a monk) and claiming to be the son of a member of the gentry from Yongji County surnamed "Cui." In 1747, when they were arrested in Yangcheng County, they had started out claiming to be the adopted son of Lu Bingchun, a prominent member of the gentry from Xiangling County: supposedly their father had lost his official post, and therefore Xinxiang had been forced to "leave the family" and become a wandering monk. They told this story to the head monk of Kaiming Temple in order to gain lodgings there and subsequently shared it with the young examination students they met.

Xinxiang's training as an actor presumably enhanced their ability to adopt new identities. On a practical level, a familiarity with costumes, props, and wigs may have helped them switch between presenting as a monk and as a member of the laity. To appear as a monk would not have been difficult, requiring simply the shaving off of one's queue and putting on a monk's robe. To switch the other way would have required more artifice, because one cannot regrow a queue on short notice, and lay clothing was more complicated than monastic attire—especially if posing as a member of the gentry. When Xinxiang was arrested in Hongtong County in lay attire, they may have been wearing a fake queue; such wigs did exist, for use by bald men.[30]

We do not know whether the alleged Mr. Cui really existed, but Lu Bingchun was certainly a real person. Lu was probably the most prominent man in Xiangling County in Xinxiang's day and, indeed, one of the most prominent the county has ever produced. His date of birth is unclear, but we know that he had outstanding success with the civil service examinations, winning his provincial *juren* degree in 1726 (one of only two from his county for that year) and his metropolitan *jinshi* degree just four years later. In fact, he was his county's only *jinshi* from 1694 to 1736. Lu is listed as a compiler of the 1732 county gazetteer, where his preface appears just after that written by the county magistrate, and he makes multiple appearances in the Republican-era gazetteer (which reproduces much of the content of earlier editions). According to his biographical sketch in the chapter on local worthies, Lu was "widely learned and an able writer," with an upright and straightforward character. After receiving his *jinshi* and initial training as a bachelor in the Hanlin Academy, he held various posts as a censor and a supervisor of civil examinations. In the early Qianlong era, however, he resigned his offices and returned home to teach. In this capacity, Lu attracted students from throughout southern Shanxi, many of whom also achieved distinction in the civil examinations. His publications included essays and poetry, several samples of which appear in the gazetteers. He seems to have been on particularly good terms with the magistrate who wrote the 1732 gazetteer's other preface, because its poetry chapter includes two poems that Lu wrote in response to a set of the magistrate's poems, which are also included.[31]

Thus, in 1747, when Xinxiang was claiming to be Lu Bingchun's adopted son, Lu himself was back home in Xiangling County and was a well-known figure with powerful regional and national connections. Lu Bingchun must have been famous, if even Xinxiang had heard of him. Moreover, it seems that Xinxiang expected people in Yangcheng County to have heard of Lu as well, or else they would not have borrowed his name. After Xinxiang's arrest, the magistrate of Yangcheng County contacted Lu Bingchun just to make sure there was no truth to the monk's claims. Lu replied by letter that "I have never met that monk."

Literacy and Cultural Knowledge

Perhaps the most interesting thing about this fraud is that it seems to have been quite convincing. We have no information about exactly what triggered Xinxiang's arrest in Hongtong County, only that they somehow provoked enough suspicion that eventually someone reported them to the authorities. We know more about how their later masquerade as Lu

Bingchun's "adopted son" was received: the young students to whom they confided this tale all believed it. The students testified that they began socializing with Xinxiang because "we saw that he was the son of an established family (*jiujia zidi*)" and "an educated person" (*wenmozhong ren*). Lu Lie further testified that he had decided to visit Xinxiang on New Year's Eve because the only other monk at the temple, Guomi, was "a vulgar, uneducated person (*suren*)" who would not make a fitting companion for Xinxiang. It also seems significant that Zhao Yuqi did not challenge Xinxiang's story when they were first introduced—it was only later, when Xinxiang claimed to be an imperial censor, that Zhao Yuqi became suspicious, and it was the fake contract that convinced him that the monk was a fraud.

Another striking detail is the testimony of the government student Wang Xu, who had reported Xinxiang to the Yongji County magistrate for prostitution in 1746. To explain how he had befriended the monk in the first place, Wang stated: "I saw that he had some education and so I socialized with him." The phrase I have translated here as "he had some education" is "*shao shi zhi hu*," which literally means "he knew some *zhi hu*"—*zhi* and *hu* being particles frequently used in classical Chinese and therefore serving as shorthand for classical literacy. It is clear that Wang Xu, like Lu Lie and his friends, considered Xinxiang to be no ordinary monk, but, rather, a respectable man of their own social class and milieu, who was worthy of befriending. In addition to literacy, Xinxiang must have made a convincing performance of the etiquette and protocols appropriate to their class, both in speech and in body language: greetings, small talk, gestures, deportment, and so on.

Wang Xu's comment about *zhi hu* raises an intriguing question—it is clear that Xinxiang could read and write, but how well? Moreover, where did they acquire whatever education they did have? There is no consensus on literacy rates in the Qing, or even the definition of "literacy" in this context. In the most generous estimate, Evelyn Rawski has argued that many people enjoyed a functional level of "popular literacy," defined as the ability to read a few dozen or hundred characters, and by this low standard she estimates that perhaps 30 to 45 percent of men "knew how to read and write." But it is doubtful that mastery of a few dozen or even a couple hundred characters really counted as "literacy" in the Qing dynasty; it might have enabled someone to decipher the shop signs in a market town, but little more. James Hayes has documented the central role played by literate specialists, who earned a living writing contracts, letters, New Year's couplets, and the like for a fee. In my own experience, very few of the contracts used by ordinary people for land sales, moneylending, household division, adoption, the sale of wives and children, and other transactions were written by the contracting parties themselves. Instead, nearly all were written by the sort of people Hayes describes—namely, scribes (*daibi*) who had been paid for their service. The high demand for such specialists suggests that a really useful level of literacy was not very common in Qing dynasty China.[32]

In the case of Xinxiang, we seem to be confronting something far more sophisticated than Rawski's minimal standard, but just how sophisticated is not entirely clear. After all, the essence of Xinxiang's scam was to persuade other people that they were more important and impressive than they really were. In eighteenth-century China, only a small percentage of men acquired the classical literacy necessary to participate in the civil service examinations, and this level seems to be what the young men who made Xinxiang's acquaintance had in mind when they described the monk as appearing to be educated and one of their own kind. It seems unlikely, however, that Xinxiang really possessed the education necessary to sit for the examinations, which required rote memorization of a vast corpus of canonical texts as well as the ability to write essays about them in classical Chinese according to a strict, standardized format. Such an education had to be acquired at private expense, and in Benjamin Elman's view this requirement alone would have excluded well over 90 percent of the population from participating even at the entry level of county-sponsored practice examinations.[33]

One of the gaps in Xinxiang's case record is that we know nothing of their family or social background except that they came from the village of Dongxu Cun, located on the Fen River in Xiangling County, and that they had one brother, who was thirteen years older. In south-central Shanxi, the term *cun* ("village") can be misleading, because some of these places hosted the mansions of wealthy merchant lineages and served as important commercial centers, even while continuing to call themselves *cun*. One example is Shangfo Cun (where the Zhaos lived and Xinxiang was arrested), which was actually a substantial entrepôt that hosted several merchant lineages. Located on the Qin River, Shangfo Cun was the site of an important ford, and the official post road ran through its center. This "village" had more than thirty different temples of various sizes, including several where students could worship literary deities such as Confucius, Wenchangdi, and Kuixing. The biggest temple hosted a school, and, over the course of the Qing, a number of local men achieved modest success in the lower stages of the civil examinations.[34]

But Xinxiang's birthplace of Dongxu Cun seems to have been a village in the most ordinary sense of the word. It still exists, currently being comprised of 290 households totaling some 1600 people and occupying about 5000 *mu*, most of which is farmland. The main crops are wheat and maize.[35] From the Google Maps satellite image it appears to be an unexceptional place: a cluster of houses near the bank of the river, surrounded by the long, narrow agricultural fields typical of North China. We know that in Xinxiang's day Dongxu Cun contained at least one temple, Chaoyang Dong, which had at least one resident monk, because that is where Xinxiang was sent when they "left the family" to become a monk themself. But, again, the presence of a temple would have been unexceptional—as David Johnson observes, rural Shanxi was "saturated" with temples. From the little we know about Dongxu Cun, it does not seem like a likely place to get a serious classical education.

In Qing legal case records, when an individual's occupation or social situation is not explicitly stated, the safest assumption is usually that they were a peasant. After all, the vast majority of the Chinese population were peasants, and that is certainly true of the people who got involved in legal cases as well. Therefore, I have assumed that Xinxiang was born into an ordinary peasant family. But, if that is correct, it raises the question of where Xinxiang acquired whatever education they did have.

Two possibilities suggest themselves. First, Xinxiang may have received at least the beginnings of a rudimentary education during their initial year as a monk, after leaving the family and moving to the local temple. A monk needed at least some familiarity with sutras and other ritual texts, and, even if most instruction involved oral recitation and memorization, we can guess that Xinxiang's master may have begun teaching them how to read before they ran away to Beijing. Second, they probably continued learning to read during those four years in Beijing with the opera. Certainly, most of the young boy apprentices, having come from very humble families, would have been illiterate, and operas were typically learned by recitation under the tutelage of a master (a process known as *shuoxi*, literally "to speak the play"). But the theater also utilized a variety of written materials, including scripts, playbills, and the notice boards that announced to actors what plays were to be performed on a given day. In that environment, total illiteracy would presumably have been a disadvantage. Moreover, at the high end of the hierarchy, boy actresses were groomed to be companions for educated men at drinking and poetry parties, much like courtesans, and that would have required at least some degree of classical literacy. We see a fictional example in chapter 28 of the eighteenth-century novel *Dream of the Red Chamber*, when the actor of female roles Jiang Yuhan participates in a drinking game with Baoyu and his elite friends that involves both composing and reciting poetry. Jiang is portrayed as an enthusiastic participant (in contrast with the vulgar Xue Pan, who is actually a member of the elite), and none of the others present seem to find that surprising.[36]

The Limits of Xinxiang's Knowledge

But just how literate was Xinxiang? Aside from the impression they made on their student acquaintances, the evidence for their literacy consists of the fraudulent marriage contract they dictated to Lu Lie and stamped with the beeswax seal. This document was what decisively exposed Xinxiang as a fraud—in fact, the Zhao family's request that Xinxiang write it may be seen as a sort of literacy test or even a trap. Nevertheless, several aspects of it are impressive, suggesting both a measure of literacy and some pretty sophisticated knowledge.

Take, for example, the fake title claimed by Xinxiang: "imperially delegated investigating censor for the Shanxi Circuit and concurrent vice minister of the right in the Board of War" (*Qinchai Shanxi dao jiancha yushi jianguan Bing Bu youshilang*). Both "investigating censor for the Shanxi Circuit" and "vice minister of the right in the Board of War" were genuine offices, and the fact that Xinxiang knew these titles and phrased them correctly in dictation indicates that they had some familiarity with the upper tier of the imperial government. Conceivably they had actually encountered such officials during their sojourn in Beijing.[37]

Nevertheless, as Zhao Yuqi commented, "even the official title did not seem quite correct" (*jiushi nage guanxian ye youxie bu shen dique*). Why not? For one thing, *jianguan* is the wrong term to use in this context, although as a piece of official jargon it may sound impressive. The correct term for "concurrent" holding of two official titles would be simply *jian*, whereas *jianguan* means something like "also managing the following" and should be followed by some task or area of responsibility rather than a title. But the biggest problem is the disproportion in rank between the two titles claimed by Xinxiang. At rank 2b, a vice minister of the right in the Board of War was one of the most senior officials in the imperial government, someone who would likely be attending imperial audiences on a regular basis. In contrast, an investigating censor ranked only 7a, and this post was usually given to brand-new recipients of the *jinshi* degree, at the beginning of their careers.[38] It strains credulity that the same man would have held these two titles at the same time. It also seems strange that the junior office would be listed before the senior one in Xinxiang's title. In short, Xinxiang's assumed title reveals both the extent and the limits of their knowledge.

Another notable feature of the contract is the phrase I have translated as "the tradition of intermarriage between the Chen and Zhu lineages and between the states of Qin and Jin" (*xu jie Zhu Chen, yong xie Qin Jin*). This phrase contains two classical literary allusions to marriage. Zhu and Chen were the surnames of two lineages that dwelled in the same village and intermarried for many generations. For this reason, ZhuChen Village (*ZhuChen Cun*) was immortalized in an eponymous poem by the Tang poet Bai Juyi, and thereafter its name became a byword for harmonious coexistence through marriage.[39] Similarly, Qin and Jin were neighboring feudal states in ancient China that maintained peace for many years by arranging marriage alliances between their respective ruling families. Xinxiang's knowledge of these allusions is perhaps less remarkable than it might at first seem, however, because they were clichés that often appeared in marriage contracts. Their use epitomizes Xinxiang's effort to pose as an educated man: superficially impressive, but unable to withstand scrutiny. Still, at very least Xinxiang must have previously seen genuine marriage contracts, or perhaps had had access to a handbook of model contracts of the kind that scribes consulted.[40]

Finally, there is the official seal that Xinxiang forged. Most of the scams documented by Mark McNicholas in his authoritative study of Qing dynasty conmen involved the forgery or misuse of official documents, and it was official seals that made such documents authentic. When a forgery was exposed, therefore, the trigger was often an unconvincing seal imprint, with errors in script, color of ink, shape, or size that a knowledgeable observer would notice immediately. In that respect, Xinxiang's case reflects a larger pattern.[41]

In the end, Xinxiang's forged seal failed to pass muster; nevertheless, what we know about it indicates that Xinxiang knew a fair amount about genuine seals. In the Qing dynasty, official seals were usually square in shape and divided vertically into two parallel columns of equal width, with Chinese characters on the right side and Manchu on the left.[42] It is not surprising that Xinxiang was familiar with the basic appearance of such seals, because they were stamped on all manner of documents readily seen by ordinary folk, including land tax receipts, "red contracts" for real estate sales ("red" because they bore official seals stamped in red ink, to confirm payment of the transaction tax), and official proclamations. Fraudsters who sought to forge an official seal might simply tear the imprint of one off a publicly posted proclamation and then copy it in secret. Moreover, nonofficial seals were carved for a variety of legitimate purposes—for example, the wooden seals used by Daoist clergy for printing talismans that they retailed to the faithful—so the basic materials and skills were not extremely rare.[43]

It is nevertheless remarkable that Xinxiang actually managed to forge a seal, which required appropriate materials and the ability to carve its surface in mirror image. Somewhere, Xinxiang had learned how to do this—for example, they knew to use beeswax (a favorite medium for forging seals) and what kind of knife to use, as well as how to fashion red ink by extracting the color from dyed cloth. Moreover, they were able to carve the seal in mirror image, with both Chinese characters and what at least looked to observers like real Manchu writing. Later on, when pressed by the magistrate whether anyone else had helped him forge the seal, Xinxiang asserted that "the Manchu and Chinese writing on the seal was all created by me" (*na Man Han wen dou shi xiaode zaochulai de*); they also denied basing it on any model. In his case report, the Yangcheng County magistrate described Xinxiang's seal as bearing "Manchu and Chinese" (*Qing Han*) characters that "lack standard calligraphic form" (*bing wu ziti*); he also derided the seal's characters as "confused" or "a mess" (*hutu*), and Zhao Yuqi noted that the seal "did not look right" (*buxiang*). But neither the magistrate nor Zhao reported that the seal was carved with random, meaningless marks. Rather, its writing was apparently recognizable to them as Chinese and Manchu (we should note that neither man was likely to have actually known how to read Manchu, but Xinxiang's effort was convincing enough that they thought it *looked* like Manchu). What betrayed the seal as a forgery was the characters' "lack of standard calligraphic form"—an apparent reference to the rules governing the design and production of official seals, which were very strict in the Qing dynasty. The imperial government designated a fixed number of standard calligraphic styles for the Chinese and Manchu writing used on seals and mandated which style should be used on what kind of seal.[44] Evidently, what the magistrate and Zhao Yuqi noticed was not that Xinxiang had failed to carve Chinese and Manchu onto the seal, but that the results had failed to conform to the mandated style.

When Zhao Yuqi heard that Xinxiang was claiming to be a senior imperial official and that they wanted to marry their sister to Zhao's nephew, he immediately rejected this tale as incredible. Lu Lie persuaded him to suspend judgment until Xinxiang had written a contract, but it is clear that Zhao Yuqi was simply waiting to have his suspicions confirmed. None of this is surprising, because the entire scenario was absurd.

First, there was Xinxiang's youth, which contradicted their claim of high office. It was inconceivable that a Han Chinese youth of twenty-one to twenty-two years old would be appointed as an investigating censor, let alone a vice minister in the Board of War. Later in the eighteenth century, the notorious Heshen would be appointed vice minister of the Board of Revenue at the age of twenty-six and grand councilor shortly thereafter. But Heshen was a Manchu bannerman, and he owed his meteoric rise to the extraordinary (and never clearly explained) affection of the elderly Qianlong emperor. In the late Qing, members of the imperial family occasionally occupied senior positions at an even younger age: for example, the sixth son of the Daoguang emperor, Yixin (Prince Gong), was appointed grand councilor at the tender age of twenty.[45] But Han Chinese had to follow the examination track, and even the youngest exam prodigies were in their late twenties or early thirties before achieving high office.

Second, that an imperial censor would disguise himself as a mendicant monk, traveling alone and on foot, without baggage or retinue, in order to make a secret investigation on the emperor's behalf seems more like an episode from folklore or fiction than something that would have happened in real life. The scenario of "incognito investigation" (*sifang*) is a favorite of court case fiction (*gong'an xiaoshuo*) and drama, and Xinxiang's inspiration for this fraud probably was the latter. For example, the famous story "The Fifteen Strings of Cash" (*Shiwu guan*), which was adapted into a play in the early Qing by Zhu Suchen, centers on an official who disguises himself as a humble fortune teller in order to solve a murder case. Scenes from this opera were often performed in eighteenth-century Beijing. There are many similar tales about the celebrated Judge Bao, who is the hero of several operas. For example, in "Judge Bao Sells Rice at Chenzhou" (*Bao Daizhi Chenzhou tiao mi*), he travels incognito, riding a mule and accompanied by a single servant, in order to investigate official corruption during a famine. In this scenario, the climax comes when the hero reveals his identity and turns the tables on the malefactors whom he has exposed.[46] But it is unlikely that a genuine Qing official would do such a thing, so it is not surprising that Zhao Yuqi found Xinxiang's story unconvincing.

Third, Xinxiang's proposal to betroth their sister, who supposedly was back home in the Yangzi Delta (about a thousand kilometers distant), to a casually encountered minor member of the regional gentry in Shanxi, made no sense at all. In reality, an official of the rank claimed by Xinxiang would have been a wealthy and powerful man, with connections throughout the elite in both the Yangzi Delta and Beijing. He certainly would have handled his family's marital affairs in a different manner.

Among the Han Chinese elite in the Qing dynasty, marriages were usually arranged through personal connections within an extended social circle, and an informal understanding between the two families would precede the engagement of matchmakers. The subsequent negotiations between the families followed elaborate customary rules. The groom's family would engage a matchmaker to deliver a letter requesting the bride in marriage (*qinghun shu*), written on red paper in classical language according to a standard format. The bride's family would express their acceptance in a similar letter (*yunhun shu*), fortune tellers would check the bride's date and time of birth for compatibility with the groom's, and, finally, the bride-price or gifts (*caili*) would be conveyed from the groom's family to the bride's family. Once an auspicious date had been chosen, the actual wedding would take place, when the bride and her dowry were delivered to the groom's household with elaborate ceremony and great fanfare. Among the elite, it was standard for the value of the dowry to exceed the value of the bride-price, in order to demonstrate that the bride was not being sold by her parents; moreover, the bride-price was often used to buy goods that would constitute part of the dowry. Details varied according to regional custom and also the wealth and status of the parties, but in general the gentry/literati followed the basic procedure described here. Moreover, the marriage of Qing officials—especially senior officials—was regulated by the imperial state's sumptuary laws.[47]

None of what Xinxiang did in offering their (fictitious) sister in marriage conformed to standard practice within the social class to which they were pretending to belong. Instead, what Xinxiang apparently proposed to do was to exchange a contract betrothing their sister for her bride-price in cash, which they would carry away. Supposedly, at a later date, they would arrange to bring the sister to Shanxi in order to finalize her marriage. No wonder Zhao Yuqi was skeptical.

Moreover, its two classical allusions notwithstanding, the document dictated by Xinxiang to Lu Lie looks nothing like a letter from one gentry family to another proposing marriage—and such a letter would normally come from the groom's family, not the bride's. It actually reads more like a contract for selling land or even a wife. For example, the phrase "fearing that afterward there will be no proof, I affix my seal as imperial delegate here [for Zhao Yuqi] to save as guarantee" (*kong hou wu ping, qinchai yin cunzheng*) is typical of such contracts (except for the reference to the "imperial delegate").[48] As the magistrate commented in his report, the contract's wording is "absurd" (*huangtang*).

Xinxiang was well aware of their limitations: they had enough literacy and cultural knowledge to bluff, but could push their luck only so far. Thus, when Xinxiang was asked to write the marriage contract in their own hand, they later recounted: "I was afraid that I would be unable to write well in front of other people (*kong dangzhe ren xie bu chu hao zi*), so I said to Lu Lie, 'Since you are the matchmaker, it's only right that you take the brush and write it for me. I'll dictate what you should write.' So Lu Lie wrote down what I dictated." This passage is highly revealing. Xinxiang understood the performative nature of writing for the literati, who prized excellent calligraphy as a hallmark of high culture and understood the ability to write correctly as a fundamental signifier of social class. Educated men would paint pictures and write colophons for each other and often took turns composing poetry for mutual entertainment. Writing was all about body language: it required a certain posture and poise, an entire ritual of grinding ink to the correct consistency, a specific way of holding the brush perpendicular to the paper, and, of course, the results had to look right. An educated man would have internalized all of this since early childhood, and Xinxiang's audience no doubt expected the entire performance to be second nature for the monk—if they were really what they claimed to be.[49]

But Xinxiang knew enough to know that they would fail this test—hence their bluff to Lu Lie. Also, Xinxiang purposely did not risk affixing the seal in the others' presence, because they would have immediately recognized the lump of beeswax as a fake. Instead, Xinxiang insisted on taking the contract back to the temple and stamping it in private. Despite these subterfuges, Xinxiang could not evade liability for the contract's text, which they had dictated, or for the seal with which they tried to validate it.

Sexual History and Transing of Gender

As far as we know, Xinxiang never had sex with a woman or, for that matter, had any association with women whatsoever. Not a single woman is mentioned in the case record, aside from the fictitious sister. Xinxiang did, however, have sex with men. Their arrest record shows that they did sex work to make ends meet, and this included seeking clients among student acquaintances. They also used sexual favors in an attempt to make an ally of Lu Lie and forestall arrest. The likelihood is that by the time these events took place, Xinxiang already had had considerable sexual experience.

Xinxiang also transed gender as a monk and as a boy actress, and both of these roles no doubt shaped their sex life, even as they formed their character and developed their talents in other ways. As we have already discussed, the Buddhist clergy should be understood as a transgender paradigm because, when they "left the family," they renounced normative gender roles defined in terms of marriage and procreation. But it is also true that Buddhist monks were one of several male subcultures in Qing dynasty China where same-sex sexual acts and relationships seem to have prevailed. There is no way to document this claim in quantitative terms, but there is plenty of qualitative evidence to support it. First of all, we have the pervasive stereotype of monks as alcohol-swilling lechers and sodomites. No doubt this stereotype is exaggerated, but, like the similar one about Catholic priests, it probably contains at least a grain of truth. In my own research in Qing legal archives, I have seen many cases of both amicable sexual relations and rapes that involved male clergy, in the resident monastic setting and among the mendicant clergy on the road. One scenario that frequently occurs is sexual exploitation of novice by master, framed by an ostensibly pedagogical hierarchy; this scenario is common enough that it appears to be a pattern. Generally speaking, it is well known that men who sexually abuse children often turn out to have been abused themselves. We can speculate that such a dynamic prevailed among the male clergy in

Ming-Qing China, reproducing itself across generations, with each penetrated novice growing up and becoming a mentor and penetrator of younger novices in turn.[50]

My point is that Xinxiang's sex life may well have begun at the temple, after they left the family. Here we are speculating, because we have no direct evidence to this effect. Nor do we know why Xinxiang ran away from the temple, after just a year—much less what prompted them to walk all the way to Beijing—but it is possible that they ran away to escape sexual abuse. Once they had been put there by their parents, that temple was the closest thing Xinxiang had to a home, but they must have been unhappy, because every time they were forced to return, they soon ran away.

Xinxiang was not a good monk. We have no evidence that Xinxiang felt any religious devotion, and it seems unlikely that they ever properly completed even whatever training was considered standard at a small rural temple. Their lying and cheating, prostitution and other sexual activity, and frequent adoption of lay attire all violated monastic vows as well as imperial law. Moreover, since they never received official license, in the eyes of the authorities even Xinxiang's role as a monk was a kind of imposture.[51] But it may be that failure as a monk reflected the unhappiness of their early experiences at the temple.

Xinxiang used monastic guise to facilitate their confidence schemes. These schemes involved claiming to be someone more important than they appeared to be, and Xinxiang explained away this discrepancy by claiming to have fallen on hard times, or to be traveling in disguise. It would have been harder to persuade anyone that they were a member of the gentry or an official if they had been dressed in lay attire that appeared too shabby for the high status they claimed. But a monk's shaven head and simple robe had a sort of "class neutrality" that Xinxiang could use to advantage.

The transgender dimension of Xinxiang's life as a performer of female roles is obvious, but, of course, there was also a sexual dimension to that life. Like the traffic in boys, sexual commerce and exploitation were absolutely integral to the theatrical scene. If Xinxiang's sexual history did not begin at the temple or on the road, then it probably began during their years as a "boy actress." In that context, an actor from the humblest of backgrounds might associate intimately with officials, banner elites, merchants, and other men of rank and status, as long as he possessed the requisite charm and erotic appeal to perform as a *dan*. We get a sense of how Xinxiang must have acquired the sophistication and polish, however superficial, that later enabled them to pose as "the son of an established family" and "an educated man."[52]

In sum, both the clergy and the theater can be thought of as "queer" milieus, both in their transing of gender and in their close association with male–male sexual relations. The two milieus also overlapped, given the regular performance of opera at temple fairs and festivals, and this overlap may well explain how Xinxiang managed to become an actor. A final, crucial piece of evidence is the testimony of the government student Wang Xu, who reported Xinxiang to the Hongtong County magistrate for prostitution. According to Wang, Xinxiang told him that "he is actually a woman" and also "behaved wildly and without regard to propriety." Xinxiang's statement appears to have been a pick-up line, part of an effort to entice Wang Xu into paying for sex. But was it something more?

For what it is worth, Xinxiang's assertion is unique in my research experience: I have never seen such a statement attributed to anyone else in a Qing legal case. For example, none of the individuals prosecuted as "men masquerading in women's attire" was recorded as making such a statement. As far as we know, Xinxiang never presented as a woman offstage, nor did they claim to be a woman in their courtroom testimony. Hence, they never endured a strip search and genital examination like those seen in previous chapters. Wang Xu's testimony aside, everyone seems to have assumed that Xinxiang was a man.

Nevertheless, we should take Xinxiang's revelation seriously. Certainly Wang Xu took it seriously: it made such an impression that he included it in his report to the Hongtong County magistrate; that magistrate later included it in the report on Xinxiang's arrest he sent to Yangcheng County; and the Yangcheng magistrate and his superiors all included it in their successive reports up the chain of command, all the way to Beijing. If we accept Xinxiang's assertion that they considered themself to be a woman, then their transgender experience in the theater, in particular, appears in a different light. Perhaps the experience of performing female roles was a process of self-discovery that revealed to Xinxiang the true persona underneath all the others they would try on. Perhaps Xinxiang's multifaceted career of roleplay and masquerade in some way reflected this deeper crisis of category.[53]

Xinxiang Strikes Again

Xinxiang was sentenced to beheading after the assizes, but they did not die—at least not yet. After a ten-year break, they suddenly reappear in the archives. In the winter of 1758, Tuoenduo, governor-general of Guangdong and Guangxi, submitted a secret palace memorial to inform the emperor of the latest crimes committed by the escaped convict Xinxiang, who by this time would have been thirty-one or thirty-two years old.[54] For background, the governor-general explains that Xinxiang's execution had been repeatedly "delayed" at the annual autumn assizes until 1753, when an imperial amnesty had reduced their sentence to "military servitude" (*chongjun*). The likely reason for this lenience is that, first, Xinxiang's impersonation of an official had failed, and, second, their motive had been pecuniary rather than political. With the amnesty, they had been released from prison and sent to serve out their sentence in Yiyang County, Hunan. Soon after arriving, however, Xinxiang had escaped and returned home to Xiangling County, Shanxi, where they were promptly recognized and arrested. This time, they were sent to Conghua County, Guangdong, which is located about one thousand kilometers south of Shanxi. They were placed under the supervision of one Zhang Yunzhong, who was the district jailer (*dianshi*) at the county yamen.

The present case being reported by the governor-general concerned Xinxiang's most recent escape from custody, which had taken place late the previous summer. After several months, Xinxiang had finally been tracked down and arrested in Leiyang County, Hunan, about three hundred kilometers directly north of Conghua County; it appears that Xinxiang was again headed home to Shanxi. When searched, they were found to be in possession of a forged official seal inscribed with the title *Shiqingong*, which translates roughly as "hereditary imperial duke"—a title that did not actually exist in the Qing dynasty. Under interrogation, Xinxiang confessed that they had also forged a seal for the Conghua County yamen and had used it to defraud people of the transaction taxes they paid on land sales (*lan shui tianqi*). To assist in this tax fraud scheme, Xinxiang had recruited two runners who guarded the yamen gate. Apparently, when people who had bought land came to the yamen to pay the transaction tax and register the transfer of title, the runners at the gate would direct them to Xinxiang, who collected their money, without turning it over to the treasury, and stamped their contracts with the fake yamen seal (ostensibly turning them into "red" contracts). In this way, Xinxiang and their confederates "amassed a considerable amount of silver."

Upon receiving this report from Hunan, the governor-general ordered the two runners arrested, conveyed to the provincial capital of Guangzhou, and interrogated in a joint investigation by the provincial judge, the provincial treasurer, and the prefect of Guangzhou Prefecture. The runners confessed to "acting together to use a fake seal on contracts to collect the transaction tax" (*huo yong jiayin shuiqi*). Moreover, the interrogators learned from them that, after Xinxiang escaped, the official responsible for the convict's custody, district jailer Zhang Yunzhong, had discovered the forged yamen seal and a quantity of silver among Xinxiang's belongings. Instead of submitting these items to the magistrate, Zhang had hidden the seal and kept the silver for himself. Zhang was arrested and brought to Guangzhou, where he, too, confessed his crimes.

The Hunan authorities also informed the governor-general that, after escaping, Xinxiang had stayed for some time in Yingde County (which neighbors Conghua County) at the home of one Su Xuanguang. Su was apparently a member of the gentry, because his house had a study where some more of Xinxiang's effects were discovered, including a prototype for the "hereditary imperial duke" seal and a sketch of its imprint that Xinxiang had apparently made when designing it. The memorial contains no further information about Su Xuanguang, but it seems likely that he had been the target of some confidence scheme in which the wily escapee had talked their way into Su's home.

The governor-general concluded his memorial by reporting that he had had the two runners escorted to Hunan in irons, to be interrogated along with Xinxiang; Zhang Yunzhong is being held in custody until the Board of Personnel strips him of his credentials, so that he, too, can be properly prosecuted. The governor-general recommended that the magistrate of Conghua County whose negligence had permitted the use of fake seals for tax fraud at his yamen, as well as Xinxiang's escape, be reported to Board of Personnel for deliberation of administrative penalties. Finally, the governor-general pledged to find out whether Xinxiang committed any other crimes while at large or was abetted by anyone else in the escape.

The Enigma of Xinxiang

A subsequent memorial reports that the magistrate of Conghua County was demoted but left at his post.[55] That document is the last mention of the indefatigable Xinxiang that I have found in the archives, so we do not know their fate. Since their new crimes included more than one capital offense, it seems unlikely that they could have escaped execution once again. But who knows?

Xinxiang had a mixed record as a con artist. Their attempt to impersonate an imperial official in order to commit marriage fraud was pathetic. However, they seem to have improved over time. The tax fraud scheme in Conghua County was very successful and seems to have been exposed only by their escape—after which Xinxiang apparently talked their way into yet another gentry home, where they forged an even more ambitious official seal. Xinxiang was a proven survivor and escape artist, so perhaps they lived to cheat another day.

How can we make sense of Xinxiang? One approach is to see them as an example of a universal type. Historians often seek external explanations of behavior in social, cultural, or economic factors that make an individual stand as a reflection of their own specific context. To be sure, the details of Xinxiang's career were "scripted" by their society and culture and were distinctive to eighteenth-century China. At the same time, however, their behavior and personality closely resemble those of con artists from other times and places—for example, the "picaresque" imposters in early modern Spain and colonial Mexico who impersonated Catholic priests; the sixteenth-century French adventurer Arnaud du Tilh, who impersonated Martin Guerre successfully enough to occupy his property and marriage bed for several years (indeed, successfully enough that he was accused of being in league with the devil); and the American check swindler Frank Abagnale (of *Catch Me If You Can* fame), who posed as an airline pilot, a medical doctor, an attorney, and even a sociology professor.[56]

Such people are motivated by money, of course, but they also crave a degree of status and prestige that they are unwilling or unable to obtain by conventional means. Abagnale, for example, appears to be intelligent, but by his own account he was far too lazy and opportunistic to do the hard work necessary actually to enter any of the professions he impersonated: "What if I were a pilot? Not an actual pilot of course. I had no heart for the grueling years of study, training, flight schooling, work, and other mundane toils that fit a man for a jet liner's cockpit. But what if I had the uniform and the trappings of an airline pilot? Why, I thought, I could walk into any hotel, bank or business in the country and cash a check. Airline pilots are men to be admired and respected. Men to be trusted. Men of means."[57] A closely related motive is the sheer thrill of deceiving people and getting away with it, which helps explain the compulsive quality of con artists' behavior. Abagnale comments that impersonating a pilot "was heady stuff and I loved it. In fact, I became instantly addicted." He used his pilot's uniform "in the same manner a junkie shoots up on heroin."[58]

But note that in Xinxiang's case, the real path to gentry status and high office—namely, the examination system—was almost certainly closed to them. The alternate route, acquisition of credentials and offices by purchase, was equally unrealistic because the prices would have been far beyond their reach.[59] In a society with extremely limited scope for upward mobility, the only way for Xinxiang to enjoy the perquisites of such status was to fake it. One can interpret their scams as an abortive attempt at upward mobility, that paralleled (and parodied) the legitimate form of upward mobility: acquiring a classical education, passing the exams, entering the gentry class, and becoming an official. Benjamin Elman has documented a variety of religious practices and superstitions that reflected people's desire for a shortcut to success in the examination system.[60] Similarly, Tristan Brown has shown that exam success was attributed to good *fengshui* (e.g., in the siting of family graves) at least as much as to individual talent or effort.[61] The popular view of exam success was similar to how people today view winning the lottery: just as wonderful but also just as arbitrary and unlikely, and certainly not as a measure of individual merit. Cheating was rumored to be widespread, as seen in the cynical portrayal of the exam system by frustrated literati like Wu Jingzi, eighteenth-century author of the black-humor novel *The Scholars* (*Rulin waishi*). One might interpret Xinxiang's impostures as a variation on this theme: a bold shortcut to high status, in a society where the odds were overwhelmingly opposed to an individual of their background achieving such success by orthodox means.

In modern psychiatry, con artists are often diagnosed with "antisocial personality disorder" (APD), more colloquially known as "sociopathy." Here is a summary of APD symptoms, from the *Diagnostic and Statistical Manual of Mental Disorders*:

Individuals with APD fail to conform to social norms with respect to lawful behavior. . . . They may repeatedly perform acts that are grounds for arrest (whether they are arrested or not), such as destroying property, harassing others, stealing, or pursuing illegal occupations. Persons with this disorder disregard the wishes, rights, or feelings of others. They are frequently deceitful and manipulative in order to gain personal profit or pleasure (e.g., to obtain money, sex, or power). . . . They may repeatedly lie, use an alias, con others, or malinger. A pattern of impulsivity may be manifested by a failure to plan ahead. . . . Decisions are made on the spur of the moment, without forethought, and without consideration for the consequences to self or others; this may lead to sudden changes of jobs, residences, or relationships. . . . They may display a glib, superficial charm and can be quite voluble and verbally facile (e.g., using technical terms or jargon that might impress someone who is unfamiliar with the topic). . . . These individuals may also be irresponsible and exploitative in their sexual relationships.[62]

Much of this description sounds like Xinxiang, especially their superficial charm, compulsive lying and manipulation, unwillingness to settle in any one place or occupation, and repeated entanglements with the law. The governor of Shanxi described them as follows: "He has been a monk since childhood, but early on he became accustomed to impersonation and confidence schemes (*jiamao kuangpian*). Despite being punished repeatedly for breaking the law, he has never reformed his conduct."

Symptoms of APD often appear in childhood; APD correlates with childhood experience of parental rejection and neglect, physical or sexual abuse, lack of supervision, and institutional living.[63] These points are especially suggestive when we consider Xinxiang's early life. For example, being sent to a temple to become a novice monk may also be considered a form of childhood institutionalization. We do not know why Xinxiang's parents did this, but it seems like a strange thing to do, given that they had only one other son and that Xinxiang was by all accounts able bodied and physically healthy. Perhaps Xinxiang chronically misbehaved in ways that anticipated their later misadventures, and the parents' hope was that religious discipline would bring them under control. But being rejected and abandoned by their parents may have traumatized Xinxiang in ways that exacerbated whatever antisocial tendencies they already displayed. Their family continued to reject them; when Xinxiang later got in trouble, their brother wanted nothing to do with them. Moreover, if they were sexually abused at the temple, or were later forced to provide sexual services as a "boy actress," those traumas may have further molded Xinxiang's character—after all, they were still a child throughout those years. Psychiatrists caution that, in some settings, "seemingly antisocial behavior may be part of a protective survival strategy," and that observation, too, would seem to apply to Xinxiang.[64] We know nothing of their vagabond life on the road, crisscrossing northern China, but it cannot have been easy, and presumably it was there that they honed the skills that enabled them to survive. To be clear, I propose nothing so presumptuous or anachronistic as a formal psychiatric diagnosis of Xinxiang's condition. But con artists the world over have long shared certain traits in common, traits that Xinxiang also seems to have shared, so I offer this perspective as one possible way to make sense of their story.

There is another way to understand Xinxiang, however, that may not be incompatible with the profile just suggested. In every society, there are some people who cannot or will not conform to gender norms, and, in many societies, the traditional dumping grounds for such people have been the clergy, the theater, the sex industry, and the prison. This one sentence neatly summarizes Xinxiang's life, and in this sense, too, they represent a universal type: as one who expressed "a defiant non-normativity." One recalls the French writer Jean Genet: the son of a prostitute, Genet was fostered at an early age, followed by childhood incarceration and sexual abuse, and a vagabond life as thief, beggar, prostitute, and user of false papers. Like Genet, Xinxiang "incarnates one understanding of *queer* as a term that brings together a range of forms of social marginality."[65]

Much of this might also apply to the American transwoman and con artist Liz Carmichael (1927–2004), whose record included forging checks, counterfeiting, bail-jumping, multiple marriages, constant changes of name and residence, and a variety of confidence schemes.[66] The most grandiose of the latter was a bogus automobile company she founded that would supposedly manufacture a revolutionary fuel-efficient car. Among other lies, she claimed to have degrees in mechanical engineering and business, and to be the widow of a NASA engineer. In 1977, Carmichael was convicted of defrauding her investors, again jumped bail, but eventually served time in prison. When investigative reporters exposed Carmichael's car company as a fraud, they simultaneously outed her as a transwoman. In the ensuing media blitz, Carmichael's transness was treated as a fraud, as a disguise designed to facilitate her financial crimes—in short, as an example of what Susan Stryker characterizes as the "evil deceivers and make-believers" stereotype that trans people are "pretending to be something that we're not."

Like Xinxiang, Liz Carmichael would seem to be a poor candidate for "queer icon" or "transgender role model." Despite her obvious intelligence and creativity, she apparently found it impossible to earn a living legally. But the one genuine and consistent thing about Carmichael seems to have been her transgender identity as a woman. She did not transition until her forties, which was typical for her generation, because there were few role models and gender-affirming medical care was rarely available. Although Carmichael's criminal activity continued after her transition, in other respects she seems to have settled down. Whereas she had abandoned previous wives and children, her (third) wife and their children together accepted her transgender identity, and this acceptance seems to have drawn the family closer. They stayed together through thick and thin, and Carmichael's children from this last marriage describe her as a loving spouse and parent.

How did Carmichael's career of lies and deception relate to her transgender identity? They may not be related, of course; it may simply be a coincidence that this con artist happened to be a transwoman. But Susan Stryker suggests a different scenario:

> If you're not being the person that you understand yourself to be, you don't often follow that normative life path. If you feel resentful that society is organized in a way that is really not good for you as a person, if you feel that interacting with people and institutions and the public and the government is something that at every step invalidates who you are as a person, maybe you're resentful about that, and maybe you engage in more so-called "anti-social behavior" out of those unresolved feelings that are based on your transness.
>
> If you're living in any kind of non-normative gender role, publicly, the employment discrimination, the housing discrimination, the kinds of police violence that get directed at you, the criminalization of your life, the psychiatrization of your life, it puts you in a very vulnerable and marginal position, where sometimes your only options are criminal ones because you want to eat, you need a place to sleep,

and how are you going to get that money? If that's what's in front of you, that's what you do.

Stryker speculates that if Liz Carmichael had been born a few decades later, in a more tolerant society, then perhaps she could have found a better way to survive in the world.

Xinxiang was a hustler who partook of at least three kinds of "drag": gender crossing, to be sure, in their capacity as a "boy actress" in Beijing; a "clerical drag," in switching between monastic robes and lay attire, which was another kind of transgender maneuver; and, finally, a "class drag," in their attempts to parlay an inadequate education and superficial charm into intimacy with young scions of the gentry—and, on that basis, to practice identity theft and impersonate officials. Xinxiang claimed at least eight different names or personae that we know of. The first three were chosen by others: their birth name, Zhao Jianlin; their Buddhist name, Xinxiang; and whatever exaggeratedly feminine stage name they were assigned in the opera. The next four, however, they chose for themself, and by listing them in chronological order we can observe a steady increase in grandiosity and ambition: the son of Mr. Cui, of the Yongji County gentry; the son of Lu Bingchun, the famous retired official and teacher from Xiangling County; Zhang Chun, imperial censor and vice minister of the Board of War; and, finally, the title inscribed on their third forged seal, "hereditary imperial duke."

Most intriguing of all, however, is the eighth persona Xinxiang claimed, with the tantalizing assertion that they were actually a woman. Perhaps, after all, this assertion is the key to making sense of Xinxiang, a decidedly "queer" nonconformist whose restless refusal to stick with any particular name or place or role acted out this more fundamental defiance of category.

Epilogue

"Brown dwarfs" are a new class of celestial bodies—new, at least, with respect to human understanding. Brown dwarfs are neither planets nor stars, but somewhere in between with regard to mass and brightness, and they complicate our very notion of what planets and stars are. Some brown dwarfs host planets, like stars do; other brown dwarfs orbit stars, like planets do. The fourth-closest star or star-adjacent object to our sun is a brown dwarf called WISE 0855 which was discovered in 2016. WISE 0855 is alone (lacking a system, like our earth is part of a solar system), cold, small, and barely visible to us. It is quite close, as these things go; yet we almost missed it, because it is at the bleeding edge of what our technology enables us to "see."

If we work from the fair assumption that our little corner of the vast universe is unexceptional, then it's likely that outer space is full of such rogue bodies. In other words, the fact that we managed to see WISE 0855 despite every limitation invites us to imagine the entire field in a different way. I appreciate this strategy, because it means the humble method of looking is also the imaginative one, the one that presents the probability of a more diverse cosmos. It is this invitation to imagine what else is out there— darkness, twinkling with worlds we cannot see—that excites me.

—TRANS ARTIST AND RESEARCHER JANANI BALASUBRAMANIAN

After reading a draft of this book, my former student Janani Balasubramanian offered the celestial brown dwarf as a metaphor for the transgender people glimpsed, however imperfectly, in the legal cases I have collected from the Qing archives and other sources. In Balasubramanian's view, "the fact that we can 'see' trans people in late imperial China, despite every limitation and absence/erasure, invites us to imagine the many more lives that we *cannot* see."[1]

Transgender people existed in imperial China. By "transgender people," I have in mind Susan Stryker's practice-based definition: "People who move away from the gender they were assigned at birth, people who cross over (*trans-*) the boundaries constructed by their culture to define and contain their gender."[2] In this book, I have tried to show how gender-transing

[248]

individuals were situated, and how their personae developed through the ways they negotiated their circumstances and moved through the world. Instead of positing a stable, shared identity, I have excavated from my sources a range of transgender practices pursued by a variety of people. These practices intersected with family, sexual behavior, occupation, religion, and class in historically specific ways. From an intersectional perspective, gender transing was never an isolated practice; on the contrary, it was always bound up with these other dimensions of life, and those who transed gender typically blurred or crossed other boundaries as well. But transgender practices were also framed by paradigms in the broader culture, including the ideology that informed the law, and literary conventions of "the strange" seen in fiction and newspaper reportage that fed a feedback loop with actual court cases, creating a shared elite discourse of predatory deviation.

Broadly speaking, we can divide transgender people in the Ming-Qing era into two categories. First, there were those who were *compelled* to trans, notably boy actresses, clergy, and eunuchs. Many of these people were subjected to coercion and considerable violence, in the form of human trafficking, sexual exploitation, the disciplines of their unchosen vocation— and for eunuchs, of course, castration and enslavement. Their gender transing was acceptable and even valorized to some degree because it served the established order of hierarchy and privilege. It was safely contained within narrow institutional contexts, guided by strict protocols, and generally did not represent nonconformist self-expression. One suspects that the normative system may have needed this kind of gender transing, in order to define the normative by contrast and to clarify its boundaries.

The second category consisted of those people who *chose* to trans gender, and who are represented in this book by our protagonists who lived as women despite having been assigned male at birth. These people were the object of paranoid fantasies of sexual predation and as a consequence were harshly punished when (on rare occasion) they came to official attention. The only plausible reason Ming-Qing authorities could imagine (or at least would admit to) for "a man to masquerade in women's attire" was to penetrate female space in order to seduce or rape the "chaste wives and daughters" cloistered within. A similar paranoid fear of male clergy as wolves in sheep's clothing focused on the wandering mendicant clergy—in other words, those who had strayed from institutional contexts, escaping the strict protocols to which they were expected to submit. The Sang Chong paradigm of the cross-dressing predator paralleled that of the predatory male clergy, and both reflected a more fundamental anxiety about the rogue male outside the Confucian family order.

Xinxiang represents a hybrid case: having begun their career as a novice monk and boy actress, they later made ends meet through sex work and confidence schemes, while wandering throughout northern China. In the process, they alternated clerical and lay attire, and transed class via a series of increasingly ambitious attempts at identity theft, impersonation, and forgery. Xinxiang combines a range of marginalized scenarios in a particularly enigmatic and "queer" persona; they also bring into focus the fundamental association between gender transing and deception that informed official paranoia.

Gender does not exist in isolation, in some sort of steady state; rather, it is a dynamic quality that is activated through encounter and interaction with other (gendered) people and with the variety of institutions that frame our lives. As Judith Butler suggests, gender comes into being through its performance—which implies both a script and an audience—and its existence depends on being repeatedly performed in interaction with others.[3] Thus, to define transgender as a set of practices in specific historical contexts (rather than a fixed transhistorical identity) is to highlight what *transgender* has in common with *all* gender. At the same time, the category-complicating reality of transgender invites us to rethink the nature of gender itself, not unlike the liminal, nonbinary brown dwarf with respect to planets and stars.

Sampling Bias in the Archives

To be clear, I have found very few cases in the legal archives of individuals assigned male at birth who lived as women, and I have found none at all of individuals assigned female at birth who lived as men. The lack of F–M transing cases in the archives, like the invisibility of sexual relations between women, strikes me as a reflection of the phallocentrism of Qing law, according to which the penis is what defines the sexual (both conjugal intercourse and rape), and therefore only those who have a penis are considered a potential threat.[4] That is why official anxiety about gender transing focused exclusively on the bogey of the male predator in disguise. In fiction, as we have seen, F–M transing is usually portrayed as a temporary solution for some predicament (rather than a transgressive act of self-expression) which is reconciled when the heroine finally returns to her normative role as a woman. Similarly, literary portrayals of sex between women tend to trivialize it and contain it safely within polygyny (the typical scenario being a main wife with her husband's concubine), where it poses no threat to the sexual and reproductive privileges of men. Simply put, sexual relations between women were not seen as important enough to be addressed in the legal code.

But why, then, have I found so few cases in the archives in which male-female transing was prosecuted? It is not for lack of effort. To be precise (leaving aside the cases reported in *Shenbao*), I have found only those analyzed in chapters 2, 4, and 5. Moreover, the cases of Zengliang, Zhang Yaoguniang, and Xing Shi were all briefly summarized in the *Conspectus of Penal Cases*, which suggests just how unusual they were, at least from the standpoint of the judiciary.[5]

A naive explanation would assume a direct correlation between the incidence of prosecution and that of gender-transing in real life—in other words, the paucity of cases in the archives simply reflects the extreme rarity of such behavior. But such an explanation is not very convincing, because it fails to take into account the inherent sampling bias in legal archives, specifically why cases ended up in court and how likely it was that they would do so.[6] The Qing state had a thin presence on the ground and local officials did not have the resources to micromanage the people in their jurisdictions or to seek out crime proactively.[7] Therefore, for a crime to come to the attention of the authorities, someone had to care enough to report it, a process that might entail considerable inconvenience and expense. This was true even of homicide, and the indirect evidence from the archives suggests that many homicides were dealt with by local communities in a manner that purposely avoided official attention, especially in places where powerful lineages held sway. We must assume that many of the things that actually happened never left any trace in the official record.

A specific example of an absence of legal case records not accurately reflecting social reality is male-male sexual relations. The Qing code prescribes the exact same penalties for consensual sex between men as for consensual extramarital sex between a man and a woman.[8] But my exhaustive search of *local* court archives has found very few cases of sex between males, and nearly all of them seem to involve parents accusing adult men or older boys of raping or seducing their underage sons; most seem to be straightforward cases of child molesting. In contrast, the local court archives contain many cases of extramarital sex involving women.

Should we conclude, therefore, that Chinese men never had sex with each other? No, of course not. For one thing, the *central* archives contain thousands of *xingke tiben* from all over China that document consensual sex between men. It is obvious from these and other sources that such acts and relationships were common. But, in *xingke tiben*, the focus of prosecution is some capital offense like homicide or rape, and the consensual sodomy is simply a secondary "lesser crime" (*qing zui*) that happened to come to official attention in the course of investigation. What a comparison of the local and central court archives shows is that consensual sodomy between men was rarely (if ever) prosecuted in the absence of more serious offenses, for the simple reason that nobody cared enough to report it to the authorities, and the authorities in turn did not care enough to expend resources looking for it. It may have been illegal and to some extent stigmatized, but it threatened no one. In contrast, for women to engage in extramarital sex might threaten the interests of their male kin—their fathers, husbands, or (for widows) in-laws—and it was those men who reported such cases to the local magistrate.

The lesson to bear in mind is that, when we survey the legal archives, we must always try to imagine what did not end up in court and therefore left no record for historians to scrutinize today. What are we *not* seeing, and why? The lack of cases involving sex between women or F–M transing should not mislead us into assuming that such things never actually happened. By the same token, we can hypothesize that the scarcity of M–F transing cases simply indicates a lack of motivation to report such matters to the authorities. It may indicate a general tolerance of people who transed gender in this particular way, a perception that they were essentially benign, that contrasts sharply with the official hysteria that M–F transing in particular seems to have provoked.

Q's Story

In this connection, I would like to share an account related to me by a Chinese colleague who prefers to remain anonymous—let's call her "Q."[9] Q spent several years of her childhood in the early 1990s living with her grandparents in her family's ancestral village in Shandong, on the North

China plain. In their village, there was a gender-ambiguous spirit medium surnamed Zhang, who had been born in the late 1920s or early 1930s. As their parents' only child, Zhang had been assigned male at birth and raised as a boy. Zhang dressed as a man and worked in the fields like other men. But, in other ways, their gender presentation violated normative expectations about masculinity, and their anatomy and behavior were the subject of gossip and speculation. Zhang would die in the late 1990s of natural causes, at around seventy years of age. Twenty years later, Q visited the village again and, out of curiosity, asked her surviving relatives and other villagers what they remembered about Zhang.

Zhang had a wife, and the couple were close friends with Q's grandparents. Zhang's wife and Q's grandmother had even pledged sisterhood (*ren le ganzimei*). One day when Zhang visited the family, Q was playing in the yard with other children, and an older boy declared that Zhang was an *eryizi*. Q did not understand this term—it is local dialect—so the boy explained that it means someone who is "half male, half female" (*ban nan ban nü*)—in other words a "yin-yang person" (*yinyang ren*). Then the children followed Zhang to the latrine to watch them urinate, hoping to catch a glimpse of their genitals. Zhang yelled at the children, and Q's grandmother scolded them and chased them away. Later Q heard some older children say that Zhang was "not a real man."

When questioned by Q, villagers told conflicting accounts of Zhang's anatomy, but all agreed that it was anomalous. Some said that Zhang had both male and female genitals, but that their penis was very small. Some said that, even though it was small, it worked properly, but others claimed that it was incapable of erection. Some claimed that Zhang's urine came out of a "crack" (*feng*) instead of their penis. When Q asked how people could know about such intimate matters, her relatives replied that "everyone knew!" (*dou zhidao*). Apparently, Zhang's condition had been common knowledge since their birth, even if there was no consensus about the details.[10] According to Q's uncle, a physician who had known and admired Zhang, they rarely urinated in front of other men and would always squat to urinate. During collectivization, when villagers had to share an open latrine while working in the fields, some of the men made fun of Zhang's squatting and of their genitals. Q's uncle told her that Zhang might be a "hermaphrodite" because of certain other physical characteristics: for example, they had "white skin" (*baijing de*) and "slender limbs" (*shoujiao xiliu*) and were "beardless" (*bu zhang huzi, laopo zui*).

In terms of gender presentation, too, Zhang was seen as different from other men. Zhang worked in the fields because they had to, but they were not very good at it. Zhang "cared about cleanliness" (*yao ganjing*) to an unusual degree, was "finicky" (*jiangjiu*) and "effeminate" (*jiaojiao, jiaoqi*), and could not do heavy manual labor or endure hardship—"he wasn't like the rest of us" (*he women bu yiyang*). Instead, ever since childhood, Zhang had enjoyed sewing and mending clothes together with the older women and generally seems to have preferred the company of women to that of men. Also, unlike other men, Zhang shared the housework with their wife and kept their house neat and clean. For this reason, the women in the village considered Zhang "a nice husband" who "loved his wife" (*xinteng laopo*).

The men in the village did not worry about Zhang's friendships with women, because Zhang's gender nonconformism defused any tension that such relationships might otherwise have provoked. They simply did not consider Zhang any sort of rival or threat. Instead, the men would laugh about Zhang's lack of masculinity: "He was not really a man, he only dressed up in men's clothing" (*ta you bu shi ge nanren, guang chuanzhe nanren yishang*); "he urinated while squatting, which proves he was not a man. Who knows, perhaps he was really a woman, haha!" (*dunzhe jieshou, kending bu shi yemenr, shi bu shi niangmenr zan bu zhidao, ha ha*). Note that, in the original Chinese quoted here, Q's informants were using the gender-neutral pronoun *ta*.

Because Zhang's mother had borne no other children (at a time when most women had many), people assumed there was something physically wrong with their family. Zhang's own wife bore no children and was very unhappy about this; she often came to Q's grandmother's house and cried about it. She once became pregnant but miscarried. There were many rumors about Zhang's wife. She had come from a distant village, and she was considered a "worn-out shoe" (*poxie*, i.e., slut) because supposedly she had lost her virginity by having an affair with a married man of her own village. There were also rumors that because her own husband was unable to make her pregnant, she had tried to "borrow seed" (*jie zhong*) by sleeping with other men in the village who already had sons. According to Q's uncle, if a family lacked a male heir, then it was acceptable to "borrow seed" in this way. There were several known cases in the village, so it would not be surprising if Zhang's wife had done this as well. Zhang's wife claimed that Zhang was potent, despite the smallness of their penis, but the other villagers did not believe her: they insisted that Zhang did not have "a man's capability," so, if their wife became pregnant, she must have "borrowed seed." Eventually, the couple adopted an abandoned girl, who was very pretty and grew up to become an actress in a local drama troupe, but later she moved away from the village and people lost contact with her.

Zhang's true vocation, it seems, was to serve as a medium for female spirits. When Zhang was a toddler, they fell ill and were bedridden for many days until a female medium engaged by their parents healed them. But, in order to be healed, Zhang had to become the medium's "godson" (*ganerzi*). When Zhang's medium godmother first examined them, she declared that "this child was born to serve the spirits" (*zhege haizi sheng-xialai jiushi cihou shenxian de*); presumably, there was something special about Zhang's appearance or anatomy that made her think so. Zhang first demonstrated spiritual powers as a teenager, when they were possessed by a "white animal spirit" (*Bai xian'er*). This spirit was either a fox, a hedgehog, or a rabbit—the villagers' recollections did not agree. (Unfortunately, by the time Q made her inquiries, there was no one left alive who had actually witnessed Zhang's ritual activities before the Mao era.) The assumption was that Zhang's godmother had taught them about religion and mentored them to become a medium. In those days, there were several female mediums (*shenpo*) in the vicinity who served animal spirits, the most common one being a weasel known to worshippers as "Great Yellow Immortal" (*Huang Daxian*), and in the 1990s there was still at least one female medium in Q's family village who served this spirit.[11] Zhang was the only local medium known to have been assigned male at birth.

During the "Anti-Superstition Campaign" of the 1950s, Zhang gradually stopped serving as a spirit medium. According to the villagers, "Chairman Mao was the greatest god, and he forced all the lesser gods to submit" (*Mao Zhuxi shi da shen, ba xiao xianr dou xiangfu zhu le*), and, during the Mao era, if Zhang was ever possessed by spirits, they kept it secret. Instead, if villagers sought Zhang's help, Zhang would use medicinal herbs they grew in their garden to treat them, including opium.

In the 1980s, Zhang began acting openly as a medium once again. In this new phase of their career, Zhang was possessed by "the Flowery Maiden" (*Huaniangniang*), a female attendant—either a fox or a weasel, according to Q—who serves the important female deity Grandma Taishan (*Taishan Laonainai*), also known as "the Sovereign of the Clouds of Dawn" (*Bixia Yuanjun*). (Note that Grandma Taishan is associated with fox spirits and is sometimes characterized as their leader or supervisor.)[12] During this period, Zhang only served as a means of communication with Grandma Taishan, "conveying messages" (*chuanhua* or *song xin*) to her on behalf of clients. Zhang no longer attempted to heal illnesses or solve other problems, explaining that "I am old now, so my ability is not as good as before" (*lao le, gongli bu xing le*).

Zhang chose specific days according to the lunar calendar for possession rituals. A client would bring a pack of cigarettes, and Zhang would hold several in their mouth and smoke them at the same time. Then their eyes would gradually narrow and their eyeballs sometimes rolled back into their head; their body and head would start to shake, and when the Flowery Maiden possessed Zhang, they would begin speaking in a woman's voice. Q asked a villager who had witnessed this: "But you considered Zhang to be like a woman anyway—wasn't their voice already like a woman's?" The villager answered, "No, this was completely different. When possessed, Zhang's voice was exactly like a woman's voice (*hen nüren*). His usual way of speaking wasn't like that." While Zhang was possessed, clients would ask questions, and the spirit would answer through Zhang; sometimes Zhang sang songs without giving specific answers. On other occasions, they might be possessed spontaneously and would utter predictions about people's fate that later proved to be accurate. After the spirit departed, Zhang would not remember what they had said while possessed. Zhang was not paid money for these services. Instead, villagers would bring gifts of food during the spring festival. Zhang regularly prepared food offerings for two female deities whom they worshiped: Grandma Taishan (whose attendant they served as medium) and the bodhisattva Guanyin. These meals might include tofu, salt fish, meat, lotus root, dumplings, and fruit.

Aside from their vocation as a spirit medium (which paused during the Maoist era), Zhang was literate and skilled at mathematics, and, during Land Reform, they helped the cadres measure land for redistribution and keep accounts. The fact that Zhang had attended school in childhood for several years indicates that their family was not poor, by local standards. Nevertheless, Zhang was never targeted during any of the mass campaigns of the Mao era, in part perhaps because Q's grandfather was a village cadre and used his authority to protect Zhang. But Zhang's personality and contributions to the community evidently made them popular, and they do not seem to have had any enemies. Their gender nonconformism did not make them a target of bullying; on the contrary, "he was a good person, so you couldn't bully him" (*shi ge haoren, bu neng qifu ta*). Villagers praised Zhang for having "talent" (*benshi*) and "spiritual powers" (*shentong*); they described Zhang as having an ethereal quality, a certain "transcendent aura" (*xianqi*). Q's impression is that Zhang had a good life as an accepted member of their community.

The "Way of Animals" Revisited

What can we conclude from this anecdote? Zhang remains something of a mystery, but clearly neither their anatomy nor their gender performance met the expectations of their assigned sex or gender. As to anatomy, a number of possibilities suggest themselves. For example, given their parents' need for a son, Zhang may have been assigned male through a combination of error and wishful thinking. It is also possible that Zhang's anatomy placed them somewhere on the intersex spectrum—that was the theory of Q's uncle, the physician, and would accord with the community opinion that Zhang was an *eryizi* or "yin-yang person." Recall that, ever since Zhang was born, the whole community seems to have been aware that something about their anatomy defied category, and the spirit medium's declaration that "this child was born to serve the spirits" seems to have been based on a similar judgment. Zhang's apparent infertility might also support this theory. At any rate, Zhang did not fit neatly into the normative male/female sex binary.

As to gender performance, Zhang's effeminacy, fastidiousness, manner of urinating (reminiscent of male Daoists), distaste for the arduous nature of farm work, and embrace of women's tasks all violated local expectations of masculine behavior. All of this made Zhang a figure of gossip, but it also meant that local men did not feel threatened by Zhang's affinity for female company. Zhang was able to cross gender boundaries in a way that might not have been tolerated of an ordinary man. Moreover, these ambiguities of sex and gender seem to have helped qualify Zhang to be a spirit medium who channeled female deities, a vocation that was usually held by women. In that context, Zhang's peculiarities provided a distinct advantage, and the same villagers who laughed about their effeminacy also testified that Zhang had genuine talent and spiritual power. Zhang was accepted and respected by their community and even protected by local cadres, because they played a valuable social role.

By now it is clear that ordinary people in Qing dynasty China generally did not share the elite obsession with separating the sexes or rigidly safeguarding female chastity. For example, my past work has shown that polyandry, marital prostitution, and wife selling were widespread survival strategies among the poor and were generally tolerated in rural society, despite the fact that the imperial state prohibited all of these practices as sex offenses.[13] Zhang's fellow villagers seem to have shared this relatively blasé attitude toward female chastity. Thus, for example, Zhang's wife may have been rumored to be a "worn-out shoe" who had "borrowed seed" in an effort to get pregnant, but no one really seems to have cared. Such rumors did not prevent her from pledging sisterhood with the wife of an important local cadre—after all, "borrowing seed" was accepted in that community as a last resort for a couple without a son. Moreover, it is obvious that ordinary people in the Qing did not embrace the official definition of heterodoxy, since so much of what the imperial state labeled and persecuted as such was simply quotidian religious practice.

A vast gulf separated the values and ideology of Ming-Qing elites from the social realities and mentalities of ordinary peasants.[14] The imperial state sought to enforce the orthodox moral order promoted by the Confucian canon, which required distinction between the sexes and their correct socialization into gendered kinship roles. Yet the protagonists of our case studies lived in a sociocultural milieu where foxes and weasels were worshiped with the aid of gender-nonconforming spirit mediums, and where a wife who lacked a son might be encouraged to "borrow seed" from someone else's husband. Was this not "the way of animals" of which *The Book of Rites* warns?

The fact that a person like Zhang could have a good life, without being persecuted or attracting attention outside their own community, calls to mind at least two of our gender-transing protagonists: the midwife Xiong Mumu and, especially, the fox spirit medium Xing Shi. Both lived as women for years (in Xiong's case, for decades) without any apparent difficulty, and neither came to official attention because of any complaint from their own communities. On the contrary, Xiong was outed by their brother only after filing a lawsuit against him, and Xing came to notice only because local constables decided to check up on their faith-healing activities—and anywhere but Beijing, the most heavily policed place in the empire, Xing might have avoided notice. In other words, we can posit that Xiong and

Xing's cases are "exceptions that prove the rule" that individuals who transed gender were unlikely to be prosecuted.

One can easily imagine scenarios in which neither Xiong nor Xing would have ever gotten in trouble. How many more people were there like them, and like Zhang, who lived quiet lives without attracting the malign attention of the Qing judiciary? My own guess is that, for every one who was prosecuted for heterodoxy, there must have been many others who left no trace in the official record. There is no way to be sure. But we do know, for example, that spirit mediums were ubiquitous in rural China and that they were popularly viewed as peculiar, unconventional people who should be treated with respect. The occasional appearance of gender-transing spirit mediums in *Shenbao*'s reportage also suggests that such people were not so rare, however distorted their stories may be by the newspaper's editorial prejudice and ignorance. Perhaps many villages had someone like Zhang—a distinctly "queer" figure whose gender nonconformism was seen as less a liability than a source of spiritual power. Like Zhang, they might have been a focus of speculation and gossip, but, at the same time, they might have been respected and valued for their unique abilities and contributions.

To return to the metaphor of the celestial brown dwarf: WISE 0855 may appear to be isolated and alone, but in all likelihood such "rogue bodies" are very common. We just haven't yet learned how to see them clearly, much less to grasp their implications for understanding the rest of the universe. We can say much the same of transgender people in imperial China. I offer this book as a first step toward a clearer vision.

Character List

an duo yidou　案多疑竇

an neng bian wo shi xiong ci　安能辨我是雄雌

anbing　暗病

anqing wei que　案情未確

ba xiaode pai le yi xia　把小的拍了一下

Bai Juyi　白居易

bai ta wei shi xuexi fuzhou　拜他為師學習符咒

Bai xian'er　白仙兒

baijing de　白淨的

bailianjiao　白蓮教

ban nan ban nü　半男半女

bangzi qiang　梆子腔

banzuo daogu zhuangshu　扮作道姑裝束

banzuo nigu　扮作尼姑

Bao Daizhi Chenzhou tiao mi　《包待制陳州糶米》

Bao'er　寶兒

bei hongyou　被哄誘

bei jian you tao　被姦誘逃

bei Shen suo hai　被沈所害

bei xiaode kanchu nan ban nü zhuang　被小的看出男扮女粧

Bencao gangmu　《本草綱目》

benlai mianmu　本來面目

benshi　本事

bi zhangfu, wo zhangfu, yinyang diti　彼丈夫，我丈夫，陰陽敵體

bian　變

bianxingren　變性人

bie wu xiejiao, yaoshu, guhuo renxin zhi chu　別無邪教、妖術、蠱惑人心之處

bing　病

bing wu ziti　並無字體

binü　婢女

Bixia Yuanjun　碧霞元君

bixu beiren hua fu nian zhou, fang you lingyan　必須背人畫符念咒，方有靈驗

bu bian chu　不便處

bu ci bu xiong　不雌不雄

bu duan　不端

bu ji shi　不濟事

bu nan　不男

bu neng jin　不能近

bu neng renshi　不能人事

bu neng xingfang　不能行房

bu nü　不女

bu shou dao gui　不守道規

bu shun　不順

bu xiao　不孝

bu yin bu yang　不陰不陽

bu ying zhong　不應重

bu zai bing min funü zhi lie　不在兵民婦女之列

bu zhang huzi　不長鬍子

bu zhi haodai　不知好歹

bu zhi ruhe shi po　不知如何識破

budan yinxin buxiang, jiushi na ge guanxian ye you xie bu shen dique
　不但印信不像，就是那個官銜也有些不甚的確

bude jinshen, wu cong youpian　不得近身，無從誘騙

bujun tongling yamen　步軍統領衙門

buxiang　不像

caili　財禮

caizhan　採戰

caizi jiaren　才子佳人

canfei　殘廢

caowu　草烏

chang le san si nian xidan　唱了叁肆年戲旦

chanmen　產門

Chaoyang Dong　朝陽洞

Chen　陳

Chen Fangsheng　陳芳生

Chen Jia Shi　陳賈氏

Chen Yao　陳幺

cheng fei bu neng shengyu, jianglai zhongshen wu kao　成廢不能生育，將來終身無靠

chengqin shi wo jiang bu bian chu zheyan, zhi shuo you bing bu neng xingfang,
　　　qingyuan jiao ta jijian　成親時我將不便處遮掩，只說有病不能行房，情願叫他雞姦

chidian　痴癲

chongjun　充軍

chu dao yi shi nü　初道伊是女

chu hu er, fan hu er, qianhou xiang chang　出乎爾，反乎爾，前後相償

chu jia　出家

chu yiduan yi chong zhengxue　黜異端以崇正學

chuan dai gai zhuang　穿帶改粧

chuan le sujia yifu, zai ge chu xian zou　穿了俗家衣服，在各處閒走

chuan tu　傳徒

Chuanghu xianhua　《窗戶閒話》

chuanhua　傳話

chuixian fuse　垂涎婦色

chujia　出家

chujia zuo daoshi　出家做道士

chunü　處女

ci bu xiong　雌哺雄

Ci Mulan ti fu congjun　《雌木蘭替父從軍》

ci xiong zhi mo bian　雌雄之莫辨

ciwai bing wu bei huo shouhai de ren　此外並無被惑受害的人

cong　從

cong yi er zhong　從一而終

dai wo gai ban nüzhuang　代我改扮女裝

daibi　代筆

dan　旦

dangtang yanming　當堂驗明

Dao Yuanyang　《倒鴛鴦》

daoshi　道士

daoshi wei zhuang wei yu　道士偽裝為嫗

Daxian Lou　大仙樓

de　的

Deng Lan　鄧蘭

dengshi hunmi　登時昏迷

di zhan zi chan　弟佔姊產

dianmai　典賣

dianshi　典史

Dianshizhai huabao　《點石齋畫報》

dimu　嫡母

dingxiang　頂香

dingxiang de　頂香的

Dong Shixiu　董師秀

Dongxu Cun　東徐村

dou zhidao　都知道

douke yisheng　痘科醫生

duangong daoshi　端公、道士

dunzhe jieshou, kending bu shi yemenr, shi bu shi niangmenr zan bu zhidao, ha
　　ha　蹲著解手，肯定不是爺們兒，是不是娘們兒咱不知道，哈哈

duo fang yanshi　多方掩飾

duo she guimen aimei　多涉閨門曖昧

er shi ci ye xiong ye　爾是雌耶雄耶

erxing　二形

erxing fei ren, bu neng shengyu　二形廢人，不能生育

erxing ren　二形人

erxingzi　二形子

eryizi　二刈子/二椅子

fakuang　發狂

faming　法名

fan le chulai you yao da banzi dijie　犯了出來又要打板子遞解

fang rui yuan zao　方枘圓鑿

fanjian　犯姦

fanjian duo ci　犯姦多次

fanyi　番役

Faren　法仁

Fasheng　法乘

fei　非

fei ci er shi xiong ye　非雌而實雄也

fei nan　非男

fei nü　非女

fei ren　非人

fei ren ye　非人也

fen zuo san liu　分作三柳

fenchang　糞廠

feng　縫

feng yang ze nü, feng yin ze nan　逢陽則女，逢陰則男

fengji　瘋疾

fufu shi　夫婦事

fuluan　扶鸞

fuke　婦科

funü　婦女

furen congrenzhe ye　婦人從人者也

futi　附體

fuzhou　符咒

fuzhou zhi bing　符咒治病

gai fan deng kong ling you bufa bie an　該犯等恐另有不法別案

gaiban nüzhuang　改扮女粧

gaifu　丐婦

gan　乾

gan anai　乾阿嬭

gan erzi　乾兒子

gan nüer　乾女兒

gan shou wuru　甘受污辱

ganqin　乾親

gei daxiao boke ji li neng guanshu zhi huizi wei nu　給大小伯克及力能管束之囘子為
　　奴

Gengsi bian　《庚巳編》

gong'an　公案

gong'an xiaoshuo　公案小說

gu (poison)　蠱

gu ("drum")　鼓

Gu Cai　谷才

guai　怪

guan qi juzhi xingji, si you keyi　觀其舉止形跡，似有可疑

guanggun　光棍

guhuo　蠱惑

guhuo renxin　蠱惑人心

guishi　鬼師

guiyi　詭異

guizhong shi wairen bu zhi, hefang huxiang wei le ye　閨中事外人不知，何妨互相為
　　樂耶

guoji erzi　過繼兒子

Guomi　果密

hanhu chawen shuo de shi bu shi　含糊查問說的是不是

hao nanse zhe　好男色者

haomao rongrong ran　毫毛茸茸然

he　和

he women bu yiyang　和我們不一樣

he yi wu nian zhi jiu jing bu zhi xi nanshen　何以五年之久竟不知系男身

He Yunliang　何運良

Hechun xiban　和春戲班

hejian　和姦

hen nüren　很女人

heshuang lianjia youjie shizhong　荷雙連枷游街示眾

hetong jijian　和同雞姦

Hong Da　洪大

Hong Shi　洪氏

Hongloumeng　《紅樓夢》

hongpian yumin　哄騙愚民

hongyou huxiang jijian, bici lian jian　哄誘互相難姦，彼此戀姦

hongyou nieshuo　哄誘捏說

hu　狐 (fox)

Hu　胡 (surname)

Hu De　胡德

Hu Erxiangu　胡二仙姑

Hu Laotaiye　胡老太爺

hu seng hu ni, hu nan hu nü, qi ju xin shu bu ke wen　忽僧忽尼，忽男忽女，其居心殊不可問

hu wei pinmu　互為牝牡

Hua Mulan　花木蘭

huadan　花旦

huan le su　還了俗

Huang Daxian　黃大仙

huang shulang　黃鼠狼

huangdi　皇帝

huangtang　荒唐

Huaniangniang　花娘娘

huanjue　緩決

huanshu　幻術

hui cheng　回城

hunmi gensui　昏迷跟隨

hunmi zhou　昏迷咒

huo　惑

huo shang miao wei ni, yihuo ji yu ling xing gaishi　或上廟爲妮, 抑或疾愈另行改適

huo yong jiayin shuiqi　夥用假印稅契

huozhong hanqian　惑眾歛錢

hutu　糊塗

huxian　狐仙

Imai　奕賚

ji yiqie ren deng　及一切人等

jia daoren　假道人

jia jiang xieshen　假降邪神

jiaban daoren　假扮道人

jiamai　價賣

jiamao kuangpian　假冒誆騙

jian　姦

jian qi rongmao junqiao　見其容貌俊俏

jian ren funü　姦人婦女

jian se qi yi　見色起意

jian shi nanzi　見是男子

jian yu shuobu　見於說部

jianei gongfeng huxian tuxiang, dingxiang zhibing　家內供奉狐仙圖像，頂香治病

Jiang Pu　蔣溥

jiang shennang qianyang baoqi　將腎囊前陽包起

Jiang Yuhan　蔣玉菡

jiangjiu　講究

jianguan　兼管

jiangxia　降下

jianmin　賤民

jiansu　姦宿

jianxing　間性

jianyin funü　姦淫婦女

jiao jianhou　絞監候

Jiao Laiyi　焦來儀

jiao li jue　絞立決

jiao qi zhi tou　膠漆之投

jiao wo liule toufa, suan ta nüren　叫我留了頭髮，算他女人

jiaojiao　嬌嬌

jiaoqi　嬌氣

jiaren　嫁人

jiatuo wuyi　假託巫醫

jiazhuang fengmo sapo xiahu　假裝瘋魔撒潑嚇唬

jiazhuang huxian jiangxia　假裝狐仙降下

jibing　疾病

jie bude zuo wanren yi　皆不得作完人矣

jie zhong　借種

jiehun zhou　解昏咒

Jiekuan　戒寬

jijian　雞姦

jin xiaofuren de shen　近小婦人的身

jing wei kuipo dili　竟未窺破底裏

Jinghua yuan　《鏡花緣》

jingju　京劇

jingwu　莖物

jingwu huan chuang kuilan, zhi cheng canfei　莖物患瘡潰爛，至成殘廢

Jinpingmei　《金瓶梅》

jinshen　近身

jisi　祭祀

jiu bei jijian　久被雞姦

jiuji　鬆髻

jiujia zidi　舊家子弟

jiujing shi nan shi nü　究竟是男是女

jiujing yiyu he wei　究竟意欲何為

jiushi nage guanxian ye youxie bu shen dique　就是那個官銜也有些不甚的確

jizi 繼子
jue mai 絕賣
jufa 舉發
junzi guo 君子國

Kaiming Si 開明寺
kan bing pianqian 看病騙錢
kanchu nan shen, xiaode jiu yu xing jian 看出男身，小的就與行姦
kanchu nan shen, yu zhi chengjian 看出男身，與之成姦
ke mian pangren kanpo 可免旁人看破
ke qi bu ke fu 可妻不可夫
ke yu furen tongjian 可與婦人通姦
kong dangzhe ren xie bu chu hao zi 恐當著人寫不出好字
kong hou wu ping, qinchai yin cunzheng 恐後無憑欽差印存證
kong miao 空廟
kong ta yi ge ren lengjing bu hao guo 恐他壹箇人冷靜不好過
kong tianxia nanzi zhi ci wei, renren yu jia zhangfu 恐天下男子知此味，人人欲嫁丈夫
kou cheng xi nüren 口稱伊係女人
kou cheng yi xi Yongji Xian Cui xiangshen zhi zi 口稱伊係永濟縣崔鄉紳之子
kuang xiao hun chen 狂笑昏沈
kuangpian caiwu 誆騙財物
kuangyan zuoxi hongshuo xi yun 誆言作戲哄說喜允
kuansong 寬鬆
kuansong, bing bu jincou 寬鬆並不緊湊
kun 坤

laiwang 來往
lan shui tianqi 攬稅田契
lang 郎
lao le, gongli bu xing le 老了，功力不行了
laopo zui 老婆嘴
li (substatute) 例
li (rites, ritual) 禮
Li Baozhen 李寶真
Li Changlai 李昌來
Li Huizhen 李惠貞
Li ji 《禮記》
Li Ruzhen 李如珍
Li Shizhen 李時珍
Li Yu 李漁
lian qian hu kou 斂錢糊口
liang bian beihou dou shi menghu dushe 兩邊背後都是猛虎毒蛇
liang ru pingta 兩乳平塌
liang ru pingta, yinhu bu neng rong zhi 兩乳平塌，陰戶不能容指

Liang Shanbo 梁山伯

liangjia funü 良家婦女

liangjia nüzi 良家女子

liangjia zidi 良家子弟

liangmin 良民

liangpang you shui you huo, houtou you hu you gou 兩旁有水有火，後頭有虎有狗

lianshang de hanmao 臉上的寒毛

Lianxiang ban 《憐香伴》

liji 立繼

lijia 立枷

ling funü gan ren wuru er bu gan yanzhe 令婦女甘任污辱而不敢言者

Ling Mengchu 凌濛初

ling qu xiaoxing 另娶小星

lingchi 凌遲

lingyue 領約

Liu Ba'er 劉八兒

Liu Jinxi 劉進喜

Liu Liu 劉六

Liu Liu xin yi wei shi, jiu jiang wo jijian le 劉六信以為實，就將我雞姦了

Liu Xiaoyoujie 劉小有姐

Liu Xing Shi 劉邢氏

Longyang zhi pi 龍陽之癖

lou chu pozhan 露出破綻

Lu Bingchun 盧秉純

Lu Can 陸粲

Lu Lie 路烈

lufu zouzhe 錄副奏摺

lun zuodao zhi hai 論左道之害

lunjian 輪姦

lü 律

Lü Yushan 呂玉山

lüe ren lüe mai ren 略人略賣人

Ma Wanbao 馬萬寶

mai bu 賣卜

maijian 賣姦

Mao Zhuxi shi da shen, ba xiao xianr dou xiangfu zhu le 毛主席是大神，把小仙兒都降服住了

meiyou jinshen yi ci 沒有近身一次

meng xiaode toushang 朦小的頭上

menghanyao 朦汗藥

miren sawang zhou 迷人撒網咒

miren zhouyu 迷人咒語

miao pan 妙判

miguai yange　迷拐閹割

miguai youxiao zinü　迷拐幼小子女

mihu qilai　迷糊起來

mili　迷離

mili pushuo zhi an　「迷離撲朔」之案

mimi huhu de genzhe ta zou　迷迷糊糊的跟著他走

ming bian cixiong　明辨雌雄

Ming shilu　《明實錄》

ming xi yaoshu miguai　明係藥術迷拐

mishi　密室

miyao　迷藥

Mizi Xia　彌子瑕

momei　魔魅

mousha　謀殺

mu　姆

mu wu faji　目無法紀

Mudanting　《牡丹亭》

mumu　姆姆

na Man Han wen dou shi xiaode zao chulai de　那滿漢文都是小的造出來的

nan　男

nan ban nüzhuang　男扮女裝/粧/妝

Nan Meng mu jiaohe san qian　《男孟母教合三遷》

nan nü you bie　男女有別

nan yao shang hua　男妖傷化

nan yi wei qi　難以為妻

nan zhuang nü ban, youjie shizhong　男裝女扮，遊街示眾

nanbao renjia nüzi bu bei yi jianyou　難保人家女子不被伊奸誘

nanzi ye　男子也

naoyanghua　鬧楊花

ni zheyang yi ge ren jiu bu gai qi xin tao laopo kenghai bieren wo rujin bu ken
　　tong ni zuo liang kouzi de le ni zaoxie ba wo xiu le ba　你這樣一個人就不該起
　　心討老婆坑害別人，我如今不肯同你做兩口子的了，你早些把我休了罷

niang　娘

nianqing mao mei　年輕貌美

nianshao funü jian ta huiwu duo bu jin shen　年少婦女見他穢污多不近身

niseng　尼僧

nü　女

nü ban nanzhuang, nan ban nüzhuang, jun gan lijin　女扮男裝、男扮女裝，均于例禁

nü guo　女國

nü huxian　女狐仙

nü xia　女俠

nü'er guo　女兒國

nüren guo　女人國

nüren shenshang de anbing　女人身上的暗病
nüxian　女仙
nüzi yuanhong　女子元紅

Pai an jing qi　《拍案驚奇》
pai hua　拍花
paiwei　牌位
pan　判
Peng Xinchou'er　彭辛丑兒
peng zhao wo bu bian chu　碰著我不便處
Peng Ziren　彭自仁
pengjian rongyin　朋奸容隱
penjing　盆景
pi ti ru miao wei ni　披剃入廟為妮
Pian jing　《騙經》
pianqian shouduan　騙錢手段
pingkong zhacheng　憑空詐稱
pingta de　平塌的
po lanbu nügua　破藍布女袿
poshen　破身
poxie　破鞋
Pu Songling　蒲松齡
pushuo　撲朔

qi (main wife)　妻
qi (to discard)　棄
qi wo fuqi yisheng bu neng tongfang hu　豈我夫妻一生不能同房乎
qian　乾
qian shen zuo nie, jin shen shou bao　前身作孽，今身受報
qiang　強
qiangbao　強暴
qiangdao　強盜
qiangjian　強姦
qie　妾
qie nanbao wu xie yin qingshi　且難保無邪淫情事
qie yin yinsi you chaishi zai shen bu neng tongfang　妾因陰司有差使在身不能同房
qieji touguan　切忌偷觀
Qin qiang　秦腔
Qinchai Shanxi dao jiancha yushi jianguan Bing Bu youshilang　欽差山西道監察御
　史兼管兵部右侍郎
Qing Han　清漢
qing zui　輕罪
qinghun shu　請婚書
qingjing zhi fashen　清淨之法身

qingshuo yun shi nüni　輕說云是女尼

qingyuan gencong xiaode　情願跟從小的

qingyuan luo fa wei ni　情願落髮爲妮

qingyuan ting xiaode jijian, ren wei fufu　情願聽小的雞姦，認為夫婦

qinshou zhi dao　禽獸之道

qiu hou chu jue　秋後處決

Qiu Jin　秋瑾

qiushen　秋審

qiyi gaizuo nü zhuang, ji ren lianmin duo gei qian mi　起意改作女粧，冀人憐憫多
　　給錢米

qu (Cantonese: keoi)　佢

qu qi wei zi ye, ru neng shengyu hu　娶妻為子也，汝能生育乎

quan zhen　全貞

quju qi gu yi tunqiao shou yin　曲舉其股以臀竅受淫

ren　人

ren cai liang kong　人財兩空

ren dao　人道

ren gong xin zhi　人共信之

ren le ganzimei　認了幹姊妹

ren naozi　人腦子

ren shi　人事

ren xingcao zhe　任刑曹者

reng wei zhengshi　仍位正室

renkui　人傀

renyao　人妖

Renyao　《人妖》

Renyao gong'an　《人妖公案》

renyao huanghou　人妖皇后

ru guitou chu ke　如龜頭出殼

ruan rouzhuang yitiao　軟肉樁一條

rui zao　枘鑿

Ruiniang　瑞娘

Rulin waishi　《儒林外史》

ruo nüzi chu jian liangren　若女子初見良人

sancong　三從

sanfasi　三法司

Sang Chong　桑冲/沖/翀/衝

Sanqing xiban　三慶戲班

se shuai ai shi　色衰愛弛

sengren　僧人

sengshe　僧舍

shan　煽

shang bu zhi si　尚不至死

shang jing xue zuo xizi, chang le san si nian xidan　上京學做戲子，唱了叁肆年戲旦

Shangfo Cun　上佛村

Shangfu Cun　上伏村

Shanhai jing　《山海經》

shanhuo　煽惑

shanhuo renmin　煽惑人民

shanhuo renxin　煽惑人心

shansha zuiren　擅殺罪人

shanshuo　閃爍

shao shi zhi hu　稍識之乎

shaonian kuangdang, lianjian qingmi, yi ji xinyuan yingyun　少年狂蕩，戀姦情密，亦即心願應允

she nan nü　捨男女

she qian qu hou　舍前趨後

shejing　蛇精

shen　神

shen dai er xing, bu nan bu nü, shi wei yaowu　身帶二形，不男不女，是謂妖物

shen jia　身價

shen suo zhi shu　伸縮之術

shen xi shinü　身係石女

shen you canji, bu neng shengyu　身有殘疾，不能生育

Shen Yunting　沈雲亭

Shen Zhiqi　沈之奇

Shenbao　《申報》

shendao jianglin　神道降臨

shenfen　神粉

shengyu　聖諭

shengyuan　生員

shenpo　神婆

shentong　神通

Shi (surname of Buddhist clergy)　釋

shi (spirit radical)　示

shi bei Liu Liu kanchu xi shu nanshen　始被劉六看出係屬男身

shi bu zhi Xing Shi shi nanren　實不知邢氏是男人

Shi Daogu　石道姑

shi e　十惡

shi fei furen xingzhuang　實非婦人形狀

shi ge haoren, bu neng qifu ta　是個好人，不能欺負他

shi ge jiujia zidi, you xiang shi wenmozhong ren　是箇舊家子弟，又像是文墨中人

shi ge suren, bu shi Xinxiang de banr　是箇俗人，不是心祥的伴兒

shi nü bao zhongshen zhi tong　使女抱終身之痛

shi wei chuan tu huozhong, yi wu ling you xieshu feiwei ji xi jiao bu fa qingshi　實未傳徒惑眾，亦無另有邪術匪為及習教不法情事

shi wu ling you jianyin funü zhi shi　實無另有姦淫婦女之事

shi xi chuzi chu poshen　實係處子初破身

shi xi nanzi　實係男子

shi xi yinyang ren　實是陰陽人

Shi'er lou　《十二樓》

Shijiamuni　釋迦牟尼

shinü ("stone maiden")　石女

shinü ("solid maiden")　實女

shiqingong　世親公

Shiwu guan　《十五貫》

shiwu xieshu　師巫邪術

shou mentu juzhong liancai　受門徒聚眾斂財

shouchu jia zhuang qingshi　首出假粧情事

shoujiao xiliu　手腳細溜

shouliu huxiang jijian　收留互相雞姦

shu　贖

shu shi　屬實

shu shu bu he　殊屬不合

shuangxing　雙性

shuoxi　說戲

si ci bailun shanghua zhi ren bu ke gurong yu shengshi　似此敗倫傷化之人不可姑容
　　於聖世

si damen　四大門

sifang　私訪

siren　寺人

sixing wuji　肆行無忌

song xin　送信

su chang　宿娼

sui shichang yu funü yizhi, bing wu jianwu qingshi　雖時常與婦女醫治，並無姦污情
　　事

suikou hunbian kuangyan　隨口混編狂言

Sun Tanzhang　孫談章

Suolun, Dahu'er　索倫、達呼爾

suren　俗人

ta (until the nineteen-twenties, gender neutral; since then, he/him)　他

ta (she/her)　她

ta (it)　它

ta (He/Him, referring to the Christian God)　祂

ta (new gender-neutral third person pronoun)　X也

ta you bu shi ge nanren, guang chuanzhe nanren yishang　他又不是個男人，光穿著
　　男人衣裳

tai huan yin shi　胎患陰實

taijian　太監

Taishan Laonainai　泰山老奶奶

teng de yi tiao gunzi zhi tong chulai, qie shi jianying bu dao　騰的一條棍子直統出
　　來，且是堅硬不倒

ti jian nan nü　體兼男女

ti qi fa　薙其髮

tiandihui　天地會

tianhuan　天宦

tiao gui　跳鬼

tiaoxi　調戲

ting　廳

Tongzhi　通誌

toubai wei shi　投拜為師

tsukurareta daisan no sei　作られた第三の性

tu yu funü xiangjin, chengji jianguai　圖與婦女相近，乘機姦拐

tuxiebing　吐血病

Wang　王

wang cheng　妄稱

Wang Erxi　王二喜

Wang Hu Shi　王胡氏

Wang Lu Shi　王盧氏

wangmao　妄冒

wangzi zhi tian chi ci you ling you gan you yu, chi chi ling ling, you qing
　　dajiangjun lingfu yi dao jianglin baohu　王子之天敕賜有靈有感有餘，敕敕令令，
　　有請大將軍靈符一道降臨保護

wei cong　為從

wei renjia chanfu shousheng　為人家產婦收生

wei shou　為首

wei xiao　痿小

weimian you xiukui qingsheng zhi shi　未免有羞愧輕生之事

wenmo zhong ren　文墨中人

wenpo　穩婆

wo cong gong le huxian de xiang zong wei yu Liu Liu xingfang, zhuanyi kan xiang
　　zhi bing　我從供了狐仙的像總未與劉六行房，專意看香治病

wo fei zhennü　我非真女

wo ti ni tuo le yifu, zanmen dahuo guangzhe shenzi shui ba　我替你脫了衣服，咱們
　　大夥光著身子睡罷

Wofo Si　臥佛寺

wu bie wu yi, qinshou zhi dao ye　無別無義，禽獸之道也

Wu Chichang　吳熾昌

wu qu shinü　誤娶石女

wu ren guikun　污人閨閫

wu shengyu zhi dao　無生育之道

Wu Zetian　武則天

wu zhuang　無狀

wu zi er you zi　無子而有子

wuchi nianshao youseng　無恥年少遊僧

wuren mi chu　無人密處

wuyong　無用

wuzuo　仵作

xi jiao xieshu wei fei bu fa de shi　習教邪術為匪不法的事

xi nanzi　係男子

xi nügong, wei furen zhuang　習女工、為婦人裝

xi shu nanshen　係屬男身

Xi yuan lu　《洗冤錄》

xia you　狎優

xian (county)　縣

xian (transcendant, spirit)　仙

xian you jianyin funü bu fa qingshi　顯有姦淫婦女不法情事

xian you tongtong zhuangshi qingbi　顯有通同裝飾情弊

xiangshen　鄉紳

xianqi　仙氣

xianren futi　仙人附體

xianzou　閒走

xiao fazi　小法子

xiaode haipa, ting ta jijian, ren wei fufu　小的害怕，聽他雞姦，認為夫婦

Xiaolongjie　小龍姐

xiaoshou　梟首

xiashen　下身

xiati　下體

xie　邪

Xie Jianshun　謝尖順

xiejiao　邪教

xiejiao, yaoshu, guhuo renxin　邪教、妖術、蠱惑人心

xieshu　邪術

xieshu huozhong, jianwu funü　邪術惑眾、姦污婦女

xieshu yi ren li　邪術醫人例

xin　心

xin zhen　新針

xinchou　辛丑

Xing Da　邢大

Xing Shi　邢氏

xing yi kuangpian qianwen　行醫誆騙錢文

xing yi pian qian　行醫騙錢

Xing'an huilan　《刑案匯覽》

xingji guiyi zhi ren　形跡詭異之人

xingke tiben　刑科題本

xinkou chu jue fa leng, hou jue mihu　心口初覺發冷，後覺迷糊

xinteng laopo　心疼老婆

Xinxiang　心祥

Xiong Erliang　熊爾諒

Xiong Ersheng　熊爾聖

Xiong Mumu　熊姆姆

xitu hongyou liangjia funü　希圖哄誘良家婦女

Xiyou ji　《西遊記》

xu jie Zhu Chen, yong xie Qin Jin　許結朱陳、永偕秦晉

Xu Jifang　許季芳

Xu Jinpingmei　《續金瓶梅》

Xu Lun　許倫

Xu Wei　徐渭

xue zuo nügong zhenzhi, chuan yong furen yishi　學作女工針黹，穿用婦人衣飾

xue zuo xizi　學做戲子

xufa chuan'er banzuo furen　蓄髮穿耳扮作婦人

xufa chuan'er chanzu, gaizhuang wei nü　蓄髮穿耳纏足，改粧為女

Yaji Shan Niangniang　雅髻山娘娘

yan funü shi　驗婦女屍

yang　陽

yang wei buyong　陽痿不用

yang xiu shanshi　佯修善事

yangfen shi wei nüshen, yi jiao yinfen ze hua wei nan yi　陽分時為女身，一交陰分則
　　化為男矣

yangshan zhongshen　養贍終身

Yangxiu　陽秀

yanli guo hao nü　豔麗過好女

yanran guose　儼然國色

yanran nanzi ye　儼然男子也

yanshen　嚴審

yao　妖

yao ganjing　要乾淨

yao wu huozhong　妖巫惑眾

yaobing ji yiqie xieshu　藥餅及一切邪術

yaodao　妖道

yaofa　妖法

yaoguai　妖怪

yaoni　妖尼

yaoni bailou　妖尼敗露

yaoren　妖人

Yaoren Xing Da　《妖人邢大》

yaoseng　妖僧

yao/xieshu　妖/邪術

yaowu   妖物

yao/xieyan   妖/邪言

yaoyan huozhong   妖言惑衆

yaoyi   妖異

Yaoyi   《妖醫》

Yesou pu yan   《野叟曝言》

yi   伊

yi banzuo nüzhuang   已扮作女裝

yi bian yongyuan jiansu   以便永遠姦宿

yi bu shi heshang, shi nigu   伊不是和尚，是尼姑

yi canfei wangmao jiaren   以殘廢妄冒嫁人

yi jing jianxie   以儆奸邪

yi ke tuilei   已可推類

yi nanzi zhuang nü   以男子粧女

yi sengren er chuandai sujia yimao   以僧人而穿戴俗家衣帽

yi shu yaoyi   已屬妖異

yi xieshu mi yin liangjia funü   以邪術迷淫良家婦女

yi yao miren   以藥迷人

yi yaobing ji yiqie xieshu miguai youxiao zinü   以藥餅及一切邪術迷拐幼小子女

yi youyin liang jia nüfu   以誘淫良家女婦

yi zhi wu ren zhongshen   以致誤人終身

yiduan   異端

yiduan fashu   異端法術

yin   陰

yin shi   陰實

yin tu youjian funü shi yi gai zhuang   因圖誘姦婦女是以改粧

ying zao ming ji   應遭冥殛

yinjian zuo te   陰奸作慝

yintian jun fu   陰天君符

yinyang ren   陰陽人

yishi hutu suo zhi   一時糊塗所致

yitu maijian shu shi   意圖賣姦屬實

yong liangshui guanjiu shi neng kaikou   用涼水灌救始能開口

yong xieyao milong   用邪藥迷籠

yong yao miren tucai   用藥迷人圖財

yongyi sha shang ren   庸醫殺傷人

you   誘

you fu zhi fu   有夫之婦

you gan xiandian   有干憲典

you jiao zuo erxingzi   又叫做二形子

You Ruilang   尤瑞郎

you shang fenghua   有傷風化

you shendao jianglin youhu   有神道降臨佑護

youdang du ri   遊蕩度日

youguai wei cheng　誘拐未成

youjian　誘姦

youling　誘令

yu nanren de ru yiban　與男人的乳一般

yu nanzi wu yi　與男子無異

yu nüren you xie liang yang　與女人有些兩樣

yu shui zhi huan　魚水之歡

yu zhenxi zhi jian wei cheng Zhang Shi zhi xin　於枕席之間未稱張氏之心

Yuan Mei　袁枚

yuanguang huafu　圓光畫符

yuantu youjian funü　原圖誘姦婦女

yue su zui xin guishen　粵俗最信鬼神

yuehu　樂戶

yunhun shu　允婚書

Yunxian xiao　《雲仙笑》

yuren zi yu　愚人自愚

yushi　御史

yuyan huangtang, yin wenzi hua hutu, mingxi jianie　語言荒唐，印文字畫糊塗，明係假捏

zai tian zhi dao yue yin yu yang, zai ren zhi dao yue nan yu nü　在天之道曰陰與陽，在人之道曰男與女

zai wai yunyou　在外雲遊

ze pingri jianwu zhi shi bu wen ke zhi　則平日姦污之事不問可知

zeng xian xiaode xiashen xiao　憎嫌小的下身小

Zengliang　增亮

Zhang Chun　張椿

Zhang Er　張二

Zhang Jun　張浚

Zhang Yaoguniang　張幺姑娘

Zhang Yunzhong　張允中

zhanlong　站籠

Zhao jia dayuan　趙家大院

Zhao Jianlin　趙建林

Zhao Silun　趙思論

Zhao Sipu　趙思樸

Zhao Yuqi　趙毓玘

zhawei　詐偽

zhe　磔

zhege haizi shengxialai jiushi cihou shenxian de　這個孩子生下來就是伺候神仙的

zhengdao　正道

zhengjing renjia shaonian funü jian xiaode shenshanghuiwu duo, jie zou bi buli　正經人家少年婦女見小的身上穢污多，皆走避不理

zhengxue　正學

zhi hu　之乎

zhi nan ji nü, zhi nü ji nan　值男即女，值女即男

zhiguai　志怪

zhitou dou jin bu qu　指頭都進不去

zhitouding ye bu neng ru　指頭頂也不能入

zhongshen　終身

zhongxing　中性

zhou　州

zhoushui　咒水

Zhu　朱

Zhu Akun　朱阿坤

zhu xiaode ban zuo nüren　囑小的扮作女人

Zhu Ying　朱英

Zhu Yingtai　祝英台

zhuandian　轉典

Zhuang Qinwang　莊親王

zhuang wei daoshi　裝為道士

ZhuChen Cun　朱陳村

zhupi　硃批

zhupi zouzhe　硃批奏摺

zhuzi junfen　諸子均分

Zi bu yu　《子不語》

zi bu yu guai, li, luan, shen　子不語怪、力、亂、神

zi xing hunhun, ren qi jianwu　自形昏昏，任其姦污

zui miren zhi yao　醉迷人之藥

zuo daoshi zhuang　作道士裝

zuo nüzi zhuang　作女子裝

zuodao　左道

zuodao huozhong　左道惑眾

zuodao yiduan　左道異端

zuodao yiduan lü　左道異端律

zuodao yiduan shanhuo renmin lü　左道異端煽惑人民律

zuodao yiduan zhi shu　左道異端之術

zuowei qishi　作為妻室

Notes

Conventions in the Text

1. Susan Stryker, *Transgender History* (Berkeley, Calif.: History Seal, 2008); Susan Stryker, *Transgender History: The Roots of Today's Revolution*, rev. ed. (New York: Seal, 2017).
2. Jen Manion, *Female Husbands: A Trans History* (Cambridge: Cambridge University Press, 2020), 11.

Introduction

1. See Michael Nylan, *The Five "Confucian" Classics* (New Haven, Conn.: Yale University Press), 2001. For the civil service examination system and its role in elite formation, see Benjamin Elman, "Political, Social, and Cultural Reproduction via Civil Service Examinations in Late Imperial China," *Journal of Asian Studies* 50, no. 1 (1991): 7–28; *A Cultural History of Civil Examinations in Late Imperial China* (Berkeley: University of California Pres, 2000); and *Civil Examinations and Meritocracy in Late Imperial China* (Cambridge, Mass.: Harvard University Press, 2013).
2. *Li ji zhengyi* [The book of rites, correct meaning], in *Shisan jing zhushu* [The thirteen classics, annotated] (Shanghai: Shanghai Guji Chubanshe, 1997), 26:1456.
3. Other traditions offer a similar view. In Genesis, for example, the Creation proceeds via a series of binary distinctions: light and darkness, the heavens and the earth, land and sea, animals and man, culminating with man and woman. After they become aware of their sexed bodies (having eaten the forbidden fruit from the

tree of knowledge), Adam and Eve experience shame and are cast out of Eden, thereby setting in motion human history.

4. *Li ji zhengyi*, 61:1680–81. In the imperial legal tradition, "moral duty" (*yi*) was the basis for a legitimate marriage; if that moral duty was "broken" (*yijue*) by, for example, a husband pimping his wife or tolerating her adultery, then Ming-Qing law mandated divorce. See Matthew H. Sommer, *Sex, Law, and Society in Late Imperial China* (Stanford, Calif.: Stanford University Press, 2000), 54–64; and Sommer, *Polyandry and Wife-Selling in Qing Dynasty China: Survival Strategies and Judicial Interventions* (Berkeley: University of California Press, 2015), 279–80.

5. Arthur Waley, trans., *The Analects of Confucius* (New York: Vintage, 1938), 83. For the relationship between sexual order and political order in classical Chinese thought, see Sommer, *Sex, Law, and Society*, 30–36; Paul Goldin, *The Culture of Sex in Ancient China* (Honolulu: University of Hawai'i Press, 2002); and Hsiao-wen Cheng, "Before Sexual and Normal: Shifting Categories of Sexual Anomaly from Ancient to Yuan China," *Asia Major* 31, no. 2 (2018): 1–39.

6. *Li ji zhengyi*, 26:1456. Here I have slightly modified Legge's translation. James Legge, trans., *Li Chi: Book of Rites* (New Hyde Park: University Books, 1967) 1:441.

7. There is debate about how to interpret the word *cong* in this context: Should the emphasis be on obedience and submission, or on "following" in the sense of having one's status determined by? The word contains both meanings. See Dorothy Ko, *Teachers of the Inner Chambers: Women and Culture in Seventeenth-Century China* (Stanford, Calif.: Stanford University Press, 1994), 6–7.

8. From the "feixiang" chapter, Xunzi, *Xunzi jijie* [Xunzi, with collected commentaries], in *Xinbian zhuzi jicheng* [Collected works of the sages, new edition] (Taipei: Shijie Shuju, 1991), 2:50.

9. For the cult of female chastity, see Mark Elvin, "Female Virtue and the State in China," *Past and Present* 104 (1984): 111–52; Susan Mann, *Precious Records: Women in China's Long Eighteenth Century* (Stanford, Calif.: Stanford University Press, 1997); Sommer, *Sex, Law, and Society*; and Janet Theiss, *Disgraceful Matters: The Politics of Chastity in Eighteenth-Century China* (Berkeley: University of California Press, 2004). For footbinding, see Dorothy Ko, *Cinderella's Sisters: A Revisionist History of Footbinding* (Berkeley: University of California Press, 2005); Hill Gates, *Footbinding and Women's Labor in Sichuan* (New York: Routledge, 2015); and John Shepherd, *Footbinding as Fashion: Ethnicity, Labor, and Status in Traditional China* (Seattle: University of Washington Press, 2018). Strict standards of female chastity and separation of the sexes were practical impossibilities for the poor and therefore served as status symbols for the wealthy and upwardly mobile. See Sommer, *Sex, Law, and Society*, chapter 5; Sommer, *Polyandry*; and Theiss, *Disgraceful Matters*, chapter 6. For attempts to ban women from visiting temples, see Vincent Goossaert, "Irrepressible Female Piety: Late Imperial Bans on Women Visiting Temples," *Nan Nü* 10 (2008): 212–41.

10. The original version of the Qing code was an almost exact copy of the Ming code; it was later amended substantially through the addition of substatutes (*li*),

although the original statutes (*lü*) remained largely unchanged. The statutes of the Ming and Qing codes are classified according to the six boards or ministries of the central government: Rites, Punishment, Personnel, Revenue, Public Works, and War.

11. Matthew H. Sommer, "Abortion in Late Imperial China: Routine Birth Control or Crisis Intervention?," *Late Imperial China* 31, no. 2 (2010): 97–165.

12. Matthew H. Sommer, "The Gendered Body in the Qing Courtroom," *Journal of the History of Sexuality* 22, no. 2 (2013): 281–311.

13. Susan Stryker, *Transgender History* (Berkeley, Calif.: Seal, 2008); Stryker, *Transgender History: The Roots of Today's Revolution*, rev. ed. (New York: Seal, 2017).

14. For the history of the transgender rights movement in the United States, see Stryker, *Transgender History*; and Stryker, *Transgender History: Roots*.

15. Transgender studies is a rapidly growing field. Key works include Susan Stryker, "My Words to Victor Frankenstein Above the Village of Chamounix: Performing Transgender Rage," *GLQ* 1 (1994): 237–54; Stryker, *Transgender History*; Stryker, *Transgender History: Roots*; Susan Stryker and Stephen Whittle, eds., *The Transgender Studies Reader* (New York: Routledge, 2006); Susan Stryker and Aren Aizura, eds., *The Transgender Studies Reader 2* (New York: Routledge, 2013); Leslie Feinberg, *Transgender Warriors: Making History from Joan of Arc to Dennis Rodman* (Boston: Beacon, 1996); Feinberg, *Stone Butch Blues: 20th Anniversary Edition* (self-published by author for open access, 2014, www.lesliefeinberg.net); J. Halberstam, *Female Masculinity* (Durham, N.C.: Duke University Press, 1998); David Valentine, *Imagining Transgender: An Ethnography of a Category* (Durham, N.C.: Duke University Press, 2007); C. Riley Snorton, *Black on Both Sides: A Racial History of Trans Identity* (Minneapolis: University of Minnesota Press, 2017); and Jules Gill-Peterson, *Histories of the Transgender Child* (Minneapolis: University of Minnesota Press, 2018). See also the historical studies cited in endnotes 22 through 27 of this chapter. For changing terms and definitions, see, for example, Paisley Currah, "Gender Pluralisms Under the Transgender Umbrella," in *Transgender Rights*, ed. Paisley Currah, Richard Juang, and Shannon Price Minter (Minneapolis: University of Minnesota Press, 2006), 3–31; Susan Stryker, Paisley Currah, and Lisa Jean Moore, "Introduction: Trans-, Trans, or Transgender?," *Women's Studies Quarterly* 36, nos. 3–4 (2008): 11–22; and T. J. Jourian, "Evolving Nature of Sexual Orientation and Gender Identity," *New Directions for Student Services* 152 (2015): 11–23.

16. See Talia Mae Bettcher's discussion of "the natural attitude" in "Evil Deceivers and Make-Believers: On Transphobic Violence and the Politics of Illusion," *Hypatia* 22, no. 3 (2007): 48–50.

17. The term "transsexual," which has fallen out of fashion in recent years, refers to people who have had gender-confirming surgery. For an amusing reflection on how rapidly discourse has changed, see Riki Wilchins, "I Was Recently Informed I'm Not a Transsexual," *Advocate*, June 7, 2017, https://www.advocate.com/commentary/2017/6/07/i-was-recently-informed-im-not-transsexual. For a history of the transformation of bodily sex in the United States, see Joanne

Meyerowitz, *How Sex Changed: A History of Transsexuality in the United States* (Cambridge, Mass.: Harvard University Press, 2002).

18. The ur-text for this perspective is Michel Foucault, *The History of Sexuality, Volume 1: Introduction* (New York: Random House, 1978); see also David Halperin's analysis of how sexual acts were understood as a performance of citizenship in ancient Athens in "Is There a History of Sexuality?," *History and Theory* 28, no. 3 (1989): 257–74. To be clear, Foucault seems to have believed that subjectivities (including sexuality) are *produced* by the larger political economy, and that the democratic-capitalist ideal of free choice is, therefore, largely an illusion.

19. For example, in *Professing Selves: Transsexuality and Same-Sex Desire in Contemporary Iran* (Durham, N.C.: Duke University Press, 2014), Afsaneh Najmabadi suggests that in Iran, sexuality and gender identities are configured and experienced in a very different way: rather than being understood necessarily as the free expression of one's true inner self, they are produced through "contingent conduct" that is "situationally enacted." Thus, trans identity is not "something necessarily arising from within one person," but "something whose meaning is shaped by one's location in many (in principle, innumerable) sites" (297). In this way, whether one is trans or gay becomes "a question of not some inner truth but of figuring out and navigating one's relationship-in-conduct vis-à-vis others" (298). Moreover, under the Islamic Republic, same-sex desire is taboo, and same-sex sexual acts are severely punished, but sex-reassignment-surgery is approved and even subsidized by the state; given that reality, to transition is sometimes simply a tactical option for same-sex desiring people that makes their lives livable (introduction and 289–90).

20. Stryker, *Transgender History*, 1; see also Stryker, *Transgender History: Roots*, 1. Compare with Leslie Feinberg's definition: "Trans*gender* people traverse, bridge, or blur the boundary of the *gender expression* they were assigned at birth" (*Transgender Warriors*, x).

21. Stryker, *Transgender History*, 1; Stryker, *Transgender History: Roots*, 1.

22. Peter Boag, *Re-Dressing America's Frontier Past* (Berkeley: University of California Press, 2011), 15–18; Clare Sears, *Arresting Dress: Cross-Dressing, Law, and Fascination in Nineteenth-Century San Francisco* (Durham, N.C.: Duke University Press, 2015), 8–10, 139–40; Jen Manion, *Female Husbands: A Trans History* (Cambridge: Cambridge University Press, 2020), 10–12.

23. Manion, *Female Husbands*, 11.

24. Sears, *Arresting Dress*, 139. In similar vein, Howard Chiang proposes a broadly inclusive "transgender continuum," which "is concerned less with who qualifies as transgender than with how different actors relate to one another *through* the category of transgender"; see *Transtopia in the Sinophone Pacific* (New York: Columbia University Press, 2021), 20–21.

25. Manion, *Female Husbands*, 2, 11.

26. Chiang, *Transtopia*, xi; see also 63.

27. Howard Chiang, ed., *Transgender China* (New York: Palgrave Macmillan, 2012), chapter 2; Howard Chiang, *After Eunuchs: Science, Medicine, and the Transformation*

of Sex in Modern China (New York: Columbia University Press, 2018), introduction, chapters 1 and 5; Chiang, *Transtopia*, 58–63. In tracing this genealogy, Chiang's focus is the emergence of modern discourses of sex, gender, and sexuality; his primary interest in eunuchs is not their social history, but the *image* of "the eunuch" in Orientalist discourse about China as "a castrated nation," and in the development of the concept of "the transsexual."

28. Other innovations included gender-neutral pronoun characters to denote "it" (for inanimate objects) and to refer to animals. A fifth character uses the spirit radical (*shi*) and is used to refer to a deity in the third person, usually the Christian God. It has an older provenance, but it came into widespread use only with Protestant missionaries' translations of the Bible. All of these pronouns continue to be pronounced in the same way: *ta*.

29. Most Chinese characters are constructed with a "radical," which is a clue to meaning and used to classify characters, plus a "phonetic," which is a clue to pronunciation.

30. Gina Tam, personal communication, March 2019. For the invention of the female *ta* and related controversies, see Lydia Liu, *Translingual Practice: Literature, National Culture, and Translated Modernity—China, 1900–1937* (Stanford, Calif.: Stanford University Press, 1995), 36–39; Huang Xingtao, *"Ta" zi de wenhuashi—Nüxing xin daici de faming yu rentong yanjiu* [A cultural history of the Chinese character "*Ta*" / She: on the invention and identity of a new female pronoun] (Fuzhou: Fujian Jiaoyu Chubanshe, 2009); and Coraline Jortay, "Pronominal Politics: (Un)Gendering Narrative and Framing Ambiguity in Chinese Literature, 1917–1937" (PhD diss., University libre de Bruxelles, 2020).

31. Judith Zeitlin, *Historian of the Strange: Pu Songling and the Chinese Classical Tale* (Stanford, Calif: Stanford University Press, 1993) 101–2. See also my discussion of this tale in chapter 5 in this volume. Another example of the narrative benefits of nonbinary pronouns is the account of the "Kingdom of Women" in the early nineteenth-century novel *Jinghua yuan* [Romance of flowers in the mirror]; see chapter 1 in this volume.

32. Cathy Lai, "'X 也'and 'Ta': The Gradual Rise of Gender-Neutral Pronouns in Chinese," *Ariana*, July 10, 2020, www.arianalife.com; Helen Hok-Sze Leung, "Epilogue: On *Keoi* and the Politics of Pronouns," *Inter-Asia Cultural Studies* 22, no. 2 (2021): 215–17. For *keoi/qu* and gendered pronouns in Cantonese, see Julie Abbou and Angela Tse, "A Hermeneutical Approach of Gender Linguistic Materiality: Semiotic and Structural Categorisation of Gender in Hong Kong Cantonese," in *Gender, Language, and the Periphery: Grammatical and Social Gender from the Margins*, ed. Julie Abbou and Fabienne Baider (Amsterdam: John Benjamins, 2016), 89–128.

33. Rachel Mesch, *Before Trans: Three Gender Stories from Nineteenth-Century France* (Stanford, Calif.: Stanford University Press, 2020), 24–25.

34. Gill-Peterson, *Histories*, 15.

35. Gill-Peterson, 13.

36. Emily Skidmore, *True Sex: The Lives of Trans Men at the Turn of the Twentieth Century* (New York: New York University Press, 2017), 10.

37. Boag, *Re-dressing*, 12, 18–19; Chiang, *After Eunuchs*, chapter 5; Sears, *Arresting Dress*, 20–21, 81.

38. Manion, *Female Husbands*, 9. My own preference is to use "themself" in this context, in the interest of clarity, because the gender-neutral pronoun is singular.

39. Some scholars have blithely assumed that people in the past assigned female at birth who presented as masculine were simply lesbians, when they might just as plausibly be claimed as transmen, and when, in fact, there is usually no way to know how they would identify were they alive today. See, for example, Terry Castle's nostalgic reverie about "Ed" in her *The Apparitional Lesbian: Female Homosexuality and Modern Culture* (New York: Columbia University Press, 1993), 21–27; and the review of Manion's book by Selina Todd, "Significant Others," *The Critic*, https://thecritic.co.uk/issues/june-2020/significant-others/ (accessed July 17, 2023). Another approach has been to explain away "female transvestism" as an expedient strategy to pursue occupations open only to men and therefore not a reflection of gender identity at all: see, for example, Rudolf Dekker and Lotte van de Pol, *The Tradition of Female Transvestism in Early Modern Europe* (New York: St. Martin's, 1989), 30–40; and Terry Castle, *The Female Thermometer: Eighteenth-Century Culture and the Invention of the Uncanny* (Oxford: Oxford University Press, 1995), 70–71. The "border wars" around the identity of Brandon Teena show that even figures from the recent past may provoke heated but ultimately futile debate: see, for example, J. Halberstam and C. Jacob Hale, "Butch/FTM Border Wars: A Note on Collaboration," *GLQ* 4, no. 2 (1998): 311–48; C. Jacob Hale, "Consuming the Living, Dis(re)membering the Dead in the Butch/FTM Borderlands," *GLQ* 4, no. 2 (1998): 283–85; and J. Halberstam, "Telling Tales: Brandon Teena, Billy Tipton, and Transgender Biography," *a/b: Auto/Biography Studies* 15, no. 1 (2000): 62–81.

40. Manion, *Female Husbands*, 13–14, 265–66; see also the use of gender-neutral pronouns by Kate Redburn, "Before Equal Protection: The Fall of Cross-Dressing Bans and the Transgender Legal Movement, 1963–86," *Law and History Review* 40 (2022): 679–723.

41. We find the same policy in other times and places; see, for example, Manion, *Female Husbands*, 2–3, 39.

42. Melissa Dale, *Inside the World of the Eunuch: A Social History of the Emperor's Servants in Qing China* (Hong Kong: Hong Kong University Press, 2018), 39.

43. Melissa Dale usefully distinguishes between "Confucian society's labeling of eunuch gender as feminine" and eunuchs' own preferred sense of themselves as being "gendered male" (*Inside the World*, 55).

44. For example, DC: 372-00 and the substatutes that follow, having been added as amendments to the basic statute. For a list of abbreviations used in citation, see the references.

45. An exception is the cross-dressing clergy discussed in chapter 3, for whom I use gender-neutral pronouns.

46. For the Qing code and judiciary, see Derk Bodde and Clarence Morris, *Law in Imperial China: Exemplified by 190 Ch'ing Dynasty Cases, Translated from the Hsing-an*

hui-lan (Cambridge, Mass.: Harvard University Press, 1967); and Sommer, *Polyandry*, appendices D and E. For local government in the Qing, see T'ung-tsu Ch'ü, *Local Government in China under the Ch'ing*, rev. ed. (Cambridge, Mass: Harvard University Press, 1962); and Bradly Reed, *Talons and Teeth: County Clerks and Runners in the Qing Dynasty* (Stanford, Calif: Stanford University Press, 2000).

47. Sommer, *Sex*, 18–22; Sommer, *Polyandry*, 14, 392–93.

48. Silas Wu, *Communication and Imperial Control in China: Evolution of the Palace Memorial System, 1693–1735* (Cambridge, Mass.: Harvard University Press, 1970). Other sources for this book include county-level court cases (cited in chapter 6 in this volume); "lateral communications" within the central government; and casebooks such as *Xing'an huilan* [*Conspectus of Penal Cases*] and its sequels: Zhu Qingqi, Bao Shuyun, Pan Wenfang, and He Weikai, eds., *Xing'an hui lan san bian* [*Conspectus of Penal Cases*, with two sequels), 4 vols. (Beijing: Beijing Guji Chubanshe, 2004), henceforth cited as XA.

49. Sommer, *Sex*; Sommer, *Polyandry*.

50. Yuan Mei's collected works include a volume of his judicial decisions. See Jin Xiage, ed., *Yuan Zicai pandu jinghua* [Highlights of Yuan Mei's legal judgments], in *Yuan Mei quanji xinbian* [A new edition of Yuan Mei's collected works], vol. 19 (Hangzhou: Zhejiang Guji Chubanshe, 2015). I cite one of his cases involving a stone maiden in chapter 6 in this volume.

51. Hsiao-wen Cheng (in "Before Sexual and Normal") traces the concept of *renyao* from antiquity through the Yuan dynasty. Beginning in the thirteenth century, this term came to refer exclusively to sexual anomalies (e.g., spontaneous sex change, bodies with the genitalia of both sexes), but in the Ming-Qing era it mainly referred specifically to M–F cross-dressers who committed sexual transgressions against women. See also chapter 2 in this volume. For twentieth-century usage of *renyao*, see Chiang, *Transtopia*, chapter 3.

52. Here, I follow in the footsteps of other historians who have used newspapers to study trans history, including Peter Boag, Howard Chiang, Jen Manion, Clare Sears, and Emily Skidmore; see their works cited in endnotes 22 through 27 of this chapter. For early Chinese journalism in general and *Shenbao* in particular, see Madeleine Dong, "Communities and Communication: A Study of the Case of Yang Naiwu, 1873–1877," *Late Imperial China* 16, no. 1 (1995): 79–119; Rania Huntington, "The Weird in the Newspaper," in *Writing and Materiality in China: Essays in Honor of Patrick Hanan*, ed. Judith Zeitlin and Lydia Liu, with Ellen Widmer (Leiden: Brill, 2003), 341–96; Barbara Mittler, *A Newspaper for China? Power, Identity, and Change in Shanghai's News Media, 1872–1912* (Cambridge, Mass.: Harvard University Asia Center, 2004); and Weipin Tsai, *Reading Shenbao: Nationalism, Consumerism and Individuality in China, 1919–37* (New York: Palgrave Macmillan, 2010). For *Dianshizhai Pictorial*, see Christopher Reed, "Re/Collecting the Sources: Shanghai's 'Dianshizhai Pictorial' and Its Place in Historical Memories, 1884–1949," *Modern Chinese Literature and Culture* 12, no. 2 (2000): 44–71; Xiaoqing Ye, *The Dianshizhai Pictorial: Shanghai Urban Life, 1884–1898* (Ann Arbor: University of Michigan Press, 2003); Nanny Kim, "New Wine in Old Bottles? Making and

Reading an Illustrated Magazine from Late Nineteenth-Century Shanghai," in *Joining the Global Public: Word, Image, and City in Early Chinese Newspapers, 1870–1910*, ed. Rudolf Wagner (Albany: State University of New York Press, 2007), 175–200; Rudolf Wagner, "Joining the Global Imaginaire: The Shanghai Illustrated Newspaper *Dianshizhai huabao*," in *Joining the Global Public: Word, Image, and City in Early Chinese Newspapers, 1870–1910*, ed. Rudolf Wagner (Albany: State University of New York Press, 2007), 105–73; and Shen Guandong, *Xushi yuyan yu shikong biaoda:* Dianshizhai huabao *tuxiang xushi yanjiu* [Narrative language and the representation of time and space: studies of image and narrative in the *Dianshizhai Pictorial*] (Zhenjiang: Jiangsu Daxue Chubanshe, 2018).

53. Huntington, "Weird in the Newspaper," 341.

54. Huntington, 349.

55. Huntington, 349. See, for example, *Shenbao*'s coverage of the famous Yang Naiwu case in Dong, "Communities and Communication."

56. I searched for "nan ban nüzhuang," "Sang Chong," "renyao," "yinyang ren," "erxing ren," and variations.

57. For example, "Qi an nan duan," *Shenbao*, July 24, 1892; and "Jinshi juhuo qiaozhuang nüzi," *Shenbao*, October 18, 1934. See also the two late Qing cases from other newspapers cited in Chiang, *Transtopia*, 114–16.

58. Natalie Zemon Davis, *The Return of Martin Guerre* (Cambridge, Mass.: Harvard University Press, 1983), 5.

1. Transgender Paradigms in Late Imperial China

1. Roland Altenburger, "Is It the Clothes That Make the Man? Cross-Dressing, Gender, and Sex in Pre-Twentieth-Century Zhu Yingtai Lore," *Asian Folklore Studies* 64, no. 2 (2005): 165–205; Roland Altenburger, *The Sword or the Needle: The Female Knight-errant (xia) in Traditional Chinese Narrative* (Bern: Peter Lang, 2009). Charlotte Furth argues that beginning in the late Ming, female-to-male sex change was increasingly represented as socially nonthreatening, in contrast with heightened anxiety about male-to-female change. See "Androgynous Males and Deficient Females: Biology and Gender Boundaries in Sixteenth- and Seventeenth-Century China," *Late Imperial China* 9, no. 2 (1988): 18.

2. Xu Wei, *Ci Mulan ti fu congjun* [The female Mulan joins the army in place of her father], in *Xuxiu siku quanshu* [Continuing edition of the complete library of the Four Treasuries] (Shanghai: Shanghai Guji Chubanshe, 2002), 1764:405–11; Siu Leung Li, *Cross-Dressing in Chinese Opera* (Hong Kong: Hong Kong University Press, 2003), 83–89; Louise Edwards, *Woman Warriors and Wartime Spies of China* (Cambridge: Cambridge University Press, 2016), chapter 2. For English translations of the original ballad and of Xu Wei's play, see Shiamin Kwa and Wilt Idema, ed. and trans., *Mulan: Five Versions of a Classic Chinese Legend with Related Texts* (Indianapolis: Hackett, 2010).

3. Judith Zeitlin, *Historian of the Strange: Pu Songling and the Chinese Classical Tale* (Stanford, Calif: Stanford University Press, 1993), 116–25; Edwards, *Woman Warriors*, chapter 2.

4. Altenburger, *Sword or Needle*, 29–31. Shi Jianqiao, who in 1935 assassinated the warlord Sun Chuanfang in order to avenge her father's death, is a modern example of self-conscious emulation of the female knight errant. See Eugenia Lean, *Public Passions: The Trial of Shi Jianqiao and the Rise of Popular Sympathy in Republican China* (Berkeley: University of California Press, 2007).

5. Wai-yee Li, *Women and National Trauma in Late Imperial Chinese Literature* (Cambridge, Mass.: Harvard University Asia Center, 2014), chapters 2 and 3.

6. Wang Zheng, *Women in the Chinese Enlightenment: Oral and Textual Histories* (Berkeley: University of California Press, 1999), 21–22, 179–80, 350–51; Antonia Finnane, *Changing Clothes in China: Fashion, History, Nation* (New York: Columbia University Press, 2008), 87–92; Joan Judge, *The Precious Raft of History: The Past, the West, and the Woman Question in China* (Stanford, Calif.: Stanford University Press, 2008), chapter 5; Edwards, *Woman Warriors*, chapters 2 and 3. Mulan's ethnicity was also transformed, from a mutton-eating, camel-riding warrior who served the Tuoba "Khan," into a Han Chinese patriot; see James Millward, "More Hun than Han: Reading the Tabghach 'Ballad of Mulan' in 2020," #AsiaNow, September 17, 2020, https://www.asianstudies.org/more-hun-than-han-reading-the-tabghach-ballad-of-mulan-in-2020/.

7. Christina Gilmartin, *Engendering the Chinese Revolution: Radical Women, Communist Politics, and Mass Movements in the 1920s* (Berkeley: University of California Press, 1995), 189–90, photographs following 114; Finnane, *Changing Clothes*, 198–200, 227–40; Wang Zheng, *Finding Women in the State: A Socialist Feminist Revolution in the People's Republic of China, 1949–1964* (Berkeley: University of California Press, 2017), chapter 8.

8. For gender crossing and androgyny in the scholar-beauty romance, see Zuyan Zhou, "The Androgynous Ideal in Scholar-Beauty Romances: A Historical and Cultural View," in *Transgender China*, ed. Howard Chiang (New York: Palgrave Macmillan, 2012), 97–125. For the "fragile" masculinity of the scholar, see Geng Song, *The Fragile Scholar: Power and Masculinity in Chinese Culture* (Hong Kong: Hong Kong University Press, 2004), chapter 1.

9. In the early Qing, failure to shave the front of the head was a capital offense; later, after the tonsure had been universally accepted, cutting off the queue became a sign of defiance and rebellion. See Philip Kuhn, *Soulstealers: The Chinese Sorcery Scare of 1768* (Cambridge, Mass.: Harvard University Press, 1990), 53–59.

10. Guojun Wang, *Staging Personhood: Costuming in Early Qing Drama* (New York: Columbia University Press, 2020), chapter 2.

11. For English translations of four versions of this tale, see Wilt Idema, *The Butterfly Lovers: The Legend of Liang Shanbo and Zhu Yingtai, Four Versions with Related Texts* (Indianapolis: Hackett, 2010). See also Wilt Idema, "Female Talent and Female Virtue: Xu Wei's *Nü zhuangyuan* and Meng Chengshun's *Zhenwen ji*," in *Ming-Qing xiqu guoji yantaohui lunwen ji* [Papers from the International Symposium on

Ming-Qing Drama], ed. Hua Wei and Wang Ailing (Taipei: Zhongyangyuan Wenzhesuo Choubeichu, 1998), 2:551–571; Altenburger, "Is It Clothes."

12. Idema, *Butterfly Lovers*, xxxv.

13. Altenburger, "Is It Clothes," 179–83.

14. Altenburger, 193; see also Idema, *Butterfly Lovers*, xxxv.

15. For the trope of the Kingdom of Women in Qing travel writing, especially with regard to Taiwan, see Emma Teng, *Taiwan's Imagined Geography: Chinese Colonial Travel Writing and Pictures, 1683–1895* (Cambridge, Mass.: Harvard University Asia Center, 2004), chapters 6 and 7. See also Norma Diamond, "The Miao and Poison: Interactions on China's Southwest Frontier," *Ethnology* 27, no. 1 (1988): 1–25, on the stereotype of Miao women as hypersexual and dangerous; and Sophie Volpp's analysis of the "ethnographic" perspective in late Ming writing that located male homoeroticism in the far south, on the margins of civilization: "Classifying Lust: The Seventeenth-Century Vogue for Male Love," *Harvard Journal of Asiatic Studies* 61, no. 1 (2001): 77–79, 94–97.

16. For a detailed overview of early sources, see Paul Pelliot, *Notes on Marco Polo* (Paris: Imprimerie nationale, 1959), 2:671–725; I am grateful to Jon Felt for bringing this text to my attention. For Tang sources, see Jennifer Jay, "Imagining Matriarchy: 'Kingdoms of Women' in Tang China," *Journal of the American Oriental Society* 116, no. 2 (1996): 220–29. Such ethnographic texts combine fantastic, mythical accounts with what appear to be descriptions of actual matriarchal societies encountered by the Chinese.

17. Wu Cheng'en, *Xiyou ji* [Journey to the West] (Beijing: Beijing Renmin Wenxue Chubanshe, 1980), chapters 54 and 55.

18. Li Ruzhen, *Jinghua yuan* [Romance of flowers in the mirror] (Beijing: Renmin Wenxue Chubanshe, 1990), chapters 32–38. For the gendered symbolism and structure of this novel, see Maram Epstein, "Engendering Order: Structure, Gender, and Meaning in the Qing Novel *Jinghua yuan*," *Chinese Literature: Essays, Articles, Reviews (CLEAR)* 18 (1996): 101–27.

19. See, for example, Paul Ropp, "The Seeds of Change: Reflections on the Condition of Women in the Early and Mid-Ch'ing," *Signs* 2, no. 1 (1976): 5–23. Hu Shi may have been the first to make this argument; see Epstein, "Engendering Order," 1–2.

20. For the life and career of Wu Zetian, see Denis Twitchett, ed., *The Cambridge History of China, Volume 3: Sui and T'ang China, 589–906, Part 1* (Cambridge: Cambridge University Press, 1979), chapters 5 and 6; and Keith McMahon, "Women Rulers in Imperial China," *Nan Nü* 15, no. 2 (2013): 179–218. The novel's relatively "muted" portrayal of Wu Zetian "contrasts sharply with the cruel and pornographic image of her prevalent in other works of fiction" from the Ming-Qing era (Epstein, "Engendering Order," 118).

21. Maram Epstein points out "the vulnerability of the orthodox order" in Li Ruzhen's novel, despite the ultimate "triumph of orthodoxy over heterodoxy" (121). See also Keith McMahon, *Misers, Shrews, and Polygamists: Sexuality and Male-Female Relations in Eighteenth-Century Chinese Fiction* (Durham, N.C.: Duke University Press, 1995),

285–86; and my discussion of Judith Butler's theory of the performative nature of gender in chapter 6 in this volume.

22. Arthur Waley, trans., *The Analects of Confucius* (New York: Vintage, 1938), 127.

23. See Rania Huntington, *Alien Kind: Foxes and Late Imperial Chinese Narrative* (Cambridge, Mass.: Harvard University Asia Center, 2003); Xiaofei Kang, *The Cult of the Fox: Power, Gender, and Popular Religion in Late Imperial and Modern China* (New York: Columbia University Press, 2006); and chapter 5 in this volume.

24. For the "legal containment of licentiousness" in the Ming-Qing era, see Y. Yvon Wang, *Reinventing Licentiousness: Pornography and Modern China* (Ithaca, N.Y.: Cornell University Press, 2021), 44–48.

25. See, for example, Zeitlin, *Historian*; Sophie Volpp, "The Discourse on Male Marriage: Li Yu's 'A Male Mencius's Mother,'" *Positions* 2, no. 1 (1994): 113–32; and chapter 6 in this volume.

26. See, for example, Colin Mackerras, *The Rise of the Peking Opera, 1770–1870* (London: Oxford University Press, 1972); Mackerras, "Peking Opera Before the Twentieth Century," *Comparative Drama* 28, no. 1 (1994): 19–42; Volpp, "Classifying Lust"; Volpp, "The Literary Circulation of Actors in Seventeenth-Century China," *Journal of Asian Studies* 61, no. 3 (2002): 949–84; Volpp, *Worldly Stage: Theatricality in Seventeenth-Century China* (Cambridge, Mass.: Harvard University Asia Center, 2011); Wu Cuncun, "Beautiful Boys Made Up as Beautiful Girls: Anti-Masculine Taste in Qing China," in *Asian Masculinities: The Meaning and Practice of Manhood in China and Japan*, ed. Kam Louie and Morris Low (London: RoutledgeCurzon, 2003), 19–40; Wu, *Homoerotic Sensibilities in Late Imperial China* (London: RoutledgeCurzon, 2004); Wu, *Xiwai zhi xi: Qing zhongwanqi Jingcheng de xiyuan wenhua yu liyuan siyu zhi* [The drama outside the play: opera culture and the private apartment brothel system in mid-late Qing Beijing] (Hong Kong: Hong Kong University Press, 2017); and Andrea Goldman, *Opera and the City: The Politics of Culture in Beijing, 1770–1900* (Stanford, Calif.: Stanford University Press, 2012).

27. Mackerras, "Peking Opera," 21.

28. Mackerras, *Rise of the Peking Opera*, 145–152; Wu, *Homoerotic Sensibilities*, chapter 5.

29. Wu, 127–32; Goldman, *Opera and the City*, 28–33.

30. *Qingbai leichao* [Qing miscellany], quoted in Wu, 128.

31. Wu, 130.

32. Wu, *Homoerotic Sensibilities*, chapter 5; Wu, *Xiwai zhi xi*; see also Wu Cuncun and Mark Stevenson, "Male Love Lost: The Fate of Male Same-Sex Prostitution in Beijing in the Late Nineteenth and Early Twentieth Centuries," in *Embodied Modernities: Corporeality, Representation, and Chinese Cultures*, ed. Fran Martin and Larissa Heinrich (Honolulu: University of Hawai'i Press, 2006), 42–59.

33. Goldman, *Opera and the City*, 18.

34. Wu, *Homoerotic Sensibilities*, 162–63.

35. Wu, chapters 2 and 3; Volpp, "Classifying Lust"; Volpp, "Literary Circulation"; Volpp, *Worldly Stage*.

36. Matthew H. Sommer, *Sex, Law, and Society in Late Imperial China* (Stanford, Calif.: Stanford University Press, 2000), chapters 4 and 6.

37. Wu, *Homoerotic Sensibilities*, 163–64.

38. Sommer, *Sex*, chapter 4; Matthew H. Sommer, "Review of Wu Cuncun, *Homoerotic Sensibilities in Late Imperial China*," *Journal of Asian Studies* 64, no. 4 (2005): 1017–19; Wenqing Kang, *Obsession: Male Same-Sex Relations in China, 1900–1950* (Hong Kong: Hong Kong University Press, 2009), chapter 1.

39. Sommer, "Review of Wu Cuncun"; see also Song, *Fragile Scholar*, chapter 5.

40. See, for example, Annalisa Anzani, Louis Lindley, Giacomo Tognasso, M. Paz Galupo, and Antonion Prunas, " 'Being Talked to Like I Was a Sex Toy, Like Being Transgender Was Simply for the Enjoyment of Someone Else': Fetishization and Sexualization of Transgender and Nonbinary Individuals," *Archives of Sexual Behavior* 50 (2021): 897–911.

41. This misogyny is parodied hilariously by Li Yu in his story "A Male Mencius's Mother." Ironically, the narrator argues that the femininity of boys is more *natural* than that of women, who supposedly must depend on artifice (such as makeup and foot-binding) for their appeal. But he also expresses disgust at women's bodies (e.g., their breasts, menstruation, the effects of childbirth). See Volpp, "Discourse on Male Marriage," 119–20.

42. For natural versus bound feet, see Dorothy Ko, "The Body as Attire: The Shifting Meanings of Footbinding in Seventeenth-Century China," *Journal of Women's History* 8, no. 4 (1997): 8–27; and Ko, *Cinderella's Sisters*, chapters 1 and 6. For literati obsession with rocks, see Zeitlin, *Historian*, 74–88. The Manchu tonsure was imposed on *dan* actors, although at first there was confusion on this point. In a 1653 case from Mancheng County, Zhili, two *dan* were arrested for failing to shave heads. Their defense was that, since they were actors of female roles, they had to have long hair; surely the tonsure was not meant to apply to them. An investigation confirmed that the two were telling the truth, and it appears they were spared execution. XT #661, SZ 10.12.13; see also Matthew H. Sommer, "Dangerous Males, Vulnerable Males, and Polluted Males: The Regulation of Masculinity in Qing Dynasty Law," in *Chinese Femininities/Chinese Masculinities: A Reader*, ed. Susan Brownell and Jeffrey Wasserstrom (Berkeley: University of California Press, 2002), 78–79.

43. Sommer, *Sex, Law, and Society*, chapters 6 and 7; Sommer, *Polyandry and Wife-Selling in Qing Dynasty China: Survival Strategies and Judicial Interventions* (Berkeley: University of California Press, 2015), 278–87. See also Anders Hansson, *Chinese Outcasts: Discrimination and Emancipation in Late Imperial China* (Leiden: E. J. Brill, 1996), chapter 3.

44. Cited in Chün-fang Yü, *Chinese Buddhism: A Thematic History* (Honolulu: University of Hawai'i Press, 2020), 123.

45. Edward Rhoads, *Manchus and Han: Ethnic Relations and Political Power in Late Qing and Early Republican China, 1861–1928* (Seattle: University of Washington Press, 2000), 60; Adeline Herrou, *A World of Their Own: Daoist Monks and Their Community in Contemporary China* (St. Petersburg, Fl.: Three Pines, 2013), 49–54.

46. Yü, *Chinese Buddhism*, 120–24; John Kieschnick, *The Eminent Monk: Buddhist Ideals in Medieval Chinese Hagiography* (Honolulu: University of Hawai'i Press, 1997), 17–21, and personal communication, May 2021; Daniel Burton-Rose, "Gendered Androgyny: Transcendent Ideals and Profane Realities in Buddhism, Classicism, and Daoism," in *Transgender China*, ed. Howard Chiang (New York: Palgrave Macmillan, 2012), 67–96.

47. Hsiao-wen Cheng, *Divine, Demonic, and Disordered: Women Without Men in Song Dynasty China* (Seattle: University of Washington Press, 2021), 138.

48. Cheng, *Divine Demonic, and Disordered*, 137.

49. Cheng, 119.

50. Chün-fang Yü, *Passing the Light: The Incense Light Community and Buddhist Nuns in Contemporary Taiwan* (Honolulu: University of Hawai'i Press, 2013), 139. Similarly, Cheng cites a Buddhist nun in contemporary Sri Lanka who asserts that "we are not women; we are renunciants" (119).

51. Yü, *Passing the Light*, 139.

52. Yü, 138–39.

53. The same was true of parents who had their sons become eunuchs. See Evelyn Rawski, *The Last Emperors: A Social History of Qing Imperial Institutions* (Berkeley: University of California Press, 1998), 163–64.

54. John Powers, *A Bull of a Man: Images of Masculinity, Sex, and the Body in Indian Buddhism* (Cambridge, Mass.: Harvard University Press, 2009), 9, 13–15, 23; Nobuyoshi Yamabe, "Indian Myth Transformed in a Chinese Apocryphal Text: Two Stories of the Buddha's Hidden Organ," in *India in the Chinese Imagination: Myth, Religion, and Thought*, ed. John Kieschnick and Meir Shahar (Philadelphia: University of Pennsylvania Press, 2014), 61–80.

55. Vincent Goossaert, "The Quanzhen Clergy, 1700–1950," in *Religion and Chinese Society*, ed. John Lagerwey (Hong Kong: Chinese University Press, 2004), 699–772; Goossaert, *The Taoists of Peking, 1800–1949: A Social History of Urban Clerics* (Cambridge, Mass.: Harvard University Asia Center, 2007), 93–97, and personal communication, June 2021. The Qing dynasty officially recognized only those clergy who were associated with registered temples; see Goossaert, "Counting the Monks: The 1736–1739 Census of the Chinese Clergy," *Late Imperial China* 21, no. 2 (2000): 40–85.

56. Adeline Herrou, "Daoist Monasticism at the Turn of the Twenty-First Century: An Ethnography of a Quanzhen Community in Shaanxi Province," in *Daoism in the Twentieth Century: Between Eternity and Modernity*, ed. David Palmer and Xun Liu (Berkeley: University of California Press, 2012), 93–99; Herrou, *World of Their Own*, 164–67.

57. Herrou, 231, 243–44.

58. Roger Ames, "Taoism and the Androgynous Ideal," *Historical Reflections / Réflexions Historiques* 8, no. 3 (1981): 21–45; Kristofer Schipper, *The Taoist Body* (Berkeley: University of California Press, 1993), 128, 156–58; Catherine Despeux and Livia Kohn, *Women in Daoism* (Cambridge, Mass.: Three Pines, 2003), chapter 10; Goossaert,

Taoists of Peking, 234; Herrou, "Daoist Monasticism," 91–93; Herrou, *World of Their Own*, 235–36, 241.

59. Herrou, 236; Hsiao-wen Cheng, "Before Sexual and Normal: Shifting Categories of Sexual Anomaly from Ancient to Yuan China," *Asia Major* 31, no. 2 (2018): 18–21.

60. Rhoads, *Manchus and Han*, 60; Herrou, 49–54; Goossaert, personal communication, June 2021.

61. Herrou, 230.

62. Ames, "Taoism and the Androgynous Ideal"; Schipper, *Taoist Body*, 128; Herrou, 246.

63. Melissa Dale, *Inside the World of the Eunuch: A Social History of the Emperor's Servants in Qing China* (Hong Kong: Hong Kong University Press, 2018), 1–2. In the Qing there were no privately employed eunuchs; all were members of the imperial establishment. The definitive studies of Qing dynasty eunuchs are Dale, *Inside the World*; and Norman Kutcher, *Eunuch and Emperor in the Great Age of Qing Rule* (Berkeley: University of California Press, 2018). See also Rawski, *Last Emperors*, chapter 5; and Goossaert, *Taoists of Peking*, chapter 5. Howard Chiang portrays the eunuch as a sort of genealogical ancestor to the modern transsexual, at least on the level of discourse; see Howard Chiang, ed., *Transgender China* (New York: Palgrave Macmillan, 2012), chapter 2; and Chiang, *After Eunuchs: Science, Medicine, and the Transformation of Sex in Modern China* (New York: Columbia University Press, 2018), introduction and chapter 1.

64. Howard Chiang (citing a tomb figurine from the second century BCE) questions whether the penis was amputated along with the testes, but, as he acknowledges, the Chinese and foreign physicians who actually examined Qing eunuchs testified that the external genitalia were completely amputated (30–45). Prospective eunuchs were physically examined before being approved for service, and incomplete amputation was grounds for rejection. See Dale, *Inside the World*, xi, 37–39, 41–42; and Kutcher, *Eunuch and Emperor*, 11, 171.

65. New names were usually assigned by eunuch superiors. There was a small number of names that were frequently assigned, to the point that historians today sometimes have difficulty distinguishing between individuals with the same name. Dale, 66–67, 71; Kutcher, 175–77.

66. This is the title of the first chapter of Mitamura's book. Mitamura Taisuke, *Kangan: Sokkin seiji no kōzō* [Eunuchs: the structure of intimate politics], rev. ed. (Tokyo: Chūō Kōron Shinsha, 2012), 3. See also Taisuke Mitamura, *Chinese Eunuchs: The Structure of Intimate Politics*, trans. Charles Pomeroy (Rutland, Vt.: Tuttle, 1970), 21.

67. Thus, Chiang argues that castration itself "reproduces eunuchs socially and culturally," and that eunuchs exercised "agency" in their own "social and cultural reproduction" (*After Eunuchs*, 50).

68. For the employment of eunuchs as an expression of "fear of the penis out of place," see Sommer, "Dangerous Males," 68. For the "transcendence of gender norms" by Han dynasty eunuchs, see Yunxin Li, "The Inner Court and Politics in the Han Empire" (PhD diss., Stanford University, 2022), chapter 2.

69. For example, in 1789, thirty-seven sons of participants in the Lin Shuangwen Rebellion were handed over to the Imperial Household Department for service as eunuchs; their ages ranged from four to fifteen *sui*; Kutcher, *Eunuch and Emperor*, 169–70. See also David Ownby, *Brotherhoods and Secret Societies in Early and Mid-Qing China: The Formation of a Tradition* (Stanford, Calif.: Stanford University Press, 1996), 110; and Dale, *Inside the World*, 34–35.

70. Dale, 29, 34–35, 42–43, 57; Kutcher, 12, 168–70.

71. While acknowledging their unfree status, Dale suggests that eunuchs were different from slaves, because one penalty for eunuchs who ran away was exile to Heilongjiang to become slaves of local officials (119–20). But the point of that particular punishment was not enslavement per se but, rather, exile to the remote northern frontier, where conditions would have been far less comfortable than in a palace in Beijing.

72. Dale, 51, 81–82; Kutcher, *Eunuch and Emperor*, 10–13, 21.

73. Goossaert, *Taoists of Peking*, 209–18; Dale, 46, 60, 79–81, 160–62; Kutcher, 210–14.

74. Kutcher, 213–14; see also Mitamura, *Chinese Eunuchs*, 127.

75. Goossaert, *Taoists of Peking*, 218–31.

76. Goossaert, 234. For consistency, I have substituted "Daoist" for "Taoist."

77. Kutcher, *Eunuch and Emperor*, 162.

78. Jennifer Jay cites five cases of eunuch adoption, only one of which dates to the Qing: the Empress Dowager Cixi's famous favorite Li Lianying. See "Another Side of Chinese Eunuch History: Castration, Marriage, Adoption, and Burial," *Canadian Journal of History* 28 (1993): 459–78. Michael Hoeckelmann focuses on the Tang: "Celibate but Not Childless: Eunuch Military Dynasticism in Medieval China," in *Celibate and Childless Men in Power: Ruling Eunuchs and Bishops in the Pre-Modern World*, ed. Almut Hofert, Matthew Mesley, and Serena Tolino (New York: Routledge, 2018), 111–28. Gilbert Chen focuses on the Ming: "Castration and Connection: Kinship Organization Among Ming Eunuchs," *Ming Studies* 74 (2016): 27–47. For eunuchs in the Han adopting sons and taking concubines, see Li, *Inner Court*, chapter 2; she sees the powerful eunuchs of the inner court as "incomplete men" whose "initial weakening of masculinity was compensated by power, wealth, and social status," but she also emphasizes that it was precisely eunuchs' "crossing of gender boundaries" that enabled some of them to gain power (85).

79. Kutcher, *Eunuch and Emperor*, 164.

80. Kutcher, 163.

81. Kutcher, 162–64. Thus, for example, Kutcher cites a 1751 case in which a eunuch who adopted a palace lady and then stole a set of clothes for her was ordered beaten to death.

82. Goossaert, *Taoists of Peking*, 209; Dale, *Inside the World*, 93–94.

83. For the Qing "consensus" on the evils of eunuch power, see Kutcher, *Eunuch and Emperor*, chapter 1; for the image of the eunuch in modern discourses of China as "the sick man of Asia," see Chiang, *After Eunuchs*, chapter 1.

84. Jay, "Another Side," 459; but see also Dale (*Inside the World*, 53–56) and Chiang (18–19, 50–51), who both cite Jay with approval. Kutcher, in contrast, has little interest in such "abstract" questions, preferring to focus on the roles that eunuchs played in the Qing imperial system and how their regulation changed over time (xviii).

85. See, for example, R. Keith McMahon, "A Case for Confucian Sexuality: The Eighteenth-Century Novel *Yesou Puyan*," *Late Imperial China* 9, no. 2 (1988): 32–55; and McMahon, "The Art of the Bedchamber and *Jin Ping Mei*," *Nan Nü* 21 (2019): 1–37. For the image of the "criminal monk" in Ming fiction, see Junqing Wu, "Sex in the Cloister: Behind the Image of the 'Criminal Monk' in Ming Courtroom Tales," *T'oung Pao* 105 (2019): 545–86.

86. *Jinpingmei cihua* [Plum in the golden vase] (Hong Kong: Xianggang Taiping Shuju, 1988, reprint), chapter 49; see also McMahon, "Art of the Bedchamber," 31–33.

87. *Jinpingmei*, chapter 93; see also Sommer, *Sex*, 142, 159.

88. McMahon, "Case for Confucian Sexuality."

89. Zhang Yingyu, *The Book of Swindles: Selections from a Late Ming Collection*, trans. Christopher Rea and Bruce Rusk (New York: Columbia University Press, 2017), 179–82; for a similar account, see Barend J. ter Haar, *Telling Stories: Witchcraft and Scapegoating in Chinese History* (Leiden: Brill, 2006), 127–28.

90. Kieschnick, *Eminent Monk*, 17–22; Beata Grant, *Eminent Nuns: Women Chan Masters of Seventeenth-Century China* (Honolulu: University of Hawai'i Press, 2009): 1–5; Yü, *Passing the Light*, 14–18, 228–38; Zhang Yingyu, *Book of Swindles*, 138–43.

91. Yasuhiko Karasawa, "Between Oral and Written Cultures: Buddhist Monks in Qing Legal Plaints," in *Writing and Law in Imperial China: Crime, Conflict, and Judgment*, ed. Robert Hegel and Katherine Carlitz (Seattle: University of Washington Press, 2007), 64–80; see also Wu, "Sex in the Cloister."

92. For example, DC: 42-00; 077-00 and substatutes; 114-00; 372-00 and substatutes.

93. Goossaert, "Counting the Monks"; Vincent Goossaert, "Irrepressible Female Piety: Late Imperial Bans on Women Visiting Temples," *Nan Nü* 10 (2008): 212–41; Yü, *Chinese Buddhism*, 125–28. For official suspicion of mendicant clergy, see chapter 3 in this volume.

94. Kieschnick, *Eminent Monk*, 17–22, 64.

95. In medieval and early modern Europe, it was evidently common for a priest to have what amounted to a live-in concubine (often euphemized as his "housekeeper"). See, for example, Janelle Werner, "Promiscuous Priests and Vicarage Children: Clerical Sexuality and Masculinity in Late Medieval England," in *Negotiating Clerical Identities: Priests, Monks and Masculinity in the Middle Ages*, ed. Jennifer Thibodeaux (New York: Palgrave Macmillan, 2010), 159–81; and Werner, "Living in Suspicion: Priests and Female Servants in Late Medieval England," *Journal of British Studies* 55 (2016): 658–79. For the scene inside the contemporary Vatican, see Frederic Martel, *In the Closet of the Vatican: Power, Homosexuality, Hypocrisy* (London: Bloomsbury Continuum, 2020). For the mocking of Catholic clergy in French literature, see Wu, "Sex in the Cloister," 572–73.

96. The theory of "situational homosexuality" was developed to try to explain (away) sexual behavior in American prisons that seemed to confound any notion of a stable hetero/homosexual binary. See Regina Kunzel, *Criminal Intimacy: Prison and the Uneven History of Modern American Sexuality* (Chicago: University of Chicago Press, 2008). But the seventeenth-century literati Shen Defu and Xie Zhaozhe articulated their own "substitution" theory of male love that bears strong resemblance to situational homosexuality. See Volpp, "Classifying Lust," 97–100.

97. See, for example, Lillian Faderman's argument that all women are potentially lesbians—especially her new introduction to the 1998 edition of her classic *Surpassing the Love of Men: Romantic Friendship and Love Between Women from the Renaissance to the Present* (New York: Morrow, 1981). On sexual culture in women's prisons, see Kunzel, *Criminal Intimacy*, chapter 4,.

98. See, for example, George Chauncey, *Gay New York: Gender, Urban Culture, and the Making of the Gay Male World* (New York: Basic Books, 1994), 91; and Kunzel, 183. The high percentage of gay men and lesbians in the Catholic clergy has been documented many times and is a focus of controversy within the church; see, for example, Martel, *In the Closet*.

99. Citing Karasawa, Gilbert Chen argues that the popular image of Buddhist clergy as lascivious constitutes a gross exaggeration, but his dissertation has an entire chapter about clergy who were prosecuted for sex offenses: "Living in this World: A Social History of Buddhist Monks and Nuns in Nineteenth-Century Western China" (PhD diss., Washington University in St. Louis), 2019.

100. Sima Qian, *Shiji* [Records of the grand historian], 10 vols (Beijing: Zhonghua Shuju, 1992), *juan* 85; see also Sommer, "Dangerous Males," 88n47. In the same account, Sima Qian casts doubt on the paternity of the First Emperor of Qin by recounting that Lü Buwei was forced to yield his favorite concubine to the heir to the throne, who was nominally the First Emperor's father; in fact, Lü kept secret the fact that his concubine was already pregnant, and she gave birth to the prince who would later found the Qin Empire.

101. Dale, *Inside the World*, 56.

102. Dale, 41–42, 57–58; Kutcher, *Eunuch and Emperor*, 11. *The Book of Swindles* tells of a eunuch who murders boys and cooks them to fashion a "Tonic of Male Essence" that will regrow his lost organs; see Zhang Yingyu, *Book of Swindles*, 145–49. Similarly, in the novel *A Country Codger Puts His Words Out to Sun*, a deviant eunuch kidnaps the hero (who possesses a highly pure and potent *yang* essence) in an attempt to secure his semen for occult purposes; see Epstein, "Engendering Order," 117.

103. Dale, 60. Suspicion of eunuchs greatly increased after several participated in the Eight Trigrams Rebellion of 1813; with their help, the rebels had managed to enter the palace in an attempt to assassinate the Jiaqing emperor. Afterward, the emperor decreed that only eunuchs emasculated by the age of sixteen *sui* who had never been married or fathered children would be permitted to work inside the palace. See Susan Naquin, *Millenarian Rebellion in China: The Eight Trigrams*

Uprising of 1813 (New Haven, Conn.: Yale University Press, 1976), 50–51, 95–97, 170–71; Kutcher, *Eunuch and Emperor*, 235; and Dale, 25, 43.

104. Volpp, "Literary Circulation," 960.

105. Volpp, 960; see also Volpp, "Classifying Lust," 100–1n50.

106. Sommer, *Sex*, chapters 4 and 7.

107. Mackerras, *Rise of the Peking Opera*, 211–18; Goldman, *Opera and the City*, 71–76.

108. Sommer, *Sex*; Sommer, "Dangerous Males"; Matthew H. Sommer, "Legal Understandings of Sexual and Domestic Violence in China," in *The Cambridge World History of Violence, Volume III—AD 1500–AD 1800*, ed. Robert Antony, Stuart Carroll, and Dodds Pennock (Cambridge: Cambridge University Press, 2020), 219–35.

109. See Talia Mae Bettcher, "Evil Deceivers and Make-Believers: On Transphobic Violence and the Politics of Illusion," *Hypatia* 22, no. 3 (2007); Gayle Salamon, *The Life and Death of Latisha King: A Critical Phenomenology of Transphobia* (New York: New York University Press, 2018); and discussion in chapter 2 in this volume.

2. The Paradigm of the Cross-Dressing Predator

1. Jiang Pu (1708–1761) hailed from Changshou County, Jiangsu; he won the *jinshi* degree in 1730 (scoring first place in the second tier; i.e., no. 4 for his year). He served as governor of Hunan from 1743 to 1745 and later held senior positions in the capital, ending as a grand secretary. He was also an accomplished painter. Qian Shifu, ed., *Qingdai zhiguan nianbiao* [Chronological list of Qing officials] (Beijing: Zhonghua Shuju, 1980), 1595–96; Pan Rongsheng, ed., *Ming Qing jinshi lu* [A record of Ming and Qing dynasty presented scholars] (Beijing: Zhonghua Shuju, 2006), 896; Arthur Hummel, ed., *Eminent Chinese of the Qing Period*, rev. ed. (Great Barrington, Mass.: Berkshire, 2018), 276.

2. Two copies of the memorial survive in the First Historical Archive in Beijing: the original (ZP 04-01-01-0106-057) and the official copy (LF 03-1349-028), both dated QL 9.7.9. I have found no other primary sources on this case, and all information and quotations related to this case are drawn from the memorial. For a brief account of this case, see Li Erqin, "Qingdai 'kuaxingbiezhe' de richang shenghuo, shengji qiantan" [A prelimary discussion of the daily life and survival of "transgender people" in the Qing dynasty], *Hebei Shifan Daxue Xuebao* [Journal of Hebei Normal University] 45, no. 3 (2022): 39–44.

3. For the Sacred Edict, see Victor Mair, "Language and Ideology in the Written Popularizations of the Sacred Edict," in *Popular Culture in Late Imperial China*, ed. David Johnson, Andrew Nathan, and Evelyn Rawski (Berkeley: University of California Press, 1985), 325–59; and discussion later in this chapter.

4. These are approximate distances between county seats and, hence, only rough estimates of how far Xiong traveled.

5. For the discourse of widow chastity and tensions between widows and their in-laws during the Qing, see Matthew H. Sommer, *Sex, Law, and Society in Late Imperial China* (Stanford, Calif.: Stanford University Press, 2000), chapter 5.

6. Kath Weston, *Families We Choose: Lesbians, Gays, Kinship* (New York: Columbia University Press, 1991); Matthew H. Sommer, *Polyandry and Wife-Selling in Qing Dynasty China: Survival Strategies and Judicial Interventions* (Berkeley: University of California Press, 2015), 35–47.

7. Jiayan Zhang, personal communication, April 8, 2018. One *mu* equals approximately one-third of an acre.

8. Household division between brothers usually took place after their father died, but its timing varied. David Wakefield, *Fenjia: Household Division and Inheritance in Qing and Republican China* (Honolulu: University of Hawai'i Press, 1998).

9. For examples, see Fabien Simonis, "Mad Acts, Mad Speech, and Mad People in Late Imperial Chinese Law and Medicine" (PhD diss., Princeton University, 2010), 579–80; and Philip Kuhn, *Soulstealers: The Chinese Sorcery Scare of 1768* (Cambridge, Mass.: Harvard University Press, 1990), 110–11.

10. Sommer, *Sex*, chapter 5; Sommer, *Polyandry*, chapters 2, 3, and 7.

11. Byungil Ahn, "Modernization, Revolution, and Midwifery Reforms in Twentieth-Century China" (PhD diss., University of California, Los Angeles, 2011), 46.

12. Charlotte Furth, "Concepts of Pregnancy, Childbirth, and Infancy in Ch'ing Dynasty China," *Journal of Asian Studies* 46, no. 1 (1987): 7–35; Yi-Li Wu, *Reproducing Women: Medicine, Metaphor, and Childbirth in Late Imperial China* (Berkeley: University of California Press, 2010), 178–86. One partial exception to this generalization was male physicians' treatment of war wounds and other trauma, which in practice overlapped with the work of forensic coroners, who were also male; see Yi-Li Wu, *The Injured Body: A Social History of Medicine for Wounds in Late Imperial China*, forthcoming.

13. Matthew H. Sommer, "Abortion in Late Imperial China: Routine Birth Control or Crisis Intervention?," *Late Imperial China* 31, no. 2 (2010): 97–165.

14. Furth, "Concepts of Pregnancy"; Furth, "Androgynous Males," 22; Charlotte Furth, *A Flourishing Yin: Gender in China's Medical History, 960–1665* (Berkeley: University of California Press,), 282; Angela Leung, "Women Practicing Medicine in Pre-Modern China," in *Chinese Women in the Imperial Past: New Perspectives*, ed. Harriet Zurndorfer (Leiden: Brill, 1999), 101–34; Matthew H. Sommer, "The Gendered Body in the Qing Courtroom," *Journal of the History of Sexuality* 22, no. 2 (2013): 281–311.

15. Wakefield, *Fenjia*.

16. Robert Mnookin and Lewis Kornhauser, "Bargaining in the Shadow of the Law: The Case of Divorce," *Yale Law Journal* 88, no. 5 (1979): 950–57.

17. Philip C. C. Huang, *Civil Justice in China: Representation and Practice in the Qing* (Stanford, Calif.: Stanford University Press, 1996), 116–22; Sommer, *Polyandry*, 343.

18. *Ming shilu* [Veritable records of the Ming dynasty], 183 vols. (Nangang: Zhongyang Yanjiuyuan Lishi Yuyan Yanjiusuo, 1962–1968), 172:4.

19. Endymion Wilkinson, *Chinese History: A New Manual*, 5th ed. (published by author, 2018), 678, 886–87.

20. Laura Stokes, *Demons of Urban Reform: Early European Witch Trials and Criminal Justice, 1430–1530* (New York: Palgrave Macmillan, 2011), 1.

21. *Taiyuan fuzhi* [Taiyuan prefecture gazetteer], Ming, Wanli era (Taiyuan: Shanxi Renmin Chubanshe, 1991), 25:416.

22. See the account in the chapter on "miscellaneous records," which provides no date for the case: *Shanxi tongzhi* [Shanxi provincial gazetteer], Ming, Wanli era, in Erudition Chinese Local Gazetteers Database, http://server.wenzibase.com/spring/user/alogin?jumppage=hello_gd (accessed via Stanford's East Asian Library, August 13, 2022), 27:33b–34a. A briefer account in the chapter on "disasters and portents" dates the case to Chenghua 13: *Shanxi tongzhi*, 26:37a.

23. Charlotte Furth ("Androgynous Males," 22–23) and Judith Zeitlin (*Historian of the Strange: Pu Songling and the Chinese Classical Tale* (Stanford, Calif.: Stanford University Press, 1993), chapter 4, have analyzed some of these later accounts, and Zeitlin provides a full English translation of Pu Songling's story "Renyao," or "The Human Prodigy" (98–100). See also Wenjuan Xie's dissertation, which characterizes Sang Chong as "the archetype female-impersonator sex criminal"; Xie lists a number of fictional accounts inspired by the Sang Chong case: "(Trans)Culturally Transgendered: Reading Transgender Narratives in (Late) Imperial China" (PhD diss., University of Alberta, 2015), 78–84.

24. As Judith Zeitlin notes, "Pu Songling clearly assumed his readers' familiarity with the case, for he added no explanation of his reference to Sang Chong and his gang" (*Historian of the Strange*, 111).

25. Usage is not consistent, but, where the terms are clearly distinguished, *renyao* refers to weird but natural phenomena ("monsters"), whereas *yaoren* refers to a sorcerer who practices occult techniques that he has learned. See, for example, Chen Fangsheng's story collection, which has separate chapters on these two categories: the chapter entitled "Renyao" includes a story about a shape-shifting, "two-formed" person, whereas the chapter entitled "Yaoren" includes a version of Sang Chong's story. Chen Fangsheng. *Yi yu jian* [Notes on difficult cases], in *Xu xiu si ku quan shu* [A continuation of the complete works of the Four Treasuries], vol. 974 (Shanghai: Shanghai Guji Chubanshe, 1691); see also chapter 3 in this volume. For a history of the term *yao*, especially as related to the *zhiguai* genre, see Rania Huntington, *Alien Kind: Foxes and Late Imperial Chinese Narrative* (Cambridge, Mass.: Harvard University Asia Center, 2003), 309–22. Hsiao-wen Cheng traces the evolution of the term *renyao* from antiquity down through the Yuan: "Before Sexual and Normal: Shifting Categories of Sexual Anomaly from Ancient to Yuan China," *Asia Major* 31, no. 2 (2018): 1–39. Howard Chiang documents the term's transformation in the early twentieth century and in postwar Taiwan: *Transtopia in the Sinophone Pacific* (New York: Columbia University Press, 2021), chapter 3.

26. Petcharat (a.k.a. Poy, Poyd, Nong Poy, and, in Chinese, *Baoer*, "Precious") won Thailand's Miss Tiffany transwoman beauty pageant in 2004. She has starred in a

number of Chinese films, including a horror thriller entitled *Yao yi* [*Witch Doctor*], which plays on traditional Chinese tropes of the randomly encountered beautiful woman being a potential sexual vampire (see chapter 4 in this volume), but also on the long-standing Hollywood trope of the transwoman as insane serial killer. See the articles about her on Baidu and Sogou.

27. Zeitlin, *Historian of the Strange*, 110–15; see also Furth, "Androgynous Males," 23n55.

28. See, for example, Ling Mengchu, *Chuke pai an jing qi* [Slapping the table in amazement, first volume] (Changsha: Yuelu Shushe, 2003), chapter 34; Chen Fangsheng, *Yi yu jian* [Notes on difficult cases], in *Xu xiu si ku quan shu* [A continuation of the complete works of the Four Treasuries], vol. 974 (Shanghai: Shanghai Guji Chubanshe, 1691), 3:36a–37b. See chapter 3 in this volume.

29. Lu Can, *Gengsi bian* [Notes from the last two years of the Zhengde reign], in *Ming Qing biji shiliao* [Historical materials from Ming-Qing notation books], vol. 99, ed. Zhongguo Guji Zhengli Yanjiuhui (Beijing: Zhongguo Shudian, 2000), 4:7a–8a. Both Charlotte Furth ("Androgynous Males," 22) and Judith Zeitlin (*Historian of the Strange*, 256, n 36) cite Lu Can as the earliest account of Sang Chong, and Zeitlin seems to accept Lu Can's claim that his account is a genuine record of the actual case.

30. Mengdie Zhao, personal communication, October 2020. Mengdie Zhao's dissertation explores the connections between this fictional genre and actual legal records and casebooks: "Shades of Justice: Debating Law and Legal Culture in Early Modern China" (PhD diss., Harvard University, 2022).

31. I am grateful for the expert assistance of Che-chia Chang (personal communication, October 2020) and Yi-Li Wu (personal communication, August 2022) in interpreting this passage.

32. Chün-fang Yü, *Chinese Buddhism: A Thematic History* (Honolulu: University of Hawai'i Press, 2020), 227–28; John Powers, *A Bull of a Man: Images of Masculinity, Sex, and the Body in Indian Buddhism* (Cambridge, Mass.: Harvard University Press, 2009), 172–74; Daniel Burton-Rose, "Gendered Androgyny: Transcendent Ideals and Profane Realities in Buddhism, Classicism, and Daoism," in *Transgender China*, ed. Howard Chiang (New York: Palgrave Macmillan, 2012), 71–74; Cheng, "Before Sexual and Normal," 19–22.

33. Acute phobia focused on the supposed pollution of menstrual blood and childbirth fluids, which was closely linked to the Buddhist idea that women are inherently sinful because of their role in perpetuating the karmic cycle by giving birth. See Emily Ahern, "The Power and Pollution of Chinese Women," in *Studies in Chinese Society*, ed. Arthur Wolf (Stanford, Calif.: Stanford University Press, 1978), 269–90; Gary Seaman, "The Sexual Politics of Karmic Retribution," in *The Anthropology of Taiwanese Society*, ed. Emily Ahern and Hill Gates (Berkeley: University of California Press, 1981), 381–96; Beata Grant and and Wilt Idema, *Escape from Blood Pond Hell: The Tales of Mulian and Woman Huang* (Seattle: University of Washington Press, 2011), 17–19, 23–34; and Yü, *Chinese Buddhism*, 233–37.

34. Wilt Idema, "Female Talent and Female Virtue: Xu Wei's *Nü zhuangyuan* and Meng Chengshun's *Zhenwen ji*," in *Ming-Qing xiqu guoji yantaohui lunwen ji* [Papers from the International Symposium on Ming-Qing drama], ed. Hua Wei and Wang Ailing (Taipei: Zhongyangyuan Wenzhesuo Choubeichu, 1998), 2:571; Roland Altenburger, "Is It the Clothes that Make the Man? Cross-Dressing, Gender, and Sex in Pre-Twentieth Century Zhu Yingtai Lore," *Asian Folklore Studies* 64, no. 2 (2005): 165–205; Altenburger, *The Sword or the Needle: The Female Knight-errant (xia) in Traditional Chinese Narrative* (Bern: Peter Lang, 2009), 171. Furth ("Androgynous Males") argues that beginning in the late Ming, female-male sex change was increasingly portrayed as relatively benign, whereas heightened anxiety focused on male-female change.

35. See the documentary film *Disclosure: Trans Lives on Screen*, dir. Sam Feder (Netflix, 2020).

36. Susan Stryker, *Transgender History: The Roots of Today's Revolution*, rev. ed. (New York: Seal, 2017), 227.

37. Stryker, *Transgender History: The Roots*, 127–38, 160; see also Susan Stryker, "My Words to Victor Frankenstein Above the Village of Chamounix: Performing Transgender Rage," *GLQ* 1 (1994): 238–39; and Gayle Salamon, *The Life and Death of Latisha King: A Critical Phenomenology of Transphobia* (New York: New York University Press, 2018), 161–69. For analysis of the claims that transgender people are "deceivers," and that transwomen are rapists, see Talia Mae Bettcher, "Evil Deceivers and Make-Believers: On Transphobic Violence and the Politics of Illusion," *Hypatia* 22, no. 3 (2007): 48–50.

38. Bettcher, "Evil Deceivers," 52.

39. Bettcher, 50–52; Kristen Schilt and Laurel Westbrook, "Doing Gender, Doing Heteronormativity: 'Gender Normals,' Transgender People, and the Social Maintenance of Heterosexuality," *Gender & Society* 23, no. 4 (2009): 453–58.

40. Janet Mock, *Redefining Realness: My Path to Womanhood, Identity, Love, and So Much More* (New York: Atria, 2014), 247.

41. In Leslie Feinberg's classic *Stone Butch Blues*, the protagonist and other butch or transmasculine characters are repeatedly subjected to gang rape as a means of identity enforcement. This use of rape to reimpose normative gender is an extreme but logical extension of the gender disciplining that the protagonist has endured from parents and peers since childhood. Like the rape of Brandon Teena, it confirms the feminist insight that under patriarchy, "rapability" is a defining feature of being a woman. See, for example, Catherine Mackinnon, *Toward a Feminist Theory of the State* (Cambridge, Mass.: Harvard University Press, 1989), 178.

42. Bettcher, "Evil Deceivers"; Cynthia Lee and Peter Kwan, "The Trans Panic Defense: Masculinity, Heteronormativity, and the Murder of Transgender Women," *Hastings Law Journal* 66 (2014): 77–132. See also Salamon, *Life and Death*; and Schilt and Westbrook, "Doing Gender," 453–58.

43. The Qianlong Emperor was notoriously obsessed with enforcing the tonsure; see Kuhn, *Soulstealers*.

44. Compare with Magnus Hirschfeld's case 13, of a young transwoman whose genital status was repeatedly exposed by men who sexually harassed or tried to rape her, or who blackmailed her into having sex: *Transvestites: The Erotic Drive to Cross-Dress*, trans. Michael A. Lombardi-Nash (Buffalo, N.Y.: Prometheus, 1991), 88–92. Forcible exposure by a would-be rapist is also a theme in the fiction inspired by Sang Chong— for example, Li Yu's *The Human Prodigy* and Wu Chichang's version of the case of Liu Xing Shi; see chapter 5 in this volume.

45. DC: 162-00. See also Sir George Staunton, trans., *Ta Tsing Leu Lee; Being the Fundamental Laws, and a Selection from the Supplementary Statutes, of the Penal Code of China* (London: T. Cadell and W. Davies, 1810), 175–76; William Jones, trans., *The Great Qing Code* (Oxford: Clarendon, 1994), 174; and Kuhn, *Soulstealers*, 85–87.

46. Huang Zhangjian, ed., *Ming dai lü li hui bian* [Compendium of Ming dynasty statutes and substatutes] (Taipei: Zhongyang Yanjiuyuan Lishi Yuyan Yanjiusuo, 1994), 589; DC: 162-00. For the Ming dynasty origins of the law, see Barend J. ter Haar, *The White Lotus Teachings in Chinese Religious History* (Honolulu: University of Hawai'i Press, 1992), 123–25, 129–30; Tian Dongkui, "Ming Qing lüdianzhong de wushu fanzui" [Sorcery crimes in the Ming and Qing codes], *Tangdu xuekan* (Tangdu Journal) 21, no. 1 (2005): 88–91; and Junqing Wu, *Mandarins and Heretics: The Construction of "Heresy" in Chinese State Discourse* (Leiden: Brill, 2017), 83–84.

47. Richard Von Glahn, *The Sinister Way: The Divine and the Demonic in Chinese Religious Culture* (Berkeley: University of California Press, 2004), 4. For a full translation of the relevant passage in *The Book of Rites*, see von Glahn, *Sinister Way*, 3–4. For an overview of Chinese terms for heterodoxy, see Kwang-Ching Liu, "Appendix: A Note on the Usage of the Chinese Terms for Heterodoxy," in *Heterodoxy in Late Imperial China*, ed. Kwang-Ching Liu and Richard Shek (Honolulu: University of Hawai'i Press, 2004), 477–89; and Junqing Wu, "Words and Concepts in Chinese Religious Denunciation: A Study of the Genealogy of *Xiejiao*," *Chinese Historical Review* 23, no. 1 (2016): 1–22.

48. See, for example, Stephen Flowers, *Lords of the Left-Hand Path: A History of Spiritual Dissent* (Rochester, Vt.: Inner Traditions, 1997).

49. Handian, https://www.zdic.net (accessed October 15, 2020).

50. Mair, "Language and Ideology," 325.

51. This translation is Mair's (326).

52. Kung-chuan Hsiao expresses deep skepticism whether the community lecture program was ever fully implemented or had any impact at all: *Rural China: Imperial Control in the Nineteenth Century* (Seattle: University of Washington Press, 1960), 184–201. Mair (357–58) suggests that by 1850 at latest, the program was a dead letter. Ting Zhang, in contrast, argues that the lectures were highly effective in disseminating legal knowledge among "ordinary people" throughout the empire: *Circulating the Code: Print Media and Legal Knowledge in Qing China* (Seattle: University of Washington Press, 2020), chapter 5.

53. Staunton's translation—"inveigle and mislead the multitude"—is accurate (*Ta Tsing Leu Lee*, 175–76), but Jones's "incite the people" leaves out the element of deception (*Great Qing Code*, 174).

54. Norma Diamond, "The Miao and Poison: Interactions on China's Southwest Frontier," *Ethnology* 27, no. 1 (1988): 1–25. I have never seen any reliable source that documents the existence of *gu* poison, let alone its use in the manner described. It appears to be a myth, but one that is widely believed even today. I have encountered several otherwise sophisticated students from China who firmly believed (without evidence) that Miao women use *gu* poison to bewitch or murder Han men—in their view, this was simply common knowledge.

55. DC: 002-00, 289-00.

56. Handian, https://www.zdic.net (accessed October 15, 2020).

57. Ter Haar, *White Lotus*, chapters 6 and 7; David Ownby, *Brotherhoods and Secret Societies in Early and Mid-Qing China: The Formation of a Tradition* (Stanford, Calif.: Stanford University Press, 1996), 159–61.

58. Kuhn, *Soulstealers*, 86, 90.

59. See, for example, Susan Naquin, *Millenarian Rebellion in China: The Eight Trigrams Uprising of 1813* (New Haven, Conn.: Yale University Press, 1976), 31–45.

60. "Yaoni bailou," *Shenbao*, January 12, 1890.

61. XA, 10:22b–23a; a nearly identical summary of the case appears in Xu Lian and Xiong E., eds., *Xingbu bizhao jiajian chengan* [Board of Punishment cases where the penalty was raised or lowered by analogy] (Beijing: Falü Chubanshe, 2009), 46. See also the brief discussion in Marinus Meijer, "Homosexual Offenses in Ch'ing Law," *T'oung Pao* 71 (1985): 115.

62. DC: 366-01. For Qing sodomy law, see Sommer, *Sex*, chapter 4 and appendix B; and Matthew H. Sommer, "Legal Understandings of Sexual and Domestic Violence in China," in *The Cambridge World History of Violence, Volume 3—AD 1500-AD 1800*, ed. Robert Antony, Stuart Carroll, and Caroline Dodds Pennock (Cambridge: Cambridge University Press, 2020), 230–33.

3. Clergy as Wolves in Sheep's Clothing

1. Two statutes in the Qing code are most relevant: DC: 175-00 states the general principle that everyone should wear only the clothing and accessories appropriate to their station in life; DC: 175-11 applies this principle specifically to Buddhist and Daoist clergy. Dressing in lay attire was one of the crimes of Xinxiang, protagonist of chapter 7 in this volume.

2. See sources cited in chapter 1 in this volume.

3. All information about this case and related quotations come from XT: 143-8, QL 6.4.25.

4. Prince Zhuang (*Zhuang Qinwang*) was one of the twelve "iron cap" first-rank peerages in the Qing aristocracy that enjoyed "perpetual inheritance" (i.e., did not degrade with each generation). See Mark Elliott, *The Manchu Way: The Eight Banners and Ethnic Identity in Late Imperial China* (Stanford, Calif.: Stanford University Press, 2001), 80.

5. The gendarmerie (*bujun tongling yamen*) were the military police charged with security in the imperial capital. See Alison Dray-Novey, "Spatial Order and Police in Imperial Beijing," *Journal of Asian Studies* 52, no. 4 (1993): 885–922.

6. Philip Kuhn, *Soulstealers: The Chinese Sorcery Scare of 1768* (Cambridge, Mass.: Harvard University Press, 1990); Matthew H. Sommer, *Sex, Law, and Society in Late Imperial China* (Stanford, Calif.: Stanford University Press, 2000).

7. Chinese azalea (*Rhododendron molle*) contains grayanotoxins; Xia Liying, ed., *Xiandai Zhongyao dulixue* [Modern toxicology of Chinese materia medica] (Tianjin: Tianjin Keji Fanyi Chuban Gongsi, 2005), 247–48; Suze Jansen, Iris Kleerekooper, Zonne Hofman, Isabelle Kappen, Anna Stary-Weinzinger, and Marcel van der Heyden, "Grayanotoxin Poisoning: 'Mad Honey Disease' and Beyond," *Cardiovascular Toxicology* 12 (2012): 208–15.

8. Melissa Dale, *Inside the World of the Eunuch: A Social History of the Emperor's Servants in Qing China* (Hong Kong: Hong Kong University Press, 2018), 66–67, 71; Norman Kutcher, *Eunuch and Emperor in the Great Age of Qing Rule* (Berkeley: University of California Press, 2018), 175–77.

9. DC: 266-00; for other laws related to the use of knockout drugs, see DC: 266-26, DC: 275-02, QH: 828/1020.

10. All information about this case and related quotations come from two documents: XT: 449-12, QL 16.7.29 and 467-5, QL 17.3.24.

11. This substatute was created in 1725 by combining an old Ming dynasty law with a more recent one from the Kangxi era; DC: 275-02.

12. Kuhn, *Soulstealers*, chapters 2 and 5. For *guanggun* and related legislation, see Sommer, *Sex*, 12–15, 96–101.

13. Kuhn, 42–46.

14. Daniel Overmyer, *Religions of China: The World as a Living System* (San Francisco: Harper and Row, 1986), 76.

15. For an overview of that tradition, see Lisa Raphals, "Chinese Philosophy and Chinese Medicine," in *The Stanford Encyclopedia of Philosophy*, ed. Edward Zalta, Winter 2020, https://plato.stanford.edu/archives/win2020/entries/chinese-phil-medicine/ (accessed July 24, 2023).

16. Yasuhiko Karasawa, "Between Oral and Written Cultures: Buddhist Monks in Qing Legal Plaints," in *Writing and Law in Imperial China: Crime, Conflict, and Judgment*, ed. Robert Hegel and Katherine Carlitz (Seattle: University of Washington Press, 2007), 64–80.

17. Zhang Yingyu, *Pian jing* [The book of swindles] (Guilin: Guangxi Shifan Daxue Chubanshe, 2008), 159–60.

18. For judicial torture in the Qing, see Alison Conner, "Chinese Confessions and the Use of Torture," in *La torture judiciaire: approaches historiques et juridiques*, ed. Bernard Durand and Leah Otis-Cours (Lille: Centre de Histoire Judiciare, Universite de Lille, 2002), 1:63–91; Nancy Park, "Imperial Chinese Justice and the Law of Torture," *Late Imperial China* 29, no. 2 (2008): 37–67; and Matthew H. Sommer, "Some Problems with Corpses: Standards of Validity in Qing Homicide Cases," in *Powerful Arguments: Standards of Validity in Late Imperial China*, ed. Martin Hoffman,

Joachim Kurtz, and Ari Levine (Leiden: Brill, 2020), 431–70. For the ankle press, see Kuhn, *Soulstealers*, 14–17.

19. For examples of this process see Kuhn; Barend J. ter Haar, *The White Lotus Teachings in Chinese Religious History* (Honolulu: University of Hawai'i Press, 1992); Laura Stokes, *Demons of Urban Reform: Early European Witch Trials and Criminal Justice, 1430–1530* (New York: Palgrave Macmillan, 2011); and Sommer, "Some Problems."

20. "Daoshi bu fa," *Shenbao*, April 8, 1891; "Xing xun yaodao," *Shenbao*, April 4, 1891; "Yu jing [] zha," *Shenbao*, April 29, 1891; "Lun zuodao zhi hai," *Shenbao*, May 1, 1891; "Du xia shu wen," *Shenbao*, May 18, 1891; "Ni zui tai qing," *Shenbao*, May 27, 1891; "Jing [] yu shu," *Shenbao*, June 5, 1891 (all accessed online, January 2023).

21. "Daoshi bu fa," *Shenbao*, April 8, 1891.

22. "Daoshi bu fa," *Shenbao*, April 8, 1891; "Lun zuodao zhi hai," *Shenbao*, May 1, 1891.

23. "Daoshi bu fa," *Shenbao*, April 8, 1891.

24. "Xing xun yaodao," *Shenbao*, April 4, 1891. Beatings and being forced to kneel on chains are examples of cruel treatment designed to induce cooperation that were permitted and that were not officially defined as judicial torture. See Conner, "Chinese Confessions."

25. "Lun zuodao zhi hai," *Shenbao*, May 1, 1891.

26. "Xing xun yaodao," *Shenbao*, April 4, 1891.

27. "Jing [] yu shu," *Shenbao*, June 5, 1891.

28. By the end of the Ming, "White Lotus Teachings" had come to refer to a supposedly pervasive heterodox sect that conspired against the imperial state. In fact, no such sect existed, except in the paranoid fantasies of officials who confirmed their fears via the torture-driven confessions of suspected sectarians. See ter Haar, *White Lotus*.

29. In fact, one can find similar rhetoric in *Shenbao* even in the late 1940s (e.g., "Hangshi buhuo renyao," *Shenbao*, August 26, 1948).

30. "Jing [] yu shu," *Shenbao*, June 5, 1891.

31. "Lun zuodao zhi hai," *Shenbao*, May 1, 1891.

32. See, for example, *Shenbao*'s coverage of the famous Yang Naiwu case: Madeleine Dong, "Communities and Communication: A Study of the Case of Yang Naiwu, 1873–1877," *Late Imperial China* 16, no. 1 (1995): 79–119.

33. "Daoshi bu fa," *Shenbao*, April 8, 1891.

34. "Jing [] yu shu," *Shenbao*, June 5, 1891. For Qing rape law, see Sommer, *Sex*, chapter 3.

35. Wenjuan Xie's dissertation lists a number of fictional accounts of "two-formed persons," including the two cases of shapeshifting nuns analyzed here: "(Trans) Culturally Transgendered: Reading Transgender Narratives in (Late) Imperial China" (PhD diss., University of Alberta, 2015), chapter 2.

36. Li Shizhen, *Bencao gangmu xin jiaozhu ben* [New annotated edition of *Systematic Materia Medica*] (Beijing: Huaxia Chubanshe, 1998), 1942.

37. John Powers, *A Bull of a Man: Images of Masculinity, Sex, and the Body in Indian Buddhism* (Cambridge, Mass.: Harvard University Press, 2009), 9, 13–15, 23.

38. Ling Mengchu, *Chuke pai an jing qi* [Slapping the table in amazement], vol. 1 (Changsha: Yuelu Shushe, 2003), chapter 34.

39. This is the sort of vampiric parasitism usually attributed to fox spirits and other demons. See Rania Huntington, *Alien Kind: Foxes and Late Imperial Chinese Narrative* (Cambridge, Mass.: Harvard University Asia Center, 2003); and Xiaofei Kang, *The Cult of the Fox: Power, Gender, and Popular Religion in Late Imperial and Modern China* (New York: Columbia University Press, 2006).

40. Ling Mengchu, *Chuke pai an jing qi* [Slapping the table in amazement], vol. 1 (Changsha: Yuelu Shushe, 2003), chapter 34.

41. See ter Haar, *White Lotus*; and chapter 4 in this volume.

42. Chen Fangsheng, *Yi yu jian* [Notes on difficult cases], in *Xu xiu si ku quan shu* [A continuation of the complete works of the Four Treasuries], vol. 974 (Shanghai: Shanghai Guji Chubanshe, 1691), 3:36a–37b.

43. See Li Shizhen, *Bencao gangmu*, 1942; and chapter 6 in this volume.

44. Chen Fangsheng, *Yi yu jian*, 3:36a–37b.

45. It is a near verbatim copy of Lu Can's story, which we discussed in chapter 2.

46. For stone maidens becoming nuns, see chapter 6 in this volume.

47. "Min shi yi xin," *Shenbao*, July 17, 1887.

48. The "standing cangue," also known as the "standing cage" (*zhanlong*), was a tall, rectangular cage with an ordinary cangue mounted horizontally on its top: the prisoner's neck would be enclosed in the cangue, requiring them to stand on tiptoe inside the cage, and, when exhaustion set in, they would hang by the neck until dead. This cruel device was not a standard form of capital punishment—it is nowhere mentioned in the Qing code—but it became quite common in the late Qing, when the imperial center lost its monopoly of capital punishment and local officials increasingly took matters into their own hands. See Weiting Guo, "The Speed of Justice: Summary Execution and Legal Culture in Qing Dynasty China, 1644–1912" (PhD diss., University of British Columbia, 2016), 105.

49. I have found a total of seven articles in *Shenbao* and one illustration with text in *Dianshizhai Pictorial* that relate to this story: "Mili pushuo zhi an," *Shenbao*, October 24, 1888; "Panduan sengni," *Shenbao*, October 25, 1888; "Fashen lü bian," *Shenbao*, October 26, 1888; "Nan ban nüzhuang," *Shenbao*, November 8, 1889; "Gongren fanjian," *Shenbao*, November 9, 1889; "Qiaozhuang ding yan," *Shenbao*, November 10, 1889; "Qiaozhuang an jie," *Shenbao*, December 9, 1889; and "Er ren tong zhuo," *Dianshizhai Huabao* wei/8 (1889): 62.

50. Par Cassel, *Grounds of Judgment: Extraterritoriality and Imperial Power in Nineteenth-Century China and Japan* (Oxford: Oxford University Press, 2012). The Mixed Courts were abolished in 1927.

51. According to *Shenbao*, this monk also went by at least three other names: "Fasheng" and "Faren," which were Buddhist clerical names, and the alias "Li Huizhen," which they adopted upon returning to Shanghai in 1889. A plurality of names is one of several features that Baozhen shared with Xinxiang, the protagonist of chapter 7 in this volume. For clarity, I refer to this individual by the name Baozhen, even though *Shenbao*'s reports have the witnesses using one or another of their four names.

52. "Mili pushuo zhi an," *Shenbao*, October 10, 1888.

53. The translation is from Shiamin Kwa and Wilt Idema, ed. and trans., *Mulan: Five Versions of a Classic Chinese Legend with Related Texts* (Indianapolis: Hackett, 2010), xiv.

54. "Mili pushuo zhi an," *Shenbao*, October 10, 1888.

55. Shi Rujie and Gongtian Yilang (Miyata Ichiro), eds., *Ming Qing Wu yu cidian* [Dictionary of Ming-Qing–era Wu dialect] (Shanghai: Shanghai Cishu Chubanshe, 2005), 93.

56. "Mili pushuo zhi an," *Shenbao*, October 24, 1888.

57. "Panduan sengni," *Shenbao*, October 25, 1888. Today, the preferred Chinese terms for an intersex person are *shuangxing* (literally, "both sexes") and *jianxing* ("intermediate sex"), although *yinyang ren* is still used.

58. "Fashen lü bian," *Shenbao*, October 26, 1888.

59. "Nan ban nüzhuang," *Shenbao*, November 8, 1889.

60. "Nan ban nüzhuang," *Shenbao*, November 8, 1889.

61. "Nan ban nüzhuang," *Shenbao*, November 8, 1889.

62. "Gongren fanjian," *Shenbao*, November 9, 1889.

63. For the notorious "trans panic" legal defense, see Cynthia Lee and Peter Kwan, "The Trans Panic Defense: Masculinity, Heteronormativity, and the Murder of Transgender Women," *Hastings Law Journal* 66 (2014): 77–132; and Victoria Steinberg, "A Heat of Passion Offense: Emotions and Bias in 'Trans Panic' Mitigation Claims," *Boston College Third World Law Journal* 25, no. 2 (2005): 499–524.

64. "Qiaozhuang an jie," *Shenbao*, December 9, 1889.

65. *Rui zao* is short for *fang rui yuan zao* ("a square tenon versus a round mortise").

66. "Nan ban nüzhuang," *Shenbao*, November 8, 1889.

67. "Gongren fanjian," *Shenbao*, November 9, 1889.

68. "Qiaozhuang an jie," *Shenbao*, December 9, 1889.

69. "Gongren fanjian," *Shenbao*, November 9, 1889.

70. "Qiaozhuang an jie," *Shenbao*, December 9, 1889.

71. "Gongren fanjian," *Shenbao*, November 9, 1889.

72. "Qiaozhuang an jie," *Shenbao*, December 9, 1889. *Shenbao* says in one article that the sentence was for two months ("Qiaozhuang ding yan," *Shenbao*, November 10, 1889), but it is clear from the date of the next article that the term had ended after just a month ("Qiaozhuang an jie," *Shenbao*, December 9, 1889).

73. "Yingjie gongtang suo an," *Shenbao*, June 3, 1884; "Nan ban nüzhuang you jie shi zhong," *Shenbao*, February 24, 1907; "Diaochayuan faxian renyao bai lei," *Shenbao*, June 23, 1911.

74. "Er ren tong zhuo," *Dianshizhai Huabao* wei/8 (1889): 62.

75. "Gongren fanjian," *Shenbao*, November 9, 1889.

76. "Er ren tong zhuo," *Dianshizhai Huabao* wei/8 (1889): 62.

77. "Nan ban nüzhuang," *Shenbao*, November 8, 1889.

78. Rania Huntington, "The Weird in the Newspaper," in *Writing and Materiality in China: Essays in Honor of Patrick Hanan*, ed. Judith Zeitlin and Lydia Liu (Leiden: Brill, 2003), 341–96.

4. Creativity Inspired by Torment?

1. All information about this case and related quotations come from a single document, XT: 2697-11, JQ 23.9.28, unless otherwise noted.

2. Hanchao Lu, *Street Criers: A Cultural History of Chinese Beggars* (Stanford, Calif.: Stanford University Press, 2005), especially chapters 6 and 7; for women beggars in Shanghai, see 169–74. See also Philip Kuhn, *Soulstealers: The Chinese Sorcery Scare of 1768* (Cambridge, Mass.: Harvard University Press, 1990),115–17. In his research on Chinese beggars, Hanchao Lu has seen no evidence of instrumental cross-dressing (personal communication, November 2020).

3. See, for example, the illustrations in Kuhn, *Soulstealers*, 116; and Lu, *Street Criers*, 160 and accompanying captions.

4. Daniel Overmyer, *Religions of China: The World as a Living System* (San Francisco: Harper and Row, 1986), 75–76; see also 52.

5. Michael Saso, "Orthodoxy and Heterodoxy in Taoist Ritual," in *Religion and Ritual in Chinese Society*, ed. Arthur Wolf (Stanford, Calif.: Stanford University Press, 1974), 329–31.

6. Lu, *Street Criers*, 76, 158–66.

7. See Matthew H. Sommer, *Sex, Law, and Society in Late Imperial China* (Stanford, Calif.: Stanford University Press, 2000), conclusion. For the Ming-Qing chastity cult, see Mark Elvin, "Female Virtue and the State in China," *Past and Present* 104 (1984): 111–52; Susan Mann, *Precious Records: Women in China's Long Eighteenth Century* (Stanford, Calif.: Stanford University Press, 1997); Sommer, *Sex*; Janet Theiss, *Disgraceful Matters: The Politics of Chastity in Eighteenth-Century China* (Berkeley: University of California Press, 2004); Weijing Lu, *True to Her Word: The Faithful Maiden Cult in Late Imperial China* (Stanford, Calif.: Stanford University Press, 2008).

8. Here I draw on my own ongoing, long-term research on male same-sex relations and masculinity in the Qing, based on nearly 2000 legal cases, which will be the topic of a future book. See Sommer, *Sex*, chapter 4; Matthew H. Sommer, "Dangerous Males, Vulnerable Males, and Polluted Males: The Regulation of Masculinity in Qing Dynasty Law," in *Chinese Femininities/Chinese Masculinities: A Reader*, ed. Susan Brownell and Jeffrey Wasserstrom (Berkeley: University of California Press, 2002), 78–79; Sommer, "The Gendered Body in the Qing Courtroom," *Journal of the History of Sexuality* 22, no. 2 (2013): 281–311; and Sommer, "Legal Understandings of Sexual and Domestic Violence in China," in *The Cambridge World History of Violence, Volume 3—AD 1500-AD 1800*, ed. Robert Antony, Stuart Carroll, and Caroline Dodds Pennock (Cambridge: Cambridge University Press, 2020), 219–35. The Ming writer Shen Defu did mention a form of "male marriage" supposedly practiced in Fujian, but, as Sophie Volpp has shown, this account (part of a broader discourse associating male love with "the South") should not be taken at face value, but, rather, must be understood as part of an exoticizing ethnographic genre in which bizarre phenomena were attributed to distant

places. There is no evidence that male-male union was seen as a form of marriage, or as a socially acceptable equivalent to marriage, anywhere in late imperial China. Sophie Volpp, "The Discourse on Male Marriage: Li Yu's 'A Male Mencius's Mother,' " *Positions* 2, no. 1 (1994): 113–32.

9. I have seen two legal cases in which blackmail is cited as the reason an older male submitted to being penetrated by a younger partner in an ongoing relationship (e.g., Sommer, *Sex*, 151–54). In both, the ostensible explanation is that the older male had already submitted once (perhaps having agreed to take turns in a casual sexual encounter) and then was compelled to continue submitting by his partner's threat to expose the fact that he had been penetrated by a younger man. In both cases, however, it seems likely that "blackmail" gave the older partner an excuse to continue playing a sexual role that he preferred, despite its violation of conventional age hierarchy.

10. Case 13, in Magnus Hirschfeld, *Transvestites: The Erotic Drive to Cross-Dress*, trans. Michael A. Lombardi-Nash (Buffalo, N.Y.: Prometheus, 1991), 59–60.

11. DC: 162-01.

12. XT: 2697-11, JQ 23.9.28.

13. For the Qing penal system, the autumn assizes, and judicial review, see Derk Bodde and Clarence Morris, *Law in Imperial China: Exemplified by 190 Ch'ing Dynasty Cases, Translated from the Hsing-an hui-lan* (Cambridge, Mass.: Harvard University Press, 1967), chapters 3 and 4; and Matthew H. Sommer, *Polyandry and Wife-Selling in Qing Dynasty China: Survival Strategies and Judicial Interventions* (Berkeley: University of California Press, 2015), appendices D and E.

14. XA, 10: 2b–23a.

15. DC: 162-00.

16. See, for example, the descriptions of spirit mediums, divination, spirit writing, and exorcism in Brigitte Baptandier, *The Lady of Linshui: A Chinese Female Cult* (Stanford, Calif.: Stanford University Press, 2008); Erin Cline, "Female Spirit Mediums and Religious Authority in Contemporary Southeastern China," *Modern China* 36, no. 5 (2010): 520–55; Alan Elliott, *Chinese Spirit-Medium Cults in Singapore* (London: London School of Economics and Political Science, 1955); David Jordan, *Gods, Ghosts, and Ancestors: The Folk Religion of a Taiwanese Village* (Berkeley: University of California Press, 1972); David Jordan and Daniel Overmyer, *The Flying Phoenix: Aspects of Chinese Sectarianism in Taiwan* (Princeton, N.J.: Princeton University Press, 1986); Li Weizu (Li, Wei-tsu), "On the Cult of the Four Sacred Animals (*Szu ta men*) in the Neighbourhood of Peking," *Folklore Studies* 7 (1948): 1–94; Lin Fushi, "Yizhe huo bingren—Tongji zai Taiwan shehui zhong de juese yu xingxiang" [Healers or patients: the shamans' role and image in Taiwan], *Zhongyang Yanjiuyuan Lishi Yuyan Yanjiusuo jikan* [Quarterly Journal of the Institute of History and Philology, Academia Sinica] 76, no. 3 (2005): 511–68; Jack Potter, "Cantonese Shamanism," in *Religion and Ritual in Chinese Society*, ed. Arthur Wolf (Stanford, Calif.: Stanford University Press, 1974), 207–31; and Saso, "Orthodoxy and Heterodoxy."

17. This substatute was a revision of a law from the Kangxi era. See QH: 806/85; DC: 297-01.

18. "Drawing halo talismans" apparently refers to a technique of divination that involved drawing circles with ritually charged water.

19. DC: 297-01.

20. The classic study is J. J. M. de Groot, *Sectarianism and Religious Persecution in China* (Leiden: Brill, 1901). See also ter Haar, *White Lotus*; Kwang-Ching Liu and Richard Shek, eds., *Heterodoxy in Late Imperial China* (Honolulu: University of Hawai'i Press, 2004); Vincent Goossaert, "The Destruction of Immoral Temples in Qing China," in *Institute of Chinese Studies Visiting Professor Lectures Series 2* (Hong Kong: Chinese University Press, 2009), 131–53; and Junqing Wu, *Mandarins and Heretics: The Construction of "Heresy" in Chinese State Discourse* (Leiden: Brill, 2017).

21. Vincent Goossaert, "Counting the Monks: The 1736–1739 Census of the Chinese Clergy," *Late Imperial China* 21, no. 2 (2000): 40–85.

22. Ter Haar, *White Lotus*; David Ownby, *Brotherhoods and Secret Societies in Early and Mid-Qing China: The Formation of a Tradition* (Stanford, Calif.: Stanford University Press, 1996).

23. Donald Sutton, "From Credulity to Scorn: Confucians Confront the Spirit Mediums in Late Imperial China," *Late Imperial China* 21, no. 2 (2000): 1–39, 37; see also Donald Sutton, "Shamanism in the Eyes of Ming and Qing Elites," in *Heterodoxy in Late Imperial China*, ed. Kwang-Ching Liu and Richard Shek (Honolulu: University of Hawai'i Press, 2004), 209–37.

24. Mayfair Yang, "Shamanism and Spirit Possession in Chinese Modernity: Some Preliminary Reflections on a Gendered Religiosity of the Body," *Review of Religion and Chinese Society* 2 (2015): 57.

25. Saso, "Orthodoxy and Heterodoxy," 336.

26. All information about this case and related quotations come from Quan Shichao and Zhang Daoyuan, eds., *Boan huibian* [Compilation of cases overturned on review] (Beijing: Falü Chubanshe, 2009): 113–15.

27. Hindu Datura (*Datura metel*) is an alkaloid-containing plant from the nightshade family that has a history in many cultures of use as a poison and a hallucinogen. Intoxication can cause delirium, panic attacks, and vivid hallucinations, and children are especially susceptible to its effects. See Molly Bliss, "Datura Plant Poisoning," *Clinical Toxicology Review* 23, no. 6 (2001): 1–2; Miguel Glatstein, Fatoumah Alabdulrazzaq, and Dennis Scolnik, "Belladonna Alkaloid Intoxication," *American Journal of Therapeutics* 23 (2016): 74–77; and Xia Liying, ed., *Xiandai Zhongyao dulixue* [Modern toxicology of Chinese materia medica] (Tianjin: Tianjin Keji Fanyi Chuban Gongsi, 2005), 587–89.

28. The same text recommends the drug for use as a surgical anesthetic; see Li Shizhen, *Bencao gangmu xin jiaozhu ben* [New annotated edition of *Systematic Materia Medica*] (Beijing: Huaxia Chubanshe, 1998), 830.

29. DC: 266-00; see discussion in chapter 3 in this volume.

30. One defendant poisoned his own nephew, who died; he was sentenced to strangulation after the assizes, for planned murder of a junior relative.

31. XA: 1213–15; Quan Shichao and Zhang Daoyuan, eds., *Boan huibian* [Compilation of cases overturned on review] (Beijing: Falü Chubanshe, 2009), 113, 120–21; Xu Lian and Xiong E., eds., *Xingbu bizhao jiajian chengan* [Board of Punishment cases where the penalty was raised or lowered by analogy] (Beijing: Falü Chubanshe, 2009), 46–47; Wu, *Mandarins and Heretics*, 85–90. See also *Shenbao's* graphic report from 1890 entitled "A Perverse Shaman Deludes the People," on the persecution of a female spirit medium by Qing authorities in Yangzhou: "Yao wu huozhong," *Shenbao*, July 29, 1890.

32. Some animal spirits communicated through their mediums by singing, and Zhao may have been such a medium. See Li Weizu (Li, Wei-tsu), "On the Cult of the Four Sacred Animals (*Szu ta men*) in the Neighbourhood of Peking," *Folklore Studies* 7 (1948): 53–54.

33. The snake was one of four sacred animals (*sidamen*) worshiped throughout rural north China, along with the fox, the hedgehog, and the weasel; all four were channeled by spirit mediums, most of whom were poor women. See Li Weizu, "On the Cult of the Four"; Li Weizu, *Si da men: Lishi yu shehui* [The four sacred animals: history and society], ed. Zhou Xing (Beijing: Beijing Daxue Chubanshe, 2011); and chapter 5 in this volume.

34. This may be an alternate name for the female deity the Sovereign of the Clouds of Dawn (*Bixia Yuanjun*), also known as the Goddess of Mount Tai, or it may be the name of one of her attendant spirits. According to some sources, she has authority over fox spirits and shares some of their traits. See Xiaofei Kang, *The Cult of the Fox: Power, Gender, and Popular Religion in Late Imperial and Modern China* (New York: Columbia University Press, 2006), 137–47; Kenneth Pomeranz, "Power, Gender, and Pluralism in the Cult of the Goddess of Taishan," in *Culture and State in Chinese History: Conventions, Accommodations, and Critiques*, ed. Theodore Huters, Roy Wong, and Pauline Yu (Stanford, Calif.: Stanford University Press, 1997), 182–204; and Kenneth Pomeranz, "Orthopraxy, Orthodoxy, and the Goddess(es) of Taishan," *Modern China* 33, no. 1 (2007): 22–46. There is a Yaji Mountain in Zhejiang, and another near Beijing; the latter is a sacred Daoist mountain that bears a temple to the Sovereign of the Clouds of Dawn.

35. XA: 1213–15; Xu Lian et al., *Xingbu bizhao*, 46–47.

36. Sommer, *Sex*, 17–22, 26–29.

37. It was officially permitted to twist a suspect's ears, force them to kneel on chains or broken pottery, or slap their face with the palm of the hand or with a specially designed leather device. See Alison Conner, "Chinese Confessions and the Use of Torture," in *La torture judiciaire: approaches historiques et juridiques*, vol. 1., ed. Bernard Durand and Leah Otis-Cours (Lille: Centre de Histoire Judiciare, Universite de Lille, 2002), 72; and Nancy Park, "Imperial Chinese Justice and the Law of Torture," *Late Imperial China* 29, no. 2 (2008): 43. Even less formal methods known to jailers the world over include deprivation of sleep, food, or water; subjection to

cold; and being forced to share a cell with abusive cellmates. Such measures are rarely recorded in official sources.

38. Laura Stokes, *Demons of Urban Reform: Early European Witch Trials and Criminal Justice, 1430–1530* (New York: Palgrave Macmillan, 2011), 1.

39. Stokes, *Demons of Urban Reform*, 156–57.

40. Ter Haar, *White Lotus*, especially chapters 7 and 8; see also Matthew H. Sommer, "Some Problems with Corpses: Standards of Validity in Qing Homicide Cases," in *Powerful Arguments: Standards of Validity in Late Imperial China*, ed. Martin Hoffman, Joachim Kurtz, and Ari Levine (Leiden: Brill, 2020), 460–62. The "White Lotus" rebel leaders whose confessions informed Susan Naquin's research were interrogated under torture, sometimes around the clock, and sometimes in the presence of the emperor. See Susan Naquin, *Millenarian Rebellion in China: The Eight Trigrams Uprising of 1813* (New Haven, Conn.: Yale University Press, 1976), 131–32, 187–88, 271–79; and Naquin, *Shantung Rebellion: The Wang Lun Uprising of 1774* (New Haven, Conn.: Yale University Press, 1981), 139–42. We see a similar process at work in the Qing campaign to extirpate "the Heaven and Earth Society" (*tiandihui*) after the Lin Shuangwen Rebellion (Ownby, *Brotherhoods*, 114–17).

41. Kuhn, *Soulstealers*. For a more mundane example of how pressure from dissatisfied superiors would compel local magistrates to torture suspects, see Sommer, "Some Problems," 438–39.

42. Thus, for example, in early modern England, long after judicial torture had largely been replaced by juries, it was still employed in cases of sedition and witchcraft. Lynn Hunt, *Inventing Human Rights: A History* (New York: W. W. Norton, 2007), 77.

43. Stokes, *Demons of Urban Reforms*, offers many examples of such confessions. And yet it was long believed (in Europe, at least) that "the body in pain would tell the truth," and that truly innocent people would not make false confessions even if tortured. It was only in the late eighteenth century that these eternal verities were seriously challenged, and judicial opinion began to change (Hunt, *Inventing Human Rights*, chapter 2).

44. Ter Haar, *White Lotus*, 254; see also Sommer, "Some Problems," 461–62.

45. For example, this was done to the defrocked Daoist Jiao Laiyi in the case discussed in chapter 3 in this volume.

5. The Fox Spirit Medium

1. I have located four sources for this case: the gendarmerie's memorial reporting the arrest (ZP: 03-2446-035, JQ 12.3.17); a lateral communication recording the Board of Punishment's investigation and findings, as well as the emperor's judgment (NG: 109625-001, JQ 12.3.29, from the Academia Sinica's *Neige Daku Dang'an* online database, https://catalog.digitalarchives.tw/item/00/27/f9/d8.html (accessed March 24, 2015); a brief summary of the case in *Conspectus of Penal Cases* (XA: 10/22b–23a); and a much later fictionalized account, Wu Chichang, "Yaoren

Xing Da" [The cross-dressing sorcerer Xing Da], in *Kechuang xianhua* [Gossip at the inn], sequel, by Wu Chichang (n.p.: Zibentang, 1875) 5:7a–11b.

2. ZP: 03-2446-035, JQ 12.3.17.

3. ZP: 03-2446-035, JQ 12.3.17.

4. My account of the first interrogation is based on ZP: 03-2446-035, JQ 12.3.17.

5. The laborers who collected nightsoil throughout the city would dump it at these sites to dry in the sun, after which it would be sold to peasants from the surrounding countryside for fertilizer. In the Qing dynasty's last decade, Beijing's nightsoil drying yards were relocated outside the city as a public health measure. The one at Nanxiawa was the last to go. He Jiangli, *Minguo Beijing de gonggong weisheng* [Public health in republican-era Beijing] (Beijing: Beijing Shifan Daxue Chubanshe, 2016), 79–80.

6. For wife-selling in Qing dynasty China, see Matthew H. Sommer, *Polyandry and Wife-Selling in Qing Dynasty China: Survival Strategies and Judicial Interventions* (Berkeley: University of California Press, 2015).

7. For widow remarriage as a form of wife sale, see Sommer, *Polyandry*, 250–58; for fraudulent wife sale, see 263–74.

8. Worth about 12.5 strings of standard cash (i.e. the rough equivalent of two to three years' wages for a hired laborer like Liu Liu). For prices in wife sales, see Sommer, chapter 5.

9. My account of the second interrogation is based on NG: 109625-001, JQ 12.3.29.

10. QH 766:434, interlinear commentary. Over the course of the dynasty, the basic penalty for "accomplices" to heterodoxy was life exile to the frontier and slavery, but the choice of frontier and specific recipients of the slaves changed a number of times.

11. NG: 109625-001, JQ 12.3.29; XA: 10/22b–23a.

12. In the Qing, it was standard for the death penalty to be executed in the county seat of the jurisdiction where the capital crime had been committed.

13. For foxes in Ming-Qing literature, see Judith Zeitlin, *Historian of the Strange: Pu Songling and the Chinese Classical Tale* (Stanford, Calif.: Stanford University Press, 1993); Charles Hammond, "Vulpine Alchemy," *T'oung Pao* 82, nos. 4–5 (1996): 364–80; Leo Tak-hung Chan, *The Discourse on Foxes and Ghosts: Ji Yun and Eighteenth-Century Literati Storytelling* (Honolulu: University of Hawai'i Press, 1998); and Rania Huntington, *Alien Kind: Foxes and Late Imperial Chinese Narrative* (Cambridge, Mass.: Harvard University Asia Center, 2003. Xiaofei Kang, *The Cult of the Fox: Power, Gender, and Popular Religion in Late Imperial and Modern China* (New York: Columbia University Press, 2006) is a study of religion that draws heavily on literary sources.

14. Kang, *Cult of the Fox*, 2–3.

15. Kang, 7–8.

16. Justus Doolittle, *Social Life of the Chinese* (New York: Harper and Brothers, 1865), 288–89, 357–358; Kang, 185–89.

17. The author saw this shrine on a visit to Pingyao in September 2016.

18. Donald Sutton, "From Credulity to Scorn: Confucians Confront the Spirit Mediums in Late Imperial China," *Late Imperial China* 21, no. 2 (2000): 1–39, 37; Sutton, "Shamanism in the Eyes of Ming and Qing Elites," in *Heterodoxy in Late Imperial China*, ed. Kwang-Ching Liu and Richard Shek (Honolulu: University of Hawai'i Press, 2004), 209–37; Vincent Goossaert, "The Destruction of Immoral Temples in Qing China," in *Institute of Chinese Studies Visiting Professor Lectures Series* 2 (Hong Kong: Chinese University Press, 2009), 131–53; Mayfair Yang, "Shamanism and Spirit Possession in Chinese Modernity: Some Preliminary Reflections on a Gendered Religiosity of the Body," *Review of Religion and Chinese Society* 2 (2015): 57.

19. Barend J. ter Haar, *The White Lotus Teachings in Chinese Religious History* (Honolulu: University of Hawai'i Press, 1992), 228; see also 227–34.

20. Every study of fox cults that I have seen cites Li Weizu's (Li, Wei-tsu) classic English-language paper "On the Cult of the Four Sacred Animals (*Szu ta men*) in the Neighbourhood of Peking," *Folklore Studies* 7 (1948), 1–94. A longer Chinese version of the same paper has been published in a book that includes valuable supplementary material: Li Weizu, *Si da men: Lishi yu shehui* [The four sacred animals: history and society], ed. Zhou Xing (Beijing: Beijing Daxue Chubanshe, 2011). For Ding County, Hebei, see Li Jinghan, *Dingxian shehui diaocha* [Social survey of Ding County, Hebei] (Beijing: Zhonghua Pingmin Jiaoyu Cujinhui, 1933), 398–401. For representative missionary accounts, see Rev. G. Owen, "Animal Worship Among the Chinese," *Chinese Recorder and Missionary Journal* 18, no. 7 (1887): 249–55, and T. Watters, "Chinese Fox-Myths," *Journal of the North China Branch of the Royal Asiatic Society* 8 (1873): 45–65. For the geographic distribution of animal cults in north China and local variation in terminology and ritual, see Zhou Xing, "Sidamen: Zhongguo beifang de yizhong minsu zongjiao" [The four sacred animals: a north Chinese folk religion], in Li Weizu, *Si da men: Lishi yu shehui* [The four sacred animals: history and society], ed. Zhou Xing (Beijing: Beijing Daxue Chubanshe, 2011), 155–66.

21. Ishibashi Ushio, *Hokuhei no shamankyō ni tsuite* [Shamanism in Beiping] (n.p.: Cultural Affairs Department, Japanese Foreign Ministry, 1934), chapter 13; a Chinese translation is provided in Li Weizu, *Si da men*. Nagao Ryūzō, *Shina minzokushi* [Chinese folk customs] (Tokyo: Shina Minzokushi Kankōkai, 1940–1942), 2:86–114, 6:52; Takizawa Shunryō, *Manshū no gaison shinkō* [Religious beliefs in rural Manchuria] (Shinkyō: Kōa Yinsatsu Kabushika Kaisha, 1940), part 6; Uchida Tomoo, *Chūgoku nōson no kazoku to shinkō* [Family and religious beliefs in Chinese Villages] (Tokyo: Kōmeisha, 1970), chapter 7.

22. *Shangfucun zhi* [Shangfu village gazetteer] (Shangfucun, Shanxi: Shangfucun Gazetteer Editorial Committee, 1994), 184, 190, 196; Diane Dorfman, "The Spirits of Reform: The Power of Belief in Northern China," *Positions* 4, no. 2 (1996): 253–89; Thomas Dubois, *The Sacred Village: Social Change and Religious Life in Rural North China* (Honolulu: University of Hawai'i Press, 2005), chapter 3; Thomas Dubois, "Religious Healing in the People's Republic of China," in *Chinese Medicine and Healing: An Illustrated History*, ed. T. J. Hinrichs and Linda Barnes

(Cambridge, Mass.: Belknap Press of Harvard University Press, 2013), 277–78; Zhou Xing, "Sidamen: Zhongguo beifang de yizhong minsu zongjiao" [The four sacred animals: a North Chinese folk religion] in Li Weizu, *Si da men: Lishi yu shehui* [The four sacred animals: history and society], ed. Zhou Xing (Beijing: Beijing Daxue Chubanshe, 2011), 146–96; Mikkel Bunkenborg, "Popular Religion Inside Out: Gender and Ritual Revival in a Hebei Township," *China Information* 26, no. 3 (2012): 359–76; Claire Qiuju Deng, "Action-Taking Gods: Animal Spirit Shamanism in Liaoning, China" (master's thesis, McGill University, 2014).

23. In chapter 4 in this volume, I briefly summarized the case of Ding Sha Shi, a woman from Zhili (Hebei) who acted as medium for a snake spirit and was prosecuted for "using heterodox magic to treat illness."

24. Li Weizu, *Sidamen*, 7; Zhou, "Sidamen," 151–52.

25. Nagao, *Shina minzokushi*, 2: figures 7 and 8; Takizawa, *Manshū*, 211; Anne Goodrich, *Peking Paper Gods: A Look at Home Worship* (Nettetal: Steyler Verlag, 1991), 100.

26. Li Weizu, "On the Cult," 26.

27. Li Weizu, 26–27, 30–31; Kang, *Cult of the Fox*, 100–101.

28. Dubois, *Sacred Village*, 80.

29. For a schematic diagram of such a spirit tablet, see Nagao, *Shina minzokushi*, 2:91.

30. Li Weizu, "On the Cult," 54.

31. Ishibashi, *Hokuhei*, 215–16.

32. Dubois, *Sacred Village*, 79.

33. Dubois, 80. In modern Taiwan, the behavior of spirit mediums has provoked debate about whether they are legitimate healers or should themselves be considered mentally ill. See Lin Fushi, "Yizhe huo bingren—Tongji zai Taiwan shehui zhong de juese yu xingxiang" [Healers or patients: the shamans' role and image in Taiwan], *Zhongyang Yanjiuyuan Lishi Yuyan Yanjiusuo jikan* [Quarterly Journal of the Institute of History and Philology, Academia Sinica] 76, no. 3 (2005): 511–68. This debate seems to recapitulate in modern, medicalized form Ming-Qing elites' contempt for mediums. See Donald Sutton, "From Credulity to Scorn"; Sutton, "Shamanism"; and Yang, "Shamanism."

34. Li Weizu, "On the Cult," 76. In the original text, Li uses the term "magician," for which I have substituted "medium."

35. For North China, see Li Weizu, 76–77; Dorfman, "Spirits of Reform"; Dubois, *Sacred Village*, 78–84; Bunkenborg, "Popular Religion"; and Kang, *Cult of the Fox*, 98–101. For South China, see Jack Potter, "Cantonese Shamanism," in *Religion and Ritual in Chinese Society*, ed. Arthur Wolf (Stanford, Calif.: Stanford University Press, 1974), 207–31; Meir Shahar, *Crazy Ji: Chinese Religion and Popular Literature* (Cambridge, Mass.: Harvard University Asia Center, 1998), 177; Baptandier, *Lady of Linshui*, chapter 10; Cline, "Female Spirit Mediums"; and Yang, "Shamanism."

36. Kang, 97–98.

37. ZP: 03-2446-035, JQ 12.3.17.

38. Compare the case of Ding Da Shi (briefly summarized in chapter 4 in this volume) who served as medium to a snake spirit and treated illnesses by burning incense and preparing tea for her patients.

39. Ishibashi, *Hokuhei*, 215–16; Li Weizu, "On the Cult," 54–55; Brigitte Baptandier, "The Lady Linshui: How a Woman Became a Goddess," in *Unruly Gods. Divinity and Society in China*, ed. Meir Shahar & Robert Weller (Honolulu: University of Hawai'i Press, 1996), 116–17, 121; Brigitte Baptandier, *The Lady of Linshui: A Chinese Female Cult* (Stanford, Calif.: Stanford University Press, 2008), 226; Donald Sutton, "From Credulity to Scorn: Confucians Confront the Spirit Mediums in Late Imperial China," *Late Imperial China* 21, no. 2 (2000): 34.

40. Aisin-Gioro Pu Yi, *From Emperor to Citizen: The Autobiography of Aisin-Gioro Pu Yi*, trans. W. J. F. Jenner (Oxford: Oxford University Press, 1987), 67–68; Nagao, *Shina minzokushi*, 2:86–93; Zhou Xing, *Sidamen*, 153–54.

41. Gayatri Reddy, *With Respect to Sex: Negotiating Hijra Identity in South India* (Chicago: University of Chicago Press, 2005), 2.

42. For Hijras, see Serena Nanda, *Neither Man nor Woman: The Hijras of India* (Belmont, Calif.: Wadsworth, 1999), Reddy, *With Respect to Sex*; and Jessica Hinchy, *Governing Gender and Sexuality in Colonial India: The Hijra, c. 1850–1900* (Cambridge: Cambridge University Press, 2019). For Native American cultures, see Sue-Ellen Jacobs, Wesley Thomas, and Sabine Lang, eds., *Two-Spirit People: Native American Gender Identity, Sexuality, and Spirituality* (Urbana: University of Illinois Press, 1997); and Sabine Lang, *Men as Women, Women as Men: Changing Gender in Native American Cultures* (Austin: University of Texas Press, 1998). "Two-spirit" is an English neologism that has provoked some controversy, because (like the outdated "berdache") it elides the enormous diversity among Native cultures, each of which has its own norms and customs, as well as appropriate vocabulary in its own language.

43. ZP: 03-2446-035, JQ 12.3.17.

44. NG: 109625-001, JQ 12.3.29.

45. NG: 109625-001, JQ 12.3.29.

46. ZP: 03-2446-035, JQ 12.3.17.

47. Among the nearly two thousand Qing legal cases I have collected that involve male-male "sodomy" (*jijian*), I have found only seven in which an ongoing relationship seems to have involved alternation of sexual roles. The evidence internal to these exceptional cases makes clear that such flouting of convention was considered strange and worthy of comment by those who knew about it.

48. The definitive account of this case by a *New York Times* reporter was produced with the cooperation of Boursicot: Joyce Wadler, *Liaison* (New York: Bantam, 1993).

49. At their trial, the murderers argued that Araujo had "raped" them, by failing to disclose her transgender identity before having sex. This bizarre victim-blaming represents yet another variation of the "transwoman as fraud/predator" theme. For analyses of this "trans panic" legal defense (which was subsequently banned in California), see Victoria Steinberg, "A Heat of Passion Offense: Emotions and Bias in 'Trans Panic' Mitigation Claims," *Boston College Third World Law Journal* 25, no. 2

(2005): 499–524; Talia Mae Bettcher, "Evil Deceivers and Make-Believers: On Transphobic Violence and the Politics of Illusion," *Hypatia* 22, no. 3 (2007): 48–50; and Cynthia Lee and Peter Kwan, "The Trans Panic Defense: Masculinity, Heteronormativity, and the Murder of Transgender Women," *Hastings Law Journal* 66 (2014): 77–132.

50. "Qu fu bei pian," *Shenbao*, March 22, 1878; "Chuan pian xiang yu," *Shenbao*, June 20, 1878; "Nan ban nüzhuang you jie shi zhong," *Shenbao*, February 24, 1907; "Hubei," *Shenbao*, March 13, 1916; "Dong san sheng tongxun," *Shenbao*, January 27, 1920. For "falconing," see Sommer, *Polyandry*, xii, 271–74.

51. "Nan ban nüzhuang," *Shenbao*, June 17, 1879.

52. "Diaochayuan faxian renyao bailei," *Shenbao*, June 23, 1911; "Renyao yinghuo bingshi," *Shenbao*, July 4, 1911.

53. It is also worth noting that the women who married "female husbands" often claimed to have been deceived (some for years) and denied that they had known their husbands had female anatomy. Manion is skeptical of such testimony, but there is no way to prove that it was false. Jen Manion, *Female Husbands: A Trans History* (Cambridge: Cambridge University Press, 2020), 147–48.

54. Wu Chichang, "Yaoren Xing Da" [The cross-dressing sorcerer Xing Da], in *Kechuang xianhua* [Gossip at the inn], sequel, by Wu Chichang (n.p.: Zibentang, 1875) 5:7a–11b.

55. It is conceivable that Wu learned of the case from reading old copies of the *Peking Gazette*, the official news bulletin issued in the capital recording major government decisions. See Emily Mokros, *The Peking Gazette in Late Imperial China: State News and Political Authority* (Seattle: University of Washington Press, 2021).

56. This four-character saying is an allusion to Han Fei's famous account of Mizi Xia, who was a male concubine of Duke Ling of Wei. In his youth, Mizi Xia could do no wrong in the duke's eyes, but as he aged and lost his looks, he lost the duke's favor. Han Fei used this parable to warn of the fickleness of rulers. The "shared peach" metaphor for male love also comes from this account. See Bret Hinsch, *Passions of the Cut Sleeve: The Male Homosexual Tradition in China* (Berkeley: University of California Press, 1992), 20–22.

57. Kang, *Cult of the Fox*, 45–46.

58. Huntington, *Alien Kind*, chapter 3.

59. Huntington, chapter 6.

60. Xing's offer to finance Liu's acquisition of a concubine parallels the scenario found in some of the legal and fictional treatments of "stone maidens" (discussed in chapter 6 in this volume) in which the stone maiden would be allowed to maintain her position as main wife while a concubine performed the biological role.

61. Pu Songling, *Liaozhai zhi yi* [Strange tales from the Liao Studio] (Shanghai: Shanghai Guji Chubanshe, 1978), 12:1711–13. See Zeitlin, *Historian*, chapter 4, for a full translation and analysis of this story.

62. Later, when the widow landlady inquires, Ma Wanbao explains that Double Joy is Ma's maternal niece, who was expelled by her husband's family because she suffers from "natural sterility" (*tianyan*); in other words, that she is a "stone maiden" (see

chapter 6 in this volume). In this way, Ma deflects the neighbors' attention and perpetuates the ruse that Double Joy is a woman.

63. For a similarly miraculous "cure" in a Li Yu story about a "stone maiden," see chapter 6 in this volume.

64. Sophie Volpp, "The Discourse on Male Marriage: Li Yu's 'A Male Mencius's Mother,' " *Positions* 2, no. 1 (1994): 118. For Patrick Hanan's translation of the story, see Li Yu, *Silent Operas*, ed. and trans. Patrick Hanan (Hong Kong: Chinese University of Hong Kong, 1990), 97–134.

65. Zeitlin, *Historian of the Strange*, 102.

66. Susan Stryker, *Transgender History* (Berkeley, Calif.: Seal, 2008), 1.

6. The Truth of the Body

1. Some of the material in this chapter previously appeared in Matthew H. Sommer, "The Gendered Body in the Qing Courtroom," *Journal of the History of Sexuality* 22, no. 2 (2013): 281–311.

2. Judith Butler, *Gender Trouble: Feminism and the Subversion of Identity* (New York: Routledge, 1990), 114. This debate has generated a vast literature, which I shall not attempt to summarize here; for an overview of key issues, see Linda Alcoff, "Cultural Feminism Versus Post-Structuralism: The Identity Crisis in Feminist Theory," in *The Second Wave: A Reader in Feminist Theory*, ed. Linda Nicholson (New York: Routledge, 1997), 330–55; and Mary Hawkesworth, "Confounding Gender," *Signs* 22 (1997): 649–85. For a sense of how perspectives have changed in recent years and continue to change, compare the original 2008 text of Susan Stryker's classic *Transgender History* with her revised version that appeared in 2017, especially the introductory chapter: Susan Stryker, *Transgender History* (Berkeley, Calif.: Seal, 2008); and *Transgender History: The Roots of Today's Revolution*, rev. ed. (New York: Seal, 2017).

3. Thomas Laqueur, *Making Sex: Body and Gender from the Greeks to Freud* (Cambridge, Mass.: Harvard University Press, 1990).

4. Laqueur, *Making Sex*, 16.

5. Jeffrey Weeks, *Sexuality and Its Discontents* (New York: Routledge, 1990), 122–23.

6. Butler, *Gender Trouble*, 112.

7. For a pioneering and prescient conceptualization of the policing of sexuality, see Gayle Rubin, "Thinking Sex: Notes for a Radical Theory of the Politics of Sexuality," in *Pleasure and Danger: Exploring Female Sexuality*, ed. Carole Vance (Boston: Routledge & Kegan Paul, 1984), 267–319.

8. Arthur Wolf and Theo Engelen, "Fertility and Fertility Control in Pre-Revolutionary China," *Journal of Interdisciplinary History* 38, no. 3 (2008): 362.

9. The phrase, of course, belongs to Adrienne Rich; see her classic essay "Compulsory Heterosexuality and Lesbian Existence," *Signs: Journal of Women in Culture and*

Society 5, no. 4 (1980): 631–60. On the intensifying imperative in the Ming-Qing era that every woman be a wife, seee Matthew H. Sommer, *Sex, Law, and Society in Late Imperial China* (Stanford, Calif.: Stanford University Press, 2000), chapter 1.

10. Charlotte Furth, *A Flourishing Yin: Gender in China's Medical History, 960–1665* (Berkeley: University of California Press, 1999), 49 and figure 3.

11. Furth, *Flourishing Yin*, 306.

12. Furth, 183; see also Sommer, "Review of *A Flourishing Yin: Gender in China's Medical History, 960–1665*, by Charlotte Furth," *Harvard Journal of Asiatic Studies* 61, no. 1 (2001): 273–79; and Yi-Li Wu, *Reproducing Women: Medicine, Metaphor, and Childbirth in Late Imperial China* (Berkeley: University of California Press, 2010), 230–35.

13. All information and quotations related to Xie Shi's case come from XT: 92-10, Qianlong 4.3.27.

14. For midwives as forensic examiners of female anatomy, see Charlotte Furth, "Androgynous Males and Deficient Females: Biology and Gender Boundaries in Sixteenth- and Seventeenth-Century China," *Late Imperial China* 9, no. 2 (1988): 22; Furth, *Flourishing Yin*, 282; Sommer, *Sex*, 83–84; and Janet Theiss, *Disgraceful Matters: The Politics of Chastity in Eighteenth-Century China* (Berkeley: University of California Press, 2004), 139–40. For the contrasting roles of female midwives and male doctors in women's medicine, see Charlotte Furth, "Concepts of Pregnancy, Childbirth, and Infancy in Ch'ing Dynasty China," *Journal of Asian Studies* 46, no. 1 (1987): 7–35.

15. The language used by both midwives echoes the forensic manual *Xi yuan lu* [The washing away of wrongs]: a stone maiden's "breasts are flat, and her vagina cannot admit even a finger" (*liang ru pingta, yinhu bu neng rong zhi*). Lüliguan [Bureau of the Code, Board of Punishment], ed. *Lüliguan jiaozheng Xiyuan lu* [The washing away of wrongs], ed. and corrected by the Bureau of the Code, in *Xuxiu siku quanshu* (Shanghai: Shanghai guji chubanshe, 1995) 972:1, 42a.

16. DC: 101-001.

17. Sommer, *Sex*, chapter 5. For the chastity cult during the High Qing, see Theiss, *Disgraceful*; and Weijing Lu, *True to Her Word: The Faithful Maiden Cult in Late Imperial China* (Stanford, Calif.: Stanford University Press, 2008).

18. In contrast, Olivia Milburn feels no inhibition in making highly specific biomedical diagnoses of people in the Chinese past whom she identifies as "intersex." See "Bodily Transformations: Responses to Intersex Individuals in Early and Imperial China," *Nan Nü* 16, no. 1 (2014): 1–28.

19. In many cultures, infants with ambiguous genitalia tend to be raised as girls by default, reflecting the widespread assumption that a female is somehow an incomplete or lesser version of a male (Furth, "Androgynous Males," 19).

20. Li's *Systematic Materia Medica* remains the foundational text for traditional Chinese medicine even today. See Carla Nappi, *The Monkey and the Inkpot: Natural History and Its Transformations in Early Modern China* (Cambridge, Mass.: Harvard University Press, 2009); and He Bian, *Know Your Remedies: Pharmacy and Culture in*

Early Modern China (Princeton, N.J.: Princeton University Press, 2020). For the taxonomy of anomalies, see Li Shizhen, *Bencao gangmu xin jiaozhu ben* [New annotated edition of *Systematic Materia Medica*] (Beijing: Huaxia Chubanshe, 1998), 192.

21. *Hanyu dacidian* [Great dictionary of Chinese] (Shanghai: Shanghai Cishu Chubanshe, 2008), 11:778. The mutilating punishments were abolished by Emperor Wen of the Han dynasty. See Derk Bodde and Clarence Morris, *Law in Imperial China: Exemplified by 190 Ch'ing Dynasty Cases, Translated from the Hsing-an hui-lan* (Cambridge, Mass.: Harvard University Press, 1967), 76. Nevertheless, even in the Qing, the juvenile sons of executed rebels and mass murderers were sometimes castrated and drafted into imperial service as eunuchs. See Melissa Dale, *Inside the World of the Eunuch: A Social History of the Emperor's Servants in Qing China* (Hong Kong: Hong Kong University Press, 2018), 34–35; and Norman Kutcher, *Eunuch and Emperor in the Great Age of Qing Rule* (Berkeley: University of California Press, 2018), 169–70.

22. Furth translates *fei nan* and *fei nü* as "those who are neither male nor female; or false males and false females" ("Androgynous Males," 4–5). Tani Barlow translates these terms as "non-males" and "non-females" in her "Theorizing Woman: *Funü, Guojia, Jiating* (Chinese Women, Chinese State, Chinese Family)," in *Body, Subject, and Power in China*, ed. Angela Zito and Tani Barlow (Chicago: University of Chicago Press, 1994), 258, 279n8. Later in the same passage, Li Shizhen also uses the terms *bu nan* and *bu nü*, which seem closer to Furth and Barlow's translations.

23. Li Shizhen, *Bencao gangmu*.

24. Furth, "Androgynous Males," 5.

25. Barlow, "Theorizing Woman," 279n6.

26. See also Robert McRuer's analysis of the connection between "compulsory heterosexuality" and "compulsory able-bodiedness" in contemporary society in *Crip Theory: Cultural Signs of Queerness and Disability* (New York: New York University Press, 2006), introduction; and Alison Kafer, "Compulsory Bodies: Reflections on Heterosexuality and Able-bodiedness," *Journal of Women's History* 15, no 3 (2003): 77–89.

27. Sommer, *Sex*, 162–63, 306–7.

28. "Stone maiden" is Charlotte Furth's apt translation of *shinü* ("Androgynous Males"). In the context of this term, *nü* means "maiden" or "unmarried daughter," rather than the "female" of the male/female binary, reinforcing the implication of arrested maturation.

29. Furth.

30. The phrase is Laqueur's (*Making Sex*, 236). See also Kafer, "Compulsory Bodies"; and McRuer, *Crip Theory*.

31. All information and quotations related to Zou Shi's case come from NB: 6-30-318, Tongzhi 4.5.13.

32. For example, an early Qing story contains the following line: "That woman was a 'stone maiden' (*shinü*), also known as a 'two-formed person' (*you jiao zuo erxingzi*)." Tianhua Zhuren, [Master of heavenly flowers], in *Yunxian xiao* [Laughter of cloud fairies] (Shenyang: Chunfeng Wenyi Chubanshe, 1983), 2:29.

33. Francesca Bray, *Technology and Gender: Fabrics of Power in Late Imperial China* (Berkeley: University of California Press, 1997), 335–68. Bray's specific claim that elite wives used abortifacient drugs to avoid childbearing is controversial and probably mistaken (see Sommer, "Abortion"). It is clear that many elite wives did bear children of their own. For the division of labor among females within the elite household, see also Susan Mann, *Precious Records: Women in China's Long Eighteenth Century* (Stanford, Calif.: Stanford University Press, 1997); and Susan Mann, *The Talented Women of the Zhang Family* (Berkeley: University of California Press, 2007).

34. Thirty strings of cash (nominally equal to thirty thousand cash) was a large amount of money for most people. To put this price in perspective, in the wife-selling cases I have collected from Nanbu County the average price of a wife in open sales during the nineteenth century was fourteen thousand cash (Sommer, *Polyandry*, 164–65, appendix C.4).

35. Similar logic guided one of the forms of "delayed transfer marriage" practiced in Shunde County, Guangdong: in "compensation marriage," a woman with an independent income who did not wish to play the biological role of wife could buy her husband a concubine to perform that role in her place. This maneuver enabled the main wife to live independently, while securing the right to move into her husband's household in old age and to claim a place on his ancestral altar after death. Janice Stockard, *Daughters of the Canton Delta: Marriage Patterns and Economic Strategies in South China, 1860–1930* (Stanford, Calif.: Stanford University Press, 1989), 48–69.

36. Jin Xiage, ed., *Yuan Zicai pandu jinghua* [Highlights of Yuan Mei's legal judgments], in *Yuan Mei quanji xinbian* [A new edition of Yuan Mei's collected works] (Hangzhou: Zhejhiang Guji Chubanshe, 2015), 19:6–7 and preface. Similarly, in an 1813 case from Huoqiu County, Anhui, a landlord bought a concubine because his wife was "crippled" (*canfei*) and "could not give birth" (*bu neng shengyu*); XT: 2500-15, JQ 18.6.7. This scenario recalls the fictionalization of Xing Shi's case discussed in chapter 5 in this volume, when Xing offered to finance Liu Liu's acquisition of a concubine to continue his family line.

37. All information and quotations related to Zhanggu's case come from BX: 4-4919, XF 1.8.14,

38. See also Furth, "Androgynous Males," 5n9.

39. We find similar solutions in other cases. In an 1863 example from Ba County, the groom's family paid the stone maiden's natal family thirteen taels of silver in exchange for a divorce; the divorce contract authorized the woman "to enter a temple as a nun," but also stipulated that "if she recovers from her disability, she is entitled to marry someone else (*huo shang miao wei ni, yihuo ji yu ling xing gaishi*)"; BX: 5-7213, TZ 2.7.8. In a 1907 example from Baodi County, Zhili, a stone maiden rejected by her husband "agreed to cut off her hair to become a nun" (*qingyuan luo fa wei ni*); BD: 170, GX 33.11.19.

40. XT: 98-13, QL 4.11.12, for one Daoist novice with some sort of mental or neurological illness (*fengji*) and another with "crippled legs"; XT: 857-3, QL 28.7.20, for

a Buddhist monk described as "short in stature and physically weak"; and BX: 6-43076, GX 4 and BX: 6-44043, GX 13.3, for two cases of Buddhist novices with "crippled feet" (perhaps club feet?). All were donated to temples by their parents.

41. Furth, "Androgynous Males," 21.

42. Cyril Birch, trans., *The Peony Pavilion* (Boston: Cheng and Tsui, 1980), 70.

43. Tang Xianzu, *Mudanting* [Peony pavilion] (Beijing: Renmin Wenxue Chubanshe, 1997), 83–86. Hsiao-wen Cheng relates a case from 1124 in which a woman who grew a moustache was ordered ordained as a Daoist nun by the Song emperor, Huizong. Hsiao-wen Cheng, "Before Sexual and Normal: Shifting Categories of Sexual Anomaly from Ancient to Yuan China," *Asia Major* 31, no. 2 (2018): 15–16.

44. Li Mengsheng, *Zhongguo jinhui xiaoshuo baihua* [One hundred tales from banned Chinese novels] (Shanghai: Shanghai Guji Chubanshe, 1994), 252. In Ming-Qing fiction, infertility is portrayed as one of the negative effects of licentiousness. See R. Keith McMahon, *Causality and Containment in Seventeenth-Century Chinese Fiction* (Leiden: Brill, 1988), 102.

45. Tianhua Zhuren, *Yunxian xiao*, 29–36.

46. XT: 198-8, QL 8.3.20. In this case, the magistrate had not brought a midwife to the inquest, so he ordered two neighbor women to examine the corpse's pelvis, and they confirmed that she was "truly a stone maiden." In an 1829 case from Xiangfu County, Henan, a widow adopted a young girl, planning to make her work as a prostitute. But prostitution, like being a wife, required vaginal intercourse, and the girl turned out to be a stone maiden, thereby frustrating the widow's plans. The widow tried to sell the girl, without success, and became cruel and abusive, finally driving her to suicide. Xu Lian and Xiong E., eds., *Xingbu bizhao jiajian chengan* [Board of Punishment cases where the penalty was raised or lowered by analogy] (Beijing: Falü Chubanshe, 2009), 581.

47. All information and quotations related to Ren Mei's case come from MQ: 156-87.

48. This statement sounds euphemistic and literary in the original Chinese: "*yu zhenxi zhi jian wei cheng Zhang Shi zhi xin*" (literally, "between pillow and sleeping mat, he failed to fulfill Zhang Shi's heart").

49. Li Shizhen, *Bencao gangmu*.

50. For "the court of matrons," see R. H. Helmholz, *Marriage Litigation in Medieval England* (Cambridge: Cambridge University Press, 1974), 89; see also Guido Ruggiero, *The Boundaries of Eros: Sex Crime and Sexuality in Renaissance Venice* (New York: Oxford University Press, 1985), 114–15, 146–47. In China, after reforms based on Western models introduced impotence as grounds for divorce, court-ordered physicians would apply alcohol to a man's penis to determine whether he was capable of erection. See Margaret Kuo, *Intolerable Cruelty: Marriage, Law, and Society in Early Twentieth-Century China* (Lanham, Md.: Rowman and Littlefield, 2012), chapter 8.

51. See Sommer, *Sex*, 41; and sources cited therein.

52. DC: 315-00.

53. Sommer, *Sex*, 40–43; Sommer, *Polyandry*, 214–16.

54. All information and quotations related to Chen Erchuan's case come from XT: 3671-23, TZ 6.12.20; the case is also summarized briefly in XA: 4/546–47.

55. Penalties varied greatly, depending on what crime the criminal had committed before being killed, and it is not clear how this law would have been applied to Yue Shi. See DC: 388-00 and substatutes that follow.

56. The standard solution for an infertile marriage would have been to adopt a nephew to serve as the husband's successor and heir. But adoption does not seem to have been discussed in this case, perhaps because the couple's mutual alienation became so extreme so quickly.

57. All information and quotations related to Zhou Sijie's case come from Ruan Qixin, *Chongkan buzhu Xiyuanlu jizheng* [The washing away of wrongs, reprinted with amendments, examples, and commentaries] (Taipei: Wenhai Chubanshe, [1807] 1968), 1:33a–b; see also the brief summary in Wenjuan Xie, "(Trans)Culturally Transgendered: Reading Transgender Narratives in (Late) Imperial China" (PhD diss., University of Alberta, 2015), 54–55.

58. Ruan Qixin, *Chongkan buzhu Xiyuanlu*, 1:33a-b.

59. Sommer, *Sex*, chapters 2 and 3. In the Qing, the legal category of *jian* was expanded to include anal intercourse between males (*jijian*). See Sommer, chapter 4.

60. Sommer, 35–36.

61. A famous example is Li Yu's play *Lianxiang ban* [Pitying the fragrant companion]. See H. Laura Wu, "Through the Prism of Male Writing: Representation of Lesbian Love in Ming-Qing Literature," *Nan Nü* 4, no. 1 (2002): 1–34.

62. Wu, "Through the Prism." See also Bret Hinsch, *Passions of the Cut Sleeve: The Male Homosexual Tradition in China* (Berkeley: University of California Press, 1992), appendix; and Tze-lan Deborah Sang, *The Emerging Lesbian: Female Same-Sex Desire in Modern China* (Chicago: University of Chicago Press, 2003), chapters 2 and 3.

63. Sommer, *Sex*, 115, 163; see also Sommer, "Dangerous"; and "Legal Understandings."

64. Sang, *Emerging Lesbian*.

65. Zhou Sijie's case suggests comparison to that of Thomas/ine Hall, a seventeenth-century Virginian colonist who provoked controversy and eventually litigation by alternating male and female dress. Hall's genitals were examined several times in order to ascertain their sex, but they were so ambiguous in appearance that observers could not agree whether Hall was male or female (some recognized a penis, others did not). In the end, the court ordered Hall to wear a combination of male and female dress, as a public marker of Hall's defiance of anatomical and social categories. See Kathleen Brown, " 'Changed . . . into the Fashion of Man': The Politics of Sexual Difference in a Seventeenth-Century Anglo-American Settlement," *Journal of the History of Sexuality* 6, no. 2 (1995): 171–93.

66. The newspaper also characterizes this individual as "neither *yin* nor *yang*" (*bu yin bu yang*) and "neither female nor male" (*bu ci bu xiong*). "Sucheng faxian renyao," *Shenbao*, December 5, 1912; "Renlei jinhua xin lun," *Shenbao*, December 11, 1912.

67. Sommer, *Sex*, 8–12, 308–16. Barlow ("Theorizing Woman") argues that gender discourse recognized no general category of woman based on anatomy; instead,

individuals were gendered exclusively by performance of family roles—in other words, strictly speaking, there were no "women" or "men," but only wives/mothers/sisters/daughters, and husbands/fathers/brothers/sons.

68. All information and quotations related to Zhao Wan's case come from XT: 288-11, QL 10.12.10.

69. The three rapists in this case were precisely the sort of rogue males outside the family system that Qing jurists had in mind when they promulgated harsh laws against "bare sticks" (*guanggun*, also translated "rootless rascals"), including the sub-statute against gang rape cited here. See Sommer, *Sex*, 96–101; and Sommer, "Dangerous Males," 67–88.

70. For Qing rape law and trial procedure, see Sommer, *Sex*, chapter 3.

71. Sommer, 79–84.

72. QH, 403:508. Women whose chaste martyrdom was recognized by imperial edict would be honored by the local magistrate in the Confucian temple and have memorial arches erected in their honor by their families at state expense. In English-language scholarship, it is conventional to refer to this process as "canonization."

73. One is reminded of Susan Brownmiller's classic argument that a shared vulnerability to rape is what defines women politically, in her *Against Our Will: Men, Women, and Rape* (New York: Simon and Schuster, 1975); and Catherine MacKinnon's observation that "to be rapable, a position that is social not biological, defines what a woman is," in her *Toward a Feminist Theory* (Cambridge, Mass.: Harvard University Press, 1989), 178. See Sommer, *Gendered Body*, 298–99.

74. I have treated this subject in detail elsewhere, so here I confine myself to a brief summary. See Matthew H. Sommer, "The Penetrated Male in Late Imperial China: Judicial Constructions and Social Stigma," *Modern China* 23, no. 2 (1997): 140–80; Sommer, *Sex*, 132–138; Sommer, "Dangerous Males"; and Sommer, "Legal Understandings."

75. Quoted in Ruan Qixin, *Chongkan buzhu Xiyuanlu*, 1:35a–b.

76. Ruan Qixin, *Chongkan buzhu Xiyuanlu*, 1:35a–b.

77. For a detailed example, see Sommer, *Sex*, 127–28.

78. XT: 143-8, QL 6.4.25.

79. Li Yu, *Silent Operas*, ed. and trans. Patrick Hanan (Hong Kong: Chinese University of Hong Kong, 1990), 11:3504–13.

80. Another miraculous cure of a stone maiden occurs in chapters 96 and 97 of the eighteenth-century novel *A Country Codger Puts his Words Out to Sun*. The protagonist Wen Suchen, whose heroic Confucian virtue and sexual self-discipline have endowed him with extraordinary yang energy, lies down next to the stone maiden naked and vigorously massages her breasts and crotch. After several nights of this treatment, her abnormally cold body warms up, a membrane sloughs off to reveal female genitals, her breasts fill out, and her menses begin to flow. See R. Keith McMahon, "A Case for Confucian Sexuality: The Eighteenth-Century Novel *Yesou Puyan*," *Late Imperial China* 9, no. 2 (1988): 41.

81. Weeks, *Sexuality and Its Discontents*, 122–23.

82. DC: 366-03; see also Sommer, *Sex*, 125.

7. The Hustler

1. I have found four sources on Xinxiang's case. A *xingke tiben* from the governor of Shanxi (XT: 378-9, QL 13.11.5) covers all events up through 1748, including Xinxiang's arrest in Yangcheng County, prosecution for impersonating an imperial official, and initial death sentence. Two secret palace memorials (*zhupi zouzhe*) from the Liangguang governor-general (ZP: 04-01-28-0002-011, QL 23.11.12; ZP: 04-01-01-0229-007, QL 24.1.29) and a memorial from the Board of Personnel (LK: 2-81-5599-3, QL 24.2.3) cover subsequent events up through 1758.

2. For the structure of the examination system in the Qing dynasty, see Benjamin Elman, *Civil Examinations and Meritocracy in Late Imperial China* (Cambridge, Mass.: Harvard University Press, 2013), figure 3.1.

3. For Shangfo Cun (renamed "Shangfu Cun" after 1949), see *Shangfu Cun zhi* [Shangfu village gazetteer] (Shangfu Cun, Shanxi: Shangfu Cun Gazetteer Editorial Committee, 1994); and *Jinshang shiliao quanlan* [Historical materials on the Shanxi merchants], 11 vols., ed. Shanxi Provincial Government's "Historical Materials on the Shanxi Merchants" Editorial Committee (Taiyuan: Shanxi Renmin Chubanshe, 2006–), 8:164–66; for the Zhao merchant lineage based there, see *Jinshang shiliao*, 8:253–257.

4. Here I estimate the distance between county seats as the crow flies, as a rough approximation. In the Qing, Xiangling County was part of Pingyang Prefecture; it is now part of Xiangfen County in Linfen Municipality.

5. Mark McNicholas, *Forgery and Impersonation in Imperial China: Popular Deceptions and the High Qing State* (Seattle: University of Washington Press, 2016), 57–61.

6. In the Qing code, DC: 175-00 states the general principle that everyone should wear only the clothing and accessories appropriate to their station in life; DC: 175-11 applies this principle to Buddhist and Daoist clergy.

7. McNicholas, *Forgery and Impersonation*, 106.

8. The Guanyin Temple, which still exists, was modest by Shangfo Cun standards, with just three main rooms for worship; it was one of more than thirty temples of various sizes in Shangfo Cun. See *Shangfucun zhi*, 184–88.

9. DC: 361-00. For alternative translations, see Sir George Staunton, trans., *Ta Tsing Leu Lee; Being the Fundamental Laws, and a Selection from the Supplementary Statutes, of the Penal Code of China* (London: T. Cadell and W. Davies, 1810), 399–400; and William Jones, trans., *The Great Qing Code* (Oxford: Clarendon, 1994), 344–45.

10. McNicholas, *Forgery and Impersonation*, 4; for a detailed study of this category of law, see chapter 7 in McNicholas.

11. Susan Naquin, *Millenarian Rebellion in China: The Eight Trigrams Uprising of 1813* (New Haven, Conn.: Yale University Press, 1976), 24, 59, 84, 90–93; Susan Naquin, *Shantung Rebellion: The Wang Lun Uprising of 1774* (New Haven, Conn.: Yale University Press, 1981), 112–15; David Ownby, *Brotherhoods and Secret Societies in Early and Mid-Qing China: The Formation of a Tradition* (Stanford:, Calif. Stanford University Press, 1996), 83–85.

12. Andrea Goldman, *Opera and the City: The Politics of Culture in Beijing, 1770–1900* (Stanford, Calif.: Stanford University Press, 2012).

13. Alternative routes continued north to Taiyuan or even Guihuacheng (modern Hohot) before heading east via Zhangjiakou. These routes were longer and more arduous, but were often taken by merchants who had business in those cities. Zhijian Qiao, personal communication, April 2021. For the Shanxi merchants, see Zhijian Qiao, "The Rise of Shanxi Merchants: Empire, Institutions, and Social Change in Qing China, 1688–1850" (PhD diss., Stanford University, 2017).

14. For hospitality at temples in Beijing, see Susan Naquin, *Peking: Temples and City Life, 1400–1900* (Berkeley: University of California Press, 2000), 86–88.

15. David Johnson, *Spectacle and Sacrifice: The Ritual Foundations of Village Life in North China* (Cambridge, Mass.: Harvard University Asia Center, 2009), 174. On the religious habitus of peasants who joined the Boxer movement, see Joseph Esherick, *The Origins of the Boxer Uprising* (Berkeley: University of California Press, 1987).

16. Naquin, *Peking*, 83–86, 634–36; Goldman, *Opera and the City*, 87–97.

17. Colin Mackerras, *The Rise of the Peking Opera, 1770–1870* (London: Oxford University Press, 1972), 7–9, chapter 4; Wu Cuncun, *Homoerotic Sensibilities in Late Imperial China* (London: RoutledgeCurzon, 2004), chapter 5.

18. Wu, *Homoerotic Sensibilities*, 127ff.

19. Mackerras, *Rise of the Peking Opera* , 44–45, 150–52; Wu, chapter 5.

20. According to Goldman, "playhouses, winehouses, and brothels for boy actresses clustered just outside the three southern gates in the wall of the Inner City" (*Opera and the City*, 69).

21. For the traffic in boys that supplied *dan* to the opera, see Mackerras, *of the Peking Opera*, 41–42, 145–49; and Wu, *Homoerotic Sensibilities*, 124–25.

22. For conditional sale of land, see Matthew H. Sommer, *Polyandry and Wife-Selling in Qing Dynasty China: Survival Strategies and Judicial Interventions* (Berkeley: University of California Press, 2015), 191–93 and sources cited therein; for conditional sale of wives, see Sommer, *Polyandry*, 104–13; for conditional sale of boys to opera troupes, see Mackerras, *Rise of Peking Opera*, 146–47.

23. LK: 2-123-10094-33, DG 14.4.18. Zhang Shichen's prosecution focused on whether he had bought the boy in order to have sex with him. After all, the boy had been trained as an actor, and the presiding officials in the Board of Punishment explicitly stated that the only plausible reason for taking an actor into service was to use him for sex. But Zhang denied having sex with the boy, and witnesses from his household backed him.

24. Prince Zhuang (*Zhuang qinwang*) was one of the twelve "iron cap" first-rank princely peerages in the Qing aristocracy that enjoyed "perpetual inheritance" (i.e., did not degrade with each generation); see Mark Elliott, *The Manchu Way: The Eight Banners and Ethnic Identity in Late Imperial China* (Stanford, Calif.: Stanford University Press, 2001), 80. Imai was an incorrigible troublemaker, having previously been fined for multiple infractions (e.g., hosting gambling parties, having his servants beat up a lesser Manchu noble who had offended him). Eventually, he would be stripped of his rank and exiled to Manchuria for having

embarrassed the Daoguang emperor by getting caught smoking opium in public, shortly after the proclamation of an empire-wide ban on the drug. Only his exalted rank as one of the highest men in the land had prevented him from being punished more severely for his previous offenses. LF: 03-3780-034, DG 17.2.22; see also XA: 4/431.

25. See multiple references to both troupes in Mackerras, *Rise of Peking Opera*; and Goldman, *Opera and the City.*

26. See Sommer, "Scandal in the Garden: *The Story of the Stone* as a 'Licentious Novel,'" in *Approaches to Teaching The Story of the Stone (Dream of the Red Chamber)*, ed. Andrew Schonebaum and Tina Lu (New York: Modern Language Association of America, 2012), 204–6.

27. Here Mackerras appears to be citing ages in terms of *sui*, rather than "years old" (*Rise of Peking Opera*, 145–52).

28. Wu, *Homoerotic Sensibilities*, 153–54.

29. For the training regimen of boy actresses, see Wu, 127–32.

30. Kuhn mentions a peasant "who was growing bald and wore a false queue." Philip Kuhn, *Soulstealers: The Chinese Sorcery Scare of 1768* (Cambridge, Mass.: Harvard University Press, 1990), 167.

31. *Xiangling Xian zhi* [Xiangling county gazetteer], compiled and ed. Li Shiyou and Liu Shiliang, in *Zhongguo fangzhi congshu* [Chinese gazetteer series], North China, No. 402 (Taipei: Chengwen Chubanshe, 1923), 1:224; 2:510–11, 533; 3:1105–8, 1154–56, 1453–54, 1464, 1499, 1534–37; Qian Shifu, ed., *Qingdai zhiguan nianbiao* [Chronological list of Qing officials] (Beijing: Zhonghua Shuju, 1980), 2915, 3271.

32. Evelyn Rawski, *Education and Popular Literacy in Ch'ing China* (Ann Arbor: University of Michigan Press, 1979), 140; James Hayes, "Specialists and Written Materials in the Village World," in *Popular Culture in Late Imperial China*, ed. David Johnson, Andrew Nathan, and Evelyn Rawski (Berkeley: University of California Press, 1985), 75–111; Sommer, *Polyandry*, 269–71.

33. Benjamin Elman, "Political, Social, and Cultural Reproduction via Civil Service Examinations in Late Imperial China," *Journal of Asian Studies* 50, no. 1 (1991): 15–19.

34. *Shangfucun zhi*, 91, 93, 96–99, 123, 128–29, 184–88. Similar examples are Fancun and Yangyicun, which were major entrepots on the main trade route through Taigu County (Zhijian Qiao, personal communication, July 2021).

35. Sogou Baike, entry on "Dongxu Cun," https://baike.sogou.com/v73821615.htm (accessed May 28, 2021). One *mu* equals approximately one-third of an acre.

36. I am grateful to Andrea Goldman, Tina Lu, and Catherine Yeh for their insights on this point (personal communications, June 2021).

37. For accounts of senior officials consorting (openly but illegally) with boy actresses, see Wu, *Homoerotic Sensibilities*, 136–49.

38. Thus, for example, Lu Bingchun had been appointed an Investigating Censor for Yunnan after completing his initial training in the Hanlin Academy (see sources cited in endnote 31 of this chapter). Charles Hucker, *A Dictionary of Official Titles in Imperial China* (Stanford, Calif.: Stanford University Press, 1985), nos. 795 and 5278.

39. Bai Juyi, *Bai Juyi quanji* [Collected works of Bai Juyi], ed. Nie Shimei and Ding Ruming (Shanghai: Shanghai Guji Chubanshe, 1999), 121.

40. See, for example, three contracts transcribed in Guo Songyi and Ding Yizhuang, *Qingdai minjian hunshu yanjiu* [Qing dynasty marriage contracts] (Beijing: Renmin Chubanshe, 2005), 13, 53, 292, which all use one or both of these allusions. For handbooks of model contracts, see Hayes, "Specialists," 86–87.

41. McNicholas, *Forgery and Impersonation*, 119.

42. For examples, see McNicholas, figures 5.1 and 5.2.

43. McNicholas, chapter 5. Some of the clergy arrested in the famous soul-stealing dragnet had such paraphernalia in their possession. See Kuhn, *Soulstealers*, 155–56, 160–62.

44. McNicholas, chapter 5.

45. Arthur Hummel, ed., *Eminent Chinese of the Qing Period*, rev. ed. (Great Barrington, Mass.: Berkshire, 2018), 215–18, 793–97. I am grateful to Macabe Keliher and Zhijian Qiao for their thoughts on this matter (personal communications, May 2023).

46. I am grateful to Andrea Goldman and Zhao Mengdie for sharing their insights on this topic (personal communications, June 5, 2021).

47. Guo and Ding, *Qingdai minjian hunshu*, chapter 1. See also Sommer, *Polyandry*, 6–11, 51–54, 302–3.

48. Sommer, 135–40 and sources cited therein.

49. Elman, *Civil Examinations*, 50–53.

50. Matthew H. Sommer, *Sex, Law, and Society in Late Imperial China* (Stanford, Calif.: Stanford University Press, 2000), 99–100, 144–47, 159–61.

51. For the relevant laws, see DC: 42-00; 077-00 and substatutes; 114-00; 175-11; 372-00 and substatutes.

52. Wu, *Homoerotic Sensibilities*, 132–49.

53. All information about Xinxiang's case and related quotations up to this point in the chapter come from XT: 378-9, QL 13.11.5.

54. All information about developments after 1748 comes from this memorial (ZP: 04-01-28-0002-011, QL 23.11.12); some of it is repeated in ZP: 04-01-01-0229-007, QL 24.1.29, which adds nothing new.

55. LK: 2-81-5599-3, QL 24.2.3; otherwise, this document adds no new information.

56. John Moore, *Mulatto, Outlaw, Pilgrim, Priest: The Legal Case of Jose Soller, Accused of Impersonating a Pastor and Other Crimes in Seventeenth-Century Spain* (Leiden: Brill, 2020); William Taylor, *Fugitive Freedom: The Improbable Lives of Two Imposters in Late Colonial Mexico* (Berkeley: University of California Press, 2021); Natalie Zemon Davis, *The Return of Martin Guerre* (Cambridge, Mass.: Harvard University Press, 1983); Frank Abagnale (with Stan Redding), *Catch Me If You Can: The Amazing True Story of the Most Extraordinary Liar in the History of Fun and Profit* (New York: Grosset and Dunlap, 1980).

57. Abagnale, *Catch Me*, 26–27.

58. Abagnale, 45–46.

59. Lawrence Zhang, "Legacy of Success: Office Purchase and State-Elite Relations in Qing China," *Harvard Journal of Asiatic Studies* 73, no. 2 (2013): 268–69.

60. Benjamin Elman, *A Cultural History of Civil Examinations in Late Imperial China* (Berkeley: University of California Pres, 2000), chapter 6.

61. Tristan Brown, *Laws of the Land: Fengshui and the State in Qing Dynasty China* (Princeton, N.J.: Princeton University Press, 2023), chapter 3.

62. *Diagnostic and Statistical Manual of Mental Disorders*, 4th ed. (Washington, D.C.: American Psychiatric Association, 1994), 646–47; for the corresponding diagnosis in children, "conduct disorder," see 85–91.

63. *Diagnostic and Statistical Manual*, 88.

64. *Diagnostic and Statistical Manual*, 647.

65. Thus Kadji Amin characterizes Genet, an "icon of queer radicalism" whose pederasty, racism, and thuggish behavior have attracted increasingly critical attention. See Amin, *Disturbing Attachments: Genet, Modern Pederasty, and Queer History* (Chapel Hill, N.C.: Duke University Press, 2017), 1, 4. As Heather Love quips, Genet might have been "sent over from the deviance studies central casting office"; see *Underdogs: Social Deviance and Queer Theory* (Chicago: University of Chicago Press, 2021), 16.

66. My account of Liz Carmichael is based on the documentary miniseries *The Lady and the Dale*, dir. Nick Cammilleri and Zackary Drucker (HBO, 2021); the quotations from Susan Stryker are from the same source.

Epilogue

1. Personal communication, September 2022, quoted with permission.

2. Susan Stryker, *Transgender History* (Berkeley, Calif.: Seal, 2008), 1.

3. Judith Butler, *Gender Trouble: Feminism and the Subversion of Identity* (New York: Routledge, 1990).

4. Matthew H. Sommer, *Sex, Law, and Society in Late Imperial China* (Stanford, Calif.: Stanford University Press, 2000), especially 162–63, 306–7. The one exception I have found to this invisibility is the case of Zhou Sijie discussed in chapter 6 in this volume.

5. XA, 10: 22b–23a. See also the brief discussion in Marinus Meijer, "Homosexual Offenses in Ch'ing Law," *T'oung Pao* 71 (1985): 115, which is based on the relevant passage in the *Conspectus*.

6. Matthew H. Sommer, *Polyandry and Wife-Selling in Qing Dynasty China: Survival Strategies and Judicial Interventions* (Berkeley: University of California Press, 2015), 17–18.

7. T'ung-tsu Ch'ü, *Local Government in China Under the Ch'ing*, rev. ed. (Cambridge, Mass.: Harvard University Press, 1962); Bradly Reed, *Talons and Teeth: County Clerks and Runners in the Qing Dynasty* (Stanford, Calif.: Stanford University Press, 2000); Sommer, *Polyandry*, conclusion.

8. Sommer, *Sex*, 124–26.

9. Personal communications, spring 2021 and summer 2022.

10. The community's confusion about Zhang is reminiscent of that in the case of Virginian colonist Thomas/ine Hall, who was forcibly stripped and examined more than once, but whose ambiguous anatomy confounded observers. See Kathleen Brown, " 'Changed... into the Fashion of Man': The Politics of Sexual Difference in a Seventeenth-Century Anglo-American Settlement," *Journal of the History of Sexuality* 6, no. 2 (1995): 171–93.

11. The actual animal is the Siberian weasel *Mustela sibirica* (*huang shulang*, literally "yellow weasel").

12. Xiaofei Kang, *The Cult of the Fox: Power, Gender, and Popular Religion in Late Imperial and Modern China* (New York: Columbia University Press, 2006), 137–47; see also Kenneth Pomeranz, "Power, Gender, and Pluralism in the Cult of the Goddess of Taishan," in *Culture and State in Chinese History: Conventions, Accommodations, and Critiques*, ed. Theodore Huters, Roy Wong, and Pauline Yu (Stanford, Calif.: Stanford University Press, 1997), 182–204; and Pomeranz, "Orthopraxy, Orthodoxy, and the Goddess(es) of Taishan," *Modern China* 33, no. 1 (2007): 22–46.

13. Sommer, *Sex*; and Sommer, *Polyandry*.

14. Sommer, *Polyandry*; see also Susan Naquin, *Millenarian Rebellion in China: The Eight Trigrams Uprising of 1813* (New Haven, Conn.: Yale University Press, 1976); Joseph Esherick, *The Origins of the Boxer Uprising* (Berkeley: University of California Press, 1987); Pomeranz, "Power, Gender, and Pluralism"; and Donald Sutton, ed., "Ritual, Cultural Standardization, and Orthopraxy in China: Reconsidering James L. Watson's Ideas," special issue of *Modern China* 33, no. 1 (2007).

References

Abbreviations Used in Citations

BD—Baodi County (Shuntian Prefecture) Archive. Held at the First Historical Archive, Beijing, microfilm available at Stanford University's East Asia Library (each case is cited by the number of the bundle in which it was stored in 1992 and by the date of the earliest dated document in the case; all are from the archival category of "Marriage, Sex Offenses, and Family Disputes").

BX—Ba County Archive. Held at Sichuan Provincial Archive, Chengdu (each case is identified by serial number and Chinese date).

DC—Xue Yunsheng. *Duli cunyi chongkanben* (A new edition of *Lingering doubts upon perusing the substatutes*), punctuated and edited by Huang Jingjia. Taipei: Chinese Materials and Research Aids Service Center, 1970 (cited by serial number).

LF—*Lufu zouzhe* (Grand Council files copies of secret palace memorials), held at the First Historical Archive, Beijing (cited by serial number).

LK—*Like tiben* (Grand Secretariat routine memorials on personnel matters), held at the First Historical Archive, Beijing (cited by serial number, Chinese date).

MQ—Chang We-jen [Zhang Weiren], ed. *Zhongyang Yanjiuyuan Lishi-yuyan Yanjiusuo xian cun Qingdai Neige Daku yuan cang Ming-Qing dang'an* (Ming-Qing documents from the Qing dynasty Grand Secretariat archive in the possession of the History and Language Research Institute, Academia Sinica). Taipei: Academia Sinica, 1986 (cited by serial number).

NB—Nanbu County Archive. Held at the Nanchong Municipal Archive, Nanchong (each case is cited by serial number, Chinese date).

QH—*Qing huidian shili* (Collected statutes of the Qing, with substatutes based on precedent). Beijing: Zhonghua Shuju [1899] 1991.

XA—Zhu Qingqi, Bao Shuyun, Pan Wenfang, and He Weikai, eds. *Xing'an huilan san bian* (*Conspectus of Penal Cases*, with two sequels). 4 vols. Beijing: Beijing Guji Chubanshe, 2004.

XT—*Neige xingke tiben* (Grand Secretariat routine memorials on criminal matters), held at the First Historical Archive, Beijing (cases are cited by serial number, Chinese date; all are from the archival category "marriage and sex offenses").

ZP—*Zhupi zouzhe* (Secret palace memorials), held at the First Historical Archive, Beijing (cited by serial number).

Online Media Cited

Baidu search engine, https://baike.baidu.com/.

Dianshizhai Pictorial, https://www.bnasie.eu/BN/Books?ID=346, accessed at Stanford University's East Asia Library.

Google Maps, https://google.com/maps/.

Handian Chinese dictionary, https://www.zdic.net/.

Neige Daku Dang'an (Grand Secretariat Archives) online database, Academia Sinica, Taiwan, https://digitalarchives.tw/, accessed at Stanford University's East Asia Library.

Shenbao, http://shunpao.egreenapple.com/WEB/INDEX.html, accessed at Stanford University's East Asia Library.

Sogou search engine, https://baike.sogou.com/v73821615.htm.

Other Works Cited

Abagnale, Frank, with Stan Redding. *Catch Me If You Can: The Amazing True Story of the Most Extraordinary Liar in the History of Fun and Profit*. New York: Grosset and Dunlap, 1980.

Abbou, Julie, and Angela Tse. "A Hermeneutical Approach of Gender Linguistic Materiality: Semiotic and Structural Categorisation of Gender in Hong Kong Cantonese." In *Gender, Language, and the Periphery: Grammatical and Social Gender from the Margins*, ed. Julie Abbou and Fabienne Baider, 89–128. Amsterdam: John Benjamins, 2016.

Ahern, Emily. "The Power and Pollution of Chinese Women." In *Studies in Chinese Society*, ed. Arthur P. Wolf, 269–90. Stanford, Calif.: Stanford University Press, 1978.

Ahn, Byungil. "Modernization, Revolution, and Midwifery Reforms in Twentieth-Century China." PhD diss., University of California, Los Angeles, 2011.

Aisin-Gioro Pu Yi. *From Emperor to Citizen: The Autobiography of Aisin-Gioro Pu Yi*. Translated by W. J. F. Jenner. Oxford: Oxford University Press, 1987.

Alcoff, Linda. "Cultural Feminism Versus Post-Structuralism: The Identity Crisis in Feminist Theory." In *The Second Wave: A Reader in Feminist Theory*, edited by Linda Nicholson, 330–55. New York: Routledge, 1997.

Altenburger, Roland. "Is It the Clothes That Make the Man? Cross-Dressing, Gender, and Sex in Pre-Twentieth-Century Zhu Yingtai Lore." *Asian Folklore Studies* 64, no. 2 (2005): 165–205.

———. *The Sword or the Needle: The Female Knight-Errant (xia) in Traditional Chinese Narrative.* Bern: Peter Lang, 2009.

Ames, Roger. "Taoism and the Androgynous Ideal." *Historical Reflections / Reflexions Historiques* 8, no. 3 (1981): 21–45.

Amin, Kadji. *Disturbing Attachments: Genet, Modern Pederasty, and Queer History.* Chapel Hill, N.C.: Duke University Press, 2017.

Anzani, Annalisa, Louis Lindley, Giacomo Tognasso, M. Paz Galupo, and Antonio Prunas. "'Being Talked to Like I Was a Sex Toy, Like Being Transgender Was Simply for the Enjoyment of Someone Else': Fetishization and Sexualization of Transgender and Nonbinary Individuals." *Archives of Sexual Behavior* 50 (2021): 897–911.

Bai Juyi. *Bai Juyi quanji* [Collected works of Bai Juyi]. Edited by Nie Shimei and Ding Ruming. Shanghai: Shanghai Guji Chubanshe, 1999.

Baptandier, Brigitte. *The Lady of Linshui: A Chinese Female Cult.* Stanford, Calif.: Stanford University Press, 2008.

———. "The Lady Linshui: How a Woman Became a Goddess." In *Unruly Gods: Divinity and Society in China*, edited by Meir Shahar & Robert Weller, 105–49. Honolulu: University of Hawai'i Press, 1996.

Barlow, Tani. "Theorizing Woman: *Funü, Guojia, Jiating* (Chinese Women, Chinese State, Chinese Family)." In *Body, Subject, and Power in China*, edited by Angela Zito and Tani Barlow, 253–89. Chicago: University of Chicago Press, 1994.

Bettcher, Talia Mae. "Evil Deceivers and Make-Believers: On Transphobic Violence and the Politics of Illusion." *Hypatia* 22, no. 3 (2007): 43–65.

Bian, He. *Know Your Remedies: Pharmacy and Culture in Early Modern China.* Princeton, N.J.: Princeton University Press, 2020.

Birch, Cyril, trans. *The Peony Pavilion.* Boston: Cheng and Tsui, 1980.

Bliss, Molly. "Datura Plant Poisoning." *Clinical Toxicology Review* 23, no. 6 (2001): 1–2.

Boag, Peter. *Re-Dressing America's Frontier Past.* Berkeley: University of California Press, 2011.

Bodde, Derk, and Clarence Morris. *Law in Imperial China: Exemplified by 190 Ch'ing Dynasty Cases, Translated from the Xing-an hui-lan.* Cambridge, Mass.: Harvard University Press, 1967.

Bray, Francesca. *Technology and Gender: Fabrics of Power in Late Imperial China.* Berkeley: University of California Press, 1997.

Brown, Kathleen. "'Changed . . . into the Fashion of Man': The Politics of Sexual Difference in a Seventeenth-Century Anglo-American Settlement." *Journal of the History of Sexuality* 6, no. 2 (1995): 171–93.

Brown, Tristan. *Laws of the Land: Fengshui and the State in Qing Dynasty China.* Princeton, N.J.: Princeton University Press, 2023.

Brownmiller, Susan. *Against Our Will: Men, Women, and Rape.* New York: Simon and Schuster, 1975.

Bunkenborg, Mikkel. "Popular Religion Inside Out: Gender and Ritual Revival in a Hebei Township." *China Information* 26, no. 3 (2012): 359–76.

Burton-Rose, Daniel. "Gendered Androgyny: Transcendent Ideals and Profane Realities in Buddhism, Classicism, and Daoism." In *Transgender China*, edited by Howard Chiang, 67–96. New York: Palgrave Macmillan, 2012.

Butler, Judith. *Gender Trouble: Feminism and the Subversion of Identity*. New York: Routledge, 1990.

Cammilleri, Nick, and Zackary Drucker, dirs. *The Lady and the Dale*. HBO, 2021.

Cassel, Par. *Grounds of Judgment: Extraterritoriality and Imperial Power in Nineteenth-Century China and Japan*. Oxford: Oxford University Press, 2012.

Castle, Terry. *The Apparitional Lesbian: Female Homosexuality and Modern Culture*. New York: Columbia University Press, 1993.

——. *The Female Thermometer: Eighteenth-Century Culture and the Invention of the Uncanny*. Oxford: Oxford University Press, 1995.

Chan, Leo Tak-hung. *The Discourse on Foxes and Ghosts: Ji Yun and Eighteenth-Century Literati Storytelling*. Honolulu: University of Hawai'i Press, 1998.

Chauncey, George. *Gay New York: Gender, Urban Culture, and the Making of the Gay Male World*. New York: Basic Books, 1994.

Chen Fangsheng. *Yi yu jian* [Notes on difficult cases]. In *Xu xiu si ku quan shu* [A continuation of the complete works of the Four Treasuries], vol. 974. Shanghai: Shanghai Guji Chubanshe, 1691.

Chen, Gilbert Zhe. "Castration and Connection: Kinship Organization Among Ming Eunuchs." *Ming Studies* 74 (2016): 27–47.

——. "Living in This World: A Social History of Buddhist Monks and Nuns in Nineteenth-Century Western China." PhD diss., Washington University in St. Louis, 2019.

Cheng, Hsiao-wen. "Before Sexual and Normal: Shifting Categories of Sexual Anomaly from Ancient to Yuan China." *Asia Major* 31, no. 2 (2018): 1–39.

——. *Divine, Demonic, and Disordered: Women Without Men in Song Dynasty China*. Seattle: University of Washington Press, 2021.

Chiang, Howard. *After Eunuchs: Science, Medicine, and the Transformation of Sex in Modern China*. New York: Columbia University Press, 2018.

——. *Transtopia in the Sinophone Pacific*. New York: Columbia University Press, 2021.

Chiang, Howard, ed. *Transgender China*. New York: Palgrave Macmillan, 2012.

Ch'ü, T'ung-tsu. *Local Government in China under the Ch'ing*. Rev. ed. Cambridge, Mass.: Harvard University Press, 1962.

Cline, Erin. "Female Spirit Mediums and Religious Authority in Contemporary Southeastern China." *Modern China* 36, no. 5 (2010): 520–55.

Conner, Alison. "Chinese Confessions and the Use of Torture." In *La torture judiciaire: approaches historiques et juridiques*, vol. 1., edited by Bernard Durand and Leah Otis-Cours, 63–91. Lille: Centre de Histoire Judiciare, Universite de Lille, 2002.

Currah, Paisley. "Gender Pluralisms under the Transgender Umbrella." In *Transgender Rights*, ed. Paisley Currah, Richard Juang, and Shannon Price Minter, 3–31. Minneapolis: University of Minnesota Press, 2006.

Dale, Melissa. *Inside the World of the Eunuch: A Social History of the Emperor's Servants in Qing China*. Hong Kong: Hong Kong University Press, 2018.

Davis, Natalie Zemon. *The Return of Martin Guerre*. Cambridge, Mass.: Harvard University Press, 1983.

De Groot, J. J. M. *Sectarianism and Religious Persecution in China*. Leiden: Brill, 1901.

Dekker, Rudolf, and Lotte van de Pol. *The Tradition of Female Transvestism in Early Modern Europe*. New York: St. Martin's, 1989.

Deng, Claire Qiuju. *Action-Taking Gods: Animal Spirit Shamanism in Liaoning, China*. Master's thesis, McGill University, 2014.

Despeux, Catherine and Livia Kohn. *Women in Daoism*. Cambridge, Mass.: Three Pines, 2003.

Diagnostic and Statistical Manual of Mental Disorders. 4th ed. Washington, D.C.: American Psychiatric Association, 1994.

Diamond, Norma. "The Miao and Poison: Interactions on China's Southwest Frontier." *Ethnology* 27, no. 1 (1988): 1–25.

Dong, Madeleine. "Communities and Communication: A Study of the Case of Yang Naiwu, 1873–1877." *Late Imperial China* 16, no. 1 (1995): 79–119.

Doolittle, Justus. *Social Life of the Chinese*. New York: Harper and Brothers, 1865.

Dorfman, Diane. "The Spirits of Reform: The Power of Belief in Northern China." *Positions* 4, no. 2 (1996): 253–89.

Dray-Novey, Alison. "Spatial Order and Police in Imperial Beijing." *Journal of Asian Studies* 52, no. 4 (1993): 885–922.

DuBois, Thomas. "Religious Healing in the People's Republic of China." In *Chinese Medicine and Healing: An Illustrated History*, edited by T. J. Hinrichs and Linda Barnes, 277–78. Cambridge, Mass.: Belknap Press of Harvard University Press, 2013.

——. *The Sacred Village: Social Change and Religious Life in Rural North China*. Honolulu: University of Hawai'i Press, 2005.

Edwards, Louise. *Woman Warriors and Wartime Spies of China*. Cambridge: Cambridge University Press, 2016.

Elliott, Alan. *Chinese Spirit-Medium Cults in Singapore*. London: London School of Economics and Political Science, 1955.

Elliott, Mark. *The Manchu Way: The Eight Banners and Ethnic Identity in Late Imperial China*. Stanford, Calif.: Stanford University Press, 2001.

Elman, Benjamin. *Civil Examinations and Meritocracy in Late Imperial China*. Cambridge, Mass.: Harvard University Press, 2013.

——. *A Cultural History of Civil Examinations in Late Imperial China*. Berkeley: University of California Press, 2000.

——. "Political, Social, and Cultural Reproduction via Civil Service Examinations in Late Imperial China." *Journal of Asian Studies* 50, no. 1 (1991): 7–28.

Elvin, Mark. "Female Virtue and the State in China." *Past and Present* 104 (1984): 111–52.

Epstein, Maram. "Engendering Order: Structure, Gender, and Meaning in the Qing Novel *Jinghua yuan*." *Chinese Literature: Essays, Articles, Reviews (CLEAR)* 18 (1996): 101–27.

Esherick, Joseph. *The Origins of the Boxer Uprising.* Berkeley: University of California Press, 1987.

Faderman, Lillian. *Surpassing the Love of Men: Romantic Friendship and Love Between Women from the Renaissance to the Present.* New York: William R. Morrow, 1981.

Feder, Sam, dir. *Disclosure: Trans Lives on Screen.* Netflix, 2020.

Feinberg, Leslie. *Stone Butch Blues: 20th Anniversary Edition.* Self-published by author for open access, 2014 (www.lesliefeinberg.net).

——. *Transgender Warriors: Making History from Joan of Arc to Dennis Rodman.* Boston: Beacon, 1996.

Finnane, Antonia. *Changing Clothes in China: Fashion, History, Nation.* New York: Columbia University Press, 2008.

Flowers, Stephen. *Lords of the Left-Hand Path: A History of Spiritual Dissent.* Rochester, Vt.: Inner Traditions, 1997.

Foucault, Michel. *The History of Sexuality, Volume 1: Introduction.* New York: Random House, 1978.

Furth, Charlotte. "Androgynous Males and Deficient Females: Biology and Gender Boundaries in Sixteenth- and Seventeenth-Century China." *Late Imperial China* 9, no. 2 (1988): 1–31.

——. "Concepts of Pregnancy, Childbirth, and Infancy in Ch'ing Dynasty China." *Journal of Asian Studies* 46, no. 1 (1987): 7–35.

——. *A Flourishing Yin: Gender in China's Medical History, 960–1665.* Berkeley: University of California Press, 1999.

Gates, Hill. *Footbinding and Women's Labor in Sichuan.* New York: Routledge, 2015.

Gilmartin, Christina. *Engendering the Chinese Revolution: Radical Women, Communist Politics, and Mass Movements in the 1920s.* Berkeley: University of California Press, 1995.

Gill-Peterson, Jules. *Histories of the Transgender Child.* Minneapolis: University of Minnesota Press, 2018.

Glatstein, Miguel, Fatoumah Alabdulrazzaq, and Dennis Scolnik. "Belladonna Alkaloid Intoxication." *American Journal of Therapeutics* 23 (2016): 74–77.

Goldin, Paul. *The Culture of Sex in Ancient China.* Honolulu: University of Hawai'i Press, 2002.

Goldman, Andrea. *Opera and the City: The Politics of Culture in Beijing, 1770–1900.* Stanford, Calif.: Stanford University Press, 2012.

Goodrich, Anne. *Peking Paper Gods: A Look at Home Worship.* Nettetal: Steyler Verlag, 1991.

Goossaert, Vincent. "Counting the Monks: The 1736–1739 Census of the Chinese Clergy." *Late Imperial China* 21, no. 2 (2000): 40–85.

——. "The Destruction of Immoral Temples in Qing China." In *Institute of Chinese Studies Visiting Professor Lectures Series* 2, 131–53. Hong Kong: Chinese University Press, 2009.

——. "Irrepressible Female Piety: Late Imperial Bans on Women Visiting Temples." *Nan Nü* 10 (2008): 212–41.

——. "The Quanzhen Clergy, 1700–1950." In *Religion and Chinese Society*, edited by John Lagerwey, 699–772. Hong Kong: Chinese University Press, 2004.

——. *The Taoists of Peking, 1800–1949: A Social History of Urban Clerics.* Cambridge, Mass.: Harvard University Asia Center, 2007.

Grant, Beata. *Eminent Nuns: Women Chan Masters of Seventeenth-Century China*. Honolulu: University of Hawai'i Press, 2009.

Grant, Beata, and Wilt Idema. *Escape from Blood Pond Hell: The Tales of Mulian and Woman Huang*. Seattle: University of Washington Press, 2011.

Guo Songyi, and Ding Yizhuang. *Qingdai minjian hunshu yanjiu* [Qing dynasty marriage contracts]. Beijing: Renmin Chubanshe, 2005.

Guo, Weiting. "The Speed of Justice: Summary Execution and Legal Culture in Qing Dynasty China, 1644–1912." PhD diss., University of British Columbia, 2016.

Halberstam, J. *Female Masculinity*. Durham, N.C.: Duke University Press, 1998.

——. "Telling Tales: Brandon Teena, Billy Tipton, and Transgender Biography." *a/b: Auto/Biography Studies* 15, no. 1 (2000): 62–81.

Halberstam, J., and C. Jacob Hale. "Butch/FTM Border Wars: A Note on Collaboration." *GLQ* 4, no. 2 (1998): 311–48.

Hale, C. Jacob. "Consuming the Living, Dis(re)membering the Dead in the Butch/FTM Borderlands." *GLQ* 4, no. 2 (1998): 283–85.

Halperin, David. "Is There a History of Sexuality?" *History and Theory* 28, no. 3 (1989): 257–74.

Hammond, Charles. "Vulpine Alchemy." *T'oung Pao* 82, 4/5 (1996): 364–80.

Hansson, Anders. *Chinese Outcasts: Discrimination and Emancipation in Late Imperial China*. Leiden: Brill, 1996.

Hanyu dacidian [Great dictionary of Chinese]. Shanghai: Shanghai Cishu Chubanshe, 2008.

Hawkesworth, Mary. "Confounding Gender." *Signs* 22 (1997): 649–85.

Hayes, James. "Specialists and Written Materials in the Village World." In *Popular Culture in Late Imperial China*, edited by David Johnson, Andrew Nathan, and Evelyn Rawski, 75–111. Berkeley: University of California Press, 1985.

He Jiangli. *Minguo Beijing de gonggong weisheng* [Public health in Republican-era Beijing]. Beijing: Beijing Shifan Daxue Chubanshe, 2016.

Hejiang xianzhi [Hejiang County Gazetteer]. Taibei: Taiwan Xuesheng Shuju, [1929] 1967.

Helmholz, R. H. *Marriage Litigation in Medieval England*. Cambridge: Cambridge University Press, 1974.

Herrou, Adeline. "Daoist Monasticism at the Turn of the Twenty-First Century: An Ethnography of a Quanzhen Community in Shaanxi Province." In *Daoism in the Twentieth Century: Between Eternity and Modernity*, edited by David Palmer and Xun Liu, 82–107. Berkeley: University of California Press, 2012.

——. *A World of Their Own: Daoist Monks and Their Community in Contemporary China*. St. Petersburg, Fla.: Three Pines, 2013.

Hinchy, Jessica. *Governing Gender and Sexuality in Colonial India: The Hijra, c. 1850–1900*. Cambridge: Cambridge University Press, 2019.

Hinsch, Bret. *Passions of the Cut Sleeve: The Male Homosexual Tradition in China*. Berkeley: University of California Press, 1992.

Hirschfeld, Magnus. *Transvestites: The Erotic Drive to Cross-Dress*. Translated by Michael A. Lombardi-Nash. Buffalo, N.Y.: Prometheus, 1991.

Hoeckelmann, Michael. "Celibate but Not Childless: Eunuch Military Dynasticism in Medieval China." In *Celibate and Childless Men in Power: Ruling Eunuchs and Bishops in the Pre-Modern World*, edited by Almut Hofert, Matthew Mesley, and Serena Tolino, 111–28. London: Routledge, 2018.

Hsiao, Kung-chuan. *Rural China: Imperial Control in the Nineteenth Century*. Seattle: University of Washington Press, 1960.

Huang, Philip C. C. *Civil Justice in China: Representation and Practice in the Qing*. Stanford, Calif.: Stanford University Press, 1996.

Huang Xingtao. *"Ta" zi de wenhuashi—Nüxing xin daici de faming yu rentong yanjiu* [A cultural history of the Chinese character *"ta"* / she: on the invention and identity of a new female pronoun]. Fuzhou: Fujian Jiaoyu Chubanshe, 2009.

Huang Zhangjian, ed. *Ming dai lü li hui bian* [Compendium of Ming dynasty statutes and substatutes]. Taipei: Zhongyang Yanjiuyuan Lishi Yuyan Yanjiusuo, 1994.

Hucker, Charles. *A Dictionary of Official Titles in Imperial China*. Stanford, Calif.: Stanford University Press, 1985.

Hummel, Arthur. *Eminent Chinese of the Qing Period*. Rev. ed. Great Barrington, Mass.: Berkshire, 2018.

Hunt, Lynn. *Inventing Human Rights: A History*. New York: W. W. Norton, 2007.

Huntington, Rania. *Alien Kind: Foxes and Late Imperial Chinese Narrative*. Cambridge, Mass.: Harvard University Asia Center, 2003.

——. "The Weird in the Newspaper." In *Writing and Materiality in China: Essays in Honor of Patrick Hanan*, edited by Judith Zeitlin and Lydia Liu, 341–96. Leiden: Brill, 2003.

Idema, Wilt. "Female Talent and Female Virtue: Xu Wei's *Nü zhuangyuan* and Meng Chengshun's *Zhenwen ji*." In *Ming-Qing xiqu guoji yantaohui lunwen ji* [Papers from the International Symposium on Ming-Qing drama], vol. 2, edited by Hua Wei and Wang Ailing, 551–71. Taipei: Zhongyangyuan Wenzhesuo Choubeichu, 1998.

——. *The Butterfly Lovers: The Legend of Liang Shanbo and Zhu Yingtai, Four Versions with Related Texts*. Indianapolis: Hackett, 2010.

Ishibashi Ushio. *Hokuhei no shamankyō ni tsuite* [Shamanism in Beijing]. Japan (n.p.): Cultural Affairs Department, Japanese Foreign Ministry, 1934.

Jacobs, Sue-Ellen, Wesley Thomas, and Sabine Lang, eds. *Two-Spirit People: Native American Gender Identity, Sexuality, and Spirituality*. Urbana: University of Illinois Press, 1997.

Jansen, Suze, Iris Kleerekooper, Zonne Hofman, Isabelle Kappen, Anna Stary-Weinzinger, and Marcel van der Heyden. "Grayanotoxin Poisoning: 'Mad Honey Disease' and Beyond." *Cardiovascular Toxicology* 12 (2012): 208–15.

Jay, Jennifer. "Another Side of Chinese Eunuch History: Castration, Marriage, Adoption, and Burial." *Canadian Journal of History* 28 (1993): 459–78.

——. "Imagining Matriarchy: 'Kingdoms of Women' in Tang China." *Journal of the American Oriental Society* 116, no. 2 (1996): 220–29.

Jiang, Yonglin, trans. *The Great Ming Code*. Seattle: University of Washington Press, 2005.

Jin Xiage, ed. *Yuan Zicai pandu jinghua* [Highlights of Yuan Mei's legal judgments]. In *Yuan Mei quanji xinbian* [A new edition of Yuan Mei's collected works], vol. 19. Hangzhou: Zhejhiang Guji Chubanshe, 2015.

Jinpingmei cihua [Plum in the golden vase]. Hong Kong: Xianggang Taiping Shuju, (Ming) 1988.

Jinshang shiliao quanlan [Historical materials on the Shanxi merchants), 11 vols., edited by Shanxi Provincial Government's "Historical Materials on the Shanxi Merchants" Editorial Committee. Taiyuan: Shanxi Renmin Chubanshe, 2006–.

Johnson, David. *Spectacle and Sacrifice: The Ritual Foundations of Village Life in North China.* Cambridge, Mass.: Harvard University Asia Center, 2009.

Jones, William, trans. *The Great Qing Code.* Oxford: Clarendon, 1994.

Jordan, David. *Gods, Ghosts, and Ancestors: The Folk Religion of a Taiwanese Village.* Berkeley: University of California Press, 1972.

Jordan, David, and Daniel Overmyer. *The Flying Phoenix: Aspects of Chinese Sectarianism in Taiwan.* Princeton, N.J.: Princeton University Press, 1986.

Jortay, Coraline. "Pronominal Politics: (Un)Gendering Narrative and Framing Ambiguity in Chinese Literature, 1917–1937." PhD diss., University libre de Bruxelles, 2020.

Jourian, T. J. "Evolving Nature of Sexual Orientation and Gender Identity." *New Directions for Student Services* 152 (2015): 11–23.

Judge, Joan. *The Precious Raft of History: The Past, the West, and the Woman Question in China.* Stanford, Calif.: Stanford University Press, 2008.

Kafer, Alison. "Compulsory Bodies: Reflections on Heterosexuality and Able-bodiedness." *Journal of Women's History* 15, no 3 (2003): 77–89.

Kang, Wenqing. *Obsession: Male Same-Sex Relations in China, 1900–1950.* Hong Kong: Hong Kong University Press, 2009.

Kang, Xiaofei. *The Cult of the Fox: Power, Gender, and Popular Religion in Late Imperial and Modern China.* New York: Columbia University Press, 2006.

Karasawa, Yasuhiko. "Between Oral and Written Cultures: Buddhist Monks in Qing Legal Plaints." In *Writing and Law in Imperial China: Crime, Conflict, and Judgment,* edited by Robert Hegel and Katherine Carlitz, 64–80. Seattle: University of Washington Press, 2007.

Kieschnick, John. *The Eminent Monk: Buddhist Ideals in Medieval Chinese Hagiography.* Honolulu: University of Hawai'i Press, 1997.

Kile, Sarah. "Transgender Performance in Early Modern China." *Differences: A Journal of Feminist Cultural Studies* 24, no. 2 (2013): 130–49.

Kim, Nanny. "New Wine in Old Bottles? Making and Reading an Illustrated Magazine from Late Nineteenth-Century Shanghai." In *Joining the Global Public: Word, Image, and City in Early Chinese Newspapers, 1870–1910,* edited by Rudolf Wagner, 175–200. Albany: State University of New York Press, 2007.

Ko, Dorothy. "The Body as Attire: The Shifting Meanings of Footbinding in Seventeenth-Century China." *Journal of Women's History* 8, no. 4 (1997): 8–27.

——. *Cinderella's Sisters: A Revisionist History of Footbinding.* Berkeley: University of California Press, 2005.

——. *Teachers of the Inner Chambers: Women and Culture in Seventeenth-Century China.* Stanford, Calif.: Stanford University Press, 1994.

Kuhn, Philip. *Soulstealers: The Chinese Sorcery Scare of 1768.* Cambridge, Mass.: Harvard University Press, 1990.

Kunzel, Regina. *Criminal Intimacy: Prison and the Uneven History of Modern American Sexuality.* Chicago: University of Chicago Press, 2008.

Kuo, Margaret. *Intolerable Cruelty: Marriage, Law, and Society in Early Twentieth-Century China.* Lanham, Md.: Rowman and Littlefield, 2012.

Kutcher, Norman. *Eunuch and Emperor in the Great Age of Qing Rule.* Berkeley: University of California Press, 2018.

Kwa, Shiamin, and Wilt Idema, eds. and trans. *Mulan: Five Versions of a Classic Chinese Legend with Related Texts.* Indianapolis: Hackett, 2010.

Lai, Cathy. "'X 也'and 'Ta:' The Gradual Rise of Gender-Neutral Pronouns in Chinese." *Ariana,* July 10, 2020. www.arianalife.com.

Lang, Sabine. *Men as Women, Women as Men: Changing Gender in Native American Cultures.* Austin: University of Texas Press, 1998.

Laqueur, Thomas. *Making Sex: Body and Gender from the Greeks to Freud.* Cambridge, Mass.: Harvard University Press, 1990.

Lean, Eugenia. *Public Passions: The Trial of Shi Jianqiao and the Rise of Popular Sympathy in Republican China.* Berkeley: University of California Press, 2007.

Lee, Cynthia, and Peter Kwan. "The Trans Panic Defense: Masculinity, Heteronormativity, and the Murder of Transgender Women." *Hastings Law Journal* 66 (2014): 77–132.

Legge, James, trans. *Li Chi: Book of Rites.* 2 vols. New Hyde Park, N.Y.: University Books, [1885] 1967.

Leung, Angela. "Women Practicing Medicine in Pre-Modern China." In *Chinese Women in the Imperial Past: New Perspectives,* edited by Harriet Zurndorfer, 101–34. Leiden: Brill, 1999.

Leung, Helen Hok-Sze. "Epilogue: On *Keoi* and the Politics of Pronouns." *Inter-Asia Cultural Studies* 22, no. 2 (2021): 215–17.

Li Erqin. "Qingdai 'kuaxingbiezhe' de richang shenghuo, shengji qiantan" [A preliminary discussion of the daily life and survival of "transgender people" in the Qing dynasty]. *Hebei Shifan Daxue Xuebao* [Journal of Hebei Normal University] 45, no. 3 (2022): 39–44.

Li Jinghan. *Dingxian shehui diaocha* [Social survey of Ding County, Hebei]. Beijing: Zhonghua Pingmin Jiaoyu Cujinhui, 1933.

Li Mengsheng. *Zhongguo jinhui xiaoshuo baihua* [One hundred tales from banned Chinese novels]. Shanghai: Shanghai Guji Chubanshe, 1994.

Li Ruzhen. *Jinghua yuan* [Romance of flowers in the mirror]. Beijing: Renmin Wenxue Chubanshe, 1990.

Li Shizhen. *Bencao gangmu xin jiaozhu ben.* New annotated edition of *Systematic Materia Medica.* Beijing: Huaxia Chubanshe, 1998.

Li, Siu Leung. *Cross-Dressing in Chinese Opera.* Hong Kong: Hong Kong University Press, 2003.

Li, Wai-yee. *Women and National Trauma in Late Imperial Chinese Literature.* Cambridge, Mass.: Harvard University Asia Center, 2014.

Li Weizu [Li, Wei-tsu]. "On the Cult of the Four Sacred Animals (*Szu ta men*) in the Neighbourhood of Peking." *Folklore Studies* 7 (1948): 1–94.

——. *Sidamen: Lishi yu shehui* [The four sacred animals: history and society). Edited by Zhou Xing. Beijing: Beijing Daxue Chubanshe, 2011.

Li ji zhengyi [The book of rites, correct meaning]. In *Shisan jing zhushu* [The thirteen classics, annotated]. Shanghai: Shanghai Guji Chubanshe, 1997.

Li Yu. *Shi'er lou* [Twelve towers]. In *Si jia mi cang jinhui xiaoshuo jinghua* [Best banned books from private collections], vol. 11. Beijing: Xinhua Shudian, 2001.

——. *Silent Operas*. Edited and translated by Patrick Hanan. Hong Kong: Chinese University of Hong Kong, 1990.

Li, Yunxin. "The Inner Court and Politics in the Han Empire." PhD diss., Stanford University, 2022.

Lin Fushi. "Yizhe huo bingren—Tongji zai Taiwan shehui zhong de juese yu xingxiang" [Healers or patients: the shamans' role and image in Taiwan]. *Zhongyang Yanjiuyuan Lishi Yuyan Yanjiusuo jikan* [Quarterly Journal of the Institute of History and Philology, Academia Sinica] 76, no. 3 (2005): 511–68.

Ling Mengchu. *Chuke pai an jing qi* [Slapping the table in amazement, vol. 1]. Changsha: Yuelu Shushe, 2003.

Liu, Kwang-Ching. "Appendix: A Note on the Usage of the Chinese Terms for Heterodoxy." In *Heterodoxy in Late Imperial China*, edited by Kwang-Ching Liu and Richard Shek, 477–89. Honolulu: University of Hawai'i Press, 2004.

Liu, Kwang-Ching and Richard Shek, eds. *Heterodoxy in Late Imperial China*. Honolulu: University of Hawai'i Press, 2004.

Liu, Lydia. *Translingual Practice: Literature, National Culture, and Translated Modernity—China, 1900–1937*. Stanford, Calif.: Stanford University Press, 1995.

Love, Heather. *Underdogs: Social Deviance and Queer Theory*. Chicago: University of Chicago Press, 2021.

Lu Can. *Gengsi bian* [Notes from the last two years of the Zhengde reign]. In *Ming Qing biji shiliao* [Historical materials from Ming-Qing notation books], vol. 99, edited by Zhongguo Guji Zhengli Yanjiuhui. Beijing: Zhongguo Shudian, 2000.

Lu, Hanchao. *Street Criers: A Cultural History of Chinese Beggars*. Stanford, Calif.: Stanford University Press, 2005.

Lu, Weijing. *True to Her Word: The Faithful Maiden Cult in Late Imperial China*. Stanford, Calif.: Stanford University Press, 2008.

Lüliguan [Bureau of the Code, Board of Punishment], ed. *Lüliguan jiaozheng Xiyuan lu* [*The Washing Away of Wrongs*], edited and corrected by the Bureau of the Code]. In *Xuxiu siku quanshu*, vol. 972, 253–24. Shanghai: Shanghai guji chubanshe, [1742] 1995.

Mackerras, Colin. "Peking Opera Before the Twentieth Century." *Comparative Drama* 28, no. 1 (1994): 19–42.

——. *The Rise of the Peking Opera, 1770–1870*. London: Oxford University Press, 1972.

MacKinnon, Catherine. *Toward a Feminist Theory of the State*. Cambridge, Mass.: Harvard University Press, 1989.

Mair, Victor. "Language and Ideology in the Written Popularizations of the Sacred Edict." In *Popular Culture in Late Imperial China*, edited by David Johnson, Andrew Nathan, and Evelyn Rawski, 325–59. Berkeley: University of California Press, 1985.

Manion, Jen. *Female Husbands: A Trans History.* Cambridge: Cambridge University Press, 2020.

Mann, Susan. *Precious Records: Women in China's Long Eighteenth Century.* Stanford, Calif.: Stanford University Press, 1997.

——. *The Talented Women of the Zhang Family.* Berkeley: University of California Press, 2007.

Marcus, Sharon. "Fighting Bodies, Fighting Words: A Theory and Politics of Rape Prevention." In *Feminists Theorize the Political,* edited by Judith Butler and Joan Scott, 385–403. New York: Routledge, 1992.

Martel, Frederic. *In the Closet of the Vatican: Power, Homosexuality, Hypocrisy.* London: Bloomsbury Continuum, 2020.

Maurer, David. *The Big Con: The Story of the Confidence Men.* New York: Anchor, 1999.

McMahon, R. Keith. "The Art of the Bedchamber and *Jin Ping Mei.*" *Nan Nü* 21 (2019): 1–37.

——. "A Case for Confucian Sexuality: The Eighteenth-Century Novel *Yesou Puyan.*" *Late Imperial China* 9, no. 2 (1988): 32–55.

——. *Causality and Containment in Seventeenth-Century Chinese Fiction.* Leiden: Brill, 1988.

——. *Misers, Shrews, and Polygamists: Sexuality and Male-Female Relations in Eighteenth-Century Chinese Fiction.* Durham, N.C.: Duke University Press, 1995.

——. "Women Rulers in Imperial China." *Nan Nü* 15, no. 2 (2013): 179–218.

McNicholas, Mark. *Forgery and Impersonation in Imperial China: Popular Deceptions and the High Qing State.* Seattle: University of Washington Press, 2016.

McRuer, Robert. *Crip Theory: Cultural Signs of Queerness and Disability.* New York: New York University Press, 2006.

Meeks, Lori. "Women and Buddhism in East Asian History: The Case of the Blood Bowl Sutra, Part 1: China." *Religion Compass* 14, no. 4 (2020): 1–14.

Meijer, Marinus. "Homosexual Offenses in Ch'ing Law." *T'oung Pao* 71 (1985): 109–33.

——. *Murder and Adultery in Late Imperial China: A Study of Law and Morality.* Leiden: Brill, 1991.

Mesch, Rachel. *Before Trans: Three Gender Stories from Nineteenth-Century France.* Stanford, Calif.: Stanford University Press, 2020.

Meyerowitz, Joanne. *How Sex Changed: A History of Transsexuality in the United States.* Cambridge, Mass.: Harvard University Press, 2002.

Milburn, Olivia. "Bodily Transformations: Responses to Intersex Individuals in Early and Imperial China." *Nan Nü* 16, no. 1 (2014): 1–28.

Millward, James. "More Hun than Han: Reading the Tabghach 'Ballad of Mulan' in 2020." #AsiaNow, September 17, 2020. https://www.asianstudies.org/more-hun -than-han-reading-the-tabghach-ballad-of-mulan-in-2020/.

Ming shilu [Veritable records of the Ming dynasty]. 183 vols. Nangang: Zhongyang Yanjiuyuan Lishi Yuyan Yanjiusuo, 1962–1968.

Mitamura, Taisuke. *Chinese Eunuchs: The Structure of Intimate Politics.* Trans. Charles Pomeroy. Rutland, Vt.: Tuttle, 1970.

——. *Kangan: Sokkin seiji no kōzō* [Eunuchs: the structure of intimate politics]. Rev. ed. Tokyo: Chūō Kōron Shinsha, 2012.

Mittler, Barbara. *A Newspaper for China? Power, Identity, and Change in Shanghai's News Media, 1872–1912.* Cambridge, Mass.: Harvard University Asia Center, 2004.

Mnookin, Robert, and Lewis Kornhauser. "Bargaining in the Shadow of the Law: The Case of Divorce." *Yale Law Journal* 88, no. 5 (1979): 950–57.

Mock, Janet. *Redefining Realness: My Path to Womanhood, Identity, Love, and So Much More.* New York: Atria, 2014.

Mokros, Emily. *The Peking Gazette in Late Imperial China: State News and Political Authority.* Seattle: University of Washington Press, 2021.

Moore, John. *Mulatto, Outlaw, Pilgrim, Priest: The Legal Case of Jose Soller, Accused of Impersonating a Pastor and Other Crimes in Seventeenth-Century Spain.* Leiden: Brill, 2020.

Nagao Ryūzō. *Shina minzokushi* [Chinese folk customs]. Vols. 1, 2, and 6. Tokyo: Shina Minzokushi Kankōkai, 1940–1942.

Najmabadi, Afsaneh. *Professing Selves: Transsexuality and Same-Sex Desire in Contemporary Iran.* Durham, N.C.: Duke University Press, 2014.

Nanda, Serena. *Neither Man nor Woman: The Hijras of India.* Belmont, Calif.: Wadsworth, 1999.

Nappi, Carla. *The Monkey and the Inkpot: Natural History and Its Transformations in Early Modern China.* Cambridge, Mass.: Harvard University Press, 2009.

Naquin, Susan. *Millenarian Rebellion in China: The Eight Trigrams Uprising of 1813.* New Haven, Conn.: Yale University Press, 1976.

——. *Peking: Temples and City Life, 1400–1900.* Berkeley: University of California Press, 2000.

——. *Shantung Rebellion: The Wang Lun Uprising of 1774.* New Haven, Conn.: Yale University Press, 1981.

Nylan, Michael. *The Five "Confucian" Classics.* New Haven, Conn.: Yale University Press, 2001.

Owen, Rev. G. "Animal Worship Among the Chinese." *Chinese Recorder and Missionary Journal* 18, no. 7 (1887): 249–55.

Overmyer, Daniel. "Attitudes Toward Popular Religion in Ritual Texts of the Chinese State: *The Collected Statutes of the Great Ming.*" *Cahiers d'Extreme-Asie* 5 (1989): 191–221.

——. *Religions of China: The World as a Living System.* San Francisco: Harper and Row, 1986.

Ownby, David. *Brotherhoods and Secret Societies in Early and Mid-Qing China: The Formation of a Tradition.* Stanford, Calif.: Stanford University Press, 1996.

Pan Rongsheng, ed. *Ming Qing jinshi lu* [A record of Ming and Qing dynasty presented scholars]. Beijing: Zhonghua Shuju, 2006.

Park, Nancy. "Imperial Chinese Justice and the Law of Torture." *Late Imperial China* 29, no. 2 (2008): 37–67.

Pelliot, Paul. *Notes on Marco Polo.* 3 vols. Paris: Imprimerie nationale, 1959.

Pilling, Arnold R. "Cross-Dressing and Shamanism Among Selected Western North American Tribes." In *Two-Spirit People: Native American Gender Identity, Sexuality, and Spirituality,* ed. Sue-Ellen Jacobs, Wesley Thomas, and Sabine Lang, 69–99. Urbana: University of Illinois Press, 1997.

Pomeranz, Kenneth. "Orthopraxy, Orthodoxy, and the Goddess(es) of Taishan." *Modern China* 33, no. 1 (2007): 22–46.

———. "Power, Gender, and Pluralism in the Cult of the Goddess of Taishan." In *Culture and State in Chinese History: Conventions, Accommodations, and Critiques*, edited by Theodore Huters, Roy Wong, and Pauline Yu, 182–204. Stanford, Calif.: Stanford University Press, 1997.

Potter, Jack. "Cantonese Shamanism." In *Religion and Ritual in Chinese Society*, edited by Arthur Wolf, 207–31. Stanford, Calif.: Stanford University Press, 1974.

Powers, John. *A Bull of a Man: Images of Masculinity, Sex, and the Body in Indian Buddhism*. Cambridge, Mass.: Harvard University Press, 2009.

Pu Songling. *Liaozhai zhi yi* [Strange tales from the Liao studio]. Shanghai: Shanghai Guji Chubanshe, 1978.

Qian Shifu, ed. *Qingdai zhiguan nianbiao* [Chronological list of Qing officials]. Beijing: Zhonghua Shuju, 1980.

Qiao, Zhijian. "The Rise of Shanxi Merchants: Empire, Institutions, and Social Change in Qing China, 1688–1850." PhD diss., Stanford University, 2017.

Quan Shichao, and Zhang Daoyuan, eds. *Bo'an huibian* [Compilation of cases overturned on review]. Beijing: Falü Chubanshe, 2009.

Raphals, Lisa. "Chinese Philosophy and Chinese Medicine." In *The Stanford Encyclopedia of Philosophy*, edited by Edward Zalta, October 7, 2020. https://plato.stanford.edu /archives/win2020/entries/chinese-phil-medicine/.

Rawski, Evelyn. *Education and Popular Literacy in Ch'ing China*. Ann Arbor: University of Michigan Press, 1979.

———. *The Last Emperors: A Social History of Qing Imperial Institutions*. Berkeley: University of California Press, 1998.

Redburn, Kate. "Before Equal Protection: The Fall of Cross-Dressing Bans and the Transgender Legal Movement, 1963–86." *Law and History Review* 40 (2022): 679–723.

Reddy, Gayatri. *With Respect to Sex: Negotiating Hijra Identity in South India*. Chicago: University of Chicago Press, 2005.

Reed, Bradly. *Talons and Teeth: County Clerks and Runners in the Qing Dynasty*. Stanford, Calif.: Stanford University Press, 2000.

Reed, Christopher. "Re/Collecting the Sources: Shanghai's '*Dianshizhai* Pictorial' and Its Place in Historical Memories, 1884–1949." *Modern Chinese Literature and Culture* 12, no. 2 (2000): 44–71.

Rhoads, Edward. *Manchus and Han: Ethnic Relations and Political Power in Late Qing and Early Republican China, 1861–1928*. Seattle: University of Washington Press, 2000.

Rich, Adrienne. "Compulsory Heterosexuality and Lesbian Existence." *Signs: Journal of Women in Culture and Society* 5, no. 4 (1980): 631–60.

Ropp, Paul. "The Seeds of Change: Reflections on the Condition of Women in the Early and Mid-Ch'ing." *Signs* 2, no. 1 (1976): 5–23.

Ruan Qixin. *Chongkan buzhu Xiyuanlu jizheng* [*The Washing Away of Wrongs*, reprinted with amendments, examples, and commentaries]. Taipei: Wenhai Chubanshe, [1807] 1968.

Rubin, Gayle. "Thinking Sex: Notes for a Radical Theory of the Politics of Sexuality." In *Pleasure and Danger: Exploring Female Sexuality*, edited by Carole Vance, 267–319. Boston: Routledge and Kegan Paul, 1984.

Ruggiero, Guido. *The Boundaries of Eros: Sex Crime and Sexuality in Renaissance Venice.* New York: Oxford University Press, 1985.

Salamon, Gayle. *The Life and Death of Latisha King: A Critical Phenomenology of Transphobia.* New York: New York University Press, 2018.

Sang, Tze-lan Deborah. *The Emerging Lesbian: Female Same-Sex Desire in Modern China.* Chicago: University of Chicago Press, 2003.

Saso, Michael. "Orthodoxy and Heterodoxy in Taoist Ritual." In *Religion and Ritual in Chinese Society*, edited by Arthur Wolf, 325–36. Stanford, Calif.: Stanford University Press, 1974.

Schilt, Kristen, and Laurel Westbrook. "Doing Gender, Doing Heteronormativity: 'Gender Normals,' Transgender People, and the Social Maintenance of Heterosexuality." *Gender & Society* 23, no. 4 (2009): 440–64.

Schipper, Kristofer. *The Taoist Body.* Berkeley: University of California Press, 1993.

Seaman, Gary. "The Sexual Politics of Karmic Retribution." In *The Anthropology of Taiwanese Society*, edited by Emily Ahern and Hill Gates, 381–96. Berkeley: University of California Press, 1981.

Sears, Clare. *Arresting Dress: Cross-Dressing, Law, and Fascination in Nineteenth-Century San Francisco.* Durham, N.C.: Duke University Press, 2015.

Shahar, Meir. *Crazy Ji: Chinese Religion and Popular Literature.* Cambridge, Mass.: Harvard University Asia Center, 1998.

Shangfu Cun zhi [Shangfu village gazetteer. Shangfu Cun, Shanxi: Shangfu Cun Gazetteer Editorial Committee, 1994.

Shanxi tongzhi [Shanxi provincial gazetteer]. Ming, Wanli era. In Erudition Chinese Local Gazetteers Database, http://server.wenzibase.com/spring/user/alogin?jumppage=hello_gd (accessed via Stanford's East Asian Library, August 13, 2022).

Shen Guandong. *Xushi yuyan yu shikong biaoda:* Dianshizhai huabao *tuxiang xushi yanjiu* [Narrative language and the representation of time and space: studies of image and narrative in the *Dianshizhai Pictorial*]. Zhenjiang: Jiangsu Daxue Chubanshe, 2018.

Shepherd, John. *Footbinding as Fashion: Ethnicity, Labor, and Status in Traditional China.* Seattle: University of Washington Press, 2018.

Shi Rujie and Gongtian Yilang [Miyata Ichiro], eds. *Ming Qing Wu yu cidian* [Dictionary of Ming-Qing era Wu dialect]. Shanghai: Shanghai Cishu Chubanshe, 2005.

Sima Qian. *Shiji* [Records of the grand historian]. 10 vols. Beijing: Zhonghua Shuju, 1992.

Simonis, Fabien. "Mad Acts, Mad Speech, and Mad People in Late Imperial Chinese Law and Medicine." PhD diss., Princeton University, 2010.

Skidmore, Emily. *True Sex: The Lives of Trans Men at the Turn of the Twentieth Century.* New York: New York University Press, 2017.

Snorton, C. Riley. *Black on Both Sides: A Racial History of Trans Identity.* Minneapolis: University of Minnesota Press, 2017.

Sommer, Matthew H. "Abortion in Late Imperial China: Routine Birth Control or Crisis Intervention?" *Late Imperial China* 31, no. 2 (2010): 97–165.

———. "Dangerous Males, Vulnerable Males, and Polluted Males: The Regulation of Masculinity in Qing Dynasty Law." In *Chinese Femininities/Chinese Masculinities: A Reader*, edited by Susan Brownell and Jeffrey Wasserstrom, 67–88. Berkeley: University of California Press, 2002.

———. "The Gendered Body in the Qing Courtroom." *Journal of the History of Sexuality* 22, no. 2 (2013): 281–311.

———. "Legal Understandings of Sexual and Domestic Violence in China." In *The Cambridge World History of Violence, Volume 3—AD 1500–AD 1800*, edited by Robert Antony, Stuart Carroll, and Caroline Dodds Pennock, 219–35. Cambridge: Cambridge University Press, 2020.

———. "The Penetrated Male in Late Imperial China: Judicial Constructions and Social Stigma." *Modern China* 23, no. 2 (1997): 140–80.

———. *Polyandry and Wife-Selling in Qing Dynasty China: Survival Strategies and Judicial Interventions*. Berkeley: University of California Press, 2015.

———. "Review of *A Flourishing Yin: Gender in China's Medical History, 960–1665*, by Charlotte Furth." *Harvard Journal of Asiatic Studies* 61, no. 1 (2001): 273–79.

———. "Review of *Homoerotic Sensibilities in Late Imperial China*, by Wu Cuncun." *Journal of Asian Studies* 64, no. 4 (2005): 1017–19.

———. "Scandal in the Garden: *The Story of the Stone* as a 'Licentious Novel.'" In *Approaches to Teaching* The Story of the Stone [*Dream of the Red Chamber*]. Edited by Andrew Schonebaum and Tina Lu, 186–207. New York: Modern Language Association of America, 2012.

———. *Sex, Law, and Society in Late Imperial China*. Stanford, Calif.: Stanford University Press, 2000.

———. "Some Problems with Corpses: Standards of Validity in Qing Homicide Cases." In *Powerful Arguments: Standards of Validity in Late Imperial China*, ed. Martin Hoffman, Joachim Kurtz, and Ari Levine, 431–70. Leiden: Brill, 2020.

Song, Geng. *The Fragile Scholar: Power and Masculinity in Chinese Culture*. Hong Kong: Hong Kong University Press, 2004.

Staunton, Sir George, trans. *Ta Tsing Leu Lee; Being the Fundamental Laws, and a Selection from the Supplementary Statutes, of the Penal Code of China*. London: T. Cadell and W. Davies, 1810.

Steinberg, Victoria. "A Heat of Passion Offense: Emotions and Bias in 'Trans Panic' Mitigation Claims." *Boston College Third World Law Journal* 25, no. 2 (2005): 499–524.

Stockard, Janice. *Daughters of the Canton Delta: Marriage Patterns and Economic Strategies in South China, 1860–1930*. Stanford, Calif.: Stanford University Press, 1989.

Stokes, Laura. *Demons of Urban Reform: Early European Witch Trials and Criminal Justice, 1430–1530*. New York: Palgrave Macmillan, 2011.

Stryker, Susan. "My Words to Victor Frankenstein Above the Village of Chamounix: Performing Transgender Rage." *GLQ* 1 (1994): 237–54.

———. *Transgender History*. Berkeley, Calif.: History Seal, 2008.

———. *Transgender History: The Roots of Today's Revolution*. Rev. ed. New York: Seal, 2017.

Stryker, Susan, Paisley Currah, and Lisa Jean Moore. "Introduction: Trans-, Trans, or Transgender?" *Women's Studies Quarterly* 36, nos. 3–4 (2008): 11–22.

Stryker, Susan, and Aren Aizura, eds. *The Transgender Studies Reader 2*. New York: Routledge, 2013.

Stryker, Susan, and Stephen Whittle, eds. *The Transgender Studies Reader*. New York: Routledge, 2006.

Sutton, Donald. "From Credulity to Scorn: Confucians Confront the Spirit Mediums in Late Imperial China." *Late Imperial China* 21, no. 2 (2000): 1–39.

——. "Shamanism in the Eyes of Ming and Qing Elites." In *Heterodoxy in Late Imperial China*, edited by Kwang-Ching Liu and Richard Shek, 209–37. Honolulu: University of Hawai'i Press, 2004.

Sutton, Donald, ed. "Ritual, Cultural Standardization, and Orthopraxy in China: Reconsidering James L. Watson's Ideas." Special issue, *Modern China* 33, no. 1 (2007).

Taiyuan Fuzhi [Taiyuan prefecture gazetteer], Ming, Wanli era. Taiyuan: Shanxi Renmin Chubanshe, 1991.

Takizawa Shunryō. *Manshū no gaison shinkō* [Religious beliefs in rural Manchuria]. Shinkyō [Changchun]: Kōa Yinsatsu Kabushika Kaisha, 1940.

Tang Xianzu. *Mudanting* (Peony pavilion]. Beijing: Renmin Wenxue Chubanshe, 1997.

Taylor, William. *Fugitive Freedom: The Improbable Lives of Two Imposters in Late Colonial Mexico*. Berkeley: University of California Press, 2021.

Teng, Emma. *Taiwan's Imagined Geography: Chinese Colonial Travel Writing and Pictures, 1683–1895*. Cambridge, Mass.: Harvard University Asia Center, 2004.

Ter Haar, Barent J. *Telling Stories: Witchcraft and Scapegoating in Chinese History*. Leiden: Brill, 2006.

——. *The White Lotus Teachings in Chinese Religious History*. Honolulu: University of Hawai'i Press, 1992.

Theiss, Janet. *Disgraceful Matters: The Politics of Chastity in Eighteenth-Century China*. Berkeley: University of California Press, 2004.

Tian Dongkui. "Ming Qing lüdianzhong de wushu fanzui" [Sorcery crimes in the Ming and Qing codes]. *Tangdu xuekan* [Tangdu Journal] 21, no. 1 (2005): 88–91.

Tianhua Zhuren [Master of Heavenly Flowers]. *Yunxian xiao* (Laughter of cloud fairies]. Shenyang: Chunfeng Wenyi Chubanshe, 1983.

Todd, Selina. "Significant Others." *The Critic*, June 2020. Accessed July 16, 2023. https://thecritic.co.uk/issues/june-2020/significant-others/.

Tsai, Weipin. *Reading Shenbao: Nationalism, Consumerism and Individuality in China, 1919–37*. New York: Palgrave Macmillan, 2010.

Twitchett, Denis, ed. *The Cambridge History of China, Volume 3: Sui and T'ang China, 589–906, Part 1*. Cambridge: Cambridge University Press, 1979.

Uchida Tomoo. *Chūgoku nōson no kazoku to shinkō* [Family and religious beliefs in Chinese villages]. Tokyo: Kōmeisha, [1948] 1970.

Valentine, David. *Imagining Transgender: An Ethnography of a Category*. Durham, N.C.: Duke University Press, 2007.

Volpp, Sophie. "Classifying Lust: The Seventeenth-Century Vogue for Male Love." *Harvard Journal of Asiatic Studies* 61, no. 1 (2001): 77–117.

——. "The Discourse on Male Marriage: Li Yu's 'A Male Mencius's Mother.'" *Positions* 2, no. 1 (1994): 113–32.

———. "The Literary Circulation of Actors in Seventeenth-Century China." *Journal of Asian Studies* 61, no. 3 (2002): 949–84.

———. *Worldly Stage: Theatricality in Seventeenth-Century China.* Cambridge, Mass.: Harvard University Asia Center, 2011.

Von Glahn, Richard. *The Sinister Way: The Divine and the Demonic in Chinese Religious Culture.* Berkeley: University of California Press, 2004.

Wadler, Joyce. *Liaison.* New York: Bantam, 1993.

Wagner, Rudolf. "Joining the Global Imaginaire: The Shanghai Illustrated Newspaper *Dianshizhai huabao.*" In *Joining the Global Public: Word, Image, and City in Early Chinese Newspapers, 1870–1910,* edited by Rudolf Wagner, 105–73. Albany: State University of New York Press, 2007.

Waley, Arthur, trans. *The Analects of Confucius.* New York: Vintage, 1938.

Wakefield, David. *Fenjia: Household Division and Inheritance in Qing and Republican China.* Honolulu: University of Hawai'i Press, 1998.

Wang, Guojun. *Staging Personhood: Costuming in Early Qing Drama.* New York: Columbia University Press, 2020.

Wang, Y. Yvon. *Reinventing Licentiousness: Pornography and Modern China.* Ithaca, N.Y.: Cornell University Press, 2021.

Wang Zheng. *Finding Women in the State: A Socialist Feminist Revolution in the People's Republic of China, 1949–1964.* Berkeley: University of California Press, 2017.

———. *Women in the Chinese Enlightenment: Oral and Textual Histories.* Berkeley: University of California Press, 1999.

Watters, T. "Chinese Fox-Myths." *Journal of the North China Branch of the Royal Asiatic Society* 8 (1873): 45–65.

Weeks, Jeffrey. *Sexuality and Its Discontents.* New York: Routledge, 1990.

Werner, Janelle. "Living in Suspicion: Priests and Female Servants in Late Medieval England." *Journal of British Studies* 55 (2016): 658–79.

———. "Promiscuous Priests and Vicarage Children: Clerical Sexuality and Masculinity in Late Medieval England." In *Negotiating Clerical Identities: Priests, Monks and Masculinity in the Middle Ages,* edited by Jennifer Thibodeaux, 159–81. New York: Palgrave Macmillan, 2010.

Weston, Kath. *Families We Choose: Lesbians, Gays, Kinship.* New York: Columbia University Press, 1991.

Wilchins, Riki. "I Was Recently Informed I'm Not a Transsexual." *Advocate,* June 7, 2017. https://www.advocate.com/commentary/2017/6/07/i-was-recently-informed-im-not-transsexual.

Wilkinson, Endymion. *Chinese History: A New Manual.* 5th ed. Published by author, 2018.

Wolf, Arthur, and Theo Engelen. "Fertility and Fertility Control in Pre-Revolutionary China." *Journal of Interdisciplinary History* 38, no. 3 (2008): 345–75.

Wu Cheng'en. *Xiyou ji* [*Journey to the West*]. Beijing: Beijing Renmin Wenxue Chubanshe, 1980.

Wu Chichang. "Yaoren Xing Da". (The cross-dressing sorcerer Xing Da). In *Kechuang xianhua* [Gossip at the inn], sequel (*xu*), by Wu Chichang. N.p.: Zibentang, 5:7a–11b, [1850] 1875

Wu Cuncun. "Beautiful Boys Made Up as Beautiful Girls: Anti-Masculine Taste in Qing China." In *Asian Masculinities: The Meaning and Practice of Manhood in China and Japan*, edited by Kam Louie and Morris Low, 19–40. London: RoutledgeCurzon, 2003.

——. *Homoerotic Sensibilities in Late Imperial China*. London: RoutledgeCurzon, 2004.

——. *Xiwai zhi xi: Qing zhongwanqi Jingcheng de xiyuan wenhua yu liyuan siyu zhi* [The drama outside the play: opera culture and the private apartment brothel system in mid–late Qing Beijing]. Hong Kong: Hong Kong University Press, 2017.

Wu Cuncun, and Mark Stevenson. "Male Love Lost: The Fate of Male Same-Sex Prostitution in Beijing in the Late Nineteenth and Early Twentieth Centuries." In *Embodied Modernities: Corporeality, Representation, and Chinese Cultures*, edited by Fran Martin and Larissa Heinrich, 42–59. Honolulu: University of Hawai'i Press, 2006.

Wu, H. Laura. "Through the Prism of Male Writing: Representation of Lesbian Love in Ming-Qing Literature." *Nan Nü* 4, no. 1 (2002): 1–34.

Wu, Junqing. *Mandarins and Heretics: The Construction of "Heresy" in Chinese State Discourse*. Leiden: Brill, 2017.

——. "Sex in the Cloister: Behind the Image of the 'Criminal Monk' in Ming Courtroom Tales." *T'oung Pao* 105 (2019): 545–86.

——. "Words and Concepts in Chinese Religious Denunciation: A Study of the Genealogy of *Xiejiao*." *Chinese Historical Review* 23, no. 1 (2016): 1–22.

Wu, Silas. *Communication and Imperial Control in China: Evolution of the Palace Memorial System, 1693–1735*. Cambridge, Mass.: Harvard University Press, 1970.

Wu, Yi-Li. *The Injured Body: A Social History of Medicine for Wounds in Late Imperial China*. forthcoming.

——. *Reproducing Women: Medicine, Metaphor, and Childbirth in Late Imperial China*. Berkeley: University of California Press, 2010.

Xia Liying, ed. *Xiandai Zhongyao dulixue* [Modern toxicology of Chinese materia medica]. Tianjin: Tianjin Keji Fanyi Chuban Gongsi, 2005.

Xiangling Xian zhi [Xiangling county gazetteer]. Compiled and edited by Li Shiyou and Liu Shiliang. In *Zhongguo fangzhi congshu* [Chinese gazetteer series], North China, No. 402. Taipei: Chengwen Chubanshe, 1923.

Xie, Wenjuan. "(Trans)Culturally Transgendered: Reading Transgender Narratives in (Late) Imperial China." PhD diss., University of Alberta, 2015.

Xunzi. *Xunzi jijie* [Xunzi, with collected commentaries]. In *Xinbian zhuzi jicheng* [Collected works of the sages, new edition], vol. 2. Taipei: Shijie Shuju, 1991.

Xu Lian et al., eds. *Xingbu bizhao jiajian chengan* [Board of Punishment cases where the penalty was raised or lowered by analogy]. Beijing: Falü Chubanshe, 2009.

Xu Wei. *Ci Mulan ti fu congjun* [The female Mulan joins the army in place of her father]. In *Xuxiu siku quanshu* [Continuing edition of the complete library of the Four Treasuries], vol. 1764, 405–11. Shanghai: Shanghai Guji Chubanshe, 2002.

Yamabe, Nobuyoshi. "Indian Myth Transformed in a Chinese Apocryphal Text: Two Stories of the Buddha's Hidden Organ." In *India in the Chinese Imagination: Myth, Religion, and Thought*, edited by John Kieschnick and Meir Shahar, 61–80. Philadelphia: University of Pennsylvania Press, 2014.

Yang, Mayfair. "Shamanism and Spirit Possession in Chinese Modernity: Some Preliminary Reflections on a Gendered Religiosity of the Body." *Review of Religion and Chinese Society* 2 (2015): 51–86.

Ye, Xiaoqing. *The Dianshizhai Pictorial: Shanghai Urban Life, 1884–1898.* Ann Arbor: University of Michigan Press, 2003.

Yü, Chün-fang. *Chinese Buddhism: A Thematic History.* Honolulu: University of Hawai'i Press, 2020.

——. *Passing the Light: The Incense Light Community and Buddhist Nuns in Contemporary Taiwan.* Honolulu: University of Hawai'i Press, 2013.

Zeitlin, Judith. *Historian of the Strange: Pu Songling and the Chinese Classical Tale.* Stanford, Calif.: Stanford University Press, 1993.

Zhang, Lawrence. "Legacy of Success: Office Purchase and State-Elite Relations in Qing China." *Harvard Journal of Asiatic Studies* 73, no. 2 (2013): 259–97.

Zhang, Ting. *Circulating the Code: Print Media and Legal Knowledge in Qing China.* Seattle: University of Washington Press, 2020.

Zhang Yingyu. *Pian jing* [The book of swindles]. Guilin: Guangxi Shifan Daxue Chubanshe, 2008.

——. *The Book of Swindles: Selections from a Late Ming Collection.* Translated by Christopher Rea and Bruce Rusk. New York: Columbia University Press, 2017.

Zhao, Mengdie. "Shades of Justice: Debating Law and Legal Culture in Early Modern China." PhD diss., Harvard University, 2022.

Zhou Xing. "Sidamen: Zhongguo beifang de yizhong minsu zongjiao" [The four sacred animals: a North Chinese folk religion). In Li Weizu, *Si da men: Lishi yu shehui* [The four sacred animals: history and society), edited by Zhou Xing, 146–96. Beijing: Beijing Daxue Chubanshe, 2011.

Zhou, Zuyan. "The Androgynous Ideal in Scholar-Beauty Romances: A Historical and Cultural View." In *Transgender China*, edited by Howard Chiang, 97–125. New York: Palgrave Macmillan, 2012.

Index

actors, 10–11, 23, 26, 33–36, 159, 207, 211, 220–26, 230–31, 238–39, 327

Altenburger, Roland, 28

anal intercourse (sodomy, *ji jian*), 117–18, 120, 144, 164, 206, 317; in Qing law, 19, 34, 46, 48, 79, 104, 123–25, 145, 157, 200–2, 206, 217, 219, 251–52, 304, 324; as surrogate for vaginal intercourse, 143–44, 153, 158–60, 187, 204. *See also* male same-sex relations

Anhui, 100, 223, 322

animal cults: 131, 146–56, 255, 312, 315–16. *See also* fox spirits

Araujo, Gwen, 71, 160, 317

Autumn Assizes, 125, 190–94

Bai Juyi, 232

Balasubramanian, Janani, 248

Bao Daizhi Chenzhou tiao mi. See "Judge Bao Sells Rice at Chenzhou"

"bare sticks" (*guanggun*), 48, 88, 200, 325

Barlow, Tani, 182, 321, 324

beggars, 19, 108–15, 117–18, 122–23, 134, 136, 309. *See also* Zhang Yaoguniang

Beijing, 18, 20, 23–24, 33–34, 42, 48, 78, 82–84, 86, 90–93, 109, 124, 129, 135, 137–41, 146, 149, 151, 162, 211, 214, 220–25, 230–31, 235, 238–39, 247, 258, 295, 298, 327

Bencao gangmu. See Systematic Materia Medica

berdache. *See* Two-Spirit

black magic, 61, 64–65, 67, 73–76, 85–87, 91, 94–95, 127, 133, 167

blackmail, 118, 120–21, 136, 310

Boag, Peter, 9, 15, 287

Board of Punishment, 3, 76, 79, 81, 84, 91–92, 125, 138, 142–46, 153, 157, 159, 170, 193, 200, 217, 220, 327

Board of Rites, 3, 72, 75, 127,

Board of War, 55, 145, 208, 231–32, 234, 247

Board of Works, 223

Book of Rites, The (Liji), 1–2, 29, 73, 111, 258, 303

Book of Swindles, The (*Pian jing*), 45, 89,
    297
"borrowing seed" (*jie zhong*), 254–55,
    258
Boursicot, Bernard, 159–61, 317
Bray, Francesca, 184–85, 322
brown dwarfs, 248, 250, 259
Brownmiller, Susan, 325
Buddha (historical), 37–39, 93
Buddhism, 39, 45. *See also* clergy
Butler, Judith, 4, 37, 174–75, 202, 204,
    250, 291

Carmichael, Liz, 245–47
Castle, Terry, 286
Chang, Che-chia, 301
"changeling" (*bian*), 93, 95, 182,
    195, 197
chastity, female, 3, 5, 9, 26, 28–29,
    37–38, 46, 51, 56–57, 63–64, 76, 95,
    97, 116, 136, 177, 180, 198–200,
    204–5, 258, 282, 299, 309, 320
Chen, Gilbert, 295, 297
Chen Fangsheng, 95, 97
Cheng, Hsiao-wen, 37, 287, 300, 323
Chiang, Howard, 10–11, 15, 284–85,
    287–89, 294–96, 300
chosen kinship, 52, 54, 56, 76–78,
    118–19
chujia. See "leaving the family"
cisgender, 35, 70, 160
civil service examinations, 1, 18, 31, 188,
    208, 213, 227, 229–30, 281, 326
clapper opera (*bangzi qiang, Qin qiang*), 222
clergy: Buddhist monks, 5, 10, 16–17, 23,
    30, 36–39, 45–46, 78–79, 81, 83, 85,
    89, 94–95, 98–106, 191, 207, 209–15,
    218–21, 226, 228, 230, 234, 237–38,
    244, 247, 250, 296, 307, 323; Buddhist
    nuns, 5, 9–10, 17, 36–37, 45, 51, 56,
    66, 76–78, 93–97, 100, 177, 186–88,

198–99, 202, 293, 322; Catholic, 46,
    237, 242, 296–97; cross-dressing by,
    97–107; Daoist monastics (female), 5,
    36, 39–40, 45, 90, 187, 199, 323;
    Daoist monastics (male), 36, 39–41;
    and eunuchs, 42–43; as sexual
    predators, 23, 44–46, 77–78, 81–107
con artists, 5, 23, 45, 89, 131, 213, 218,
    242–247. *See also The Book of Swindles*
    (*Pian jing*); Xinxiang
concubines, 68, 161, 164, 166, 168–69,
    184–85, 187, 196, 251, 296–97, 318,
    322
Confucian values, 1–3, 26–31, 37–38,
    43–44, 48, 73–75, 88, 97, 111, 127,
    168, 175–76, 180, 184, 193–94, 205–6,
    250, 258, 325. *See also* chastity, female
Conspectus of Penal Cases (*Xing'an huilan*),
    78, 129, 251, 287, 330
contracts, marriage, 208, 210, 214, 228,
    231–32, 235–37, 322
*Country Codger Puts his Words out to Sun,
    A* (*Yesou puyan*), 45, 297, 325
crip theory, 182, 321
cross-dressing. *See* transgender

Dale, Melissa, 286, 294–96
dan. See actors
Daoism. *See* clergy
Dao Yuanyang. See Lovebirds' Reversal
Davis, Natalie Zemon, 24
deadnaming, 16, 71
"deformed" males and females (*bunan/
    feinan, bunü/feinü*), 173, 181–82,
    189–90, 194–95. *See also*
    "changeling" (*bian*)
Dianshizhai Pictorial, 20–21, 82, 98–99,
    103–6, 287, 307
disability, 5, 38, 150, 178, 180–88,
    192–93, 200, 203–4, 321–22. *See also*
    crip theory; stone maidens

Dream of the Red Chamber (*Hongloumeng*), 225, 231

"dry kinship" (*ganqin*). *See* chosen kinship

Dubois, Thomas, 150, 152

Elman, Benjamin, 243

eunuchs, 6, 9, 11, 36, 40–44, 46–47, 82–84, 190, 202, 223, 285–86, 294–97, 321

exorcism. *See* faith healing

Faderman, Lillian, 297

faith healing, 22, 57, 59, 78, 113–14, 122, 124–33, 136, 144, 151–56, 258; in Qing law, 126–27, 129–32. *See also* spirit mediums

feedback loop. *See* literature, Ming-Qing

Feinberg, Leslie, 284, 302

female impersonators. *See* actors

female knight errant (*nü xia*), 22, 26–27, 289

fictive kinship. *See* chosen kinship

"Fifteen Strings of Cash, The" (*Shiwu guan*), 234–35

forced disclosure (of genital status), 70–71, 120. *See also* midwives

Foucault, Michel, 7, 284

fox spirits: in literati discourse, 147–49; in popular religious practice, 22, 59, 77, 137, 140–41, 149–55, 255, 258, 312, 315; as sexual vampires, 32, 147, 164, 307; worshiped at yamens, 148. *See also* animal cults; faith healing; spirit mediums; Xing Shi

fraud and forgery, 5, 23, 47, 48, 50, 70, 78, 88, 107, 113, 142, 188, 209, 216, 227–28, 231–33, 240–42, 245–46, 250, 317; marriage fraud, 160, 172, 179–80, 185–86, 190, 192–93, 216; in

Qing law, 75–76, 179, 185, 190, 192–93, 217–18, 326. *See also* con artists; heterodoxy

Furth, Charlotte, 176, 181, 288, 300

gan qin ("dry kinship"). *See* chosen kinship

Gendarmerie, Beijing (*bujun tongling yamen*), 83–84, 91–92, 137–43, 153, 156, 159, 162, 305

gender confirmation surgery, 6, 11, 168, 283–84

Genet, Jean, 245, 330

Gill-Peterson, Jules, 14

Goldman, Andrea, 34, 220, 327–29

Goossaert, Vincent, 42–43

gu poison, 74–75, 304

Guangdong, 85, 200, 240, 322

guanggun. *See* bare sticks

Guangxi, 128–29, 240

Hainan, 85

Hall, Thomas/ine, 324, 331

Halperin, David, 284

Hanan, Patrick, 319

Hayes, James, 228–29

Heilongjiang, 41, 55, 145, 295

Henan, 108, 115–16, 118, 122, 131, 133, 188, 191, 193, 198, 323

Herrou, Adeline, 39

heterodoxy, 54, 61, 81, 88, 95, 111, 134–35, 137, 258–59, 290, 303; in Ming-Qing law, 3, 5, 12, 22, 72–77, 79–80, 91–93, 113, 121–27, 129–31, 133, 142, 145–46, 217–18, 314. *See also* "The Book of Rites"

hijras, 155, 317

Hirschfeld, Magnus, 120, 303

homicide, 75, 126, 177–79, 189, 192, 200–1, 219, 251–52

homosexuality. *See* anal intercourse; same-sex relations; sexual orientation

Hong Da. *See* Xing Shi

Hongloumeng. See Dream of the Red Chamber

household division, 53, 59, 229, 299

Hsiao, Kung-chuan, 303

Hua Mulan, 21, 26–29, 56, 99, 107, 289

Hubei, 108, 112, 117–18, 122, 177

Huiyuan, 37

"Human Prodigy, The" (*Renyao*). *See* Pu Songling

Hunan, 50–51, 53, 76, 100, 240–41, 298

Hunt, Lynn A., 4

Idema, Wilt, 69

"illicit sex" (*jian*) in Ming-Qing law, 75–76, 123–25, 143–44, 194–202

impotence, legal significance of, 190–91, 323

"incognito investigation" (*sifang*) scenario in literature, 234–35

inheritance. *See* household division

intersex, 6, 11, 21, 155, 174, 177, 257, 308, 320. *See also* "two-formed person"

Iran, 284

Ishibashi Ushio, 151–52

Jay, Jennifer, 44, 295–96

jian. See "illicit sex"

Jiang Pu, 50–51, 54–55, 63, 65, 72–73, 78, 80, 125, 132, 136, 298,

Jiangsu, 160, 185, 194, 223, 298

Jiangxi, 85, 130

Jiaqing Emperor, 125, 297

jijian. See sodomy

jing biao. See chastity cult

Jinghua yuan. See Romance of Flowers in the Mirror

Jinpingmei cihua. See Plum in the Golden Vase

Johnson, David, 221, 230

"Judge Bao Sells Rice at Chenzhou" (*Bao Daizhi Chenzhou tiao mi*), 235

Kang, Xiaofei, 147, 152

Karasawa Yasuhiko, 45, 89, 297

kidnapping, 45, 82–89, 110, 114, 121, 202.

Kingdom of Women, The, 25, 29–32, 75, 285, 290

knockout drugs, 67–68, 82–89, 127–29, 148, 202, 305. *See also* kidnapping; rape

Kuhn, Philip, 75, 88, 134, 328

Kutcher, Norman, 42, 43, 295–96

Lao Ai, 47

Laqueur, Thomas, 174–75

"leaving the family" (*chujia*), 5–6, 9, 22–23, 36–44, 46, 81–83, 88, 97, 100, 104, 187, 198, 205, 209, 211, 225–26, 230, 237–38

lesbians. *See* same-sex relations: female

Liang Shanbo, 28

Liaozhai zhiyi (Strange Tales from the Liao Studio). *See* Pu Songling

Li Lianying, 295

Ling Mengchu, 19, 63, 93–97, 301

Lin Shuangwen Rebellion. *See* rebellion

Li Ruzhen, 30–32, 290

Li Shizhen, 93, 95, 128, 173, 181–82, 189–91, 194–97, 320–21

Li Weizu (Li, Wei-tsu), 149–50, 152–53, 315–16

Li Yu, 19, 63, 107, 203–6, 292, 319

literacy, 58, 128, 227–34, 236, 256

literature, Ming-Qing: court case fiction (*gong'an xiaoshuo*), 65, 68, 234; "feedback loop" with legal cases, 19–23, 33, 89, 99–100, 107, 249; genre of the strange (*zhiguai*), 19–22, 32–33, 63, 82, 97, 107, 146, 148, 160, 162–64,

177, 249; scholar-beauty (*caizi jiaren*) romance, 22, 27–29, 289. *See also* "incognito investigation" scenario; The Kingdom of Women; Li Yu; Ling Mengchu; Pu Songling; Yuan Mei

Liu Liu. *See* Xing Shi

Lovebirds' Reversal (*Dao Yuanyang*), 28

Lu, Hanchao, 309

Lu, Tina, 328

Lu Bingchun, 209, 226–27, 247, 328

Lu Can, 63, 65–68, 162, 301

Lü Buwei, 47, 297

Mackerras, Colin, 225, 328

MacKinnon, Catherine, 302, 325

Mair, Victor, 73–74, 303

Manchus, 17, 28, 137, 223–24, 234, 292, 327

Manchu script, 233–34

Manchu tonsure, 28, 37, 40, 42, 71, 111, 289, 292, 302

Manion, Jen, xv, 9–10, 15, 287, 318

masculinity, 16, 18, 29, 35, 71, 178, 202, 225, 253–54, 289, 295, 309

"man masquerading in women's attire" (*nan ban nü zhuang*): as understood by Qing authorities, 5, 12, 48–49, 50, 54, 60–61, 64–65, 70, 104–6, 116, 120–25, 132–33, 188, 219–20, 249–50; in Qing law, 18, 36, 54, 72–80, 116, 120–25, 135–36, 142–46, 157–59. *See also* Sang Chong; Xing Shi; Xiong Mumu; Zengliang; Zhang Yaoguniang

McNicholas, Mark, 217, 232

McRuer, Robert, 321

medical malpractice (in Ming-Qing law), 126–27, 129–30

Mesch, Rachel, 14

Miao women, 74, 290, 304

midwives, 5, 51–53, 57–59, 76, 94, 96, 108, 137, 153, 162, 173, 177–80, 182–83, 188, 190, 197–200, 203, 320, 323. *See also* Xiong Mumu

Milburn, Olivia, 320

Ming Code, 4, 73, 282

Ming shilu. See Veritable Records of the Ming Dynasty

misogyny, 35, 68–72, 292

Mitamura Taisuke, 41, 294

Mizi Xia, 318

Mock, Janet, 70

monks. *See* clergy

Mulan. *See* Hua Mulan

Najmabadi, Afsaneh, 284

Naquin, Susan, 313

nuns. *See* clergy

opera, 5, 9, 21–22, 33–34, 42, 47–48, 159, 202, 211, 221–26, 230–31, 234–35, 239, 247, 327. *See also* actors

Overmyer, Daniel, 112

Pai an jing qi. See Slapping the Table in Amazement

Peking Opera (*jingju*). *See* opera

Peng Ziren. *See* Zhang Yaoguniang

Peony Pavilion (*Mudanting*), 187

Petcharat, Treechada, 65, 300–1

Pitying the Fragrant Companion (*Lian xiangban*), 324

Plum in the Golden Vase (*Jinpingmei cihua*), 45, 187

Prince Zhuang (*Zhuang Qinwang*), 83, 224, 304, 327

pronouns: in Chinese, 12–14, 30, 100, 254, 285; for historical figures, 14–17, 44, 286

Pu Songling, 13, 19, 21, 63, 65, 120, 147, 167–68, 149, 300, 303

Qianlong Emperor, 41, 50, 55, 78, 134, 234, 302
Qiao, Zhijian, 329
Qing Code, 17, 45, 54, 72–75, 179, 190, 201, 217, 251, 282, 286, 303–4, 307, 326.
Qiu Jin, 27

rape, 5, 45, 48–49, 58, 61, 62, 68, 71, 82, 86, 94, 96, 107, 120, 132, 143, 148, 160, 166–68; of a Buddhist nun, 23, 198–200; concept of "rapability," 199–201, 205, 302; as gender enforcement, 70–72; of a male, 83–84, 89, 177, 180, 200–2; in Qing law, 93, 177, 199–202
Rawski, Evelyn, 228–29
rebellion, 10, 41, 134, 148, 218, 289, 313; Eight Trigrams, 297; Lin Shuangwen, 295, 313, 321; Wang Sen, 148–49, 162
renyao, 20, 65, 77–78, 92, 96, 106, 160, 162, 166–67, 169, 197, 287–88, 300
Renyao ("The Human Prodigy"). See Pu Songling
Rich, Adrienne, 319
Romance of Flowers in the Mirror (Jinghua yuan). See Li Ruzhen
Rulin waishi. See Wu Jingzi

Sacred Edict, 50, 73–74, 298
same-sex relations: female, 15, 38, 71, 196–97, 286, 297; male, 18–19, 46, 118–20, 123, 157, 170, 237, 284, 309–10. See also anal intercourse; sexual orientation; "situational homosexuality"; Zhou Sijie
Sang Chong, 19–23, 33, 60–72, 76–78, 81–82, 89, 92–93, 95–96, 106–7, 116, 124–25, 132, 136, 148, 161–62, 166–68, 220, 249, 288, 300–1, 303
Scholars, The (Rulin waishi). See Wu Jingzi

Sears, Clare, 9, 15, 287
self-determination: as a factor in transgender identity and politics, 6–8, 10–11, 12. See also Judith Butler
sexual orientation, 7, 35
Shaanxi, 83, 130, 222
Shandong, 86, 130, 149, 189, 252
Shanxi, 20, 61–63, 83, 148, 207–15, 219–22, 225, 227, 229–31, 235–36, 240, 244, 327,
shape-shifting, 20, 40, 45, 65, 82, 93–97, 107, 147, 149, 155, 158, 176, 195, 197, 300
Shen Defu, 47, 297, 309
Shen Zhiqi, 75
Shenbao, 20–22, 77–78, 81–82, 90–92, 97–101, 105–7, 160–61, 197, 251, 287, 306–8, 324
Shi Jianqiao, 289
Shi Peipu, 159–60
Shiwu guan. See "The Fifteen Strings of Cash"
Sichuan, 183, 186, 322
"sinister way, the" (zuodao). See heterodoxy
"situational homosexuality," 46, 297
Skidmore, Emily, 14, 287
Slapping the Table in Amazement (Pai an jing qi). See Ling Mengchu
sodomy (jijian). See anal intercourse
spirit mediums, 77–78, 127, 130–32, 137, 140–41, 146, 149–56, 159, 162, 172, 253, 255–59, 312
Stokes, Laura, 62, 134, 313
stone maidens (shinü), 4–5, 9–10, 58, 95, 97, 177–88, 190, 200, 202–6, 287, 318–19, 321–23, 325
Stryker, Susan, 8–10, 246–47, 330
Systematic Materia Medica (Bencao gangmu). See Li Shizhen

Taiwan, 29, 38, 290, 300, 316
Teena, Brandon, 71, 286, 302

ter Haar, Barend, 134–35, 148
TERFs ("trans exclusionary radical feminists"). *See* transphobia
torture, 15, 20, 22, 62, 71, 89–94, 101, 105, 133–36, 138, 143–45, 148, 153, 159, 162, 170, 211, 219–20, 305–6, 312–13
traffic in boys, 223–24, 238, 327
transgender: definition, xv, 8–10, 25, 120, 170–71, 237, 248–50, 284; as history, 8–12; as identity, 6–7. *See also* "the way of animals"
transitioning: decision to transition, 55, 109–10, 139, 144, 156–57, 171–72, 284; process of transitioning, 8–9, 51, 56–57, 66, 109–11, 173. *See also* gender confirmation surgery
trans panic defense. *See* transphobia
transphobia: similarities between Qing and today, 49, 69–70, 302; "trans panic" defense, 103, 308, 317
transsexual, 11, 69, 283, 285, 294
"two-formed person" (*erxing ren*), 23, 95–96, 176, 183–84, 194–97, 300, 306, 321. *See also* intersex
Two-Spirit, 155, 317

Veritable Records of the Ming Dynasty (*Ming shilu*), 19, 61–64, 67–68, 75
Volpp, Sophie, 47, 168, 309–10
von Glahn, Richard, 73

Wang Sen. *See* rebellion
Wang Shixian. *See* Xing Shi
"way of animals, the" (*qinshou zhi dao*). *See* The Book of Rites
Washing Away of Wrongs, The (*Xi yuan lu*), 194, 201, 320
Weeks, Jeffrey, 175
What Confucius Did Not Say (*Zi bu yu*). *See* Yuan Mei

White Lotus. *See* rebellion
wife sale, 139–40, 159, 172, 314,
Wu Chichang, 162, 167, 169–70
Wu Cuncun, 34–35
Wu Jingzi, 243
Wu Zetian, 31, 290

Xie Jianshun, 111
Xie, Wenjuan, 300, 306
Xie Zhaozhe, 63, 297
Xing'an huilan. *See* Conspectus of Penal Cases
Xing Da. *See* Xing Shi
Xing Shi (AKA Xing Da, Liu Xing Shi), 57, 119, 173, 220, 251, 258; childhood, 138–39, 171; fictional version, 20, 162–70, 303, 322; and Hong Da, 138–40, 157, 171–72; interrogation, 138, 142–45, 157–59; and Liu Liu, 138, 143–44, 157–59, 162; sexual history, 139–40, 143–44, 158–59, 171–72; as spirit medium, 137, 140–41, 152–56, 162, 172
Xinxiang (AKA Zhao Jianlin), 5, 16, 23, 250, 304, 307; as actor, 23–24, 211, 220–23, 225–26, 230–31; as con artist, 209–10, 212–13, 226–28, 240–45; education and literacy of, 227–37; as monk, 211, 230, 238; sexual history of, 214–17, 237–39; travels of, 220, 240–41. *See also* con artists; clergy
Xiong Mumu (AKA Xiong Ersheng), 22, 70–71, 74, 76, 78, 97, 124, 136, 167, 173; community acceptance, 53, 57, 258; family and chosen kin, 52–53, 56; lawsuit, 53, 59–60; as midwife, 52, 57–59. *See also* midwives; heterodoxy; Sang Chong
Xunzi, 2–3
Xu Wei, 26

yaoren. See renyao

Yeh, Catherine, 328

Yesou pu yan. See A Country Codger
Puts his Words out to Sun

yinyang ren. See intersex

Yongzheng Reforms, 36, 48, 197

Yü, Chün-fang, 38

Yuan Mei, 19, 32–33, 63, 185

Yunxian xiao. See Laughter of Cloud
Fairies

Zeitlin, Judith, 13–14, 65, 167–68, 300

Zengliang, 78–81, 124–25, 251

Zhang (gender-ambiguous spirit
medium), 253–59

Zhang, Ting, 303

Zhang Yaoguniang (AKA "Peng Ziren,"
"Peng Xinchouer"): as alleged sexual
predator, 114–16; as beggar, 110–11,
113–14; as faith-healer, 112–14,
125–26, 130–31; interrogation of, 109,
117, 132–33, 135–36; and Wang
Shixian, 117–22, 124. *See also* beggars;
faith healing; torture

Zhao Mengdie, 301, 329

Zhao Wan, 198–99

zhiguai (genre of "the strange"). *See*
literature, Ming-Qing

Zhili, 84–85, 130, 220, 292, 316, 322

Zhou Sijie, 194–97, 330

Zhu Yingtai, 22, 27–29

zuodao yiduan. See heterodoxy

Printed in the USA
CPSIA information can be obtained
at www.ICGtesting.com
JSHW021340130324
59149JS00002B/44